JAZZ
The 1980s Resurgence

Stuart Nicholson

D1290194

DA CAPO PRESS
New York

Library of Congress Cataloging in Publication Data

Nicholson, Stuart.
 Jazz: the 1980s resurgence / Stuart Nicholson.—1st Da Capo Press ed.
  p.   cm.
 Originally published: Jazz: the modern resurgence. London: Simon & Schuster, 1990.
 ISBN 0-306-80612-6
 1. Jazz—History and criticism. I. Title.
ML3506.N53 1995
781.65'5—dc20

95-199
CIP

First Da Capo Press edition 1995

This Da Capo Press paperback edition of *Jazz: The 1980s Resurgence*
is an unabridged republication of the edition published in London in 1990
under the title *Jazz: The Modern Resurgence,* with minor emendations and a new
preface by the author. It is reprinted by arrangement with the author.

Published by Da Capo Press, Inc.
A Subsidiary of Plenum Publishing Corporation
233 Spring Street, New York, N.Y. 10013

For K. W.

Preface

The 1980s was a decade when jazz buzzed with an excitement that took even the most seasoned observers by surprise. It had all begun innocuously enough. Towards the end of the 1970s, the avant-garde, after almost two decades of blood-letting, began creeping inside the changes; musicians from what had been regarded as the "cutting edge" began producing albums that were dubbed "in tradition." Although no one knew it at the time, it would provide a kind of *leitmotif* for the decade. At the same time there was general disenchantment with fusion, despite a seal of respectability bestowed on it by Miles Davis at the beginning of the 1970s that had once made it seem like the way ahead. With other areas of jazz marginalized, paradoxically, as much by its own relentless evolution as by rock and pop music, jazz seemed to be at one of its lowest ebbs ever. Yet within five years all that had turned around and by the end of the 1980s young jazz musicians were appearing in fashionable magazines and weekend color supplements.

Throughout its existence, jazz has been inexorably linked to the social fabric from which it emerged. During the 1980s the dominant theme was decentralization. The sociopolitical changes wrought in Reagan's America and Thatcher's Britain that extolled the cult of the individual were reflected in jazz. With no single musician dominating the decade—or providing a rallying point, as happened in the past, to codify the diatonic, chromatic, harmonically-free, and rock-influenced eras—the task of moving the music passed to a diversity of individual contributors. "I hear people everywhere saying the trouble with our times is that we have no great leaders anymore," wrote Laurens Van De Post. "If we look back we always had them. But it seems to me there is a very profound reason why there are no great leaders anymore. It is because they are no longer needed. The message is clear . . . every man must be his own leader. He knows enough not to follow other people."[*] Jazz, it seemed, had finally become too broad and diverse to be changed by the revelations of one great man.

---

[*]*A Walk With a White Bushman* by Laurens Van De Post (Penguin, 1988).

It marked a unique moment in the music's history. Like Mark Twain returning home after twenty years to discover how much wiser his father had grown, jazz, after decades of pursuing the future, discovered its past. The result was a new classicism that ranged from a conscious imitation of the hard-bop style at one end of the spectrum to an imaginative re-creation and distortion of stylistic devices from King Oliver to Albert Ayler at the other. Between 1910 and 1930, European art had undergone a similar transformation. In what Jean Cocteau called a "return to order," a search for an elusive, never-to-be-attained stability, art reacted first against industrialization and then to the chaos of the Great War (1914-18). *Realisme classicissant* represented a period of consolidation by artists such as Picasso, Maillol, and Stravinsky before they went on to greater triumphs. In jazz during the 1980s, the most visible manifestation of this trend was a return to the hard-bop mainstream of the mid-1950s and early 1960s.

Recording companies, responding to unprecedented media attention on trumpeter Wynton Marsalis (b.1961), who upon graduating from Art Blakey's Jazz Messengers had won simultaneous Grammy awards for a jazz album and a classical album, rushed to sign similar *wunderkinder*. It created a bandwagon effect that lasted throughout the decade as young musicians, fluent in the hard-bop idiom, became actively promoted by major record labels. Adopting Marsalis's visual signature of sartorial elegance, they connected with a young audience equally impelled towards the conservative conformity of the 1980s. It was a contrast to the late 1950s when hard-bop was heading jazz's musical agenda and the social climate was moving towards radical reform and revolutionary idealism, yet the music seemed fresh and new to an audience saturated by rock, pop, funk, or disco. "Everything I've done was new to people of my generation," explained Marsalis. "Playing *jazz* was new because people were into fusion and disco. Everyone was saying jazz was dead but when they heard me, they knew I was taking care of business."*

However, as the 1980s gave way to the 1990s, it remained to be seen if these musicians, many using the adopted voices of some of jazz's older and sometimes posthumous heroes, would realize the deferred promise of their own artistic maturity. While on the one hand these photogenic young stars focused welcome media attention on jazz and raised its public profile, on the other, their highly touted recording debuts often turned out to be invitations to jump aboard their learning curve as they searched for an individual style among their assimilated influences. The demands

---

* Interview by author, 19 October 1991.

of the marketplace meant some young musicians had record contracts thrust upon them in advance of artistic maturity. "That's not one of the situations I'm in agreement with," observed master trumpeter Jon Faddis. "A lot of times a young musician doesn't feel he's got to go out there and pay his dues. It's good for them but a little dangerous for jazz."[*]

One unexpected effect of the trend back to traditional values was a focus of attention on the older styles of jazz. Musicians who had been regarded as distinctly un-hip for decades were finally accorded respect and informed curiosity by young musicians. Wynton Marsalis played and recorded with New Orleans veteran Danny Barker and sat-in with "Doc" Cheatham, who once played lead trumpet in McKinney's Cotton Pickers; swing-era veteran Milt Hinton toured and recorded with Branford Marsalis; while the climate of rediscovery allowed Benny Carter (born 1907), one of the few universally acknowledged "giants" of jazz, to be presented with his "first chance in decades to conduct a program of his old and new music, played by a crack orchestra."[**]

In contrast, the thirty-somethings, too old to be young lions, yet too young to be elder statesmen, suddenly found themselves sidelined in the rush to sign the youngest-and-the fastest. Some, at their peak artistically, yet unable to obtain adequate recording exposure, passed the decade in relative obscurity. And while nobody would accuse the music business of being fair, the real irony of this situation became apparent when Jon Faddis spoke of two internationally respected musicians who were both unfashionably close to their fortieth birthdays. He said neither had a current recording contract, but were giving lessons to two teenage musicians who did.[***]

Even so, several talented young musicians did emerge as the decade progressed, although not quite as many as record company press offices would have had us believe. While there was certainly precedent for young genius and precocious talent in jazz, it had previously occurred two or three times a generation, rather than two or three every few months. Major-label record executives, it seemed, lost sight of the fact Duke Ellington was 40 when he recorded "Ko-Ko," Coleman Hawkins 38 when he recorded "Body and Soul," Lester Young 30 when he recorded "Lester Leaps In," John Coltrane 33 when he recorded *Giant Steps,* and Miles Davis 33 when he recorded *Kind of Blue.*

Ultimately, however, the 1980s seemed washed with history. It was quite probably the last decade when the whole history of jazz was refracted

---

[*] Interview by author, 11 July 1993.
[**] Liner notes, Music Master CIJD 20126Z/27X, by Gary Giddins.
[***] Interview by author, 11 July 1993.

through the music of its surviving practitioners. More than ever it emphasized the fact that jazz was not a single species, but rather a mass of sub-cultures divided by historical precedent that could only be properly understood by examining the component parts individually. I have therefore tried to preserve the historical primacy of each style, albeit viewed from the perspective of the 1980s, beginning in New Orleans and moving chronologically through to 1980s neo-classicism and the Loisaida scene. Vocal and Worldwide developments, which have remained apart from the main thrust of jazz, although reflecting it, have been left until the end. Occasionally this approach meant creating some artificial pigeonholing, such as placing Oscar Peterson and Stan Getz under "Past Masters and Keepers of the Faith" simply because their mainstream-modern styles did not sit well under "bop" or "post-bop." But in the main I have kept the genres as broad as possible to avoid any grotesque miscarriages of justice. Any quotes that lie in the text without references are taken from the pages of *Down Beat* and *Wire* magazines, whose perspicacious columns are heartily recommended.

When I began writing this book in the fall of 1989 it was for a tight deadline. At the time, I wanted to get my thoughts about a very exciting decade for jazz onto paper while my impressions were still fresh and, perhaps more importantly, before they were changed by the inevitable rationalization hindsight affords. The book appeared in hardback a year later in the U.K. as *Jazz: The Modern Resurgence*. Warily returning to to it five years later to write this new preface, I was relieved I could still agree with Tony Harlow's comment later in the book when he says that between the text and his discography a listener should be able to get a good idea of what jazz during the 1980s was all about. This is all the book set out to do.

This is a critical guide. It is not a complete guide. It is told through a series of snapshot critiques of musicians whose work I thought representative of what was happening in a given style or genre during the decade, sometimes to acclaim, sometimes in relative obscurity. My chief problem was space. This I tried to use as effectively as possible. For countless musicians I simply picked up their careers in the 1980s with just a few personal observations to establish historical context. There seemed little point in duplicating several excellent reference books available and anyway, this book was about a specific decade. For every musician I included, however, there were, of course, several whom I had to leave out. This was the hardest part of all. There had to be a cut-off point, but two biographies (one on Ella Fitzgerald, the other on Billie Holiday) and countless reviews, magazine articles, liner and program notes later, I am at a loss to say quite what it was. I am sure there was one, but probably no more scientific than a gut feeling based on what I had seen and heard during the decade, which included almost all the artists and albums mentioned in the text.

All the photographs are my own and I have tried to select prints that relate to the text in an attempt to create a unified perspective of the music. Throughout I tried to capture what Cartier-Bresson called the "decisive moment" to create an image that related to the individuality or style of the musician concerned, such as the photo of Lester Bowie, for example. Just as the photos of Francis Wolff for the 1950s and 1960s Blue Note album covers provided an aesthetic entry point into the music, equally I have tried to create moments of "frozen music" that convey the passion of jazz.

In preparing this book for the paperback edition, I am grateful for the faith shown in it by Yuval Taylor, the senior editor at Da Capo, in making everything possible. I am also grateful to Jed Williams and Max Harrison for their help in reaching this point. During the preparation of the original manuscript, Loren Schoenberg, Steve Kuhn, Bobby Previte, Jack Walrath, Jay Leonhart, Helen Keane, Artie Moorhead, and Steve Backer discussed at length their experiences and observations of jazz during the 1980s from their various vantage points and helped disabuse me of many preconceptions and prejudices. As the deadline loomed Tony Harlow's reading and rereading of various versions of the manuscript and his subsequent observations and criticisms helped shape the final draft; I am also grateful for his "interactive" discography of albums cut during the 1980s. Finally, thanks to my mother, the in-laws for taking the piss, and to my brother Malcolm for his constant encouragement and shrewd observations which have played an important role in shaping the way I perceive the music. My largest debt is to my wife Kath, to whom the book is dedicated with all my love.[*]

Stuart Nicholson
Woodlands St. Mary
Berkshire, England
November 1994

---

[*] Despite much temptation, the original text remains intact, with one exception where the spin on one value judgment was altered by just fourteen words. I have also tried to correct any errors of fact I became aware of.

Contents

Key To Symbols Used

(t)	Trumpet
(flhn)	Flugelhorn
(tb)	Trombone
(vtb)	Valve Trombone
(fh)	French Horn
(tba)	Tuba
(ss)	Soprano Saxophone
(as)	Alto Saxophone
(ts)	Tenor Saxophone
(bs)	Baritone Saxophone
(f)	Flute
(cl)	Clarinet
(vn)	Violin
(clo)	Cello
(p)	Piano
(k)	Keyboards
(b)	Bass
(d)	Drums
(vib)	Vibraphone
(perc)	Percussion
(v)	Vocal

1
Past Masters and Keepers of the Faith

THE WRITER AND chronicler Stanley Dance is usually credited as being the first to coin the word 'mainstream'. He used it as a generic term to accommodate the music of a group of displaced ex-Count Basie musicians still plying their craft in New York during the 1950s who continued to play within the conventions of the swing era, even though the musical climate around them had long since changed. While they were not the first casualties to be marginalized by the evolution of jazz, they were a graphic illustration of just how fast was the speed of change; less than ten years earlier they had been at the top of their profession in one of the greatest big bands in the history of jazz. Now they were scuffling for work in combos, and grateful for the occasional record date.

As history repeated itself, more and more musicians, conscious of the limit of their art, continued to love their style in humility rather than attempt to keep in step with the zealous reformers. Like Stanley Dance's 'mainstreamers' they became marooned within the confines of their style, living slices of history bypassed by the lure of the future. Away from the cutting edge, these sensible and sometimes shrewd disenchanted continued to work in their chosen area of jazz, often with a rare worldly-wise maturity and craftsmanship that only time and experience brings. As the record producer Orrin Keepnews pointed out, 'there was a reasonable amount of club work, and there were lots of independent record companies . . . willing to take a few fairly inexpensive chances on recording [them]'.[1]

However, by the end of the 1970s there was a downturn in the evolutionary cycle of jazz, the emphasis shifting to consolidation and with it a more egalitarian climate where styles from every era of the music at last found peaceful co-existence alongside each other. By the end of the 1980s, for example, it was not considered unusual for the great bass player

Milt Hinton, who had played in Cab Calloway's band in the 1930s, to appear with the young tenor star Branford Marsalis or to lead a group at the Knitting Factory that included Wayne Horvitz and Marty Ehrlich. Pluralism became cause for celebration and many musicians once bypassed and considered passe began to enjoy a profile that would have been impossible during the '60s or '70s. It meant that the 1980s provided a unique, and quite possibly the last, opportunity to view the whole history of jazz refracted through the music of its surviving past masters.

Equally, there were also a number of musicians who decided to adopt the swing/mainstream style as their musical home. They emphasized a set of values that placed premium on tone, melodic construction and paraphrase rather than cascades of semi-quavers. Less glamorous than the neo-classical hard-boppers, *these* keepers of the faith, free from institutionalized methodology, were, within the confines of their style, equally absorbing, particularly in their handling of ballads, an area that seemed to trouble many musicians from bop and beyond.

NEW ORLEANS

For some reason it didn't occur to the city elders of New Orleans until almost too late that they were sitting on a potential tourist goldmine in the way Nashville exploited country and western. However, by 1989 the city had mounted its 20th annual New Orleans Jazz & Heritage Festival with its current favourite son, Wynton Marsalis, a headliner. New Orleans was back on the jazz map with a crop of talent headed by Marsalis and his brothers that included Terence Blanchard, Donald Harrison, Marlon Jordan, Kent Jordan and Harry Connick Jr. But New Orleans was about history; it weighed heavy with jazz folklore and its brass marching bands that had spawned jazz at the turn of the century.

During the 1980s there was a revival of the music of the traditional New Orleans marching bands that moved from tired music for jaded tourists into exciting, creative traditionalism. Until the middle of the decade perhaps the most famous of the traditional-style bands were **Michael White's Original Liberty Jazz Band,** composed of the real old-timers of New Orleans jazz including Danny Barker, and the **Olympia Brass Band,** formed in 1958 by Harold Dejan. Closely associated with the famed Preservation Hall, most of the Olympians played on Sundays throughout the '80s in the Preservation Hall Band. Although Dejan died in 1987, the band continued to be one of the most popular in Gulf City; they once played for President Ford and featured extensively in the opening shots of the James Bond movie 'Live And Let Die'. Their style, very much in the tradition—dirges to the graveside, uptempo to the wake—appeared on 'New Orleans Brass Bands—Down Yonder' (Rounder).

However, during the '80s the venerable brass band tradition was revolutionized by young musicians. Tempos were changed, becoming faster and 'funkier' and the repertoire expanded to embrace bop, soul and even pop numbers. The driving force in this revival was **The Dirty Dozen Brass Band**. Formed in the early 1970s by a group of youngsters with kazoos and drums they emerged in 1975 as a marching band—all eight of them—incorporating diverse influences such as Cajun music, Professor Longhair, bebop and funk. They caused a sensation both at street parades and neighbourhood bars such as The Glass House. Such was their significance that by the mid-1980s they were the first band since the 1920s to have an international impact playing a style of jazz based on the traditional New Orleans model.

Initially, other bands objected to their inclusion of numbers like 'Bongo Beep', 'Blue Monk', the theme from 'The Flintstones' and their own originals but the second-liners and young people in the black community loved

The Olympia Brass Band: Formed in 1958 by Harold Dejan, they were closely associated with Preservation Hall and epitomized the tradition of New Orleans marching bands that stretched back to the turn of the century.

The Dirty Dozen Brass Band: They dared to dabble with the sacred precepts of New Orleans traditionalism and came up with something startlingly fresh and new.

it. Their debut album from 1984, 'My Feet Can't Fail Me Now' (Concord) included their special brand of excitement on 'I Ate Up The Apple Tree', 'Blackbird Special' and the title track. Kirk Joseph on tuba was the band's star performer with a virtuoso technique that made his playing sound like an electric bass. Gone was the familiar heterogeneous polyphony of the traditional New Orleans ensemble, in its place well-crafted arrangements with a self-perpetuating push-me-pull-you groove of such interlocking aplomb that the written and the improvised merged intro one.

Their 1985 live performance at Montreux, 'Mardi Gras in Montreux: Live' (Rounder) was typical of their exuberant in-person performances, when their repertoire was stitched together in one seemingly endless segue. A move to CBS in 1987 produced 'Voodoo' (CBS), released in 1989, but even special guests Dizzy Gillespie, Branford Marsalis and Dr. John could add nothing to such a self-contained unit. But the Dirty Dozen were very much an in-person band; captivating and original they dared to dabble with the sacred precepts of New Orleans traditionalism to come up with something new and fresh.

By the end of the 80s there were well over a dozen highly active brass bands comprising young musicians, either based on the traditional role-models, such as 'The Young Tuxedo', or contemporary brass bands inspired by the Dirty Dozen. They included **The Rebirth Brass Band** who during the '80s added significantly to the brass band revival. Led by Kermit Ruffins, their headquarters was just half a block from Louis Armstrong Park on North Vilere, the bastion of traditional black culture. 'Here To Stay' (Arhoolie) from 1984 came early in the band's development, very much in the Dirty Dozen mould but with a raw edge. By 1989 'Feel Like Funkin' It Up' (Rounder), described by the *New York Times* as 'raucous and wild,' was more refined but nevertheless compulsive and irresistible. Among the other younger bands were the Chosen Few, led by Tuba Fats comprising teen and sub-teen musicians and featured on 'Down Yonder' (Rounder), the even younger 'All Stars', as well as the Roots of Jazz Brass Band, West End Brass Band, The Pinstripes, The Young Men Brass Band and Leroy Jones and the Hurricane Brass Band.

CHICAGO

Chicago was responsible for a forthright brand of dixieland jazz made famous in the Roaring Twenties by a group of white musicians mainly, but not exclusively, from Austin High School. Based on New Orleans jazz it had the spirit and fire of youthful enthusiasm and discovery. When the Chicago school moved to New York in the 1930s many played under the aegis of Eddie Condon who brought a new meaning to the word Bacchanal. Since those heady days their style has been emasculated into the acceptable face of jazz, usually featuring at Party conventions when the balloons are released from the ceilings. But it wasn't always like that. The first real confluence between black and white musicians, the Austin High School gang learnt at the feet of masters like Armstrong, King Oliver and Earl Hines and pointed the way to the modern conception of swing.

Austin High School cornet player **Jimmy McPartland** (b.1907) replaced the legendary Bix Beiderbecke in the Woverines in 1924, and succeeded in getting a few informal cornet lessons from him during the hand-over period. Not surprisingly, this left McPartland forever smitten by Beiderbecke's style as revealed on the 1953 'Shades of Bix' (MCA) with Bobby Hackett.

Still touring during the 1980s, including a performance at the Nice Jazz Festival in 1985, he was capable of evoking Beiderbecke's style with stunning clarity. When McPartland first recorded with fellow Austin High School Gang tenor saxist **Bud Freeman** (b.1906), it was on the 1927 McKenzie/Condon Chicagoans session that virtually defined Chicago jazz.

Jimmy McPartland: Bugles for Beiderbecke.

Their 1975 collaboration, 'Jazz Meeting In Holland' (Circle), re-issued in 1982, showed two old stagers playing with the ease of masters—particularly McPartland—although the dead-cat bounce of the Dutch sidemen was too self-consciously dixieland. Freeman, wholly individual, whose cascading style played an important, but barely acknowledged role in defining the tenor sax in early jazz, remained intermittently active until the late 1980s. In 1989 he published his autobiography, *Crazeology* (University of Illinois Press).

Wild Bill Davison (1906-89) was a powerful cornettist who helped define Chicago jazz and preserved it in semi-perpetuity throughout the '40s and '50s in New York at clubs such as Nicks and those run by fellow arch-raconteur Eddie Condon. Described by James Lincoln Collier as 'a powerful and exciting player',[2] Davison's unequivocal real-ale style was celebrated with a Carnegie Hall concert in 1980. He continued to tour the world throughout the decade and at one stage planned an autobiography.

The 1981 'Running Wild' (JSP) placed him alongside two guitars and a bass that evoked the Ruby Braff/George Barnes collaborations of the late '70s, although at a shouted rather than spoken remove, and revealed an ingenious lyricism even at 75. A disappointing session with tenor saxophonist Eddie Miller, 'Wild Bill Davison and Eddie Miller Play Hoagy Carmichael' (Real Time) from the same year is just far too polite; for Davison, life began at treble forte. In October 1988 a re-union with pianist Art Hodes at the Cork Jazz Festival was such a success that it prompted the 'Together Again' CD released in 1989. Prior to his death on 14 November 1989 he had been touring with Hodes and John Petters' Dixielanders as 'The Legends of American Dixieland'.[4]

SWING INTO MAINSTREAM

When the swing era drew to a close in the late '40s, it was not simply a matter of bop taking over the vanguard of jazz. A whole entertainment infrastructure went as well. Dancehalls throughout the States were forced to close their doors for good, hastened, as persuasively argued by writer Gene Lees[3], by the demise of the urban and interurban railways which served them. Employment opportunities for musicians abruptly diminished; bandleader Andy Kirk went into hotel management while other leaders including Count Basie, Woody Herman and Cab Calloway were forced to front small groups.

It was a testament, therefore, to the ability of the survivors of this most rigorous natural selection that they were still actively performing in jazz during the 1980s. More particularly, with their verve and enthusiasm undiminished by the passage of years, many seemed to be playing better than ever.

Benny Carter (b.1907) was one of the most complete musicians in jazz; both as arranger and instrumentalist Carter was one of the few figures universally acknowledged a jazz giant. That he succeeded in garnering such unqualified admiration from peers and public alike is all the more remarkable as post-war Carter's involvement in jazz, until the 1980s, was only peripheral. His primary career during those years was writing music for the movies and television in Hollywood where he was widely credited for playing a major role in desegregating the established work practices that had long prevailed. Even so, Carter's career in jazz had provided enough material for the definitive Berger/Patrick biography *Benny Carter—A Life In American Music* (Scarecrow Press, 1982) and in 1989 he was the subject of the documentary film 'Benny Carter: Symphony In Riffs'.

Carter first started arranging for the Fletcher Henderson Orchestra in 1928 and soon established a reputation as one of the classiest arrangers in jazz whose writing for saxophones was without equal. As an instrumentalist he was, with Johnny Hodges, the pre-eminent alto saxophonist in pre-bop jazz, although he played tenor, trumpet, clarinet, trombone and piano as well. His style, melodically luminescent and resourceful, was aided by an excellent technique and a rare ability to conceive a solo as a logical whole. He relied little on vibrato and always succeeded in sounding fresh and modern, irrespective of his musical surroundings. Of all the swing era musicians, Carter's style sounded least dated.

In 1981 Carter made a three-week, 14-date tour of Japan with his All-Stars, recreating the success of the 1977 'Live And Well In Japan' (Pablo). Although Carter had recorded regularly for the Pablo label, including the excellent 1988 'Meets Oscar Peterson', other albums included the 1980 'Summer Serenade' (Storyville) and 'Gentlemen Of Swing' (East Wind), the 1982 'Skyline Drive' (Phontastic), the 1985 'A Gentleman And His Music' (Concord), and the 1987 'Benny Carter's All-Stars' (Gazell). A three-disc set, 'Swing Reunion' (Book Of The Month Club) from 1985, was recorded with pianist Teddy Wilson.

But it was not until February 1987, Carter's 80th year, that his achievements in jazz were finally placed in perspective. The occasion was a concert with the American Jazz Orchestra dedicated to his compositions and arrangements at the Great Hall of Cooper Union. The AJO provided Carter with the first opportunity in decades to conduct a programme of his music, which included the premiere of 'Central City Sketches', recorded shortly after the concert as 'The American Jazz Orchestra/Benny Carter: Central City Sketches' (Music-masters).

In 1989 he featured in a concert celebrating his songwriting skills, part of a short concert series organized by Wynton Marsalis and Stanley Crouch at Lincoln Center; 'Benny was on stage for only eight tunes,' wrote Kevin Whitehead,[4] 'playing rings around Dizzy Gillespie, ten years his junior.' But perhaps his most exciting concert appearance was at the Chicago Jazz Festival later that year when at the behest of the festival organizers he produced his 'Further Definitions' sax-section charts from the legendary 1961 'Impulse' album; on hand were original session mates Phil Woods and John Collins plus Milt Hinton, Frank Wess and Eddie Johnson, but not, sadly, a recording remote.

Trumpet player **Doc Cheatham** (b.1905) was set to retire from the music business when he was 64 in 1969 after a lifetime at the top of his profession, playing alongside most of the great swing era legends. But in the 1970s he was asked to play at Your Father's Mustache and set in train a series of events that led to a remarkable renaissance in his career, including performances at Festivals throughout the world. By the 1980s he could be numbered among the most accomplished musicians on his instrument, with admirers as diverse as Wynton Marsalis and Sun Ra.

Although originally influenced by Louis Armstrong, for whom he once substituted in the 1920s when Armstrong was playing Chicago's Vendome Theatre billed as 'The greatest trumpet in the world!', Cheatham quickly evolved a style that moved out of Armstrong's omnipresent influence. More lyrical and light-footed, it was a genuine, if at the time unfashionable, alternative to Armstrong's dominance which was so complete that both Cheatham and Henry 'Red' Allen, who had also moved out of Armstrong's spell, were virtually sidelined.

The 1979 'Black Beauty' (Sackville) was a collaboration with Sammy Price (p) and a powerful reminder that some excellent jazz was still within the ken of some of its oldest practitioners. The 1983 'The Fabulous Doc Cheatham' (Parkwood) with Dick Wellstood (p) showed Cheatham's cunningly lyrical and elegant style that was simultaneously modern and traditional. The live 'Echoes of Harlem' (Stash) from a 1985 concert at the Loeb Student Centre, New York University placed him alongside George Kelly (ts) (from Panama Francis's reformed Savoy Sultans) and young saxophonist Joey Cavaseno (b.1967) but suffers the vicissitudes of the spontaneous jam; Cheatham, however, cycled elegantly through the traffic.

In 1980 he began a Sunday brunchtime gig at the Sweet Basil, originally for four weeks. He was still there in 1990. The group appeared on the 1982 'Doc Cheatham and his New York Quartet' (Parkwood), including six vocals in a voice not too far removed from Kermit the Frog. 'I made all those plans years ago,' he said[5], 'that I would keep playing until I'm 90'. In June 1990 he celebrated his 85th birthday at the Sweet Basil backed by the Jackie Williams Trio; *The New York Times* described him as 'a national treasure.'

Milt Hinton (b.1910) has long been regarded as the dean of bass players. With Cab Calloway between 1935-51, he also performed and recorded with countless major jazz musicians. In the early 1950s his excellent tone, time, taste and technique made him one of the most sought after session musicians in New York, playing in an incredible variety of situations including recordings, radio, television and concerts with artists as varied as Louis Armstrong, John Coltrane, Frank Sinatra, Barbara Streisand, Bing Crosby and Paul McCartney.

During the 1970s he was virtually the house bassist at Michael's Pub and in the '80s he became increasingly involved as an educator at numerous colleges and workshops in New York City, mainly at Hunter and Baruch. A memorable duet with **Art Hodes** (p) (b.1904), 'Just The Two Of Us' (Muse) from 1981, featured Hodes' sophisticated bar-room piano

Benny Carter: Universally recognised as one of the true giants of jazz, Carter seemed impervious to the effects of ageing and was busier in jazz during the 1980s than he had been for decades.

and was a historical gem. The 1985 'The Judge's Decision' (Exposure), a quintet album with a saxophone front line, allowed the linear logic of Hinton's walking lines to reign supreme.

Throughout his career Hinton kept an open mind about the development of jazz, and playing alongside Dizzy Gillespie in the Calloway band in 1939-40, he pressed Gillespie to teach him about the new, emerging bop, 'He'd take it apart harmonically and give me flatted chords and very modern substitutions to use,' he said[6]. Almost 50 years later his enthusiasm to keep abreast of developments in jazz continued unabated; in 1988 he appeared on 'Trio Jeepy' (CBS) with Branford Marsalis, performing with him later in the year at the New York JVC Festival, and in 1989 he led a band at the Knitting Factory.

Throughout his long career Hinton was an avid amateur photographer and in 1989 about 200 of his photographs were published in his autobiography *Bass Line* (Temple, 1989) in collaboration with David G. Berger, who had previously arranged for a one-man exhibition of Hinton's photographs in 1981-82. It provided a unique insight into the history of jazz; one of just a handful of indispensable books on the subject, it was a profound and shrewdly observed 'aural' history of jazz, with Hinton both literally and metaphorically, playing the role of Isherwood's camera.

When pianist **Jay McShann's** (b.1916) big band made its New York debut in 1942, it caused a stir among musicians through the solos of his alto saxophonist Charlie Parker. In 1955 he had a Number 1 R&B hit 'Hands Off' (VeeJay) and in 1969 he began touring extensively. His career was given a boost in 1978 by the Becker/Farrell film 'Hootie's Blues' and his performances in the acclaimed 1979 Bruce Ricker film, 'Last Of The Blue Devils'. His percussive piano style, steeped in the Kansas City blues tradition and flavoured by boogie-woogie, was much loved by mainstream audiences, prompting Stanley Dance to enthuse in 1988: 'Judging by pure standards, we would say that McShann is now the best jazz pianist we have left'.[7]

Typical McShann horsepower was generated on his meeting with macho ex-Lunceford tenor and reborn jump-band leader Joe Thomas on 'Blowin' In From K.C.' (Uptown), but although McShann was somewhat typecast in the blues idiom, the 'money tunes', as he called them, his work with Jim Galloway on 'Thou Swell' (Sackville) did not contain one blues performance. However, it scarcely affected the gutsy aplomb of his playing. 'Airmail Special', with Neil Swainson (b) and Terry Clarke (d), and the 1981 'Saturday Night Function' (both Sackville), this time with Don

Thompson (b) plus Buddy Tate (ts) and Jim Galloway (saxes), were a mixture of swing era standards and warhorses and, of course, blues performances full of period charm and exuberance.

A regular duo during the '80s, **Al Grey** (b.1925) and **Buddy Tate** (b.1913) appeared the proverbial yin and yang of swinging mainstream jazz. Tate's style, Texas tenor pruned down to the minimum grit and gristle to qualify, came to prominence in the Basie Band of 1939 and even in the '80s he had requests for 'Blue And Sentimental', a feature he inherited from Herschel Evans. A perennial Basie-ite, he helped define the word 'mainstream jazz' and his consistent level of professionalism enabled him to continue working when the idiom became less fashionable. In 1981 a bizarre accident with a high-pressure shower scalded his arm, temporarily sidelining him, subsequently forcing him to perform for a long period bandaged.

His albums on the Sackville label included 'Quartet' from 1978 and 'The Ballad Artistry' from 1981 that demonstrate the essence of his big-toned, expressive style. His work on the Concord label included three 1981 sessions, 'The Great' with cornettist Warren Vaché, 'Scott's Buddy' with tenor saxophonist Scott Hamilton and the excellent tripartite meeting at Toranomon Hall, Japan with the addition of Al Cohn, 'Tour De Force'. A regular performer at such mainstream outlets as Dick Gibson's Jazz Party and the Nice Jazz Festival, his most frequent touring companion in the '80's was trombonist Al Grey; 'Just Jazz' (Uptown). In 1986 he commemorated 50 years in jazz with a concert at NYU Loeb Student Centre.

Al Grey was one of jazz's great journeyman trombonists, the perennial jamming musician and impeccable section player. He played in big bands led by Benny Carter, Jimmie Lunceford and Lucky Millinder in the 1940s and Lionel Hampton, Dizzy Gillespie and Count Basie in the '50s. Since a 1961 collaboration with tenor saxophonist Billy Mitchell, Grey has, from time to time, co-led several combos with a tenor/trombone front line including Jimmy Forrest in the '70's—'Live At Ricks' and 'Live In Chicago' (both Aviva)—and Buddy Tate throughout the '80's—'Just Jazz' (Uptown); he also had a brief run with Al Cohn (ts) in New York in 1986.

By the 1980s, Grey was one of the few trombonists left in jazz who was a master of the art of playing the trombone with a plunger mute, a style perfected by Joe 'Tricky Sam' Nanton (1904-46) with Duke

Ellington. The idiosyncratic charm of this almost extinct art was featured on 'Al Grey & The Jasper Thilo Quintet' (Storyville), released in 1987.

SMALL BAND SWING

The Harlem Jazz and Blues Band, formed in 1972, established a reputation for recreating the 52nd Street swing of the late '30s and early '40s. Originally, its members comprised disenfranchized swing era musicians under the nominal leadership of Clyde Bernhardt, but by 1980 the group was led by trumpeter Bobby Williams. A loose-limbed repository of swing numbers and 12-bar riffs, the band included from time to time Eddie Durham, Sammy Benskin, George Kelly, Eddie Chamblee, Al Casey and Johnny Blowers. They enjoyed a strong following in Europe, where they frequently toured throughout the '80s, their albums included the imaginatively titled 'Harlem Jazz And Blues Band 1973-80' and the 1980 'Harlem Jazz And Blues Band' (both Barron).

The original **Savoy Sultans,** formed in 1937 and led by Al Cooper, achieved a formidable reputation as the house band at the Savoy ballroom in Harlem until they disbanded around 1946. A powerfully swinging jump band, they were by all accounts very much an 'in-person' group—the sides they recorded for Decca simply do not square with the legend. The idea of recreating the Sultans was devised by the French Black and Blue label who approached drummer **Panama Francis** (b.1918) with an invitation to tour and record in 1979.

The tour was an unqualified success, and the subsequent album 'Gettin' In The Groove' (Black and Blue) was a minor hit in France and was awarded the Grand Prix du Disque. Comprising solid journeymen, the band included Francis Williams and Irvin Stokes (t), Norris Turney, Howard Johnson and George Kelly (saxes), Red Richards (p), John Smith (g) and Bill Pemberton (b). The band did not slavishly stick to the original Sultan's repertoire, but included originals and hits from other bands associated with the Savoy, including Chick Webb's 'Clap Hands Here Comes Charlie' and 'Harlem Congo', Lucky Millinder's 'Shipyard Social Function' and Erskine Hawkins' 'Norfolk Ferry'. The emphasis was on an infectious beat and capturing the spirit of the swing era—music for dancing. In 1980 they upstaged the Lionel Hampton band at the Newport Jazz Festival, New York and their jumping support lifted Jimmy Witherspoon on 'Jimmy Witherspoon Sings The Blues With Panama Francis And The Savoy Sultans' (Muse). Their relentless drive and workmanlike solos made them a popular attraction, appearing at the Rainbow Grill, New York and at countless Festivals during the early 1980s.

Jeannie and Jimmy Cheatham and their Sweet Baby Blues Band from the West Coast made their debut on Concord in 1984 with 'Sweet Baby Blues' and like all their albums it predominantly featured original material by the two leaders. With guest Charles McPherson (as), the album enjoyed some celebrity through their original composition, 'Meet Me With Your Black Drawers On'. Fronted by singer and pianist Jeannie Cheatham, around whose two-fisted piano style and powerful vocals the band was built, the group was filled by seasoned professionals that created a renaissance of the pre-war Kansas City style that was anything but sweet. They were tailor-made for the festival circuits where they unfailingly left audiences shouting for more. Jeannie Cheatham, who had worked with the likes of T-Bone Walker, Wynonie Harris, Jimmy Witherspoon, Jimmy Rushing, Joe Williams and Dinah Washington somehow eluded recognition until she emerged as the band's star performer; husband Jimmy modestly assumed a back seat role as arranger and bass trombonist.

Lead trumpeter Snooky Young (b.1919), whose solo on Jimmie Lunceford's 1939 'Uptown Blues' was one of the classics of the Swing Era, was featured on all the band's albums in the '80s, his stamina, style and creativity unaffected by *anno Domini,* with powerful support coming from Curtis Peagler (as) and Jimmie Noone (son of the famous New Orleansian) on clarinet. Their second album, 'Midnight Mama' (Concord), confirmed their unequivocal swing with another collection of originals while the 1987 'Homeward Bound' (Concord), with guest Eddie 'Cleanhead' Vinson (1917-88) sounding like a charter member of the band with his searing alto, reaffirmed this was *renaissance,* not re-creation. Humour, irony and social comment are never very far from the blues, and a new classic in the making emerged with 'Sometimes It Be That Way' with the chorus, 'You've got the blues young yuppie. . .'

The 1988 'Back To The Neighborhood' (Concord), with guest Papa John Creech on violin, continued the consistent level of controlled exuberance, one of the delights of the '80s 'mainstream' scene. Growing steadily in popularity through the decade, they were booked into New York's Blue Note for two weeks in 1989 where they did SRO business twice nightly, three times at the weekend; 'Irresistible uptown-style. . . jazz with roots broad enough for a house,' wrote Gary Giddins. 'The Cheathams are in from L.A. and they are rockers.'[8]

KEEPERS OF THE FAITH

Quite apart from the swing era musicians who were by-passed by the crusading avant garde, there were others, who, despite the vicissitudes of fashion, turned away from the work of their contemporaries at the cutting edge to reinvent the past. For some, bop proved to be the rubicon they refused to cross, its beginnings the limit of their stylistic aspirations. And while their solos might have lacked the historical primacy of a Coleman Hawkins or a Louis Armstrong, there were, by the '80s, a select few whose carefully polished work had come to assume a life of its own, like a wheel within a wheel, existing within the boundaries charted out by historical precedent. Neither slavish copy nor imitation, yet wholly at ease within the mainstream tradition, the best of this careful and shrewd derriere-garde were careful not to second-guess or recycle what had gone before or re-house it within a repertory function. Instead, they developed original voices that, although post-dated, retained a sure sense of their creative identities.

Ruby Braff (b.1927) came to the fore in the mid-1950s, when, as Whitney Balliett pointed out, 'Young trumpet players were no longer idolizing Armstrong, instead they followed the mercurial, multi-noted ways of Dizzy Gillespie and Fats Navarro . . . Braff, by contrast, was a throwback, a return to an unfashionable way of playing that was devoted to melody, lyricism and grace.'[9]

Undeterred by prevailing musical trends, Braff's music had the poise and style of a great craftsman; his perspective on creativity was such that it served to reinstate the validity of working within self-imposed stylistic limitations by appearing fresh, creative and new, a singular art that seemed to elude so many of the young neo-classicists during the '80s.

Braff's inability to suffer fools at any cost might have impeded his career, but by the 1980s he cut down possible friction points by working only with certain musicians whose playing was in accord with his own. He created a minor classic with pianist Dick Hyman on the 1984 'America The Beautiful' (Concord), a duet recorded live at the Pittsburg Area Theatre Organ Society with Hyman playing the pipe organ, 'Two Pisces with but a single groove,' said Hyman later. Two years later they filmed their unique collaboration for BBC TV at the Fairground Musuem in Norfolk with Hyman playing the mighty Wurlitzer. Hyman returned to the less imposing piano for 'Music From My Fair Lady' (Concord), another congenial and highly sympathetic mainstream summit.

Braff combined with young fellow-traveller Scott Hamilton, a tenor saxophonist whose Flip Phillips-out-of-Ben Webster style became justly praised at the end of the 1970s, on the 1985 'A Fine Match', the 1986 'A Sailboat In The Moonlight' (both Concord) and 'Mr. Braff To You' (Phontastic) from later in the same year. Braff's playing is always assured and inventive, his gift of paraphrase echoed by Hamilton, who has an equal aversion to playing the same phrase twice. Their styles are a celebration of magnificent obsolescence.

Clarinettist **Kenny Davern** (b.1935) had almost 20 years of solid playing experience behind him in mainstream/dixie bands as diverse as Henry 'Red' Allen and The Dukes Of Dixieland when he achieved international recognition as one half of the Soprano Summit duo with Bob Wilbur, formed in 1974. When the group disbanded in 1979 he decided to concentrate exclusively on clarinet, 'I think to come to terms with any instrument you have to stay with it,' he said.[10]

By then he had demonstrated on the 1978 'Unexpected' (Kharma), with Steve Lacy, Steve Swallow and Paul Motian, a vision of breadth and insight in a free jazz context. Although he subsequently remained within the mainstream orbit his playing never seemed tied dogmatically to the conventions of the idiom. He grafted ideas that were from harmonically and rhythmically more enlightened eras in flashes of wisdom and wit that simultaneously evoked Thelonious Monk and Pee Wee Russell within a style that was underpinned by the fluency of Benny Goodman. His tone was rich and centered and during the course of the 1980s his playing, although under-recorded, attained a level of maturity that marked him as a true original and a latterday master of his instrument.

By the 1980s Davern's preferred idiom was a trio, recording two albums with Ralph Sutton (p) and Gus Johnson (d) and touring with the group Blue Three with Dick Wellstood (p) and Bobby Rosengarden (d). Among the best of his trio albums were 'The Hot Three' (Monmouth Evergreen) with Art Hodes and Don DeMicheal, a homage to early clarinettists such as Noone, Dodds and Bechet, and 'Live Hot Jazz' (Statiris) with Dick Wellstood and Chuck Riggs. The 1984 'The Very Thought Of You' (Milton Keynes Music Series) won a British Phonographic Industries Award and 'This Old Gang Of Ours' (Calligraph) was a cheerful session with British bandleader Humphrey Lyttelton. The individuality of Davern's playing, however, was not translated on to record during the '80s, ironically a time when he appeared at the peak of his powers: one of the few clarinettists in jazz to remain his own man, lit by the sun of his own style rather than playing from within the shadow of Goodman.

Tenor saxophonist **Scott Hamilton's** (b.1954) solos were described by Nat Hentoff as, 'Big toned, deep-swinging melodic improvising that is the jazz equivalent of a prime steak dinner'. Certainly there was a wholesome quality about his work that did not lack for authority, purpose or direction. Although his style emerged through such swing era models as Coleman Hawkins, Ben Webster, Flip Phillips and Paul Gonsalves, Hamilton evolved an approach that was conspicuously his own, with an instantly recognizable tone and, within the context of his style, showed he had the imagination of a major jazz improviser.

During the 1970s he was encouraged by trumpeter Roy Eldridge and pianist John Bunch and by 1977 was working with Benny Goodman. Since 1978 there was a steady flow of albums on the Concord label and by the end of the 1980s he had appeared on over 40 albums as either leader or sideman. All Hamilton's albums have something to commend

Warren Vaché and Scott Hamilton: Their poise and authority could be startling in live performance.

them; for example, his solo on 'Ham Fat', a riff on the 'Rhythm' changes, from 'Apples And Oranges' (Concord) is something of a *tour de force* that illustrates the main features of his playing. Flowing and relaxed, it gradually builds in tension through its juxtaposition of melodic motifs that appear and reappear in different forms throughout his solo. Such thematic cohesiveness, while sounding spontaneous, nevertheless interlocked to form a complete improvised statement that, together with his personal tone and expressive inflections, created work of genuine substance within the mainstream idiom.

Hamilton's work with his own quintet—John Bunch (p) and his former Providence, Rhode Island blowing buddies Chris Flory (g), Phil Flanigan (b) and Chuck Riggs (d)—benefited from of working together over a long period. Their integrated group sound is at its best on 'Close Up', the 1983 concert at Yamaha Hall, Tokyo that produced the excellent 'In Concert' and 'The Second Set', a congenial 'The Right Time' and the 1989 'Scott Hamilton Plays Ballads', a mixture of easy swingers and ballads that included a well thought out 'Body And Soul', (all Concord). In fact, Hamilton's ballad performances received consistent praise during the '80s; one of the few young contemporary musicians to master this most difficult area of jazz, his poise and authority were at times startling, particularly in live performance.

Throughout the 1980s cornettist and occasional flugelhornist **Warren Vaché's** (b.1951) career was closely associated with Scott Hamilton. They first played together in 1976 and quickly realized that their thinking was developing along similar lines, in extending the swing era rather than being limited by it. Vaché's style, described by Peter Straub as 'Bunny Berigan shakes hands with Clifford Brown', was, like that of Hamilton's, immediately recognizable as his own in both tone and concept.

Vaché originally attracted attention in 1975 with recreations of Bix Beiderbecke solos with the New York Jazz Repertory at Carnegie Hall and this led to work with Benny Goodman, an association that continued until 1984. From 1976-79 he was a member of the house band at Eddie Condon's club and by the 1980s he, like Hamilton, had become a regular on the Concord label. By the end of the decade he had appeared on over 30 Concord albums including sessions with Hamilton, Rosemary Clooney, the Concord Super Band, Woody Herman and Buddy Tate.

Vaché's work as a leader in his own right include 'Jillian', the 1979 'Polished Brass' (both Concord) and the 1981 'Iridescence' (Concord). The latter, an excellent mainstream/modern date with Hank Jones (p), George

Duvivier (b) and Alan Dawson (d), featured Vaché's elegant flugel on 'Softly As In A Morning Sunrise', 'No Regrets' and 'The More I See You'. A 1982 trio date with John Bunch and Phil Flanigan, 'Midtown Jazz' (Concord), placed Vaché's style under close scrutiny in this most demanding environment and his playing checked out on all counts within the context of his adopted musical home. Intonation, articulation, originality, tone and conception: despite his slightly dated vibrato, Vaché had it all.

On the 1986 'Easy Going' (Concord), the leader democratically split the solos equally among guitar, piano and trombone leaving his own work little space, which was a shame as this was a session where he genuinely sounded relaxed. Vaché's skill in ballad interpretation was featured on 'Warren Vaché And The Beaux-Arts Quartet' (Concord); projects with strings have traditionally been fraught with problems in jazz, but Vaché's tone, warmth and maturity-beyond-his-years again demonstrated an original style worthy of close attention.

But Vaché, like Hamilton, failed to get on to record the true breadth of his individuality, something that became all too apparent in live performance; 'I'm just too painfully aware of where I am when I'm recording,' he said. Both musicians toured extensively in Europe and Japan throughout the 1980s, and in the right environment—'I'm a night club player,' confessed Hamilton—produced solos of dramatic validity within an enlightened mainstream context. But because the idiom in which they chose to express themselves was considered distinctly non-hip they continued all too often to move in the less exalted circles of pick-up bands and semi-pro rhythm sections; in late 1989, for example, Hamilton was touring as a single in New Zealand. Critical recognition that should have been universal was, generally speaking, withheld in favour of more fashionable trends.

Ken Peplowski (b.1958) had, by the end of the 1980s, developed a reputation as perhaps the finest young clarinettist in New York. After two years as a clarinet major at Cleveland State he left to go on the road playing tenor sax/clarinet with the Tommy Dorsey Orchestra directed by Buddy Morrow. Three and a half years later he decided to try his luck in New York and initially worked with Jimmy McPartland and Max Kaminsky before joining Loren Schoenberg's Orchestra. In 1985 Benny Goodman, a major influence on his clarinet style, began using Schoenberg's band for personal appearances, so fulfilling Peplowski's ambition of working with his childhood idol.

Ken Peplowski: In the King's footsteps, the young virtuoso works out on Goodman's 'Clarinade'.

Just how fluent Peplowski was in the Goodman style was demonstrated on the 1988 'In Concert Tokyo' (Concord) by Mel Torme and the Marty Paich Dek-Tette where the singer reverted to drums and Peplowski to clarinet to evoke Goodman/Krupa powerplay on 'Cottontail'. Peplowski also remained true to the King on his 1987 debut album 'Double Exposure' (Concord) where his six clarinet numbers alluded to the Goodman/Christian sextets, with Canadian guitarist Ed Bickert the soul of stylistic discretion. The remaining four tracks featured his tenor saxophone which, like his clarinet playing, showed a willingness to move occasionally beyond swing era models to include harmonic and rhythmic devices from bop. The 1989 'Sonny Side' (Concord) showed greater stylistic abandon, moving from 'Ring Dem Bells' to Monk's 'Ugly Beauty' and from Sonny Stitt's 'Sonny Side' to Roland Kirk's 'Bright Moments'.

Peplowski's versatility (he also played alto on 'Alone At Last' from 'Sonny Side' [Concord]) was also featured with George Shearing, Peggy

Lee, Susannah McCorkle, Hank Jones, Leon Redbone and Loren Schoenberg's Orchestra. His appearance with the Schoenberg Orchestra at the 1989 Goodman tribute at Carnegie Hall, playing the demanding clarinet role on Goodman features, including the tricky 1945 Mel Powell arrangement of 'Clarinade' amongst others, prompted John S. Wilson in the *New York Times*[11] to observe, 'Ken Peplowski stayed close to Goodman style and extended his performance of 'Stealin' Apples' to a true king of swing climax.'

COOL

Cool was not so much a specific style as an attitude. Most cool musicians were, in fact, bop musicians who had mastered the melodic and harmonic implications of bop but favoured the subdued lyricism of Miles Davis, Lester Young, Lennie Tristano and Count Basie. Although the cool sobriquet was primarily associated with West Coast jazz of the 1950s, often overlooked were East Coast musicians performing in Boston and New York in a similar manner. Cool soloists were usually characterized by a soft, dry and subdued tone and its orchestrators emphasized pastel tone colours inspired by the 'Birth Of The Cool' sessions by Miles Davis for Capitol Records in 1949-50, the Claude Thornhill Orchestra of the late forties and the drive of the Basie Orchestra of the late 1930s. When cool jazz was at its height in the '50s, one of its main characteristics, as compared to hard-bop, was the emphasis on written arrangements. By the '80s, the orchestral style was all but forgotten; cool existed only in the few remaining personal voices of the musicians who were associated with the style in the '50s.

Perhaps the finest exemplar of cool in the 1980s was **Lee Konitz** (b.1927), who with Lennie Tristano (1919-78) could really be considered to be one of the sources of the cool approach to improvisation (their collaborations were reissued in the 1980s to considerable acclaim, 'Lennie Tristano-Requiem' and 'The Lennie Tristano Quartet' [both Atlantic]). Tristano was in equal parts pianist, teacher and philosopher; 'He felt and communicated that the music was a serious matter. It wasn't a game or a means of making a living, it was a life force,' recalled Konitz, 'I respect what he was doing as an artist and I'm trying to keep that alive.'

Tristano helped Konitz to develop an alto style that was wholly individual and virtually unique in that it was totally unrelated to Charlie Parker's conception. Konitz's ideal was to create a solo that stood as a complete statement, rather than a series of choruses that may or may not relate one to the other. His style initially followed Tristano's with long flowing lines with the minimum of rhythmic displacement and his light, dry tone was similar to that of Lester Young on the tenor sax. Although an East Coast player, Konitz' influence was most apparent on the West Coast, touching the playing of saxophonists such as Bud Shank, Bob Cooper and Lennie Niehaus.

By the early '70s, however, Konitz was advertising for pupils in the pages of *Downbeat* magazine. Swept to the sidelines by the '60s 'New Thing' and the blind alley of fusion in the '70s, he emerged in the '80s, older, if not necessarily wiser, through his experiences as a hostage to musical fashion. Such recording exposure as he did receive between 1960-79—particularly his continued association with Warne Marsh (1927-87)—suggested his playing may have peaked, but without anyone really noticing.

Certainly, during the 1980s, both live and on record, Konitz's playing was variable. With a player of his high standards, this may have been simply a matter of degree, but his style, centered on the art of genuine spontaneous creation, of spinning melodic variations one upon the other to form a complete and self contained whole, was a fragile art. If one layer fell uneasily it upset the balance of succeeding layers, 'It's kind of easy superficially to just jump in and play some variations of "All The Things You Are". But to really account for every note, as I think a serious improviser or composer ought to do . . . I try to go in with a blank slate and not a whole vocabulary of useful licks,' he explained.

Konitz entered the 1980s at the head of a nonet based on the Miles Davis 'Birth Of The Cool' ensemble; the 1977 'Lee Konitz Nonet' (Chiaroscuro), the 1979 'Live At Laren' (Soul Note) and 'Yes, Yes, Nonet' (Steeplechase) deserved more success with soloists that included from time to time Red Rodney, Jimmy Knepper, Ronnie Cuber and a rhythm section featuring Ray Drummond and Billy Hart.

By the mid-1980s Konitz had joined the staff at Temple University, Philadelphia giving master classes and individual tuition, but continued to tour with a quartet built around longtime accompanist Harold Danko (p); the 1983 'Dovetail' (Sunnyside) was marred by seven and a half minutes of 'free' playing but the 1986 'Ideal Scene' (Soul Note) is among his best work from the decade. Konitz now fragmented his line, challenging the listener with a series of anagrams rather than spelling everything out in long rows of neat, flowing handwriting. However, 'The New York Album' (Soul Note) from the following year disappointed; Konitz's playing seemed at arm's length, the emotional distancing exacerbated by the un-credited use of his Martini-dry soprano sax on some numbers.

Other highspots included duets with Harold Danko, 'Wild As Spring-time' (GFM), Michel Petrucciani, 'Toot Suite' and 'I Hear A Rhapsody' (both Owl) and the 1988 'Songs Of The Stars' (Jazzhouse) with John Taylor. 'Round And Round' (Music Masters), was a quartet session with pianist Fred Hersch, but the 1989 'In Rio' (MA Music), a collaboration with orchestrator Allan Botschinsky, seemed an uncharacteristic lapse into the ephemeral for one of the master improvisers in jazz, 'I think they call it *easy listening*' he said.

Trumpeter/Flugelhornist **Chet Baker** (1929-88) was, perhaps, the most conspicuous victim of that well known euphemism in jazz, 'personal pro-blems'. His face told the story. Much photographed, the boyish good looks of the 1950s Pacific Jazz album covers had disappeared with the ravages of his lifestyle, his face lined and shrunken, the all too tangible evidence of the blight of addiction. 'They're laugh lines,' he once quipped to fellow trumpeter and arch-humorist Jack Sheldon, '*Nothing* in life is that funny', was the response. And while addiction was one problem, another, observed writer Mike Zwerin, was that the world was not, 'and may never be, ready to accept a redneck jazz musician'.[12]

Baker, the eternal boy-man, once enjoyed phenomenal success in the 1950s as a member of the Gerry Mulligan Quartet and subsequently with his own groups. But despite the acclaim, Baker managed to snatch defeat from the jaws of victory by profligate indulgence. His spectacular nose-dive into skid-row reached its nadir in 1968 when his teeth were knocked out, apparently at the behest of a drug dealer. A slow and painful come-back through the '70s, including a reunion with Mulligan at Carnegie Hall in 1974, gradually established his reputation, albeit as one of the most precarious bookings on the circuit, 'There were certainly off-nights,' wrote *The Times*,[13] 'but even when the trumpet tone was practically trans-parent, his singing voice a whisper and the music seemingly in imminent danger of coming to an absolute halt, his innate musicianship could still achieve small miracles of wounded grace.'

His style, like a hyper-sensitive Miles Davis, was simultaneously moving and unsettling, a musical confessional that was as honest as his life was corrupt. Such soiled romanticism was somehow fascinating and there was no shortage of independent labels willing to take a chance on Baker, who recorded prolifically during the '80s: countless musical fixes left in the wake of his peripatetic lifestyle. The 1979 'Daybreak' (Steeplechase) recorded in Denmark with his preferred latterday lineup of guitar and bass, included his limping vocals which, like James Dean's acting, were something of an acquired taste.

The 1980 'Salsamba' (Musica), recorded in Paris with the French Latin-jazz group Novos Tempos (whose lineup included an accordion) was an unusual yet successful concept, Baker's floating lyricism perfectly balancing the group's *joie de vivre*. The 1982 'Peace' (Enja), a New York date with Dave Friedman (vib), Buster Williams (b) and Joe Chambers (d), was a controlled exercise in Baker's professional introspection but the 1983 Stockholm concert with the Stan Getz Quartet, 'Line For Lyons' (Sonet), disappointed, his singing over exposed and off-key.

Two weeks before he fell to his death from a second-storey hotel window in Amsterdam on 13 May 1988, Baker's variable form drifted into focus to create a satisfying and well crafted epitaph; his best work in years. 'My Favorite Songs—The Last Great Concert' and 'Straight from The Heart—The Last Great Concert Vol. 2' (both Enja) featured his vocals and trumpet against an impressive backdrop provided by the German NDR-Big Band and the Radio Orchestra Hanover in a set of well chosen and arranged jazz standards. The session was supervised by Kurt Giese, who subsequently raised the question of Baker's mysterious death; did he fall or was he pushed? 'Things were looking good again . . . Chet had plans. He had his eye on a little house outside Paris . . . '[14] The attitude of a man with suicide on his mind?

In 1986 Baker appeared on one number in the Bertrand Tavernier film 'Round Midnight' (CBS), but in 1989 occupied centre-stage in fashion photographer Bruce Webber's documentary, 'Let's Get Lost'. Despite the self-confessed idolatry tone it showed Baker as both taker and manipulator, particularly of women. His ex-wives queued up to list his infidelities, but his fecklessness simply added to the mystique; the film became a cult success. The soundtrack was posthumously released by Novus and was a surprise hit in the 1989 *Billboard* charts. Baker had almost made it, again.

Of **Dave Brubeck** (b.1920) the English critic Benny Green said in 1961 'there is no jazz attraction of any kind in the world to challenge the mass appeal of Brubeck.'[15] Between 1951 and 1967 Brubeck's Quartet was considered by a large section of the public to be the very epitome of hip, modern jazz. His success was not without controversy, however, as his style clearly avoided the then prevailing bop conception and rhythmic feeling and was widely panned by critics.

But Brubeck was an original thinker. Quite independent of Miles Davis he organized a West Coast ensemble very similar in style to the East Coast 'Birth Of The Cool' sessions, his experiments with time signatures made unusual metres commonplace in jazz following his 1959 million-seller 'Take Five', and his percussive, polyrhythmic, polytonal and harmonically dense piano style was an acknowledged, but seldom commented, influence on Cecil Taylor's radical experimentation.[16] In fact, Brubeck as pianist was rooted in Boogie-Woogie; that unique, pounding style the starting point of every lesson when he studied with Darius Milhaud in 1947 and the point of departure for his subsequent 'progressive' piano work.

At the end of the 1970s Brubeck reformed a quartet with Jerry Bergonzi (ts), son Chris Brubeck on bass—and rather bizarrely bass trombone—and Butch Miles (d), who had just left the Basie band. 'Back Home' (Concord) from 1978, fell short of the mark, if only because Bergonzi's workmanlike post-Coltrane tenor seemed out of context in Brubeck's highly personal world. The 1980 'Tritonis' and the 1981 'Paper Moon' (Concord), with the English drummer Randy Jones who replaced Miles in 1979, failed to advance Brubeck's cause, and confirmed the uneasy Brubeck/Bergonzi mix.

When the clarinettist and classical composer William D. Smith—Bill Smith in his jazz persona—replaced Bergonzi, he restored something of the missing poise and sense of period in Brubeck's music. Smith had performed and recorded intermittently with Brubeck since the two met as students of Milhaud and was introduced on the 1982 'Concord On A Summer Night' which together with the live 1984 'For Iola' (both Concord), revealed Smith as an individual and articulate musician and not far removed from the top clarinettists in '80s jazz.

In 1987 the Brubeck Quartet was invited to tour in the USSR and returned again in 1988 as the only American artist invited to perform at the historic Reagan/Gorbachev summit; when presented to Secretary General Gorbachev, Brubeck gave him copies of 'Moscow Night' (Concord) recorded at Rossiya Concert Hall, Moscow the previous March. Other than his work with Gerry Mulligan, (1968-72), it was probably his best post-Desmond album; mercifully son Chris's trombone had remained in its case. In early 1989, Brubeck became seriously ill, but by June appeared at Carnegie Hall as part of the JVC New York Jazz Festival.

Brubeck's position in jazz has never rested well with critics, conscious that there were artists of greater talent and originality earning a fraction of Brubeck's income and virtually unknown outside the music. With the passage of time, however, his achievements were neither as bad as the critics would have had us believe or as good to warrant the enormous following he once commanded. No one has ever claimed that the music business is fair. What was remarkable about Brubeck's success was that he did not compromise *his* vision—in the light of subsequent events in jazz, a worthy achievement in itself.

Brubeck, romantic idealist and popularizer, helped make modern jazz accessible to a large predominantly white, middle-class audience—the audience that came to play a significant role in sustaining jazz through recordings, concert tickets and by patronizing jazz clubs. But popularity devoured Brubeck's reputation, relegating him to the no-man's land of contemporary critique, rather like Tchaikovsky in classical music.

WEST COAST

West Coast Jazz, once dubbed 'bourgeois bop' of the '50s and the most popular variant of cool, had passed from view by the '60s. Once a release from the mediocrity of the McCarthy era, it was subsequently savaged by critics for its bloodless and often gutless performances. But, as in all generalizations this was only partly true and certainly not true of the majority of the work of trumpeter/flugelhornist **Shorty Rogers** (b.1924).

Bud Shank and Shorty Rogers: After 20 years the 'Giants' return.

Little has been written to acknowledge Rogers' inquisitive and probing experimentalism; an exciting and exceptionally inventive arranger for both the late '40s Woody Herman band and the early '50s Stan Kenton band, his arrangements for his own studio big band for the 'Cool And Crazy' sessions in 1953 (RCA) made use of bitonality, irregular ostinatos and timbral densities.

In his small groups—The Giants—and those of Jimmy Giuffre, Shelly Manne and Teddy Charles he abandoned chord changes five years before Ornette Coleman's breakthrough, used modes before Miles Davis's 'Milestones' (CBS) and in 1954 made pioneering use in jazz of the 12-tone system. Clearly his work was in need of drastic re-appraisal and the opportunity came in 1989 with the re-issue of his EMI-Atlantic work on Mosaic. Genial and well crafted, they stood the test of time, their optimistic defiance refusing to be squashed by detractors. But it was a style that ended as abruptly as it had begun when key figures, such as Rogers, began to obtain lucrative work in the Hollywood recording studios at the end of the '50s.

One of the surprises of the '80s, therefore, was the return of Shorty Rogers plus his reformed Giants to active performance for the first time in over 20 years. Rogers, who had immersed himself in motion picture and television writing, was persuaded in 1982 to tour the United Kingdom, where his '50s big band reissues, 'Blues Express' (the 'Cool And Crazy' sessions) and 'Courts The Count' (both RCA) had topped the jazz charts a couple of years before. The subsequent tour, with the National Youth Jazz Orchestra, represented the first time in over 15 years he had played in public. In March 1983 he linked up with alto saxophonist Bud Shank, a close associate since the early '50s, and in May he reassembled The Giants for 'Re-Entry' (Atlas), a re-working of his early '50s material that earnt a 'Seal Of Approval' from Japan's *Swing Journal*.

The June 1983 'Yesterday, Today And Forever' (Concord), with Bud Shank, was in comparison a disappointment in its lack of urgency and hustle and bustle that was so much a part of Rogers' writing. In September the Giants reassembled to tour Japan and 'Aurex Festival '83/Live' (Aurex) reinstated their executive swing and highly competent, and in the case of Bud Shank on 'For The Love Of Art', impassioned soloing over the joyful swing of drummer Shelly Manne (1920-84). The Shank/Rogers combination hit their stride on the 1985 'California Concert' (Contemporary); Shank's playing was light years away from his tepid work with the LA4 in the '70s and Rogers' crafty loop-the-loop solos on flugel swung mightily.

When **Bud Shank** (b.1926) emerged from the safe haven of the Hollywood recording studios in 1980 with a move to Seattle it soon became clear that his comfortable, if slightly obscure, place in jazz was in need of drastic revision. The discovery of a 1956 session with his quartet, 'Live At The Haig' (Concept), issued in 1985, gave evidence that even in the '50s he was a far better musician than he was generally given credit for. Then his style was influenced by Lee Konitz; in the '80s it had become hard-bitten and strident with something of the emotional intensity of the late Art Pepper, for whom Shank ably substituted when the altoist was so often detained at the pleasure of the Justice Department during the '50s.

Shank made several albums during the '80s, but surprisingly few conveyed the passion of his live performances; perhaps so long in the studios made Shank err on the side of caution. However, the 1984 'This Bud's For You' (Muse) with Kenny Barron, Ron Carter and Al Foster reveal the revitalized Shank, albeit high on professionalism and low on chance-taking. A 1985 date at London's Festival Hall performing Manny Albam's 'Concerto For Alto Saxophone And Orchestra' with the Royal Philharmonic Orchestra (Mole Jazz) left no doubt as to Shank's massive technical competence, but little else. The 1986 'Bud Shank Quartet—Jazz Alley' (Contemporary), a live date at Dimitriou's Jazz Alley in Seattle, Washington still showed Shank's conservatism, on record at least, but occasionally revealed the inner-man—a born again be-bopper.

Of all the cool school, **Jimmy Giuffre** (b.1921) was the most relentless of experimenters; from his orthodox swing-into-bop writing for Woody Herman he imperceptibly became a one-man avant garde in cautious, cerebral degrees and always by dint of his own careful rationalisation than the influence of others. By the time he recorded 'Free Fall' (CBS) in 1963 he had made 15 albums as a leader. By 1990 he had made only four more, 'I look for personal creative music without addressing myself to the common market,' he said.[17]

Along with Gerry Mulligan, Giuffre was one of the first to abandon the piano in jazz, moving through folk-jazz into free jazz and then into oblivion. His re-emergence from the New England Conservatory with his quartet in 1983 revealed another incarnation, the electric Giuffre. His quartet, with Pete Levin (synths), Bob Nieske (b) and Randy Kaye (d), produced haunting electronic soundscapes that the *New York Times* described as 'atmospheric rather than linear.' The 1983 'Dragonfly' (Soul Note) had Giuffre on tenor, soprano, clarinet, flute and bass flute creating

Jimmy Giuffre: Only Miles Davis springs to mind as someone who consistently and ruth-lessly moved his music forward through radical changes.

a sinewy and occasionally jarring New Age music with teeth. The 1985 'Quasar' (Soul Note) continued his essays in cautious abandon, 'I want to sound warm and full of energy,' he said, 'but what I would like to be is unpredictable.'[18] Uncelebrated, Giuffre's small corner of jazz deserved acclaim, for rarely—and only Miles Davis springs readily to mind—had a musician consistently and ruthessly moved his music on through such radical changes.

SUI GENERIS

There has been no trumpeter or flugelhornist in jazz like **Clark Terry** (b.1920). The possessor of a tone so personal and a style so inimitable that a music contractor once told him he couldn't book him because, 'even though you might not play the lead, your sound is too individual[19],' Terry was probably the only jazz musician actively performing in the '80s whose identity could be spotted from just one note. In an age of mass cloning—the Coltrane clones, the Brecker clones, the Gadd clones, the Sanborn clones *et al*—a Clark Terry performance was always a unique event with a style and sound that answered to no-one.

By the '80s Clark Terry was comfortably off; he had invested wisely in real estate as a member of the Duke Ellington Orchestra (1951-59), as a staff member of the NBC orchestra and as a featured member of the 'Tonight Show' band (1959-72), but continued an exhausting round of clinics and master classes, festival appearances, concert tours and recording dates throughout the decade. Terry's style was the epitome of technical proficiency; one of the few brassmen to completely master circular breathing, his ability to tongue (separate) notes even at the fastest tempos was widely admired by musicians, but he went a step further: he made every note smile.

Terry's style was equally at home in hard-bop or mainstream; careful not to be pigeon-holed he explained, 'I found that to . . . stay out of the controversial categorizing thing . . . you stay yourself and play things people can recognize and you do it your way.' A consummate blues and ballad player (as a sideman, his solo with the Quincy Jones Orchestra of 'I Remember Clifford' is probably the definitive version), Terry, perhaps surprisingly, made only a handful of wholly satisfactory albums. Other than the memorable 'Oscar Peterson Plus One' (Mercury) from 1964 and his four albums with co-leader Bob Brookmeyer between 1964-66, Terry seemed to have been the victim of unimaginative record producers who, conscious of his ability to make silk purses from sows ears, seemed content to put him in the studio with a pick-up band and let him loose on a set of worn-to-death standards with the minimum of preparation.

The Big B-a-d Band he was leading in 1980-81, including Branford Marsalis and Chris Woods in the saxophone section, went unrecorded. Instead, his then current record label Pablo, whose unwritten maxim seemed to be quantity rather than quality, ground out a series of hastily convened sessions that included 'Memories Of The Duke' from 1980 with Joe Pass that oddly failed to include any number from Terry's eight-year tenure with Ellington. The 1981 'Yes, The Blues' with Eddie 'Cleanhead' Vinson included vocals by Terry's alter-ego, the 'manic Delta bluesman', Mumbles, whose humorous scat refused to wear thin through over-exposure. The session with Zoot Sims, 'Mother-Mother', and 'Alternate Blues' with Gillespie, Freddie Hubbard and Peterson kept up the Pablo numbers game, scrupulously avoiding anything profound.

Sadly, the only recorded re-union of the 'Mumbles and Grumbles' combination during the '80s (Terry's association with valve trombonist Bob Brookmeyer that dated back to the '60s when they co-led a quintet) was as a part of the 1980 'Bob Brookmeyer/Composer, Arranger with the Mel Lewis Jazz Orchestra' (Gryphon) on 'El Co' and 'Fan Club'. A re-union in 1986 at Chapel Hill, Newport County with Tommy Flanagan, Jay Anderson (b) and Kenny Washington (d) was a good recording opportunity missed. The 1986 duo 'Clark Terry—Red Mitchell' and 'To Duke And Basie' (both Enja), showed Terry's lyricism supported only by a bass, effortlessly holding centre stage with his unflagging imagination and was the kind of intense performing situation his discography was all too short of. The 1988 'Portraits' (Chesky) and a fun session with Red Holloway from 1989, 'Locksmith Blues' (Concord), are good Terry performances with quality sidemen but marred by conservative, hoary material; unfortunately Terry seemed typecast by his producers in limiting rather than expansive roles.

Over the years the work of tenor saxophonist **Stan Getz** (b.1927) has been increasingly taken for granted. Claims that he was a Lester Young copyist could be dismissed as early as 1949 with his virtuoso display through all 12 keys on the uptempo blues 'Crazy Chords' (New Jazz), or his superb ten-chorus solo at 76 bars per minute on the 1955 'Shine' from 'West Coast Jazz' (Verve)—the eight-bar unaccompanied introduction alone worth the price of the album.

Getz continually refined his style and succeeded in redefining his art in a variety of contexts; his early 1950s quintet with guitarist Jimmy Raney, the improvised counterpoint of his 'Shrine' (Verve) recordings with Bob Brookmeyer, the modest commercial success of 'Moonlight In Vermont' (Vogue) with guitarist Johnny Smith, his collaboration with Eddie Sauter that produced 'Focus' (Verve), one of his best-ever recordings, the Bossa Nova years that brought him four Grammy awards and his association with younger musicians that moved his playing from contemplative to competitive in the company of Gary Burton, Chick Corea and JoAnne Brackeen.

The 1979 'Children Of The World' (CBS), with ersatz strings and glossy pop backing was a disappointment. In live performance he was using electronic keyboards to create a post-fusion backdrop, 'I didn't realise how awful it had become until I stopped,' he said later.[20] His performance at the 1980 Midem convention, 'Midem Live '80' (Kingdom Jazz) represented the end of this unsatisfactory period in Getz's career. In 1981 he moved from New York to San Francisco, severed his ties with CBS and signed with the Concord label.

'The Dolphin' from May 1981, recorded live at Keystone Korner marked his initial collaboration with Victor Lewis, his first choice drummer throughout the 1980s, but the sustained reserve and control throughout was ultimately detracting. 'Pure Getz' from 1982, had Getz combining with Jim McNeely (p), Marc Johnson (b) and Lewis and together with 'The Stockholm Concert' (Sonet) from 1983, with George Mraz (b), represented his best work since the Grammy nominee 'Stan Getz Gold' (Inner City/Steeplechase) from 1977. A collaboration with pianist Albert Dailey in 1983 produced 'Poetry' (Elektra Musician), an album of elegant, focussed two-way invention.

In 1985 Getz's association with Dianne Schuur, a talented new young vocalist, resulted in cameo appearances on her GRP albums; 'Schuur Thing' and 'Timeless' from 1986. Getz was unequivocal in his admiration of her prowess, allowing his name to be used to advance her career. Other cameo appearances included Barry Manilow's 'Swing Street' (Arista) and 'Small World' by Huey Lewis and The News (Chrysalis).

'Voyage' (Blackhawk), a March 1986 session, ended a three-year gap since Getz's last quartet session, with Kenny Barron now on piano. The group followed Getz into his artist-in-residence appointment at Stamford University where he created a jazz division in the existing music department. In 1987, with Rufus Reid on bass, the group toured Europe. Getz was clearly at one with his art, secure in the knowledge that what he did, he did well.

He had refined his ballad interpretation to a level that hardly any musician during the 1980's could match, 'I like Stan,' said Miles Davis, 'because he has so much patience, the way he plays those melodies—other people can't get nothing from a song, but he can.'[21] Getz's playing was a model of lucid, logical thematic (rather than harmonic) development; whatever the tempo his control of tonal colouring enabled him to intensify the emotional dimension of his playing that could move from gentle caresses to powerful, steely assertions. Equally important, his musicians, chosen to challenge and stimulate him, ensured a high level of creativity.

Perhaps here lies the key to Getz's consistency. He always chose musicians to extend him, such as Chick Corea who joined him as an unknown pianist in 1966 and collaborated on what many consider one of Getz's best albums, 'Sweet Rain' (Verve). 'He's willing to go into new areas . . . even though they are sometimes very strenuous for him', observed vibraphonist Gary Burton, who featured in his group 1964-66.

Oscar Peterson (b.1925) can claim the dubious immortality as the most recorded jazz artist of all time, sometimes releasing as many as five albums in the space of a year—in 1981 the English critic Richard Palmer said he had over 250 albums featuring Peterson.[22] Such a prolific output in-

Oscar Peterson: 'Dominated his trios to the point of alienating its members'.

evitably created something of a critical *ennui,* which, it must be said, damaged his career not a bit. His piano style, like that of his *alma mater* Art Tatum, was beyond category—simply Oscar Peterson.

Undeniably flashy, Peterson's awesome command of his instrument and his strong, straightforward swing were derived from swing era/mainstream models. Superficially his playing appeared profoundly in debt to Tatum's style with his use of sophisticated harmonic substitutions, rococo flourishes and love of 'stride' piano; both Tatum and Peterson were the logical and ultimate refinement of the Harlem Stride school of the 1920s, even duplicating some of its sociological conventions, such as the Master/Pupil relationship, embodied in Peterson's friendship with Tatum. But Peterson's conception was more direct and, particularly when playing with bass and drums, orchestral in the big band sense, using block chordal passages, question and answer and ostinato riffs.

The glamour of Peterson's forceful and expansive style reached beyond jazz and it was not unusual for sections of his audiences to dress as for opera at his concerts. Many of the large audience he attracted were inclined towards displays of virtuosity for its own sake, prompting Peterson's decision in 1972 to indulge his technique in solo concerts, 'I became too involved in what I was doing and didn't listen to my group,' he said.[23] When, at the end of the 1970s he returned to the traditional trio format with bass and drums, something of the one-man-show continued to permeate his performances. Peterson seemed to want the bass, and more particularly the drums, to play with minimum interaction so as not to impede his flow.

The duo 'Digital At Montreux' (Pablo), from July 1979 with Niels-Henning Orsted Pedersen on bass, is a pretty comprehensive workout of all aspects of Peterson's style, which had been refined to the point where it had become an exposition of his technique; 'The virtuoso sign flashed incessantly', wrote Whitney Balliet,[24] 'and it hid the fact that the chief content of his solos was packed into the first eight or ten bars; what came next was largely ornamentation and hyperbole.' Such bravura was held in check on 'The Original Score From The "Silent Partner" ' (Pablo), a good, straightforward mainstream session featuring Peterson's original, uncomplicated compositions with like-minded swingers Clark Terry, Benny Carter, Zoot Sims and Milt Jackson.

From the late 1970s Peterson used the unpretentious English drummer Martin Drew, who along with Niels-Henning Orsted Pedersen, became Peterson's regular working group. With the addition of guitarist Joe Pass, a frequent collaborator since the early 1970s, they appeared on 'In Japan '82' (Pablo). Recorded live in Tokyo, both sets from late February are curiously restrained and perfunctory.

Perhaps Peterson needed stimulation; the 1981 meeting with Milt Jackson, 'Ain't But A Few Of Us Left' (Pablo) was a typical Pablo permutation that had Grady Tate and Ray Brown pushing from behind and insisting things happen; it was one of his better albums of the decade. On Good Friday 1984 Peterson premiered his somewhat meandering 'Easter Suite' on English television with his regular group. In 1985 he appeared with Ella Fitzgerald on the PBS 'On Stage At Wolftrap' series and by 1987 the Canadian bassist Dave Young had replaced N-HOP. Later in the year another Pablo collaboration, this time one of Peterson's best, 'Benny Carter Meets Oscar Peterson', made comparisons with Art Tatum's similar 1954 meeting (Verve) inevitable; Peterson and Carter effortlessly continued to extend the mainstream tradition into the 1980s. In 1988 drummer Bobby Durham replaced Drew for a European tour and later in the year Peterson appeared as a guest of Dizzy Gillespie, featuring in a duet on the PBS 'Great Performances' series.

Quite how firmly Peterson was planted in the mainstream was shown in sharp relief on the 1982 session with trumpeter Freddie Hubbard, 'Face

To Face' (Pablo). When he attempted to customize the subtle Miles Davis vehicle 'All Blues' to his usual specifications, the composition's implied stylistic rubicon proved impossible for him to cross; equally on Hubbard's post-bop theme 'Thermo' the feeling intensified with an incongruous stride piano postscript. In fact, Peterson's style, particularly when performing solo, was almost a distillation of pre-1950s piano techniques from stride through to bop, 'My roots go back to people like Coleman Hawkins, harmonically speaking, certainly Art Tatum, which you can hear, and Hank Jones too,' he said.

Early in his career Peterson realized that his phenomenal technique held the key to success. 'I decided I was going to wipe every piano player, if that was the only way I was going to get my just due. I went for broke.'[25] Certainly, within those terms, Peterson can claim to have succeeded, even if it meant he 'dominated his various trios to the point of alienating its members.'[26]

But music is not simply a matter of being held in awe by a peer group of musicians. Mastery, as Montale pointed out, is knowing how to limit yourself.[27] It also involves aesthetic direction and as Burnett James observed, it was 'often impossible to tell what artistic ends all that technique and all that vitality' were directed.[28] Ultimately, however, Peterson cast a shadow so large it went beyond jazz to stimulate curiosity about the music by breaking down barriers of musical prejudice through his great talent. It was not an inconsiderable achievement.

2

Big Bands: Ancient to Modern

THE CLOSER YOU look at big bands, the greater the distance from which they look back, never simply themselves but the sum of their place in the history of jazz. The swing era, that decade in American history when big bands dominated both jazz and popular culture, has continued to exert a powerful influence on both the sound and structure of the larger ensemble to the extent that any innovation appears more as an expansion of the tradition than a step into the future. Fresh discoveries have been rare and more often than not new revelations of old truths. By the 1980s the big bands, by remaining largely impervious to the coterie of movements that have periodically transformed jazz, appeared as much touchstones of craft as creativity.

The popularity of the big band dates back to the 1920s and whether or not Duke Ellington borrowed the theme of Fauré's 'Sicilienne' from *Pelléas Et Melisande* for his 1932 'It Don't Mean A Thing If It Ain't Got That Swing', the title at least was prophetic. By the mid-1930s swing had captured the imagination of the public to the extent that big bands suddenly seemed to be everywhere, featuring at the dancehalls that proliferated in pre-war America, dominating the radio, record charts and, for a time, popping up on the slightest pretext in Hollywood movies. But for most of the millions of fans they drew, it was not jazz improvisation that attracted them, it was because the big bands played music for dancing.

King of the musical battlefield in the early days of swing was Benny Goodman's Orchestra. His slick presentation of a series of masterful arrangements by Fletcher Henderson, in essence a fusion between jazz and the American Popular Song, became the role-model for countless bands that followed. Henderson's writing etched in stone a methodology of big band writing that soon created a kind of uniformity that was often only personalized by a bandleader's instrumental prowess.

At best, exemplified by the Count Basie Orchestra of 1939 and Duke Ellington's Famous Orchestra of 1940, big band jazz offered a powerful dualism; the individuality of the soloist threatened by the ensemble, the struggle of man versus machine. But although several bands tried to balance the putative opposites of orchestration and individual freedom, there were many that saw record sales and box office receipts as the sole arbiters of success. The dichotomy of the swing era was that the music was functional, played for dancing and the more the big bands succumbed to musical exploitation, the more equivocal became the position of jazz musicians in their ranks.

When in the late 1940s the big band business suffered a sharp downturn in fortune a number of factors were blamed, but the bottom line was cost. The expense of moving 15 or so musicians and their associated impedimenta cross-country night after night quite simply had become prohibitive. But although the swing era has long since receded into history, it has nevertheless continued to exert a profound influence on public expectation of the big band 'sound'. Its definition became fixed in time, in terms of the Benny Goodman Orchestra and other popular swing bands such as those led by Artie Shaw, Glenn Miller and Tommy Dorsey.

For the majority of post-swing era bands survival often meant that economic viability took precedence over artistic ambition. Thus developments in modifying what had become the commonly accepted status quo in both orchestrational and instrumentational terms were conservative, measured only in a series of caveats, codicils and only on occasion a total re-drafting of the basic formula worked out by Fletcher Henderson, Duke Ellington and Count Basie, the prime architects of big band jazz. The swing era, it seemed, cast a long shadow; even by the beginning of the 1980s the Willard Alexander Agency, whose Chicago and New York offices booked most of the name bands then working the circuits, confirmed the band on their books that worked the most was the Glenn Miller Orchestra directed by Larry O'Brien[1]—this almost 40 years after Miller's death.

But if public expectation helped shape the sound of the big bands, so did the educational system from which most of the musicians playing in their ranks during the '80s emerged. Performing in large ensembles demands sound instrumental technique, inch-perfect phrasing, precise intonation, dynamic control and the ability to read at first sight often complex scores. Bringing these elements together is an important process in learning to make music. Bandleader Stan Kenton realized that these virtues could be used to great effect by using the big band as a vehicle for music education; in 1959 he introduced the 'Stage Band' concept to the American educational system.

The concept was a success; big bands gradually became part of musical life in High Schools, Colleges and Universities in America so that by 1981, there were approximately 400,000 young musicians playing in some 20-25,000 bands in American—60% in High Schools, 30% in Colleges and Universities and 10% in Junior High Schools.[2] The level of musicianship achieved by the best was awesome, the level of originality less so. Sounding like Kenton, Basie or Herman provided a system of values that could be slotted into an educational concept, but the aesthetic of a Gil Evans or other rethinkers could not. What began as a Kenton influence had, by his death in 1979, become a Kenton industry with precisely the uniformity so noisome to jazz.

So the functional role big bands inherited from the swing era continued in the 1980s; once they existed to provide music for dancing but now they were mainly educational vehicles or 'Rehearsal Bands,' forums where like-minded musical craftsmen gathered to sharpen their skills. In such settings there was a tendency, observed by Toshiko Akiyoshi, of 'being what a big band is supposed to be.'[3] The 1980s saw the end of the 'Roadband' and the demise of several of the legendary big band names. It should have seemed like the end of an era. But it didn't; big bands were scarcely in short supply, but new ideas were. The idiom had not so much moved forward since the swing era as constantly rationalized with hindsight.

THE SWING ERA: LEGENDS AND LEGACY

Count Basie and his Orchestra

In many ways the post-war decline in influence of big bands could be represented by the artistic eclipse of **Count Basie** (1904-84) and his Orchestra. In short it was of structure progressively replacing personality. In the late 1930s the Basie band made history as much for the gifted improvisers within its ranks as their unique rhythmic flexibility that enabled the rhythm section to swing the band like a small group. But as Basie's gifted improvisers began to depart in the 1940s, the personality of the band suffered. He was forced to adapt and his attitude became unequivocal, 'Well, you don't try and think about Lester Young or Herschel Evans or Don Byas or anything like that,' he said, '. . . so therefore . . . you get yourself more ensemble things.'[4]

By the late 1940s that process was well under way so that when he unveiled his re-jigged sixteen-men-swinging in 1952, the arrangers, particularly Neal Hefti and Ernie Wilkins, had created an ensemble sound that was pretty well invulnerable to the comings and goings of its personnel. It was a blueprint for survival and judged on those terms it was successful. The clockwork ensemble trademarks of the '50s band were thoroughly examined and re-examined over the next 30 years to the extent that Basie's honourable institution became illuminated more by past achievements than present aspiration.

In 1980 Basie was commanding the highest fees of his career and working five days a week with a month off every six weeks. Health, however, was a concern; in the mid-1970s he had suffered a heart attack and shortly before his 76th birthday he was admitted to a Chicago hospital for treatment of fatigue and a viral infection. 'Since these ailments began to slow the old sparrow down a bit,' said Basie, 'they know what I want, so when I start somewhere on the old keys . . . they know were I'm going and that's where they take it for me.'[5] And if that sounds just a little too close to autopilot for comfort, then Basie had long since become something of an institution, any critical brickbats having all the force of calling the vicar a liar mid-sermon.

His final studio sessions with his Big Band was 'Fancy Pants' (Pablo), recorded in December 1983. In the context of contemporary jazz, the band had come to represent what Gunther Schuller described as 'little more than a resplendent travelling jazz museum',[6] albeit the most significant link with the Swing Era to survive into the 1980s. In early 1984 Basie was admitted to hospital in Hollywood, Miami for treatment of an ulcer, but doctors discovered cancer of the pancreas. When he died on 26 April 1984 his adopted son, Aaron Woodward, said Basie was never told of the disease.[7]

Ironically Basie's best latterday work was away from his big band machine. When he signed with Norman Granz's Pablo label, the impresario made it clear he wanted to record Basie in a variety of contexts. It was a radical departure for Basie whose 1962 'Kansas City 7' (Impulse) was his only small group recording since economics had forced him to lead an octet between 1948 and 1951. Granz created a series of small ensemble dates, ranging from various Basie 'Jams' to the invaluable 'For The First Time' (Pablo) trio set and the surprisingly successful head-to-heads with Oscar Peterson that were a more suitable epitaph than the series of plinks that were typecast against the treble forte blast of his ensemble.

Frank Foster directing the Count Basie Orchestra. The guitarist Freddie Green is in the foreground.

The Basie Legacy

After Basie's death most of the ensemble stayed on fulfilling engagements with Eric Dixon acting as unofficial musical director. But problems were encountered without the focus of a leader resulting in **Thad Jones** (1923-86) being approached to front the band. He accepted, moving from Copenhagen to take up the appointment on 10 February 1985 but a combination of ill health and contractual problems caused him to resign in the spring of 1986, returning to Copenhagen where he died of prostate cancer on 20 August of that year.

Jones's replacement was **Frank Foster** (b.1928), whose association with the Basie Band, like that of Jones, dated back to the 1950s. The first album under Foster's leadership was a celebration of the 50th anniversary of the band's formation, 'Long Live The Chief' (Denon) from June 1986. Although including some familiar fare, the band managed to generate some zest that was conspicuously missing from the final albums under Basie's direction. The band also brought in new young talent, including Melton Mustafa (t) and Dennis Mackrel (d), who later took over the demanding drum chair in the Mel Lewis Orchestra when Lewis died in 1990.

A collaboration with Dianne Schurr, 'Dianne Schurr & the Count Basie Orchestra' (GRP), from 1987 continued the rejuvenation, but sadly three days after the album was recorded, guitarist **Freddie Green** died after 48 years of service to the Basie Band. In January 1989, at the National Association of Jazz Educators convention in San Diego, the band debuted their 'Count Basie Jazz History Suite', a musical biography of Basie's career written by Frank Foster that included narration. The suite appeared as 'The Count Basie Remembrance Suite', minus the narration, on 'The Legend, The Legacy' (Denon), recorded in May 1989, a robust reaffirmation that showed the extent Foster's helmsmanship had restored power, precision and, more importantly, enthusiasm.

When the **Frank Capp/Nat Pierce Juggernaut** made one of its first public appearances in San Fernando Valley in 1975, the *Los Angeles Times* wrote, 'King Arthur's in Canoga Park might as well have changed its name to Basie Street when Frankie Capp and Nat Pierce took over the bandstand.' Their debut album, 'Juggernaut' (Concord), recorded live at the club in 1977, went straight to the top of the jazz charts in Japan and the United Kingdom, and caught the band improvising riffs between the brass and saxophone sections, something of a lost art in an age of gifted sight readers. The 1978 'Live At The Century Plaza' (Concord), this time with a large helping of Joe Williams vocals, repeated the excellent showing in the jazz charts.

In full cry the Juggernaut showed just how mechanical the Basie Band had become. However, further releases became few and far between when Woody Herman signed with the Concord label; 'Strikes Again' (Concord) from 1981 and the 1987 'Live At The Alley Cat' (Concord), featuring Ernestine Anderson's vocals, failed to catch the vibrancy of their earlier work, which attempted to distance themselves from the Basie image. Even so, their earlier albums were enough to raise questions as to what Basie might have achieved with a swinging drummer after the still unexplained departure of Gus Johnson in 1954. Like Ellington and his unusual choice of vocalists, Basie's Achilles heel appeared to be flashy, show-biz drummers.

Buck Clayton (b.1911), forever associated with Count Basie's great ensemble of the late 1930s and early '40s, was forced to give up playing the trumpet in the '70s because of lip trouble in later years. He continued to work as a teacher, arranger and record producer but in 1987 formed a big band that played his own compositions and arrangements, inspired by the quietly successful Loren Schoenberg Orchestra. Such was the respect Clayton commanded, he was able to call upon top New York musicians, 'I get such a kick out of having what I write played by musicians who feel the way I do,' he said.[8]

Clayton's arrangements were full of crafty touches, which the band dispensed with a gracious charm characteristic of the leader himself, 'There's a nice spirit about the band,' said Howard Alden who played guitar in the band from time to time, 'Not incredibly precise but everybody plays with feeling. In a sense it's like the Basie band Buck was in.'

The band debuted on record with 'A Swingin' Dream' (Stash) recorded live at the 16th anniversary of the New Jersey Jazz Society, and included Mel Lewis (d), Joe Temperley (bs) and Chris Flory (g). The band played fundamental swing era jazz, such as Clayton's own 'Avenue C' and new 'in the tradition' compositions such as 'One For Jazzbeaux', 'Beaujolais' and a slow 'Black Sheep Blues'; played with obvious delight by the band, Clayton was telling it like it used to be.

The King of Swing

Undoubtedly **Benny Goodman** (1909-86) was the most popular musician in jazz. Even at the age of 76, in October 1985, he was able to fill New York's Marriott Marquis by invitation at $1000 a seat. But Goodman, for all his popularity, was one of the great enigmas in jazz. Although he continued to work throughout his life, occasionally with a big band, some performances seemed to be for his own exclusive enjoyment. When in 1978 he returned to Carnegie Hall to celebrate the 40th Anniversary of his legendary concert that had 'brought a new level of recognition to jazz',[9] the result was 'a shambles'.[10]

By the early 1980s Goodman's playing, which had occasionally seemed blunted by involvement with classical music, sounded rejuvenated. His appearance at the 1980 Aurex Jazz Festival, 'King Of Swing' (Aurex), soared with a confidence that belied his age. In 1982 he re-formed his famous Quartet—with Lionel Hampton and Teddy Wilson and Panama Francis on drums in place of the late Gene Krupa—for several concert and festival appearances. But in the November he suffered from heart problems culminating in an operation to have a pace-maker fitted—something that was kept secret during his lifetime. A period of recuperation followed and in 1985 he gradually returned to playing. In the February he startled everybody by borrowing a clarinet and sitting in with the house band at a formal dinner celebrating 'Making Music Chicago Style', quipping afterwards, 'I guess it sounds as if I'm disabled.'

Benny Goodman: 'Just lived for the clarinet'.

Further unannounced sessions followed and in June 1985 he appeared at the NYC Kool Jazz Festival tribute to his brother-in-law John Hammond. From 16 August he began rehearsing with the Loren Schoenberg Orchestra to prepare for an October TV special for WNET/PBS, 'Under Schoenberg's leadership they made a fine band,' wrote Will Friedwald,

. . . but when Benny Goodman took over they became something else . . . Goodman riled them up, looked them in the eye with those ray-guns of his which saw everything and nothing, filled them with fire . . . and when he was done they weren't just 16 men, they were part of history and something truly incredible. They were Benny Goodman and his Orchestra.'[11]

Their public debut was at an outdoor concert at Waterloo Village, New Jersey on 27 September, where Goodman invited Schoenberg to take a bow, saying, 'a young man who's really been instrumental in putting these people together and he's done a wonderful job.'[12] The PBS special produced 'Let's Dance' (Music Masters) and confirmed Goodman's remarkable return to form. Featuring his library of Fletcher Henderson arrangements, including several not so well known items, it turned out to be his finest big band since the 'BG In Hi-Fi' (Capitol) date in 1954. Goodman was so taken with Schoenberg's band that he reached an agreement to use it whenever he wanted which included recording it at his own expense at Purchase, NJ; 'The Benny Goodman Yale Archives' (Music Masters).

Goodman's performances with the band included appearances at Yale, Radio City, Washington DC, Ann Arbor and a 'spectacular' with Frank Sinatra and Ella Fitzgerald, with bookings accepted to November of that year. But he was pushing himself too hard. Motivated to a level he had not enjoyed for years his playing was powerful, inventive and articulate; members of the band speak of how he would launch himself into a solo but could not stop himself giving his all, even if it meant, as on one occasion, being helped from the stage afterwards. On Saturday 7 June 1986 he appeared at Wolftrap near Washington DC but the following Friday he died unexpectedly of cardiac arrest in his New York apartment.

It ended a career fraught with paradox, contradiction, controversy and triumph. The Swing Era had made Goodman a wealthy man, but not a happy one.[13] He had spent many a long hour in psychotherapy and his inter-personal relationships created an endless fund of stories exchanged by the exasperated musicians with whom he worked. 'Later in his life,' said Milt Hinton, 'I'd see him standing alone, playing pinball machines in one of the arcades on Broadway. To me, he seemed to be a man who just found it very hard to be comfortable with people.'[14] By some accounts he later mellowed as his relationship with Carol Philips developed, but it is clear that Goodman remained a difficult man. 'He put together some wonderful bands, but he had a reputation for spoiling the fun', wrote bassist Bill Crow.[15]

A passionate player and one of the finest instrumentalists in jazz Goodman, like John Coltrane, compulsively practised throughout his life, 'Benny Goodman was a man who lived in a small cloud,' said Frank Sinatra, '. . . he only knew about the clarinet. Once I said to him, "Every time I see you, Ben, and we play somewhere . . . you're constantly noodling." I said, "Why do you do that constantly?" And he said, "Because if I'm not great, I'm good!" '[16] Equally, Loren Schoenberg, the talented young instrumentalist and bandleader who worked for several years as Goodman's personal assistant during the 1980s, was continually amazed when arriving at Goodman's office first thing in the morning to find him finishing a two-hour practice session, the first of many to be held throughout the day, 'He just lived for the clarinet', he said.[17]

In the end, the immense wealth fame brought, his professorial image, his stand-offishness and his eccentric treatment of many musicians who worked with him surely counted against him when the historical ledger was drawn up. When questioned shortly before his death by the *Wall Street Journal* about a Goodman 'ghost band', he asserted he was 'the product', what the public wanted to hear. He was wrong. On 16 January 1988 Bob Wilber fronted the Loren Schoenberg Orchestra at Carnegie Hall to celebrate the 50th anniversary of Goodman's historical concert and recreate the original programme. The concert was sold out within days. Goodman's music was bigger than even he imagined.

The Swing Era: Legends And Legacy II

Artie Shaw (b.1910), a swing era legend and in his day one of the finest clarinettists in jazz and for a time Goodman's deadly rival, left the music business in 1955 in a quest for greater intellectual fulfilment and swore never to return. When, in 1983 Shaw put his name to a band led by clarinettist and tenor saxophonist Dick Johnson, rehearsing it, using music from his old library and making personal appearances, it represented a U-turn of considerable proportions. 'There are very few people who get a second time around,' he said. 'In a way I'll be getting it. Vicariously but still getting it!'[18]

Gentle persuasion from band agent Willard Alexander moved Shaw from his previously intractable position and although he had long since ceased to play the clarinet, he set out to prove that, in his words, he could still 'play a big band'. The band debuted in December 1983 at the refurbished Glenn Island Casino, one of the legendary big band venues of the swing era. Shaw was clearly pleased with the concept, calling it a composite of the several bands he led years ago.

Full of young musicians, the band provided Shaw with the opportunity of reminiscing at concerts; as one reviewer put it after the band's appearance at the 1984 New York Kool Festival, 'like a ghost band being conducted by the ghost'. Then suddenly he wanted nothing further to do with public appearances, 'I was right the first time' he said.[19] But Shaw couldn't let go. In 1990 he hosted Princess Voyages' 11-day swing-time cruise from Miami to Barcelona.

Vibraphonist and bandleader **Lionel Hampton** (b. 1909) has always bemused critics by the spectacular tastelessness of his performances but nevertheless remained the only bandleader from the Swing Era to continue working throughout the 1980s and into the '90s. When performing in public he always adopted the role of entertainer first and musician second, which often succeeded in deflecting criticism from his musical policy. Hampton came to fame as a member of the Benny Goodman 'Quartette', joining him in 1936 and leaving in 1940. Although he was soon on the road with his own big band his best work on record was already done, both with Goodman and as a leader of several brilliant ad hoc small group sessions for RCA Victor.

As a leader of a big band Hampton had few artistic pretensions. Much of his work heartily subscribed to riffs and rhythm and projected a 'good time' feeling similar to Louis Jordan (compare the riffs of Jordan's 'Choo Choo Ch'Boogie' and Hampton's 'Hamp's Boogie'—both men were precursors of R&B). This rigorously fundamental approach seemed to be what the public wanted, however, and through careful management by his wife Gladys, Hampton had, by the 1980s, accumulated a music publishing company, record company and the Lionel Hampton Development Company which was involved in multi-million dollar property deals.

At the beginning of the 1980s he became increasingly active again as a bandleader following the death of his wife, touring, recording and record producing a number of mix 'n' match sessions for the 'Lionel Hampton Presents' series on the Who's Who label. During 1982 and 1983 he fronted a band assembled and directed by Tom Chapin that included tenor saxophonists Arnett Cobb and Ricky Ford that drew capacity crowds throughout the world. 'Made In Japan' (Timeless) comes from two concerts in Tokyo in June 1982. A mixture of old and new compositions it mercifully stops short of including the curious encores Hampton was using at the time—'In The Mood' and 'When The Saints Go Marching In'—when notable critics could be seen pulling sucking-lemon-faces as the band circled the bandstand hamming it up to the delight of their leader.

In 1986 he recorded and produced an album featuring singer Sylvia Bennett with his band, 'Sentimental Journey' (Atlantic). A surprisingly relaxed outing on nine standards, he paused for a moment to acknowledge his Benny Goodman days with the old Quartet/Band coda on 'Avalon'. By 1988 with Tom Chapin still acting as MD, Hampton had become the longest established bandleader in the history of jazz. In 1989 he guested with the Loren Schoenberg Orchestra at Carnegie Hall in a tribute to Benny Goodman; 'Mr. Hampton contributed some vibraphone solos that still danced as joyfully as they did when he first joined the Goodman troupe 53 years ago,' said John S. Wilson in the *New York Times*.

Ultimately, however, Hampton's own bands have been undistinguished despite the number of important young musicians who have passed through them or Hampton's undoubted status as a 'Giant' of jazz. While he delighted audiences, it was achieved by giving them exactly what they expected, invariably at the expense of artistic and aesthetic content. His ability to bring an audience to fever pitch, foreshadowing contemporary Rock concerts, was not only at the expense of his own playing, but that of the material he chose to perform. As Max Harrison observed, 'it must lead to Hampton's musical capabilities as a leader being questioned.'[20]

Illinois Jacquet: 'An orchestra like this competes only with records, which can never duplicate the experience of hearing an authentic swing band in the flesh.'

Illinois Jacquet (b.1922) was 19 when he recorded 'Flying Home' with Hampton on 26 May 1942. His solo was such that it has become virtually enshrined within the song itself, with countless versions quoting it in whole or in part. Jacquet, a deft and proficient musician who worked for years as a successful single or with his own small groups decided in 1983 to form his own big band, which at 61 was something more than just a mid-term career change. It was a long look over his shoulder to the swing era and a declaration of a musical manifesto he learnt in his youth.

By 1988 his band had become one of the hottest draws in New York, particularly at the Village Vanguard, and his album 'Jacquet's Got It' (Atlantic) received rave reviews. Young musicians sat side by side with seasoned pros, who from time to time included Rudy Rutherford, Eddie Barefield, Norris Turney, Cecil Payne and Richard Wyands. Although their drawing card was unashamedly a lusty power-drive, they certainly succeeded in removing a few cobwebs from numbers like 'Stompin' At The Savoy' and 'Tickletoe'; 'An orchestra like this competes only with records, which can never duplicate the experience of hearing an authentic swing band in the flesh,' said the critic Gary Giddins.[21]

Woody Herman (1913-87) was not a gifted jazz instrumentalist, rather a good, sound professional musician. For the critical fraternity, who prefer their heroes to have a far more tangible musical profile, Herman's niche in jazz has therefore been correspondingly undervalued.[22] The problem was that Herman, as alto saxophonist, soprano saxophonist and clarinettist, never had any pretensions to be a Benny Goodman or an Artie Shaw. Instead he brought to jazz the skills of man management and motivation—a rather tenuous aesthetic to introduce into the forum of musical criticism. Even so, the fact remains that for over 50 years Herman demonstrated a remarkable gift for organizing young talent to produce some of the most memorable big bands in jazz.

Although his career stretched back to the early days of swing, Herman was always conscious of the changes occurring in jazz and was careful to select musicians in tune with the times. Indeed, the few concessions he would make to his past during concert performances were perfunctory renditions of his million selling hit from 1939, 'At The Woodchoppers Ball' or his famous 1948 'Four Brothers'.

Herman wrote himself into jazz history with his two late-1940s big bands, the First and Second 'Herds'. Even now his recordings manage to convey the shock-effect that stunned audiences of the time, a big band roar that Herman succeeded in sustaining throughout his life.

Woody Herman: Man-manager and motivator, 'ought to be given credit as an outstanding figure in jazz'.

In 1980, at the age of 67, Herman could not unreasonably have been anticipating retirement. Instead, the Inland Revenue Service began putting pressure on him for settlement of huge tax irregularities dating back to a time when manager Abe Turchen mis-handled his affairs in the late 1960s. As a result Herman was forced to continue working to pay off the debt. A permanent base for the band seemed likely when Herman began a residency at 'Woody Herman's', a night club in New Orleans located at Plaza level of the Hyatt Regency-Polydras Plaza. But in one week in November 1982 he lost his wife of 46 years and the club residency. But continued pressure from the IRS forced him back to work.

Undaunted and philosophically accepting his fate[23] Herman signed with the Concord label and made a couple of jam session albums with the label's stable of mainstreamers and re-convened his Herd. 'Concord Festival 1981' (Concord) has pianist John Oddo assuming arranging duties and revealed that even at a frail 68 Herman could energize a young ensemble. A typical Herman concert of the period appeared as 'Live In Chicago March 6th 1981' (Status), a mixture of previously recorded material. In 1982 he toured Japan with his band plux ex-Herdsmen Al Cohn, Sal Nistico and Flip Phillips and Supersax-man Med Flory; the best of their performances were issued on 'World Class' (Concord) which mixes new Oddo arrangements with classics such as 'The Four Brothers'.

By 1986 the talented young trombonist John Fedchock had taken over arranging duties and '50th Anniversary Album' (Concord), recorded live at the American Music Hall, San Francisco includes a version of 'Pools' from the repertoire of Steps Ahead—Herman never remained stuck in the litany of the past. But the feeling of the band suggested the wheel had gone full circle; Herman, whose involvement in music education influenced countless Stage Bands, now, through using the very young musicians the system produced, reflected the influence of the Stage Band system in style and content. His final album, 'Woody's Gold Star' (Concord) was issued at the time of his death on 29 October 1987.[24]

Herman had been incapacitated for most of 1987, initially hospitalized in Colorado. His condition worsened when he reacted to medication and was moved to a hospital in Detroit where he recovered sufficiently to return to his California home. The IRS, however, seized his house and put it up for auction. The purchaser let it back to him, but Herman, now enfeebled and debilitated by illness, could no longer work and went into rent arrears. On 8 September 1987 he was to be evicted. 'The news media picked up the story', wrote Gene Lees. 'Woody was brought out of his bedroom to face the camera. He had a small white beard and his head looked like a skull, a pathetic little figure as helpless as a baby.'[25] His situation prompted donations and benefit concerts but he was soon back in hospital where he eventually died of congestive heart failure, emphysema and pneumonia.

Herman's achievements in jazz have either been downvalued or ignored by critics, writers and historians. Whether it was as a result of what Gunther Schuller suggested was 'Crow Jim' prejudice,[26] or because Herman was neither jazz virtuoso, innovator nor arranger, is difficult to say. But it was as a catalyst that Herman's great contribution to jazz lay, creating a remarkable forcing house for talent that stretched almost unbroken from the 1930s into the 1980s and a recorded legacy of some of the finest big band music in jazz. 'Woody Herman', wrote Schuller, 'ought to be given credit . . . as an outstanding figure in jazz.'[27]

During Herman's illness Frank Tiberi (ts), Herman's right-hand man since the '70s, took over the running of 'The Young Thundering Herd', continuing into the 1990s in conjunction with Herman's estate. 'We really aren't doing anything different than we did when Woody was with us,' said Tiberi.[28] In 1989 The Woody Herman Foundation Scholarship was announced, awarded through the music departments of California State University.

Buddy Rich (1917-87), was one of the great drummers in jazz and felt it imperative to reaffirm his status with every performance. He perfected a multi-purpose post-Swing Era style that was almost timeless and his speed and precision were legendary—even into his 70th year he appeared impervious to the effects of ageing or the occasional heart attack.

During his long career he played with most of the great names in jazz and appeared in a variety of small group settings, including the JATP roadshow, but it was long ago ordained that his optimum musical environment was the Big Band. The sheer lift and exuberance of his playing transformed formula antiphony between brass and reeds into nearly substantial musical events and leaders like Artie Shaw, Tommy Dorsey, Les Brown and Harry James were prepared to pay Rich big money to make their ensembles sound something special.

When he came to form his second big band in 1966 (the first in the '40s flopped) Rich commissioned a completely new book of arrangements from the likes of Oliver Nelson, Bill Reddie, Bill Holman, Don Piestrup, Pete Meyers and Bill Potts which were marked by punching brass and slick saxophone *solis* that were a logical extension of the swing era. Somehow Rich made virtues out of the vices of big band jazz; breakneck tempos, screeching trumpets and riff piled mercilessly upon riff. Rich's superb ensemble drumming, the ultimate marriage between lead trumpet and drums, and his crisp fills were very often more exciting and absorbing than the long drum solo that climaxed every concert; an encyclopedia of crescendo and diminuendo snare drum rolls, rapid-fire rim shots, bass drum explosions and cymbal cascades.

Rich was a driven man. In 1983, for example, he underwent open heart surgery and 54 days later opened at Ronnie Scott's jazz club in London playing two one-hour sets a night, followed it with a concert tour of the United Kingdom and a speedy return to the States to back Frank Sinatra. He led by example, expecting similar commitment from his sidemen and although it often caused an undercurrent of creative stress, it almost always ensured a consistently high level of live performance. Even so, by the 1980s Rich, perhaps surprisingly, had not made a wholly satisfactory album since his Pacific Jazz days in 1966-70.

At the beginning of the 1980s Rich continued to be in something of an artistic cul-de-sac with over-busy jazz-rock numbers and from time to time a vocal glee-club organized by his daughter Kathy. 'The Man From Planet Jazz' (Ronnie Scott Productions) disappointed and 'The Buddy Rich

Buddy Rich: One of the great drummers in jazz who felt it imperative to reaffirm his status with every performance.

Band Plays' (MCA) was branded by Rich himself as the worst ever.[29] However, in 1982 Mel Torme persuaded him to confront his honourable Swing Era past and perform three of his old feature numbers, Artie Shaw's 'Carioca' and Tommy Dorsey's 'Well Git It' and 'Not So Quiet Please', all sensitively rearranged by John LaBarbera, at Carnegie Hall. Rich raised the roof.

Perhaps coincidence, but in live performance he began to pull out more of his straight-ahead sixties and seventies repertoire and wisely began to moderate his edict of contemporary material for contemporary material's sake. Several numbers from an early Pacific Jazz album 'Big Swing Face' had all but become big band classics and one of them, 'Love For Sale', had become to his band what 'Four Brothers' was to Woody Herman or 'April In Paris' to Basie. Played by countless rehearsal bands the world over, at least one band, the Dick Melodian/Sonny Igoe orchestra recorded the entire Pete Meyers arrangement intact ('The Jersey Swing Concerts'— Progressive Jazz) while 'Willowcrest', also from 'Big Swing Face', reappeared in 1987 on 'Trash Can City' by Bob Florence (Trend).

Swing era warhorses, such as 'Cotton Tail' and 'One O'Clock Jump', were introduced, but duly arranged in the Rich style with the now familiar device of surging pedal points that brought the leader's drumming into focus through the ensemble. With the exception of Mike Abene's arrangement of 'Birdland', many of the faceless jazz-rock numbers began to recede in the face of a better balanced repertoire that favoured Rich's powerful 4/4 swing.

'Mr. Drums—Live On King Street, San Francisco' (Cafe), a three album set from April 1985 and the video produced by Gary Reber, had Rich exhorting his troops to greater deeds with shouts and yells of approval and the band responding with the appropriate level of energy, commitment and perspiration. Despite a somewhat cloth-eared sound engineer, it represents one of his best albums for years; a cheering retrospective plus solid new charts by pianist Bill Cunliffe, and of course the 'medleys', which had become *de rigeur* at his concerts after the success of 'West Side Story Medley' from his band's debut album on World Pacific in 1966.

Together with Steve Marcus, who joined the band in 1975 and became the band's 'straw boss', Rich had brought another group of young musicians to a high level of professionalism to serve as a vehicle for his electrifying drumming. Then 67, Rich, as he had done so often over the years, almost succeeded in convincing you he was the best drummer in jazz. By then he had built his band into an international attraction, continuing a busy touring schedule until three months before his death on 2 April 1987. A biting wit to the end, Rich was asked when being admitted to hospital if he was allergic to anything. 'Country and Western music', he replied.[30]

Loren Schoenberg: 'This is no nostalgia band. What I play are serious jazz compositions that deserve to be heard again.'

The Swing Era: Legacies

Loren Schoenberg (b.1958) formed what to all intents and purposes was a repertory orchestra in the spring of 1980. Schoenberg, a keen musicologist, pianist and talented tenor saxophonist, had assembled an exceptional library of arrangements, mainly from the swing era by arrangers such as Eddie Sauter, Benny Carter, Fletcher and Horace Henderson and Duke Ellington. 'This is no nostalgia band,' he asserted, 'what I play are serious jazz compositions that deserve to be heard again.'

The band debuted at the 'Red Blazer' in New York City in 1982, by which time word of the exceptional library of arrangements the young bandleader was accumulating was spreading amongst musicians, enabling him to attract an impressive roster to both rehearse and perform with his band, including Lee Konitz, Mel Lewis, Jimmy Knepper and Johnny Carisi. When Buck Clayton heard the band he was moved to write several charts for it and went on to form his own big band.

Schoenberg's first album, 'That's The Way It Goes' (Aviva) from 1984, led to his band being adopted by Benny Goodman for concerts from 1985 until his death. It also focussed attention on the young bandleader. 'After Benny hired the band we slowly started to get more work,' he said, 'We started playing the Cat Club, a rock and roll-new wave joint that every Sunday night is rented by the New York Swing Dance Society, which was important. A lot of people and a lot of musicians came to hear the band.'

In the meantime he had access to Goodman's library and unearthed several valuable charts, stretching from unrecorded items from the 1930s to Goodman's USSR tour in 1962. Several of these subsequently appeared, together with transcriptions of rare swing era material by Mark Lopeman, on the 1987 'Time Waits For No One' (Musical Heritage Society) and the 1988 'Solid Ground' (Music Masters).

By 1989 Schoenberg's long, hard struggle to establish his band was beginning to pay off. In April the band went on the road for the first time and in June they appeared in Carnegie Hall with Lionel Hampton and George Benson in a Goodman tribute. The quality and variety of his repertoire and Schoenberg's integrity and attention to detail meant that he was able to maintain a consistent personnel, including Mel Lewis (d), Dick Katz (p), Paul Cohen (t), Eddie Bert (tb), Danny Bank (bs) and fellow musicophiles Ken Peplowski (ts,c) and Richard Sudhalter (t), author of the definitive *Bix—Man and Legend* (Quartet, 1974).

Schoenberg did not seek definitive recreations but personal interpretations and left his sidemen free to present their own solos, 'I trust their aesthetic instincts, they're great players, they know the music inside out, whatever they want to do they're free to do it,' he explained. But it was the exciting repertoire Schoenberg had painstakingly assembled, interpreted by some of New York's finest musicians that was the band's drawing card, 'After all,' he said, 'where else can musicians get to play Eddie Sauter arrangements and where else can people get to hear them?'[31]

Schoenberg was also a member of **The American Jazz Orchestra**, acting as the band's manager, deputy conductor and featured tenor saxophonist. The AJO debuted in New York City's Great Hall of Cooper Union in June 1986 and was the brainchild of writer/critic Gary Giddins, 'I took off from the *Village Voice* for a year to get this thing started,' he said, adding 'Its been costing me a fortune.'[32] A repertory undertaking, often re-creating original solos, Giddins acted as Artistic Director while the MJQ's John Lewis was the Musical Director and chief conductor. In an interview with critic Gene Santaro, Lewis said, 'We want to underscore the important contributions of Big Band jazz to our American culture.'[33]

Concerts were devoted to the works of Jimmie Lunceford, Sy Oliver in 'The Dorsey Years', Fletcher Henderson and Edgar Sampson in 'The Benny Goodman Years', Gerald Wilson, Benny Carter and Count Basie. Both Gerald Wilson and Benny Carter directed their own work in concert and Benny Carter also directed and played on the AJO recording 'American Jazz Orchestra/Benny Carter Central City Sketches' (Music Masters) from February 1987. In November 1988 they recorded 'Ellington Masterpieces' (East West), featuring highlights of Ellington's great 1940-41 repertoire.

In both an act of faith and honesty in presenting the Big Band as serious art, making available past verities for contemporary audiences, the AJO cried out for public subsidy as it struggled from concert to concert. Ironically, in 1988 John Lewis was approached by the French government, who had donated $1 million to create a competing French Jazz Orchestra. 'It infuriates us,' said Giddins, 'they offered John Lewis a fortune to come over to Paris and be their consultant—a house, a chauffeur, unlimited air travel to do his MJQ dates and a big salary. He turned it down but it made us all realize what a ludicrous position we are in here.'[34] Despite lack of financial support—'What's our alternative, just not do it?' said Schoenberg[35]—the AJO managed to walk the fine line between imitation and contemporary re-creation, something that somehow eluded the New York Jazz Repertory Company and the National Jazz Ensemble in the '70s.

BEING WHAT A BIG BAND SHOULD BE

An orchestrator of ingenuity, wit and originality, **Gerry Mulligan** (b.1927) was a welcome antidote to the brassy blasts and relentless drive generated by the majority of his competitors. Mulligan achieved excitement through colour, shading and dynamics. 'He knows exactly what he wants,' said bassist Bill Crow, 'He wants a quiet band. He can swing at about 15 decibels lower than any other band.'[36] Mulligan's involvement in the Miles Davis 1948 'Birth Of The Cool' sessions, where as a 21-year-old he contributed 'Jeru', 'Venus de Milo' and 'Godchild', hold the key to his arranging style, which he has always asserted was 'based on what I wrote for Miles'[37]—a combination of low dynamics, light swing and meticulous attention to inner harmonic movement.

In 1978 he formed a 14-piece band, touring the following year. As well as new material composed and arranged by Mulligan for the project, he also featured charts from the Concert Jazz Band he led between 1960-68, such as 'Lady Chatterley's Mother', and his 1972-74 ensemble 'Age Of Steam' (A&M). A slightly expanded version of the band recorded the Grammy winning 'Walk On Water' (DRG) in September 1980, featuring five Mulligan arrangements including four new originals and some fine solos by Mulligan on both baritone and soprano saxes and Tom Harrell (t, fh). Among the better big band albums of the decade, it was a disappointment that this album remains the sole representation of the young, talented ensemble Mulligan managed to keep together for about six years.

'Even if bands are not important economically the way they were 40 years ago, young players coming along still want to play that kind of music—they need that,' observed Mulligan. 'My band offers a unique opportunity of learning and development for young players . . . What I do with my band is use dynamics—dynamics of attack as well as volume. As a consequence I think players get a particular joy out of playing that requires them to do things out of a wide range of possibilities.'[38]

Although in 1986 and 1989 he toured with a small group, he also toured as a soloist appearing with symphony orchestras performing his 'Symphonic Dreams', 'Entente For Baritone Sax And Orchestra' and 'The Sax Chronicles', which he recorded with Enrich Kunzel and the Houston Symphony; 'Symphonic Dreams' (PAR). However, he occasionally returned to the big band format, assembling a Concert Band for the Festival circuit in 1988, which included an appearance at the Glasgow Jazz Festival who had commissioned a new, extended composition, 'The Flying Scotsman'.

As a major mainstream big band work from the '80s it passed by unnoticed. Its significance lay in its conception as both composition *and* arrangement, a rarity in big band jazz since the death of Duke Ellington in 1974. The generic lines of descent and development of 'The Flying Scotsman' reached back to Mulligan's pianoless quartet of the 1950s, with fluid, intertwining counterpoint, but also looked forward with writing that made its structure sound spontaneously conceived. Like all Mulligan's writing it was unfairly surprising, with so much said in such a short space.

Despite his perspicacity as a soloist (he has recorded albums with everyone from Thelonius Monk to Barry Manilow[39]), it was as bandleader, composer and arranger that Mulligan's most valuable contribution to jazz lay, a truth that he was at pains to avoid facing: 'I don't know why I'm not writing more, there are so many reasons that there's none' he once confessed. But the fact remained that Mulligan was a major composer/arranger in big band jazz, one of only a handful of musicians able to encompass compositional *and* orchestral expressionism.

The Survival of the Species: The Rehearsal Band

Even if the days of the touring big band were all but over, big bands continued to flourish as a result of the 'Rehearsal Band' concept pioneered by the Thad Jones-Mel Lewis Jazz Orchestra. Formed in December 1965 by trumpeter/cornettist and arranger Jones and drummer Lewis, they debuted at the Village Vanguard, New York in February 1966. Depending heavily on free-lance jazz and studio musicians, the band assembled every Monday night to play for their own pleasure and that of anyone else who cared to come along.

The cost factor of transporting men and equipment was thus overcome and musicians who would otherwise have been deterred by the prospect of constant travel were free to get together on a regular basis to play primarily for enjoyment or musician's union basic scale. 'That one night a week at the Vanguard means everybody stays with the band,' said Lewis. 'We never have to change personnel. Road bands never had that kind of stability.'[40] The concept caught on; by the 1980s every major city in the States, Japan and Europe could boast its own local Big Band.

In 1979, co-leader Thad Jones dissolved his partnership with Mel Lewis to pursue his career in Denmark, leaving his wife and two children to remarry, 'I couldn't do anything about it,' said Lewis, 'and I didn't know at the time it was all over a chick. He wouldn't talk to me. That's why nothing was written about the real reason.' Conventional wisdom might have suggested that this was the end of the band.

But **Mel Lewis** (1929-90) continued on his own, turning to outside arrangers to fill the void left by Jones' departure. By 1980, both Bob Brookmeyer and Bob Mintzer had each contributed sufficient material for an album apiece of their work. 'Bob Brookmeyer/Composer, Arranger with Mel Lewis and the Jazz Orchestra' (Gryphon), recorded live at the Village Vanguard in February 1980 is an excellent showcase for Brookmeyer's talents, the careful harmonic writing in 'First Love Song' alone sufficient to wonder why Brookmeyer the orchestrator has remained so under-exposed.

Bob Mintzer, who contributed several charts to the Buddy Rich Band while a member during the '70s before joining the Jazz Orchestra sax section, contributed several arrangements of Herbie Hancock numbers that comprised 'Live At Montreux' (Pausa) from July 1980. Less given to the subtleties of Brookmeyer, Mintzer's forthright 'One Finger Snap' figured regularly in the band's performances throughout the 1980s. A video of the band, 'Jazz At The Smithsonian' (Parkfield) gave a good cross-section of the band's repertoire, and includes the emerging young alto star Kenny Garrett.

In 1985 Lewis celebrated two decades at the Village Vanguard, by now the longest continuing gig in the history of jazz, marked by the album '20 Years At The Village Vanguard' (Atlantic). Charts by Jim McNeely

Mel Lewis and the Jazz Orchestra: Monday night at the Village Vanguard, the longest continuing gig in the history of jazz until Lewis died on 2 February 1990.

(p), Thad Jones, Bill Finnegan, Jerry Dodgion, Richard DeRosa and Bob Brookmeyer illustrated the shift of emphasis from soloist to arranger. The 1988 'Soft Lights, Hot Music' (Musicmasters), this time with contributions from Bill Finnegan (who in the swing era arranged some of Artie Shaw's and Glenn Miller's most enduring hits) and pianist Kenny Werner.

The Grammy nominated 'The Definitive Thad Jones' (Musicmasters) recorded live at The Village Vanguard in 1988 re-examined some of Jones' complex, but swinging charts that made his writing style the most influential of the '70s with 'Little Pixie' the standout track. While the band occasionally emerged from its Monday night enclave for short tours (it visited Japan in 1988, for example), it continued to be a once-a-week-band throughout the '80s, true to the concept sparked by the original version.

However, after a two year battle with cancer Mel Lewis died on 2 February 1990. But the band carried on, with Dennis Mackrel (b.1963) taking over the drum chair, as Lewis intended. Mackrel had substituted for Lewis as he succumbed to his illness, sometimes sharing responsibilities in concerts. 'The decision of the players has been to carry on without any leader per se,' said tenor saxist Dick Oatts. 'Mel would have kind of wanted us all to lead the thing so we're going to have a team effort.'[41]

Pianist **Bob Florence** (b.1932) led a Californian rehearsal band formed in 1973 composed of top West Coast studio veterans which he called Limited Edition. Active throughout the 1980s several of its albums attracted Grammy nominations. Florence played in Si Zentner's band from 1959 to 1964, contributing several arrangements, including the Zentner hit 'Up A Lazy River'. Despite his involvement in a variety of commercial writing projects, in 1983, for example, he scored the Burt Reynolds movie 'Stick', Florence consistently provided a flow of new material for the band, described by trumpet player Gene Coe as 'the kind of charts big bands are supposed to play'.[42]

Working firmly within the parameter of traditional Big Band values, Florence's meticulous charts were full of interesting and surprising tone colours (the band had a six-man sax section), original melodic lines and succinct part writing. The band recorded for the Trend label, including the 1979 'Concerts By The Sea', the 1983 'Magic Time' and 'Trash Can City' from 1986. Avoiding decibel excess, Florence's writing possessed a gentle and judicious originality, balanced by the maturity of soloists such as Lanny Morgan, Bob Cooper and Steve Huffsteter.

Arranger and valve trombonist **Rob McConnell** (b.1935) formed his Boss Brass in 1968 playing commercial material and by 1976, having achieved modest success, felt confident enough to embrace the jazz repertoire with 'The Jazz Album' (Pausa). Two years later he dropped the commercial material completely to concentrate on jazz. McConnell contributed all the arrangements for the band, his repertoire a mixture of standards and his own original compositions featuring his Brookmeyer-ish valve trombone and some of Toronto's top studio veterans.

By 1983 McConnell had earnt five Grammy nominations, including one for the album 'All In Good Time' (Palo Alto) and another for the arrangement of 'I Got Rhythm' from it, and by the time they disbanded they had accumulated a further three. Despite their reputation, however, McConnell's band remained a labour of love to which he confessed only being able to devote 15 per cent of his time; in fact the busiest year of the band's existence was 1984 with just 60 engagements.

Occasionally the band emerged from Canada for limited tours, usually for engagements on the West Coast following their successful appearance at the 1981 Monterey Jazz Festival. Albums with Mel Torme (Concord) and Phil Woods (MCA) attested to their growing reputation, which was enhanced by the availability of McConnell's scores that found their way into the repertoire of rehearsal bands the world over, prompting his increasing interest in music education. In 1988 the group gave its final concert at McComb University in Michigan, when McConnell moved to California to become a full time faculty member with the Grove School Of Music.

The Boss Brass albums, endorsing a slightly modified Basie manifesto, were models of suppressed power considering the 22 head count and remained firmly in the big band 'swing' tradition; 'Present Perfect' (MPS), a Grammy nominee from 1980, was a good representation of their style with excellent solos from the leader, Ed Bickert (g) and Sam Noto (t) underpinned by Don Thompson's elegant bass; 'Live In Digital' (Dark Orchid), another Grammy nominee, restated McConnell's musical philosophy, 'I'm a traditional person. I'm not very far out. I think my band exemplifies a lot of that.'[43]

BREAKING THE MOULD

Pianist **Toshiko Akiyoshi** (b.1929) and tenor saxophonist **Lew Tabackin** (b.1940) formed a rehearsal band in Hollywood in 1973 that evolved into one of the most significant of the post-war big bands. Its importance, however, was obscured by poor marketing by RCA, the band's record label during the '70s, who never appeared to realize this was one of the great ensembles of the decade. Their series of eleven uniformly excellent recordings[44] that began with 'Kogun' in 1974 and ended with 'Farewell' in 1980 were issued on a rather haphazard basis, some available only in Japan, some only in the States and some in Europe.

The band's strength was Toshiko's magnificent writing and Ellington-like recognition of her soloists' individuality. The breadth of her writing technique was impressive; her highly personal orchestral colours (including a frequently used combination of clarinets and flutes) and detailed vertical voicings (running counter to the prevailing trend of linear, horizontal voicings) lent great emotional depth to her orchestrations. Her use of frequently changing metres (but not necessarily tempos), extended forms plus her rich melodic logic, conceived as both composition *and* arrangement, created orchestrations of stunning conceptuality unique in jazz. Underpinning her orchestrational gifts was a respect for tradition and a strong personal belief that jazz should aspire to the highest intellectual principles and not sell itself short by seeking commercial options.

'Farewell' (RCA) from January 1980 was her last album for the RCA label, dedicated to the late Charles Mingus with whom Akiyoshi played for ten months in 1966-67. By the time it was released the majority of American and Japanese critics recognized that the ensemble was the leading big band in jazz, with three *Down Beat* poll victories to its credit and a first place in the Japanese *Swing Journal* poll. However in Europe, where hardly any of the band's albums had been released, there was by no means a universal consensus.

Frustrations with RCA led to a new record label and 'Tanuki's Night Out' (JAM), from March 1981, was something of a departure in terms of repertoire. Up until this point all compositions and arrangements had been by Akiyoshi; this time the compositions were by Tabackin, the arrangements were provided by the distaff side. 'European Memories' (Baystate), from September 1982, reverted to form, with compositions and arrangements by Akiyoshi, including 'Remembering Bud' which became a regular at her concerts.

Meticulously rehearsed — Bobby Shew, lead trumpeter and soloist for the band during much of the 1970s, once said, while wryly stroking his lip, that he never gave so much blood for a big band to get so few gigs[45]—Akiyoshi and Tabackin had by now sustained a level of excellence over some 15 albums. In 1982 they unexpectedly announced their intention to move from their West Coast base to Manhattan. Done, Akiyoshi claimed, for the sake of her husband Lew Tabackin's 'artistic health', a new band with a completely new personnel debuted in 1983. Now known as the 'Toshiko Akiyoshi Jazz Orchestra featuring Lew Tabackin' it recorded several albums on their own self-produced Ascent label.

In February 1990 the band appeared at the Pasadena Auditorium in 'The Sounds Of Genius' series; '*Genius* is a term tossed around too often by hucksters,' wrote Leonard Feather, 'but if ever it was merited, this unique composer-arranger-pianist-bandleader deserves it . . . . More than any other writer in modern times except Gil Evans, she has been a wellspring of melodic invention, of textural colours that far transcend the simple brass-reeds-rhythm patterns of the traditional big band.'[46]

Gil Evans (1912-88) would have left an indelible impression on jazz even if he had never written another note after his collaboration with Miles Davis between 1957 and 1961. His orchestrations for 'Miles Ahead' (1957), 'Porgy and Bess' (1959) and 'Sketches Of Spain' (1960)—all CBS—rank among the finest recorded moments of 20th-century music. From time to time Evans assembled his own orchestra to perform and record his unique arrangements and as various editions of his orchestra came and went, they left some classic recordings of big band jazz in their wake, including 'Out Of The Cool' (MCA/Impulse), 'The Individualism Of Gil Evans' (Verve), 'Svengali' (Atlantic), 'Blues In Orbit' (Enja) and 'Priestess' (Antilles).

Gil Evans: His recorded legacy included moments of profound improvisation and orchestral majesty.

However, it took a chance meeting between James Browne, a disc jockey at station WBGO-FM-Jazz in New York, and Evans in a Greenwich Village Supermarket to set in motion a chain of events that resulted in Evans forming a Monday Night Band in the Sweet Basil jazz club in April 1983. Incredibly, at the age of 71, it was one of the few times in his life that Evans had a regular ensemble at his disposal.

Evans' gift was recomposition; on albums like 'Miles Ahead', 'Out Of The Cool' and 'The Individualism' it was achieved through meticulous orchestration, but as the '70s progressed the emphasis shifted to the bandstand and relied on the sympathetic interaction of his band members to convert and reshape numbers into new orchestral tapestries, often spontaneously conceived. He gradually began importing electronic tone colours and rock rhythm section patterns into his work and throughout the decade his compositions and arrangements became progressively looser in both form and texture, in stark contrast to the rigidities usually characteristic of big bands. Soloists had more time for self-expression and were encouraged to extend themselves while the band often improvised sympathetic backgrounds, usually dictated from the piano by Evans himself: bandleader and arranger Angel Rangelov, who studied with Evans, called the process 'like hearing birds in the forest: you don't know how it started or where its going to end.'[47]

Subsequently, his recorded work reflected the problems inherent in his high-risk policy of public experimentation. 'Live At The Public Theatre (New York 1980) Vols. 1 & 2' (Blackhawk) contain moments of inspiration with a stellar cast of musicians that include Arthur Blythe, Billy Cobham, Hamiet Bluiett and George Lewis but 'Anita's Dance', for example, drifts into rootlessness. Evans freely acknowledged the problems his methodology entailed, 'some performances are better than others . . . . We teeter on the edge of formlessness a lot of times—then someone can't stand it any longer and we'll all move on.'

Evans toured England in 1983 with his son Miles and a band of British musicians, including John Surman, John Taylor and Chris Hunter on alto saxophone, who subsequently joined him in New York. 'Gil Evans—The British Orchestra' (Mole Jazz) includes restrained but successful versions of 'Hotel Me' and 'Friday The 13th' from a tour that most of the musicians who participated regard as the experience of a lifetime.

His regular base at the Sweet Basil enabled him to maintain a consistent personnel of some of Manhattan's finest musicians and the four album set 'Live at Sweet Basil Vols. 1 & 2' (Electric Bird) from August 1984 contain versions of material Evans had been performing throughout the '70's—Mingus, Hendrix and Monk numbers, Alan Shorter's 'Parabola' and so on—while 'Bud and Bird' and 'Farewell' (both Electric Bird) from December 1986 introduce new compositions by band members Mark Egan, Bill Evans and John Clark. Their overall effect is of a spontaneous, freewheeling musical workshop running the knife-edge between success and failure—and there are episodes of both on these albums.

With his regular appearances at Sweet Basil, Evans the septuagenarian was bemused to find himself in vogue; in 1985 he arranged and conducted the soundtrack music for the British pop movie 'Absolute Beginners' (Virgin) and in 1987 the pop singer Sting appeared with the band—their concert at the Umbria Jazz Festival attracted a crowd of 30,000 and was broadcast live over Italian television. Later in the year they collaborated on Sting's album '. . . Nothing Like The Sun' (A&M) which included a version of 'Little Wing' by the band. While in London during his 75th Birthday Tour, Van Morrison, whose compositions occasionally surfaced at the Sweet Basil, sang to his entire satisfaction with the band.

During the 1980's, Evans also recorded two intimate duets, 'Collaboration' (Emarcy) with Helen Merrill (v) and 'Paris Blues' (Owl) with Steve Lacy (ss) that were both simultaneously sympathetic and probing. In early 1988 Evans underwent surgery and shortly afterwards left New York for Cuernavaca, Mexico to recuperate. On 20 March he died of peritonitis.

His recorded legacy was a unique body of recorded music that virtually created its own idiom in jazz and 20th century music, containing moments of profound improvisation and orchestral majesty. His son Miles continued with the 'Monday Night' band at the Sweet Basil with a virtually unaltered personnel; they returned to the Umbria Jazz Festival in 1988, just a few months after Evans' death, with guests Bireli Legerene (g), Urszula Dudziak (v) and Michael Urbaniak (vn); 'Tribute To Gil' (Soul Note). The band continued into the 1990s, even appearing on a Muppets production by Jim Henson, 'Ghost Of Faffner Hall.'

George Russell (b.1923) made his great contribution to jazz with his theory, 'The Lydian Chromatic Concept Of Tonal Organisation'—a study that suggested that improvisation on modes, instead of chord changes, was possible. The apotheosis of Russell's ideas came with the Miles Davis album 'Kind Of Blue' (CBS) at the end of the 1950's, resulting in an important shift in the basis of jazz improvisation.

The 1988 re-release of 'Jazz Workshop' (RCA), recorded in 1956 when Russell's conception was taking root among musicians, served to underline how Russell's role in jazz had come to be overlooked with the passage of time. For years Russell's albums had all but disappeared from the record catalogues and this, together with his appointment to the faculty of the New England Conservatory in 1969, had the effect of putting him out of sight and out of mind of the jazz public in general and jazz writers in particular, so obscuring what should have been a secure reputation in jazz.

Although he ceased to compose for a while during the 1970s to extend the ideas of his Lydian concept, Russell began recording and performing again later in the decade, observing that while his central aim was still to complete his Lydian Chromatic Concept, 'to the extent performance furthers my aim, I feel that it is a necessity.' Russell headed towards the 1980s with an impressive 1976 recording of his 'Vertical Form VI' (Soul Note) with a 24-piece Swedish orchestra which, like all Russell's work is an exercise in reconciling his brilliant and sometimes abstract imagination with the logical order suggested by his theories, 'I can't imagine any piece based on African music that didn't reflect Vertical Form because the Africans were innovators,' he said. 'In an African drum choir, one drummer is the rhythmic gravity while the others gradually layer on sophisticated rhythms on top of this tonal centre. The whole isn't really evolving in a horizontal way . . . it's vertical energy, getting higher and higher, compounding.'[48]

'New York Big Band' (Soul Note) from 1978 is by an all-star cast and both the variety of material and strong personnel make this one of his better albums in recent years. 'Live In An American Time Spiral' (Soul Note), the seventh of Russell's Vertical Forms, is again by his New York Band and dates from 1982, but is surprisingly ordinary, despite Marty Ehrlich's ingenious flute work.

Russell finally appeared on an American record company with his self-produced recording of 'The African Game', recorded in June 1983, which was picked up by Blue Note records, 'From an emotional as well as an analytical point of view [it] is one of the most significant new album releases of the past several years,' declared Robert Palmer in the *New York Times*. But the 'Living Time Orchestra', consisting mainly of NEC students, suggested that this *magnum opus* had reached them before artistic maturity. Equally 'So What' (Blue Note) from the same concert included a raunchy and exciting version of the title track, using the classic Miles Davis solo—scored by Gotz Tangerding—as its theme, but stumbled when the soloists took over. In 1988 Russell inaugurated a semi-annual New Jazz/Big Band series at the Smithsonian Institute with his Living Time Orchestra and continued to be active as a composer, debuting his 'Six Aesthetic Gravities' at the New England Conservatory.

Carla Bley (b.1938), once a student of George Russell, formed her own ten-piece band in 1976, which she managed to sustain for almost ten years even though it meant putting all her copyright royalties into the project, 'It's a losing proposition,' she said, 'any big band is.'

'European Tour 1977' (ECM) is the first of several albums with her entourage of like-minded iconoclasts. Bley's world was never what it seemed. Unpredictable and zany, clever and crude, it walked the knife edge between kitsch and avant garde, could subvert into rock or confront the audience with theatrical parody. Humour, often black or ironic, swirled through her compositions, which at their best could be affecting, profound and ultimately triumphant.

Albums like 'Dinner Music' (Watt/ECM) with Steve Gadd and his gang in the rhythm section, the minimalistic 'Social Studies' (Watt/ECM) and the excellent 'Live' (Watt/ECM), recorded at the Great American Musical Hall in 1981, each have vital moments capturing the essence of her music. Bley does not so much attempt to break the mould of the big band as take what often sounded like a Bacchanalian swipe at the establishment values the genre had come to represent. Subsequent albums suffered with an apparent desire to secure FM radio airplay; the superficial 'Heavy Heart' (Watt/ECM) and a couple of small groups outings—'Sextet' (ECM/Watt) and 'Night-Glo' (ECM/Watt)—featuring Steve Swallow, revealed the non-conformist conforming.

Bassist **Charlie Haden** (b.1937) resurrected the concept of his celebrated Liberation Music Orchestra' album (Impulse/Jasmine) from 1969, reforming the band in 1982 initially to cut 'The Ballad of the Fallen' (ECM). As with his 1969 band, he again used arrangements by Carla Bley in an affecting and at times deeply moving adaptation of songs from Central America, particularly El Salvador. Haden took the Band on several tours during the 1980s, but unfortunately the band did not aspire to the heights of the album; Haden's democratic leadership allowed solos of great length from all protagonists which not only negated the high head count by reducing the band to soloist plus rhythm, but also created the unique spectacle of both audience and band growing restive as the round robin of solos began to stretch beyond 45 minutes on one song.

Muhal Richard Abrams (b.1930) the great sage of the AACM, was both philosopher and sociologist as well as musician, pianist, orchestrator

Charlie Haden's Liberation Music Orchestra: (L to R) Haden, Bob Stewart, Sharon Freeman, Herb Robertson, Stanton Davis, Ken McIntyre, Joe Lovano.

and conceptualist. Paradoxically, however, he always seemed to avoid giving interviews or even discussing his music, preferring it to stand or fall on its own merits. The first president of the AACM after he helped form it in 1965, Abrams encouraged young musicians to become aware of the whole tradition of jazz. This has always underwritten his own work, and more particularly that of his big band. He moved to New York from Chicago in 1978 where he experimented with groups of various sizes, from his own solo piano ruminations through to a big band with his ambitious, searching compositions.

However, it was with a big band that he made some of his most impressive and original statements although 'Mama And Daddy' (Black Saint) from 1980 seemed only to get to the point on the title track after much experimental water-treading. The 1981 'Blues Forever' (Black Saint) is more cogent and washed with Ellingtonian images and Ellington-through-Mingus episodes, with powerful solos from Baikida Carroll (t) and Craig Harris (tb) rhythmically stewarded by Andrew Cyrille (d).

Although the 1985 'View From Within' (Black Saint) was only with an octet, it is so full of orchestral texture, particularly on his composition 'Laja', that it is impossible for it not to be considered a 'big band'. Abrams had acquired a reputation as a somewhat stand-offish instrumentalist, and indeed the previous two albums contain moments that project this feeling, but here the texures and conception are warmer, with excellent solos from Stanton Davis (t) on the blues 'Down At Pepper's', Marty Ehrlich (woodwinds, ts) and John Purcell (woodwinds, as).

Abrams brought all the elusive diffuse elements that had made his previous large ensemble albums shine on the powerful, impressive 'The Hearinga Suite' (Black Saint) from 1989. Dedicated to the memory of Steve McCall and Raphael Donald Garrett, the 18-piece ensemble included musicians such as Jack Walrath and Cecil Bridgewatet (t), Ehrlich and Purcell, Fred Hopkins (b) and Cyrille (d). Refracting the whole big band tradition with his wide-ranging imagination, and, as on all his albums, using strong rhythmic elements on which to hang his tapestries, it was his most impressive work to date.

Sun Ra (b.1914) and his phantasmagoric ensemble, the Arkestra, has perplexed and delighted audiences since the mid-1950s. At times his music could sound like the Portsmouth Symphonia[49] or the sound of the Fletcher Henderson Orchestra being dragged through a hedge backwards. His concerts were multi-media events; Sun Ra dwelt heavily on astrological-space-is-the-place mythology and the attendant theatre, full of costume parades and chants had to be seen to be believed. 'It's part of entertainment,' he said, 'we have to think of ourselves as actors *and* musicians, and actors wear costumes all the time.'[50]

However, Sun Ra's compositions could suggest the work of 20th-century classical composers such as Edgard Varèse and Krysztof Penderecki, subvert into post-Ellingtonian modernism or become a complete pastiche of a well-known standard, such as 'Cocktails For Two'. His intergalactic battleship could create mountains of dissonance with a thousand subjective meanings—densely layered African chants, exotic mode-based improvisations or simply sound-for-sound's-sake car smashes—which his long time associate John Gilmore (ts), an ex-Jazz Messenger who is reputed to have influenced John Coltrane, would attempt to ascend.

Sun Ra's albums, more than 100, most on his own poorly distributed Saturn label, were often baffling. But in the 1980s he began playing standards, Fletcher Henderson arrangements and oblique, straight ahead originals, 'From now on our melodies are going to be fully recognizable, but the harmonies will be celestial,' he said.[51] A Hat Art album from the early '80s caught the band in transition, moving from the outer galaxies to a more earth-bound orbit, as did 'Reflections In Blue' and 'After Hours' (both Black Saint). However, Ra's live performances, with their collective sense of showmanship and repeated ritualistic chants did not translate well on to disc, the 1988 'Live At Pit Inn' (DIW), 'Love In Outerspace' and 'A Night In East Berlin' (both Leo) suggested all the fun was in the visuals.

In 1988 he signed with A&M—who says Ra didn't have the special metaphysical powers he claimed—and 'Blue Delight' (A&M) saw him evoking Basie on the title track in *l'atmosphère très primitive,* while the oboe and bass clarinet solos on 'Sunrise', were, well, painful. The problem with such material was that it exposed him to the harsh glare of objectivity. The 'joyful noise' classics such as 'Magic City' or 'Cosmic Chaos' survived because of their subjectivity; but working out on straight ahead material the execution of the Arkestra, despite a couple of ringers, was spotty. Beneath the Arkestra gowns there seemed to be a few ankles of clay, while the impression lingered of an old man having fun.

3
The Hard-Bop Mainstream

After being regarded as passé for over two decades, hard-bop was redis-covered towards the end of the 1970s. With jazz floundering as freedom and fusion hit burn-out, the return to the hard-bop mainstream was a return to the underlying principles of improvisation that virtually under-pinned the whole jazz experience. Yet when bop took hold around 1945, it was exciting, anti-establishment and new; its musicians consciously at-tempting to create a new elite who were no longer merely entertainers but artists in their own right. But breaking stereotyped roles, particularly that of the dichotomy of black creation within a white entertainment infrastructure, was a painful transition; the audience for bop showed a marked decline from the huge following enjoyed by the big bands that had gone before.

Such a beginning has usually been portrayed as a revolution, a radical break with the swing era. However, viewed in strictly musical terms bop, was not revolution but evolution, shaped by 'hundreds of individual con-tributions, both large and small . . . which looked at closely in its day to day developments was slow and painstaking.'[1] As with so many of the great breakthroughs in the world of arts, no matter how radical they may have seemed at the time, most have flowed creatively from the major developments that preceded them.

However, the step from swing to bop marked a fundamental change in the aesthetic of jazz, in essence a move from the communal celebra-tion to private contemplation. During the swing era the top big band leaders had followers numbered in millions, but those huge audiences would have rapidly evaporated if their feet had not been immediately engaged by the music. And while this was hardly a measure of artistic stature, it was at least an unambiguous realization of commonly held values.

But with the rise of bop the music became increasingly a one-to-one experience. As jazz moved out of the dancehall and into the jazz club, audiences became correspondingly smaller and the performing situation more intimate. Equally, the simultaneous rise of the long playing record increased the intimacy between musician and audience, 'Turning the radio off may be excusable, as the show will go on without you,' wrote Evan Eisenberg, 'but if you take a record off you boorishly disrupt the performance.'[2]

Bop set in motion a quest for new and more challenging musical forms and a belief that progress could only take place by displacing the prevailing norm. Equally, the audience for the music became, as the bop pioneers intended, concerned more with artistic merit than commercial consideration. It represented a key moment in the evolution of jazz. By cutting themselves off from the consumption rate of mass audiences, the modernists ensured their music could develop at its own pace artistically.

As quickly as 1948 bop was undergoing change; the Miles Davis nonet heralded a softer, subtler approach to improvisation, even Charlie Parker's virtuosity, the *sine qua non* of bop, was being rationalized into a less frantic expressionism by musicians such as Davis and Thelonious Monk. Another key Miles Davis record date, this time the 1954 'Walkin' session (Prestige) summed up the state of bop as it entered its second decade, pointing to much of what was to come. Now dubbed hard-bop it drew on the communicative earthiness of urban blues that brought solos down to earth; arrangements became simple and uncluttered and the repertoire mixed blues and originals with just a few standards. The preferred instrumentation was two or three horns plus piano, bass and drums; bop had established itself as the mainstream style with astonishing speed, and even by the late 1940s, 'it had sucked virtually all of the young players into its vortex'.[3]

Despite successive waves of modal jazz, free jazz and jazz-rock that swept hard-bop to the sidelines, many musicians, both young and established, swam against the then prevailing tides of fashion. As the end of the '70s approached it was clear that neither freedom nor fusion had, as was widely predicted at the time, become the mainstream style. Both seemed to have run their course.

In 1975 Maxine Gregg of 'MsManagement' cleverly promoted tenor saxophonist Dexter Gordon, who had been living in Europe since 1962, in a series of concerts that celebrated his 'Homecoming', despite the fact that he had been returning regularly for short visits for years. 'When I first made calls on Dexter, nobody wanted him,' she said. 'Max Gordon [owner of the Village Vanguard] didn't want to book him. They said he'd been away to long, that he wasn't interesting.'[4]

In the end she persuaded Max Gordon to book him, and after a carefully planned publicity campaign the night he opened there were lines going around the block. He returned there in December 1976 to play a second concert (that produced the double album 'Homecoming' [CBS]) and broadcast a New Year's Eve concert from the club for Station WRVR, something he repeated over the next few years, underlining he was back to stay. A masterpiece of public relations, Gordon's 'return' is now seen as one of the major events that signposted a hard-bop revival in the 1980s.

DEXTER GORDON AND THE TENOR SAXOPHONISTS

Dexter Gordon (1923-90) was one of the key saxophonists in jazz but his significance was often overlooked by historians as he spent most of the 1950s in prison as a result of two drug busts at a time when hard-bop history was being made. A transitional figure, he played an important role in moving the nomenclature of the tenor saxophone from swing to bop and was an early influence on the styles of both Sonny Rollins and John Coltrane.

The hallmarks of his style were the unequivocal emotional force of his playing, a highly developed sense of form and structure and the ability to combine simple elements into a complex and coherent whole. He also liked to dot unlikely musical quotations throughout his solos and while in others this practice was merely irritating, Gordon somehow got away with it, rather like comedian Jack Benny's ability to make the same jokes funny for over 50 years.

The acclaim that greeted Gordon on his return to the States, including an appearance at the White House in 1978, was such that for the first time in his career he was able to sustain a regular working group. However, 'Gotham City' (CBS) from 1980 was with a pick-up group comprising Cedar Walton (p), Percy Heath (b) and Art Blakey (d) with Woody Shaw (t) on some tracks and George Benson (g) on others. Blakey's inspirational drumming and some stunning guitar work by Benson galvanized Gordon, 'He locks together giant cubes of sound in his solos,' said Whitney Balliett, 'piling one on another until he had constructed a gleaming amphitheatre.'[5]

Not all his work in the 1980s yielded amphitheatres however; the 1982 'American Classic' (Elektra Musician) was marred by inconsistency, a poor choice of material and inappropriate production. However later in the

Dexter Gordon: One of the key saxophonists in jazz.

year his appearance at the 1982 Playboy Jazz Festival with his regular group—'In Performance At The Playboy Jazz Festival' (Elektra Musician)—and an appearance in 1983 at the Paul Masson Winery for the 'Harvest Jazz' video series showed his playing to be as robust as ever.

In contrast, his work in Japan at the 'Aurex Jazz Festival '82' (Aurex) with an all-star group is only adequate. But Gordon was drinking heavily and as the 1980s unfolded some of his appearances were 'rather less than consistent'[6]; in early 1984 he was taken ill in Finland and a trip to North Africa ended in disaster when he became too sick to perform. In the latter half of 1984 Gordon's health collapsed completely and after a period of hospitalization he moved to Cuernavaca in Mexico to take an acupuncture and herbal cure.

Eighteen months later Bertrand Tavernier cast him in the role of Dale Turner, a composite character based on the final years of Bud Powell and Lester Young, in the film 'Round Midnight' (Warner Brothers); 'One of the most powerfully memorable jazz movies ever made', said the *Guardian.* Instead of the lunatic misjudgement that cast Diana Ross in the role of Billie Holiday in 'Lady Sings The Blues', Gordon seemed almost typecast as the decaying jazzman living out his last days. His performance as 'a shambling heavy drinker heading for the grave',[7] earned him a nomination as Best Actor in the 59th Academy Awards.

Herbie Hancock's musical direction earned him a Grammy, with music from the soundtrack appearing on both 'Round Midnight' (CBS) and 'The Other Side Of Round Midnight' (Blue Note). The musicians used on the soundtrack also appeared on screen, a remarkable assembly of talent that had virtually carried the Blue Note label 25 years previously.

In 1987 Gordon was celebrated at Avery Fisher Hall with the New York Philharmonic in an 'American Masters' series of three concerts. But during his subsequent tour with the 'Round Midnight' all-stars it was clear he was in frail health, just playing on a few numbers. Even so, the film seemed to confer the long overdue status as a 'Giant of Jazz' on Gordon, a role that he had been preparing to play throughout his life, but came just too late. After a long illness he died on 25 April 1990.

Like Gordon, **Johnny Griffin** (b.1928) moved to the Continent in 1962, returning in 1978 after Gordon had regaled him with stories of his own homecoming. Griffin and Gordon had performed frequently as a two-tenor combination, the last of the great 'battling tenors' tradition in jazz and one of their last recorded performances together appeared on the 1981 Chuck France film, 'Jazz In Exile'. Griffin was an exhilarating soloist renowned for a formidable technique that allowed him fast and feisty execution much admired by musicians, but his approach became more philosophical during the 1980s, with less emphasis on speed and more on expressivity. With age he had become a more commanding player.

Together with Gordon's resurgence, Griffin's late '70s, early '80s albums such as 'Return Of The Griffin', 'NYC Underground' and 'Call It Whachawana' (all Galaxy) helped generate interest in the return to the hard-bop mainstream. In 1983 Griffin appeared on 'Stop, Look, Listen' (Uptown) by Philly Joe Jones' Dameronia, contributing a memorable ballad performance on 'If You Could See me Now' in a project that provided Philly Joe Jones (1923-85), one of the great hard-bop drummers, with a perfect context for his playing.

In 1985 Griffin became a member of the Paris Reunion Band, appearing on the 1985 'French Cooking', (Sonet) but this, as with other editions of the band, failed to capitalize on the available talent. The 1988 'Isfahan' (Who's Who) confirmed Griffin's status as what producer Orrin Keepnews described as a 'B-plus musician . . . capable of specific bursts or full evenings of . . . notable creativity and joy; but never finishing first in a poll, or causing lines to form outside clubs or having a best-selling record.'[8]

Having seen out the electronic 1970s in the pit bands of Las Vegas, the alto and tenor saxophonist and flautist **James Moody** (b.1925) moved from the sunshine state to New York to make a welcome comeback in 1980. 'Liberace,' he said, 'a nice guy, but how long could I play the "Blue Danube" and "Beer Barrel Polka"?' After a two week engagement at New York's Sweet Basil in 1980 that prompted glowing reviews in the *Village Voice, Downbeat* and the daily papers he moved east.

A genial and genuinely witty man, Moody conveyed both the love and passion of making music but refused to take himself seriously; his in-person appearances contrasted humour with the vibrancy of his strongly melodic style. A remarkable technician, his 1987 'Something Special' (Novus) disappointed only because the excitement he could create in live performance failed to materialize on record. Containing an update of his perennial 'Moody's in the Mood for Love', his quartet included Kirk Lightsey (p) and the excellent Idris Muhammad (d). The 1988 'Moving Forward' (Novus) was again assured, competent and never less than highly professional but again lacked the creative tension that 'in-person' performances brought to his playing.

Moody clearly had stars in his eyes when he recorded 'Sweet And Lovely' (Novus) in 1989; played at the marriage to his wife Linda it was top heavy with saccharine synths and clearly reflective of his state of mind at the time. Best man Dizzy Gillespie weighed in on two numbers and their vocal duet on 'Get The Booty' was nominated for a Grammy. But the album seemed custom made for the cut-out bins. Six months later his performances in Europe showed that 'Sweet And Lovely' was a temporary aberration. In the autumn of 1989 he toured as a member of the Phillip Morris Superband.

Clifford Jordan (b.1931) originally attracted attention with his playing in the Max Roach Quintet in 1957 before joining Horace Silver in 1958 and going on to work with a variety of names. However, his playing reached a level of profound maturity during the 1980s where his work included 'Two Tenor Winner' (Criss Cross) from 1984, 'Royal Ballads' (Criss Cross) from 1986 and 'Dr Chicago' (Beehive) from 1987 (with Red Rodney on two tracks). But the album that set his playing apart was 'Repetition' (Soul Note) from 1984.

When Stanley Crouch reviewed the 'Repetition' quartet for the *Village Voice* in December 1981 he referred to 'a grandeur . . . the kind of breadth and depth one expects from artists once they pass forty.' Jordan's huge sound, reminiscent of Ben Webster and Coleman Hawkins, and his melodic logic suggesting Lester Young, regularly provided a foil for Art Farmer's flugelhorn, appearing with distinction on all his albums on the Contemporary label during the '80s. Managed by Helen Keane, who guided pianist Bill Evans's career with such distinction, Jordan appeared on several of her productions for the Contemporary label, including Carol Sloane's 'Love You Madly'.

Charlie Rouse's (1924-88) hard tone and economical style were matured in the Thelonious Monk Quartet from 1959 to 1970. At the height of jazz-rock in the '70s he became disenchanted with the music scene and ceased playing to take acting lessons. He eventually returned to jazz after a brief flirtation with Brazilian music with his Cinnamon Flower Band and a group with cellist Callo Scott.

In 1981 he joined Ben Riley on drums—another Monk graduate—pianist Kenny Barron and bassist Buster Williams at a 72nd Street club with the idea of forming a group committed to Monk's repertoire. The chemistry was right and in 1982 they formed Sphere, 'You're playing his music but you're not playing like him,' explained Barron. 'You're bringing to the music your own personal experiences and your own interpretations.'

Ironically their debut album 'Four In One' (Elektra Musician) was recorded, unknown to the participants, the morning of Monk's death on 17 February 1982: six Monk tunes handled with aplomb and originality. The 1983 'Flight Path' (Elektra Musician) was even better, this time only one Monk tune—the rest originals from the group's members—as the group developed their own identity. A sumptuous, haunting 'If I Should Lose You' by Rouse opens the album and was one of the band's finest cuts; Robert Palmer in the *New York Times* said Sphere 'can now be added to the short, select list of essential modern jazz bands', while the effusive Stanley Crouch wrote in *Village Voice* that they had 'evolved into one of the best small groups in jazz history'.

Certainly their enormous maturity, their common vision and unhurried craftsmanship was, with just few exceptions, unique in acoustic jazz at the time; few ensembles actually played together on a regular basis and with each succeeding year Sphere indeed gained in stature. 'On Tour' (Red Record) recorded live at Bologna in November 1985 became 'Record Of The Week' in the *New York Times;* once again with only one Monk composition, its subtle intensity underlined the fact they could live up to their press. The July 1986 'Live At Umbria Jazz' (Red Record) showed the group at a plateau, their music something more than the sum of the individual members; empathy and intuition were also helping shape their performances.

However, when the group signed with Verve in 1987, the subsequent 'Four For All' (Verve) was well mannered but lacked the inner tensile strength of the live recordings, although the subsequent 'Bird Songs' (Verve), celebrating the music of Charlie Parker, pared Parker's compositions with Monkian brevity.

In 1987 Rouse appeared with the Wynton Marsalis band at the Concord Jazz Festival and toured the United Kingdom with the Stan Tracey Quartet, the British pianist's Monk-influenced piano suitably *à la mode* in a collaboration that produced 'Playin' In The Yard' (Steam). In 1988 he appeared alongside Marsalis again on Marcus Roberts' best-selling 'The Truth Is Spoken Here' (Novus) and recorded a collection of Monk compositions with Carmen McRae for the Concord label. His last recorded performance was in October 1988 with 'Epistrophy' (Landmark), with Don Cherry on two tracks and a rhythm section that included George Cables (p). Then suddenly Rouse was gone, his career cut short by lung cancer on 30 November 1988.

ALTO SAXOPHONY

Sonny Stitt (1942-82) arrived at a style that was a virtual mirror-image of Charlie Parker's in the 1940s, but critics found the similarity just too close for comfort. Stitt hotly denied being a copyist, 'I resembled him . . .

but I was already playing like that anyhow. He just played his thing and I played mine and it came out real close.'[9]

Throughout his career Stitt relished a musical challenge and in 1977 he teamed up with fellow alto/tenor double Red Holloway, with whom he regularly toured until his death. One of the most recorded artists in jazz despite debilitating struggles with alcohol and drugs, Stitt collaborated with up and coming tenor star Ricky Ford on the 1980 'Sonny's Back' (Muse) and Art Pepper on the July 1980 'Groovin' High' (Atlas), a valedictory meeting between two shrewd alto saxophonists who had seen it all and done it all before.

Stitt demonstrated his mastery of the bop idiom with nonchalant ease on 'In Style' and the excellent 'The Last Sessions Vols. 1 & 2' (Muse); the latter with such powerful swinging creativity it seemed impossible that he would be dead some six weeks later on 22 July 1982 of cancer. Just weeks earlier he had substituted for Art Pepper in the Kool Jazz Festival where he shared the stage with Richie Cole, with whom he was reportedly planning to collaborate at the time of his death.

Stitt was one of bop's master musicians, a formidable technician who played an important and influential role in smoothing out the contours of bop. His use of patterns to move from one chord to the next became widely imitated, helping unlock the music's mysteries. On song, the lift and drive he could project as he powered through a set of changes, virtuoso lights flashing, was awesome and he was just beginning to become valued again at the time of his death. The man around whom one of the most enduring jazz legends was built, has Charlie Parker metaphorically handing him 'the keys to his kingdom'[10] shortly before he died in 1955, served as a measure of his stature. But in 1981 Stitt laughed it off: 'That was just a commercial lie' he said, 'to sell records.'

Survivor's Suite: Art Pepper and Frank Morgan

One of the few alto saxophonists to emerge from the bop tradition with a style that was not in hock to the omnipresent influence of Charlie Parker, **Art Pepper** (1925-82), in the years before his death on 15 June 1982, considered himself a living legend. But as the 1981 Don McGlynn film, 'Notes From A Jazz Survivor' showed, survivor was indeed a better sobriquet. By the end of the 1970s Pepper's comeback was something of a *cause célèbre* in the media as an archetypal 'jazzman who battled with drugs and survived', and together with Dexter Gordon's resurgence, Pepper played an important role at the beginning of the '80s in the renewal of interest in jazz in general and acoustic music in particular.

Sonny Stitt with Red Holloway. Stitt was one of bop's master musicians who played an important and influential role in smoothing out the contours of bop.

But in his book *Straight Life* (Schirmer, 1979), Pepper gives every impression that he actually enjoyed his fix and it was not until the late 1970s he was able to effect a rehabilitation. He debuted in New York in 1977 and seemed genuinely surprised that he was still alive and kicking—a garrulous talker, he was not beyond giving his audiences a medical update on the problems years of abuse had wrought on his body. 'I do not hesitate to use the word "genius" in describing Art Pepper,' said Shorty Rogers in 1989, a friend who played extensively with him during the late 1940s and throughout the 1950s. 'He was a true 100 per cent jazz musician.'[12]

Despite Pepper's several prison sentences for narcotics offences, the impassioned intensity of his playing retained a surprising stylistic unity, and it was a source of speculation how much further it might have advanced given an ordered life style. Since his renaissance in 1975, he recorded regularly and his work was both consistent and honest in the impassioned tone of one who has seen Naples and is about to die.

Even on the inevitable and dreaded 'with strings' album, the 1980 'Winter Moon' (Galaxy), he was convincing, particularly on a haunting 'Blues In The Night' on clarinet. The following day he recorded with a quartet and 'One September Afternoon' (Galaxy) continues the relaxed, West Coast feel. 'Blues For The Fisherman' and 'True Blue' (both Mole Jazz), for contractual reasons issued under Pepper's then pianist Milcho Leviev's name, are live at Ronnie Scott's club in London from June 1980. 'Roadgame', 'Art Lives' and 'APQ' (all Galaxy) are all from a live session at the Maiden Voyage, Los Angeles on 13 and 15 August 1981 with new recruit George Cables (p); taken together they capture the searing honesty of Pepper's style, always at maximum commitment in live performance, and are a good representation of his final period. His last session was a duo with George Cables from May 1982 that produced 'Goin' Home' and 'Tête-À-Tête (Galaxy), a quietly beautiful Parthian shot from a jazz maverick.

After a promising debut in the early 1950s, when scarcely out of his teens, **Frank Morgan** (b.1933) gave every indication of becoming a player of great potential. But sadly, at the age of 17, he became addicted to heroin, shooting-up with Charlie Parker during one of his visits to the West Coast. Imprisoned for drug offences, his harrowing story included long stretches at San Quentin, Chino and Synanon, where he played with Pepper and trumpeter Dupree Bolton in the prison band. When his 1955 album 'Introducing Frank Morgan' (GNP) was re-issued in 1977, Leonard Feather, who re-wrote the liner notes, initially assumed he was dead until exhaustive enquiries proved otherwise.

Morgan's first complete album as a leader since 1957 was 'Easy Living' (Contemporary) with the Cedar Walton Trio from 1985. It was immediately apparent that a great talent had been lost to jazz for almost 30 years, described by Robert Palmer in the *New York Times* as 'one of this year's surprises and musical delights'. Morgan continued to rebuild his career, including turning himself in to serve a four-month sentence for a parole violation so that he would be on the straight and narrow when 'Easy Living' was released.

In 1986, a March appearance at a West Coast club was reviewed by Leonard Feather for the *Los Angeles Times*, 'In peak form, and in terms of the post-Charlie Parker tradition,' he wrote, 'Frank Morgan is the greatest alto saxophonist living today.' In April 1986 Morgan again collaborated with the Cedar Walton Trio on 'Lament' (Contemporary), 'I didn't want to be on the streets with my life up for grabs any longer', he said.[13]

In December 1986 he made his New York debut at the Village Vanguard. 'It was like, "Where've you been",' he said. 'I felt I had come home.'[14] Musicians such as Betty Carter, Art Blakey, Max Roach, Tommy Flanagan, Freddie Hubbard and Clifford Jordon came to check him out. On the third night trumpeters Wynton Marsalis and Eddie Henderson sat in with him; the following Saturday Marsalis sat in with him again and asserted, 'Frank Morgan is an example of the finest musicianship America is capable of producing.'[15] The media rushed to interview him, 'I'm a bebopper, a person who believes in keeping the music in its purest state,'[16] he told them all. Unfortunately, 'Bebop Lives' (Contemporary), recorded live during his stay at the club, did not come up to expectations, with a lacklustre Johnny Coles on flugelhorn the party pooper.

A bop-meets-post-bop meeting with the McCoy Tyner Trio, 'Major Changes' (Contemporary), from April 1987, included a surprisingly successful 'Theme From Love Story'—believe it or not. A Parker tribute from January 1988, 'Yardbird Suite' (Contemporary), included copacetic sidemen Mulgrew Miller, Ron Carter and Al Foster who also appear on 'Reflections' (Contemporary), together with Joe Henderson (ts) and Bobby Hutcherson (vib) for another bop meets-post-bop variant. In 1989 he signed with Island/Antilles and 'Mood Indigo' included trumpeter Wynton Marsalis. Morgan's disciplined abandon, returning to the old 1940s benchmark of speed and complexity of line, was a memorable prodigal return in the 1980s that in live performance actually lived up to the hyperbole his performances had generated.

Two Generations

Profoundly influenced by Charlie Parker's playing, which formed the basis of his own accomplished and mature hard-bop style, **Phil Woods** (b.1931) has been described, with good reason, as 'the finest alto saxophonist in mainstream jazz'[17] and 'chief alto of the jazz tribe'.[18] Woods' playing has always been a model of consistency and taste and reached a new peak

Frank Morgan: In peak form and in terms of the post Charlie Parker tradition Frank Morgan is the greatest alto saxophonist living today,' said Leonard Feather.

during the 1980s with a series of uniformly excellent albums that saw his alto tone broaden and his effortless virtuosity coloured with gruff growls that recalled Ben Webster.

In the transient world of jazz with its pick-up groups and pre-fabricated festival lineups, Woods managed to maintain a consistently excellent group from 1974 and throughout the 1980s. Steve Gilmore (b) and Bill Goodwin (d) were fixtures from inception; in 1981 Hal Galper replaced Mike Melillo on piano and in 1984 trumpeter/flugelhornist Tom Harrell was added, staying until 1989 when he was replaced by trombonist Hal Crook.

Even though Concord Records turned down 'Phil Woods Quartet Vol. 1' (Adelphi), it nevertheless garnered considerable critical acclaim, including two Grammy nominations as Woods entered the 1980s; 'In short,' wrote Peter Keepnews, 'a representative set by a state of the art jazz ensemble, in other words truly good jazz.' The follow up, the Grammy winning 'More Live' (Adelphi) also came from the same live date in Austin, Texas. A performance recorded in Macerata, Italy from 1980 appeared on 'The Macerata Concert' (Philology), and if indulgent through length, it remains an important documentation of one of the notable *ensembles* of '80s jazz.

'Birds Of A Feather' (Antilles), while not particularly well recorded, was nevertheless a characteristically determined performance by the group from the blistering 'Star Eyes' to a beautiful ballad interpretation of 'Goodbye Mr. Evans'. A live date at the Village Vanguard on 7 October 1982, 'Live From New York' (Palo Alto) and 'At The Vanguard' (Antilles) from the following day, together with the brilliant 'Integrity' (Red Record) were the swan songs from the quartet; from 1984 the group toured and recorded as a quintet with the addition of Tom Harrell (t, flhn).

The December 1984 'Heaven' with the new lineup was a placid affair in comparison to the fierce blowing of the final quartet albums; in fact the quintet albums during the 1980s were altogether more restrained affairs. The 1986 'Gratitude' (Denon) was typical of the material the group used in live performance, and while the track 'Tenor Of The Times' was something of a *tour de force* for the whole group, the emphasis was on more considered, lyrical introversion and a democratic apportionment of solos which included long bass solos that effectively cut numbers in half. One of Woods' foibles in live performance was to insist his bass player had a fair hearing, upbraiding his audience if they grew restless during their spectacular length. Another was for his band to play acoustically (i.e. *no* microphones), a heroic gesture in the far from subtle world of the night club.

The group finally signed with Concord records in 1987 and their performance at the Fujitsu-Concord Jazz Festival that year was issued as 'Bop Stew' and 'Bouquet' (both Concord), followed by 'Phil Woods Little Big Band' (Concord), eight tracks with the quintet augmented by Nick Brignola (bs), Hal Crook (tb) and Nelson Hill (ts). The final album with Harrell, 'Flash' (Concord) was recorded in April 1989, an ebullient sextet session with Crook (tb).

Woods was highly active in music education, one of the causes dear to him the annual Delaware Gap Celebration Of The Arts. His appearances 'special guest' in a variety of recording situations included Carly Simon's 'Torch' (Warner Bros), Billy Joel's '52nd Street' (CBS), Ben Sidran's 'On The Live Side' (Magenta), Bob Connor's 'Boss Brass 'n Woods' (MCA), Harry Leahey's 'Live From The Showboat' (RCA), Jaki Byard's 'Musique Dubois' (Muse) and Steve Miller's 'Born 2B Blue' (Capitol) amongst others.

Richie Cole (b.1948) had lessons on alto saxophone from Phil Woods for two years and won a scholarship to Berklee College Of Music where he studied for a further two and a half years. There the concept of his 'Alto Madness' band was formed, 'My first "Alto Madness" band was in Boston, and the rhythm section was Richie Beirach, Miroslav Vitous and Harvey Mason—we were all first year students,' he said.

Immediately after Berklee he joined the Buddy Rich Big Band, featuring on albums such as 'Keep The Customer Satisfied' (Liberty), followed by six months with Lionel Hampton in 1972. An association with singer Eddie Jefferson, with whom he toured and recorded continued until the singer was killed in 1979. Subsequently Cole travelled the globe with his group Alto Madness, his swinging brand of bebop fearlessly treading where man had previously trodden, only this time laced with humour and genuine enjoyment that made many new converts for jazz.

At the beginning of the '80s Cole was among the most talked about of the emerging young musicians, featuring during October and November 1980 on the covers of *Downbeat, Jazz Times* and the Japanese *Swing Journal*. Part of his success lay in his extrovert on-stage performance, 'Personally, I appreciate people spending their hard earned money to see me. I feel obliged to do the best I can,' he said.

Cole's playing was accomplished, fluent and hot. Alongside Phil Woods, 'Side by Side' (Muse) from 1980, the master-pupil relationship was apparent, but Cole was by no means outclassed; 'The most important reason,' said Woods about their collaboration, 'was to document what I call the oral (and aural) tradition—passing on the information person to person . . . not from a book but from knowing someone.'[19]

A February 1981 concert in Japan, 'Tokyo Madness' (King), later released as 'Some Things Speak For Themselves' (Muse), and an appearance at the Village Vanguard four months later with the catalytic Bobbie Enriquez on piano, 'Richie Cole . . . Alive!' (Muse), give a good idea of a Cole concert as did a 'Jazz Life' video produced by Ben Sidran. All participants clearly enjoyed themselves and *communicated,* a humanizing factor absent in the music of many young neo-classicists.

Even though the 1982 'Alto Annie's Theme' (Palo Alto) contained one of Cole's finest solos on record—Duke Pearson's 'Jeannine'—he failed to sustain the creative intensity with diverse and occasionally hare-brained offerings. Unfortunately Cole seemed to lack the ability to create a body of work that could be taken seriously—even 'Jeannine' is undermined by a baritone overdub for no apparent reason. In live performance, however, Cole could generate a formidable head of steam, able to sustain chorus after chorus of steadily building intensity with a fluency that never seemed to falter for want of ideas.

But a huge gulf existed between what he was actually capable of in-person and what he achieved on record. The 1986 'Pure Imagination' (Concord) or the 1987 'Popbop' (Milestone), where he and producer Ben Sidran act like two kids let loose in a chocolate factory, sustained the image of court jester—entertaining, yes, but nothing of lasting value, which Cole was well capable of. A jamming band assembled for the 1987 festival circuit with Hank Crawford (as) and Emily Remler (g) had Cole and Remler stealing the show on 'Bossa International' (Milestone) recorded live at Nimes, France; it showed the importance of context to focus Cole's playing by simply putting him on the spot and forcing him to create. However, when in November 1989 Cole toured the USSR, it was difficult to think of any other musician in jazz capable of bringing goodwill and *glasnost* jazz-style with such carefree abandon to the fast-changing political landscape of that vast, sad country.

BOP BRASS

In 1976 Martin Williams wrote that **Dizzy Gillespie** (b.1917) saw himself, 'impersonally, almost reverently as part of a brass tradition which began with King Oliver's cornet and moved through Louis Armstrong, Roy Eldridge and himself. He [saw] that heritage as also having passed on to others.' Williams could have added that there was not a trumpet player in jazz who had not come under the influence of that tradition.

Gillespie's finest work on record was done in the 1940s, as he literally helped shape the direction of American music. Since then there were surprisingly few albums of significance and considering his stature as an artist, this is surprising. From 1972 Norman Granz's Pablo label recorded Gillespie at 'a ridiculously prolific rate including some dogs'.[20] Even so, under Granz's management Gillespie's career, which for the previous ten years or so had been in the doldrums, was resurrected during the 1970s.

'Digital At Montreux 1980' (Pablo) was a rather bizarre combination, pitting Gillespie alongside 'Toots' Thielemans on guitar and Bernard Purdie on drums, while 'Musician, Composer, Raconteur' (Pablo) put him back in the familiar all-star jam band situation at the same venue a year later but was flawed by the trumpeter's poor articulation. 'To A Finland Station' (Pablo) was a head-to-head with the spectacular Cuban trumpet virtuoso Arturo Sandoval from 1982 but the expected sparks were dampened by a Finnish rhythm section and Gillespie's inexplicable use of the jew's harp. Later in the year he guested on Stevie Wonder's single 'Do I Do', from the album 'Original Musiquarium' (Motown), and sounded surprisingly in sync with the new surroundings.

'New Faces' (GRP) from 1985, with a group of young stars including Branford Marsalis and Kenny Kirkland did not live up to expectation, even though six of the seven tunes were written by Gillespie. In 1987 he celebrated his 70th birthday with a widely acclaimed world tour with his '70th Birthday Big Band'. Later in the year a birthday 'all-star' concert at Wolf Trap was recorded for PBS and his appearance at the Fifth International Jazz Festival Havana formed the basis of a film by John Holland, 'A Night in Havana: Dizzy Gillespie In Cuba'.

In 1988 he ended a three-year recording hiatus with 'Endlessly' (Impulse) but conveyed the impression of emotional detachment in his playing that often crept into his latter-day work. Later in the year he appeared on the festival circuits with another big band, debuting at the Playboy Jazz Festival, pacing his playing and deferring to his protege Jon Faddis when necessary.

At the end of 1988 he formed 'Dizzy's United Nation' with a cast of thousands, including James Moody, Paquito d'Rivera, Arturo Sandoval, Flora Purim, Airto, Steve Turré, Slide Hampton and Ignacio Berroa. Their appearance at London's Royal Festival Hall in June 1989 was videoed by BBC TV. In March 1989 he played a spontaneously conceived live duet with Max Roach (d) comprising 23 numbers, 'Max + Dizzy - Paris 1989' that placed him in his most challenging environment since the hey-day of bop. At 71 he quite probably surprised even himself with his playing. The 1988 Clint Eastwood film 'Bird' (CBS), depicting Charlie Parker's life, was an awkward reminder of the drug sub-culture that was associated with the burgeoning bop movement. In the film, the Gillespie character takes Parker to task for, 'living up (or down) to the prejudices that society has about irresponsible blacks'. But Dizzy ruefully observes: 'I'm a reformer, you're a martyr and they remember the martyrs.'[21]

And in a way that was Gillespie's fate; 'To live longer than 40 years is bad manners,' said Dostoevsky's Underground Man, but Gillespie remained unromantically alive, almost a peripheral figure since the 1950s. His first love was the big band, never seeming to have his heart in organizing a really effective small group so his music suffered. But Gillespie was a survivor and by the 1980s enjoyed an emeritus status that guaranteed a walk-on part at every major jazz festival in the world. It ensured his popularity but he failed to make any advances on his art, undermining, in the minds of many, the crucial role he played in the development of bop until it was almost too late.

Red Rodney (b.1927), who replaced Kenny Dorham in Parker's quintet in late 1949, fell victim of addiction and saw his promising early career tailspin into oblivion.[22] He began to resurface around 1975 and by the end of the 1970s formed a quintet including Gerry Dial (p) and Billy Mitchell (ts).

In 1980 a chance meeting with multi-instrumentalist Ira Sullivan led to their co-leading a quintet that became widely acclaimed during the early 1980s. 'I was supposed to go into the Village Vanguard with a quintet . . . and I asked Ira,' Rodney explained in 1981. 'We rehearsed a few days and recorded live at the Vanguard . . . I think it's the best thing I ever did in my life.' In fact the three nights of recording produced both 'Live At The Village Vanguard' (Muse) and 'Hi Jinx At The Vanguard' (Muse). With an up-to-date repertoire, including several original compositions from pianist Gerry Dial, the group became so busy that by 1982 they were turning down job offers.

'Night And Day' (Muse) was another fine example of this talented quintet whose astonishing tonal variety came from Sullivan's multi-instrumental talents that included trumpet, flugelhorn, alto and tenor saxophones and flute. A change of record label produced a rather glossy 'Spirit Within' (Elektra Musician) but the Grammy-nominated 'Sprint' (Elektra Musician), recorded live at the Jazz Forum in November 1982, was back on course with the band lifted by the presence of Ornette Coleman in the audience.

In 1986 Sullivan found touring a burden and restricted his playing to occasional appearances with Rodney who continued with the band, with Dick Oatts (as,ts)—who also played extensively with the Mel Lewis Orchestra during the late 1980's—Jay Anderson (b) and Joey Baron (d) (replaced in 1988 by John Reilly) with Gerry Dial on keyboards continuing to contribute much of the repertoire. Their 1986 album 'No Turn On Red' (Denon) captured their neatness if not the excitement they generated live, 'I didn't think I'd get past 40 and here I am at 60 playing jazz with these great young musicians,' he said.

In 1987 Australian multi-instrumentalist James Morrison worked with the band including dates at Chicago's Jazz Showcase and the Village Vanguard. However, Red Alert continued with Dial and Oatts, recording 'Red Snapper' and 'One for Bird' (both Steeplechase) live during their 1988 European tour. Rodney had created a crisp, energetic ensemble with talented young players whose contemporary playing flourished as well as

Red Rodney with Gerry Dial piano; Rodney created a crisp, energetic ensemble with talented young players.

ensured the leader's style was not date-stamped in the past. In early 1989, during a stay at the Village Vanguard, they were unexpectedly joined by Wynton Marsalis who was reportedly impressed with the band.

Dick Oatts, also a member of the fusion group Flim And The BB's (dmp label), and Gerry Dial debuted as leaders in their own right with the 1989 'Dial and Oatts' (dmp), with guest Mel Lewis on an album of 15 original but glossy compositions.

Art Farmer (b. 1928) played flugelhorn exclusively and was one of the great ballad interpreters in jazz; indeed all his work had a lyrical and sapient quality that placed him among the foremost performers on his instrument. Farmer moved to Vienna in 1968, and became a regular member of the Austrian Radio Orchestra, but his move away from the hub conspired to diminish what should be have been a secure reputation in jazz.

Farmer had always returned to the States on a regular basis, most often to tour and record with Clifford Jordan, an association that dated back to the time they shared the front line in the Horace Silver Quintet in 1958. His 1970s collaborations with Jordan can be found on the Inner City label while 'Mirage' (Soul Note) from 1982 and 1985's 'You Make Me Smile' (Soul Note) chart their early '80s association. His work for the Concord label, 'Warm Valley' and 'Work of Art' are perhaps a little too introverted, but elegantly crafted for all that.

In 1982 he reformed the Jazztet with co-leader Benny Golson and trombonist Curtis Fuller. Golson's distinctive writing—he once was musical director of one of the most highly regarded versions of Art Blakey's Jazz Messengers—provided a little more pep that displayed the breadth of Farmer's style; 'Moment To Moment' (Soul Note), 'Back To The City' (Contemporary), 'Real Time' (Contemporary) and 'Live At Sweet Basil Vols. 1 & 2' (Contemporary) chart their progress, representing a classy re-union of the 1980s.

His continental work produced 'Foolish Memories' (L&R), a tasteful set of standards and originals with an all European group from 1981 and in 1984 toured Europe with Slide Hampton (tb), 'In Concert' (Enja). On his increasingly frequent Stateside returns, Farmer worked with Chico Freeman in 1983 and regularly with his Quintet that included Clifford Jordan; 'Something To Live For' (Contemporary) is a memorable 1987 reading of seven Billy Strayhorn compositions while the February 1988 'Blame It On My Youth' and the April 1989 'Ph.D' (both Contemporary) are models of good taste and quality musicianship—all produced by Helen Keane— that underlined the fact that Farmer's beautiful, lyric understatement reached new heights during the 1980s.

In October 1970 **Tom Harrell** (b.1946) made his recording debut as a member of Woody Herman's Orchestra on 'Woody' (Cadet). He was featured on an arrangement of 'Time For Love' and it was clear the 24-year-old had in place tone, technique and a flair for lucid melodic construction. Since then he worked with Horace Silver, appearing on five albums with him, and a remarkable roster of musicians including pianist Bill Evans, George Russell, Mel Lewis, Bob Brookmeyer, Lee Konitz and, in 1980, contributed some beautiful flugelhorn solos on Gerry Mulligan's Grammy winning 'Walk On Water' (DRG).

But despite Harrell's gift for lyrical invention, economy of line, wholesome tone and the high regard of his peers, he remained, like his on-stage persona, shy and withdrawn. The reason was revealed when sleeve annotator Ken Frackling pointed out on Harrell's 1988 'Stories' (Contemporary) that the trumpeter suffered from schizophrenia.

From 1983 to 1989 he was with Phil Woods' acoustic bop quintet, 'Tom is the most complete musician in my experience,' said Woods, 'I continue to be impressed by his total harmonic recall, his knowledge of tunes of the past and his compositions reflecting the future.'[23] His first important statement on record as a leader in his own right was 'Play Of Light' (Blackhawk), recorded in 1982, with Ricky Ford on tenor, but not released until 1986. Harrell's thoughtful, probing lyricism had much in common with a Bill Evans improvisation; both favoured the introspective, the slightly melancholy and an explorative, less frantic approach.

'Moon Alley' (Criss Cross) was a 1985 date with Kenny Garrett (as), while 'Open Air' (Steeplechase) from 1986, is with the Phil Woods rhythm section and Bob Rockwell (ts). Despite the hard-bop configuration of the group, what emerges is a decidedly softer approach, creating the right environment for Harrell's unfussy melodic construction to flourish. 'Stories' (Contemporary) linked him up again with Bob Berg on tenor, his blowing partner during his Horace Silver Quintet days. The 1989 'Sail Away' (Contemporary) had Joe Lovano on tenor and James Williams on piano and is notable for the supreme lyricism of Harrell's playing, especially-on the medium and slow numbers, where he seemed perhaps the only trumpeter in the 1980s able to evoke the *beauty* of the late Clifford Brown's playing.

PIANISTS

At his best **Hank Jones** (b.1918) inspired writers to describe his playing as 'impeccable' and 'elegant', qualities long appreciated by his peers and it is no exaggeration to say that he was probably the most recorded pianist in jazz. Regarded as the 'father' of the Detroit school of pianists, Jones' style had great depth, reflecting on the one hand his formative influences such as Teddy Wilson and Fats Waller and on the other early bop stylists such as Al Haig and Bud Powell.

A 1975 date for Inner City produced 'Hanky Panky' that led to a series of albums, recorded initially for Japanese consumption, under the collective heading 'The Great Jazz Trio'. Some of his best recorded work is cunningly disguised under this name and while 'The Great Jazz Trio At The Village Vanguard' (East Wind) was recorded in 1977, with Ron Carter and Tony Williams, it is one of the finest examples of his style which did not go unnoticed by young 1980s pianists such as James Williams, Benny Green, Mulgrew Miller and Geoff Keezer.

However, not all his work under the Great Jazz Trio's banner aspired to this standard; albums like the 1982 'Ambrosia' and the 1986 'Standard Collection' are patently mood music while 'The Club New Yorker' and 'Monk's Moods' (all Denon) do not fare significantly better. The 1980 'Great Jazz Trio Revisited: At The Village Vanguard' (East Wind) almost recaptured the magic, this time with Eddie Gomez and Al Foster. He also recorded and toured with fellow Detroit pianist Tommy Flanagan, 'Our Delights' (Milestone) and 'I'm All Smiles' (MPS) and with George Shearing on 'The Spirit Of 176' (Concord).

Like Jones before him, **Tommy Flanagan** (b.1930) had spent several years as Ella Fitzgerald's accompanist. When he finished his tenure with Fitzgerald, Flanagan performed jazz a great service by becoming his own boss in the late 1970s. Flanagan's work was a treasure trove of delights. Unruffled by the fastest tempos of bop, his calm creativity masked an exceptionally fertile imagination, which by common critical consensus was never at a loss for ideas. Nothing Flanagan played was gratuitous or suggested the use of technique for technique's sake; rather he was able to create solos rich with inner meaning so that his work appeared as a complete statement where nothing could be added or subtracted without destroying its closely interlocking logic.

Flanagan is one of the few artists in jazz who was able to make a convincing statement virtually every time he recorded and his work was invariably so consistent that preferences emerged more through the work of his accompanists than through his own playing; the February 1980 'Super Session' (Enja) has Elvin Jones (d) and Red Mitchell (b) with two Flanagan originals and four standards. 'Plays The Music Of Harold Arlen' (Inner City) from the same year is with the brilliant George Mraz (b) and

Connie Kay (d) with a Helen Merrill vocal on 'Last Night When We Were Young'.

The 1981 'Magnificent' (Progressive) substitutes Al Foster for Kay and together with the 1982 'Giant Steps' (Enja)—an album of Coltrane compositions—1983's 'Thelonica' (Enja) with Art Taylor substituted on drums—an album of Monk tunes—'The Master Trio' and 'Blues In The Closet' (both Baybridge) comprise as sublime a selection of Flanagan's art as any. His 1987 'Nights At The Vanguard' (Uptown) prompted Ira Gitler, writing in the *Jazz Times*, to call Flanagan, 'One of the great pianists of jazz . . . an all time great.'

Horace Silver (b.1928), Blue Note's longest serving artist, made his final album for the label during 1978-79, 'Silver N' Strings' (Blue Note), after a 28-year association with the label. One of the original Jazz Messengers, his own groups have consistently contained exciting improvisers. In the '50s and '60s Silver had one of the quintessential groups in jazz and along with fellow Blue Note artist Art Blakey, helped define hard-bop. Silver always used his own original material, his catchy themes and well conceived arrangements providing ideal launching pads for his soloists.

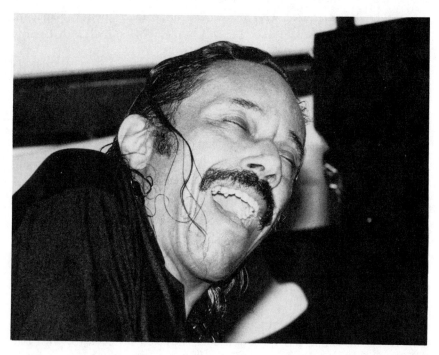

Horace Silver, whose compositions were 'meant for the upliftment of man's soul, mind and body'.

His finest group was the 1959-63 quintet with Blue Mitchell and Junior Cook, who interpreted Silver's compositions with audible delight and—as critic Martin Williams noted—a spirit akin to the early Basie band. However it was some of his mid-sixties albums that proved to be most popular with the public; 'Cape Verdean Blues' (Blue Note) and his big-seller 'Song For My Father' (Blue Note) continued their appeal into the 1980s, enjoying a renaissance in the discos of London.

In 1970 Silver began a continuing theme of self-help, evangelized through his compositions, 'We call it self-help holistic metaphysical music,' he said, 'meant for the upliftment of man's soul, mind and body.' The themes were often as catchy, sometimes suggesting past triumphs but the titles were changed to cloying slogans such as 'Smelling Our Attitude', 'Accepting Responsibilities' and 'Don't Dwell On Your Problems'. All was well until the vocals.

In 1981 Silver formed his own record company, Silveto Productions but 'Guides To Growing Up' (Silveto), was the first album on the new label and dwells rather too long on the holistic message with vocal duo Feather and Bill Cosby drafted in to emphasize the Silver's well meaning, but tedious message. 'Spiritualizing The Senses' (Silveto) from 1983 featured Eddie Harris (ts) in a front line with the fine, underrated trumpeter Bobby Shew and Ralph Moore (ts) on one of Silver's best albums since the sixties—there were no vocals. 'There's No Need To Struggle' (Silveto), without Moore but with Feather again, was only partially successful.

In 1982 Ralph Moore and Brian Lynch (t) became Silver's regular front line for personal appearances and together with Bob Maize (b) and Carl Burnett (d) established themselves as a firmly swinging, highly competent band that stayed together until late 1985. When Brian Lynch left he was replaced by the somewhat dire vocalist Andrew Bey; by 1987 Michael Mossman (t) and Ralph Bowen (ts), formerly with Out Of The Blue, the young bop band created by record producer JoAnne Jiminez for the reconstituted Blue Note label, were the front line, with Mossman being replaced by Vince Cutro in 1988. But Bey remained, 'One cannot help regarding the songs as an unnecessary interruption to the real business of the evening' said The Times.[24]

'Music To Ease Your Disease' (Silveto) was the best of Silver's homegrown productions, with Clark Terry (t), Junior Cook (ts), Ray Drummond (b) and Billy Hart (d) although Andy Bey continued to be a source of irritation. The compositions were archetypal Silver, except for the titles, but 'The Respiratory Story', and 'What Is The Sinus-Minus?' were hard-blowing and jaunty vehicles with Cook and Terry the icing on the cake.

Silver's crusade for the betterment of mankind was a noble and altruistic gesture, but doomed to failure. The therapeutic and uplifting powers of music have long been known to mankind and Silver's naive message presented an unnecessary obstacle in the path of enjoying his music. His message seemed to undermine the deeper seriousness of jazz, rather as if he were promoting a brand of soap.

With most born-again evangelizers, one dinner party in their company is usually enough. Silver, his powers undiminished but misdirected, failed to capitalize on the bop revival of the 1980s in the way that several of his contemporaries did. In contrast to fellow Jazz Messenger Art Blakey, Silver's profile in the 1980s remained low, although not helped by ill-health, while Blakey's resurgence was so strong and so much a part of what was being achieved by young musicians in their parallel neo-classic revival of hard-bop that he more properly appears elsewhere.

How is it that **Ahmad Jamal** (b.1930), who excited praise from the likes of Art Tatum, Miles Davis, Anthony Braxton, Gil Evans, pianist Bill Evans *and* the respected critic and entrepreneur John Hammond, has remained an obscure, almost peripheral figure in jazz? Hailed as a genius by Miles Davis in the fifties and saluted in the eighties by Jack DeJohnette with 'Ahmad The Terrible' on his 1984 'Album, Album' (ECM), Jamal's career has sometimes faltered as he has taken more than his share of wrong turnings; but he showed that the talent which had excited so much praise during the '50s and early '60s could still be tapped during the 1980s.

Jamal's position in the jazz hegemony is impossible to acknowledge without the perspective offered by his work on the Chicago-based Chess label, stretching from the 1955 'Chamber Music Of The New Jazz' to 'Ahmad Jamal At The Blackhawk' from 1961 with Vernell Fournier and Israel Crosby. However, these albums have been notoriously difficult to obtain, perhaps one of the reasons why Jamal's éclat has dimmed.

Certainly Jamal's influence on Miles Davis, and thus at one remove, jazz during the '50s, was profound. Ian Carr's biography of Miles Davis[25] listed ten tunes Davis used from Jamal's repertoire—omitting 'Billy Boy' which would make 11 in all—at a time when the Davis Quintet was considered the foremost group in jazz. 'I think,' said bassist Todd Coolman, 'that what Miles liked about Ahmad was the level of excitement that he achieved without being obvious . . . Miles learned from that.'[26] Jamal's style of shaping silence with a Basie-like minimalism contrasted with startling rococo flourishes that unleashed his not inconsiderable technique. The dramatic flair of his playing appealed strongly to the trumpeter.

Jamal's 1981 appearance at Midem with his trio had Gary Burton sitting-in on some tracks, 'Live In Concert' (Kingdom Jazz—also on video), demonstrate Jamal's return to form in the 1980s and his abrupt mix 'n' match juxtaposition of contrasting sections of compositions. A sell-out concert at The Great American Music Hall from 1982 eventually appeared as 'Goodbye Mr Evans' (Black Lion) and with a percussionist in the lineup, it was clear Jamal was striving for a more powerful reincarnation of his style.

When he signed for Atlantic in 1985, Jamal returned to his greatest moments for the Chess label with digital versions of 'Poinciana' and 'But Not For Me' and sophisticated contemporary compositions such as Wayne Shorter's 'Footprints' on 'Digital Works' (Atlantic); but it has always been live performances that galvanized his talent. 'Live At Montreal Jazz Festival 1985' (Atlantic) showed the extent of his sweeping style, and although the percussionist blurs the powerful duality of Jamal's piano, his talent was finally back in gear. Jamal had moved on from the lost horizons of the '50s to a more competitive plane, still serving a potent-lesson in the less-is-more ethic.

'Rossiter Road' (Atlantic) from 1986 and 'Crystal' (Atlantic) from 1987 are studio sessions that capture Jamal's touch but sacrifice the confrontation between audience and artist that so often produced creative exhilaration. The 1989 'Pittsburgh' (Atlantic) disappointed with a big band and vocal backing; Jamal's odyssey returning full cycle to the '70s when his albums lost their way artistically.

When **Andrew Hill** (b.1937) returned to the Blue Note label in 1989, David Rosenthal wrote: 'Essentially, [he] is a hard-bopper (albeit a highly idiosyncratic one).' A virtuoso pianist and occasionally eclectic stylist, Hill consolidated his approach through an expansion of Thelonious Monk's radical reassessment of the role of the piano in jazz. Monk's use of rhythm, primarily of rhythmic displacement, together with his ability to distill the melodic essence of a piece with a mixture of brevity and paraphrase were the basic syntax Hill seized upon as the starting point of his own style.

With his commanding technique, Hill avoided Monk's rugged fundamentalism with a lighter touch and a faster, fleeter use of deconstruction and fragmentation. It was as if Monk's style had taken wings; a mixture of the forceful and delicate with a clarity of expression that emphasized Hill's individual mixture of the perilous and the surprising.

Hill's Blue Note recordings in the sixties seemed to place him as the logical link between Monk, the 'high-priest of bop', and Cecil Taylor, before his profile receded against a background of study, education and musical social work. While he continued to be one of the least visible of the major jazz improvisers in the 1980s because of the serious illness of his wife, who died in 1989, he did at least record intermittently. The 1980 'Faces Of Hope' was a solo recital and 'Strange Serenade' (both Soul Note) a trio with Alan Silva (b) and Freddie Waits (d); however Hill's style was at its most lucid on the solo set. Perhaps that is why his next album, the 1986 'Verona Rag' (Soul Note) was also a solo outing; a profound discourse that showed why he was once dubbed an 'innovative enigma'.

'Shades' (Soul Note) from 1986 is an impressive album by any standards. All the pieces were composed by Hill, with an elusive form that he occasionally camouflaged further by blurring the distinction between written and improvised sections. The opening 'Monk's Glimpse' showed how far he extended Monk's vision with a series of elipses and allusions that touch base with Monk's style as they moved through Hill's crafty refractions. Clifford Jordan (ts) navigated the same firm path that Charlie Rouse did with Monk, while Ben Riley (d) and Rufus Reid (b) kept the rhythmic current flowing as Hill swims against, through and around it.

'Eternal Spirit' (Blue Note) from 1989 reaffirmed Hill's status as a master improviser and conceptualist. Bobby Hutcherson (v) was added while Greg Osby (as) replaced Jordan; it gave the young altoist the opportunity to inadvertently demonstrate how rhythmically constraining his downtown M-Base outings were. Throughout, Hill's playing had the angular suppleness of Monk's art, a conspiracy between harmony and rhythm yet at the same time remaining their servant, which had the effect of making Osby sound a major talent.

GUITAR

Joe Pass (b.1929) began playing the guitar in 1939, influenced by Charlie Christian, Django Reinhardt and in later years Barney Kessel and Tal Farlow. However, he didn't emerge in jazz until record producer Richard Bock discovered him playing in a Synanon drug rehabilitation centre in 1961, after spending several years on the fringes of society. His debut on record came with 'Sounds of Synanon' (Pacific Jazz) released in 1962, and was followed by a spell with George Shearing (1965-67), studio work and in a guitar team with Herb Ellis (1972-74).

Joe Pass, the foremost practitioner of the solo guitar in jazz.

In 1973 he was signed by Norman Granz for his Pablo label and his first album for him, 'Virtuoso' (Pablo)—followed in later years by another three volumes—was highly successful. Granz, who managed both Oscar

Peterson and Ella Fitzgerald, immediately put him to work with his two major artists and arranged countless mix 'n' match sessions on record with his stable of artists.

Soon Pass was generally accepted as one of the finest guitartists in jazz, while Granz saw to it that he also became one of the most recorded. By now it was apparent that Pass was deserving of the sobriquet 'Art Tatum of the guitar'; a stylistic consolidator who absorbed and expanded on virtually the whole post-Christian school, Pass developed into the foremost practitioner of the solo guitar in jazz. His dense, pianistic lines and rococo flourishes were set against his own simultaneous accompaniment of arpeggiating chords and an interpenetrated bass line.

Like Oscar Peterson, Pass built up a huge discography on the Pablo label, his occasionally wearying virtuosity achieving a dazzling consistency. Often it is the musicians with whom Pass recorded that gave some albums a particular bias; certainly 'Blues For Two' with Zoot Sims (ts) and 'Checkmate' with Jimmy Rowles (p) are a welcome contrast to his frantic virtuosity with Oscar Peterson. With his own group 'Live At Long Beach City College' (Pablo) and 'Live At Donte's' (Pablo) have an informality that contrasts with the sober perfection of his studio work; 'I've never really been satisfied with the sound I've gotten in the studio,' he said in 1984.

Jim Hall's (b.1930) discursive search for inner meaning within the Popular Song form was both cerebral and intimate. Since his early career in the 1950s when he established himself as a member of the Chico Hamilton Quintet and then Jimmy Giuffre's Trio he quietly stripped his playing of cliche. His albums for the Concord label, including the 1981 'Circles' and 'Live At Village West', the 1982 'Telephone' and the 1986 'Jim Hall's Trio' all reveal his subtle art; iconoclastic inversions and quartal-voiced chords, oblique assaults on metre, such as contrasting 3/4 with 4/4, and the ability to distance himself from the melodic undertow of a song, only to surface at the beginning of a new chorus with the air of an illusionist whose next trick is also impossible.

A master of the unexpectedly right, some of Hall's finest work has been in collaboration with major improvising talents such as Sonny Rollins, Paul Desmond, and pianist Bill Evans. 'First Edition' (Concord) is a duo with George Shearing (p) while in 1986 he toured with Michel Petrucciani (p). They were joined by Wayne Shorter (ss) at the Montreux Festival for 'Power Of Three' (Blue Note), a live recording that revisits the great moments of subtle empathy he reached with past collaborators. In 1987 he toured with Bob Brookmeyer (vtb) and his February 1988 album

'These Rooms' (Denon) with his trio—Steve LaSpina (b) and Joey Baron (d)—had the eloquently introspective Tom Harrell guesting on flugelhorn and trumpet. The impressive level of creativity seemed to confirm that Hall's catalytic effect on others had a reciprocal pay-off by raising the level of his own performance.

Emily Remler (1957-90) entered Berklee College Of Music when she was 16 to study guitar and after a relatively undistinguished period as a student moved to New Orleans at 18 where her studies began in earnest. 'I did weddings, shows, bar mitzvahs, club dates anything to get more experience,' she said, plus jazz work with Wynton Marsalis and Bobby McFerrin. While in New Orleans she met Herb Ellis who introduced her to Concord Records with whom she made her recording debut with the 1982 'Firefly' (Concord), which, in her own words, was 'pretty straightahead'.

At 21 she moved to New York and after three years with vocalist Astrid Gilberto, during which time she appeared as a member of Great Guitars with Ellis and Barney Kessel, she formed her own trio, with Eddie Gomez (b) and Bob Moses (d), which featured on 'Transitions' (Concord). The subsequent 'Take Two' and 'Cat Walk' fell fairly and squarely within the somewhat claustrophobic role-model hierarchy of the Charlie Christian-Wes Montgomery lineage. Looking back on her albums in 1985 she joked, ' "This Is How Much I Love Wes", that was the first one . . . the third one was "Half Me And Half This Is How Much I Love Wes".'

Her 1985 tour of Europe with guitarist Larry Coryell resulted in the duet album 'Together' (Concord). But essentially her work on Concord was a voyage of discovery to find the real Emily Remler. However that voyage was interrupted in 1985 with a brush with alcoholism causing the breakup of her marriage to Monty Alexander; but a period of study at the University of Pittsburgh with Bob Brookmeyer and avant garde composer David Stock helped effect a complete rehabilitation. Between 1987-88 she was 'Artist In Residence' at Duquesne University's School of Music.

The 1988 'East To Wes' (Concorde), her first album after getting back on course, was spurred on by Hank Jones (p), Buster Williams (b) and Marvin 'Smitty' Smith (d). Her playing, exuding neat, uncluttered logic and powerful swing, comfortably operated within the Herb Ellis/Barney Kessel/Wes Montgomery axis. However, there were moments amid her gracefully symmetric flurries of semiquavers where she could be mistaken for any of these players; rather than expanding the tradition she seemed to have merged with it. Live, however, she took more chances as the 1987 live album with Richie Cole/Hank Crawford 'Bossa International' (Milestone) showed.

'I still have to prove myself every single time,' she said, summing up the stress of a woman in a man's world. 'The only thing is that I'm not intimidated anymore . . . I have to rise above it by playing good.' But the pressures proved too great; 'personal problems' loomed as she sought escape. Sadly on 4 May 1990 she died during a tour of Australia. The cause of her death was given as a heart attack.

PERCUSSION BITTER/SWEET: MAX ROACH/THE MJQ

A member of Charlie Parker's quintet in the early days of bop, **Max Roach** (b.1924) was probably the most influential of all the bop drummers. His speed, but more particularly his independent polyrhythmic coordination (that in turn influenced Elvin Jones) and the architechtonic quality of his solos, reached beyond the usual tenets of jazz-drumming-as-timekeeping to that of a percussionist working within compositional structures, contributing significantly to the collective whole of a performance. It was a conceptual as well as philosophical step in the evolution of jazz drumming; in filling out colouristic detail within the jazz ensemble Roach reached beyond bop and his influence could be heard in the work of drummers as diverse as Sunny Murray and Tony Williams.

In 1972 he joined the faculty of the University of Massachusetts at Amherst and subsequently achieved a professorship. Throughout, he continued to perform actively and always in challenging situations. In 1970 he formed M'Boom, an occasional percussion ensemble that was still performing in 1989, and in 1972 formed an association with trumpeter Cecil Bridgewater from which evolved his regular working quartet. Reflecting an abiding commitment to hard-bop, albeit with freer harmonies and more challenging compositions, their rigorous approach anticipated the neo-classicism of the 1980s years before the trend became common currency.

The 1979 'Pictures In A Frame' (Soul Note) contained the nucleus of his band for the 1980s with fellow educator and musicologist Odean Pope (ts), Bridgewater and Calvin Hill (b). It was followed by 'Chattahoochee Red' (CBS) that included fresh-sounding interpretations of jazz standards by John Coltrane, Benny Golson and Thelonious Monk and a civil rights statement 'The Dream/Its Time' with extracts from Dr. Martin Luther King's 'I still have a dream' speech. The 1982 'In The Light' (Soul Note) was dominated by Monk and Tadd Dameron compositions but was not

Max Roach, probably the most influential of all bop drummers.

wholly successful. On 'Scott Free' (Soul Note) from May 1984, Hill was replaced by Tyrone Brown on what is an ambitious extended piece inspired by the 1931 Scottaboro Boys case. The Quartet had been playing Bridge-water's composition since 1978, but like so many pieces that are stretched over two sides of an album, it sagged a little in the middle.

Roach sought to compensate for the lack of tonal colouring a piano might have brought to his quartet with his drumming, which, however inspired, began to assume monochromatic proportions over the length of an album or in concert, creating a feeling of cold rather than hard-bop. His arrangements for the most part failed to address this problem, sticking to the typical head-solos-head format in contrast to, say, the old Gerry Mulligan quartet of the early 1950s which varied the texture of a similarly minimal ensemble with improvised counterpoint, background figures and clever part-writing. Instead, Roach's sidemen were often marooned with skeletal accompaniment which simultaneously served to expose their weaknesses as well as their strengths.

'Easy Winners' (Soul Note), from January 1985, goes a long way to redress this imbalance. On the two main tracks, 'Bird Says' and 'A Little

Booker', the arrangements (by Bridgewater and Roach respectively) integrate daughter Maxine Roach's Uptown String Quartet into the ensemble. They are among the best examples of using strings, so long the *bête noire* of jazz, within the improviser's ensemble, but the remaining two tracks surrender the initiative to rather limp writing. The formula is revived on 'Bright Moments' (Soul Note) from 1986 but unfortunately continues in the vein of the lesser items on 'Easy Winners'.

In May 1985 Roach won an Obie Award for music written for three Sam Sheppard plays and collaborated with the Alvin Ailey American Dance Theater on a ballet dedicated to Nelson and Winnie Mandela. In 1989, at 65, he appeared at the Banlieues Bleues Festival in Paris with Dizzy Gillespie, then 71, and 'Max + Dizzy, Paris 1989' (A&M) soared with spontaneous interplay. Later in the year Roach undertook his first ever tour of the United Kingdom with his quartet, his energy and enthusiasm undiminished.

The Modern Jazz Quartet

From the perspective of the 1980s it was almost impossible to imagine the ire the dignified and respectable Modern Jazz Quartet provoked among the critics of the 1950s and 1960s; 'The earthiness of jazz has been replaced by a fey tinkling'[27] asserted Benny Green, while Wilfred Mellers wrote 'Jazz can hardly survive in the improbable medium of vibraphone, piano, bass and percussion.'[28] Their hackles, in common with many others, had been raised by the MJQ's quaint and pointillistic attempts to graft European structures—particularly the conventions of Bach—on to bop through the influence of their pianist and leader John Lewis (b.1920).

He and the other members of the Quartet met in the Dizzy Gillespie Big Band of 1946, but it was not until 1952, after a couple of false starts and a name change that Lewis, together with Milt Jackson (b.1923) on vibes, Percy Heath (b.1923) on bass and Kenny Clarke (1914-85) on drums, emerged as the Modern Jazz Quartet. As Lewis assumed artistic control of the group, Clarke departed and was replaced by Connie Kay (b.1927).

Lewis realized that bop, for all its instrumental virtuosity, relied on traditional and often simplistic structures—generally no more complicated than a theme-solos-theme format—and compositional form was one way of enriching its basic design. His tight structures and clear reference to classical models prompted suggestions that Milt Jackson's fluid, clearly thought improvisations were stultified in the MJQ and given freer rein

The Modern Jazz Quartet whose collective efforts are now an indispensable part of the body jazz. (L to R) Connie Kay, John Lewis, Percy Heath and Milt Jackson.

he would thrive. But like Ellington, Lewis was careful to frame the group's key soloist in a variety of compositional contexts that drew the best from his improvisational powers.

Paradoxically, Jackson's work away from the MJQ—with the exception of his recordings with Thelonious Monk—never came up to the standard of those with the group. His firmly swinging style, to which Lewis would encourage the virtues of dynamics, range and pacing his line, brought an undercurrent of contrast and tension that added significantly to the emotional impact of the group's work. In 1974 Jackson decided to leave the MJQ and end the 22 year association that had made them the most enduring small group in jazz.

One of the high spots of the 1980s was the re-union of the MJQ. Their first appearance, after what John Lewis called their 'seven year vacation', was at Tokyo in October 1981 and 'Re-Union At Budohkan' (Pablo) included a familiar fare of their most requested numbers. Shortly afterwards bassist Ray Brown took over management of the group, occasionally appearing with them at the end of their concerts and rather curiously insisting on acoustic performances, even in large halls, 'That's how we did it in the 1940s' he explained.[29]

A European tour followed in 1982, producing 'Together Again: Live At Montreux Jazz Festival '82' (Pablo), more familiar works performed with a *joie de vivre* lacking in many albums from their previous incarnation. But their first post-re-union studio recording, 'Echoes' (Pablo) from 1984, was not distinguished, 'The Horn Pipe' and 'Sacha's March' almost a parody of their more self-conscious Third Stream efforts from the '50s. In contrast was 'This One's For Basie' (Pablo) from 1985, where the Old World verities were confronted far more convincingly on 'Valeria', 'Le Cannet' and 'Milano'—a rare Lewis piano solo, originally recorded in 1954 featuring Jackson—while the straight-ahead numbers were shaped by an easy, nonchalant swing.

By now management of the group had passed to the Monte Kay office and in 1987 they returned to the Atlantic label and collaborated with the New York Chamber Symphony on 'Three Windows' (Atlantic). It included a recomposed 'Django' that was inspired by the Gil Evans arrangement of the tune from his 1959 album 'New Bottle, Old Wine' (EMI-Manhattan), a testament to the continually evolving nature of the group's repertoire. 'If we stop changing,' said Lewis, 'we stop playing the number.' But their most successful album of the decade, and among their all time best, was the 1988 'Modern Jazz Quartet: For Ellington' (East/West). Three tracks were from Ellington's 1940 repertoire, 'Ko-Ko', 'Jack The Bear' and 'Sepia Panorama', and even allowing for disparities of scale and texture it is remarkable how well Lewis adapted the material to the small ensemble, maintaining the key ingredients of Ellington's orchestrations while at the same time stamping the MJQ's identity on them.

Francis Newton once observed that Ellington's music was 'both created by the players and fully shaped by the composer'.[30] Certainly the finest moments of the MJQ see this powerfully creative duality, and if Europe rather than Africa was the starting point for some of Lewis's compositional experiments it is now clear that it should not militate against the group's collective achievements, now an indispensable part of the body of jazz.

4
Whither Freedom?

T. S. ELIOT POINTED out that no artist can work outside the tradition because the tradition will stretch to accommodate anything artists do. He didn't, however, specify how long this process would take, and for free jazz that promise seemed long postponed. Only by the end of the 1980s could its lessons really be said to have been integrated into the mainstream. It had been a bumpy ride. In 1988, *The New Grove Dictionary Of Jazz* noted that free jazz was 'highly regarded by the critics,' but Mark Gridley, in *Jazz Styles: History And Analysis,* said it was 'one of the least popular styles in jazz history'. Such ambivalence between critical perception and public consumption had underwritten the whole development of free jazz since it was thrust into the public domain in 1959 by Ornette Coleman.

It would be an oversimplification to say free jazz emerged as a result of boredom or frustration with bop, although this was undoubtedly a factor. For almost two decades the methodology of bop had been thoroughly examined from both ends of the spectrum, by reductionists such as Miles Davis and Thelonious Monk through to John Coltrane's high-density cascades. But by the end of the 1950s several young musicians were beginning to view bop's harmonic and rhythmic conventions as limiting and were experimenting with cutting themselves free of such constraints. It was a development that became inextricably woven into the social fabric of the time.

On 13 November 1956 the Supreme Court ruled that segregation on buses and street cars was unconstitutional. In autumn the following year black students were stopped from attending school by armed national guardsmen when the Governor of Arkansas and the people of Little Rock resisted a court order for racial integration of a public high school. On 24 September 1957 the President of the United States sent in U.S. Army paratroopers to guard the students.

These events gave enormous impetus to the growing black civil rights movement that gave expression to both political awareness and rejection of racial injustice for America's black minority. 'The increasing intensity of the black rights movement through the late 1950s and into the sixties,' wrote James Lincoln Collier, 'produced a generation of angry young blacks who, not content with demanding reform of the society, wanted to over-turn it entirely.'[1] Naturally, many young black jazz musicians were swept along with the prevailing tide of opinion. They felt that by freeing them-selves from bar lines, harmony and rhythm they were participating, both literally and metaphorically, in the black crusade for freedom and social justice.

For many, free jazz became the anthem that screamed rejection of racial inequality, 'From using music to entertain the white man, the negro had moved to hating him with it,' wrote Philip Larkin in 1968.[2] Certainly much of early free jazz was inextricably linked to the social climate from which it emerged; an indigenous music used as a vehicle of social protest and political indignation was seen by many as worthier than musical merit. This inevitably posed problems of critical evaluation. Free jazz ap-peared to weigh more heavily on some critics' consciences than their pleas-ure centres and whatever the 'shock of the new', a certain critical discretion preceded valour lest history marked the denigrator of the new Picasso or Joyce.

In fact, what seemed to be missed was that the best free jazz has always offered truth in exchange for the pain it inflicted; it was not a passport to musical apostasy. However, the early blossoming of free jazz left sur-prisingly few records of genuine significance. While the avant garde need not be immediately accessible, many albums intentionally rejected the possibility and thus disqualified themselves as art; 'For every one Cole-man,' pointed out Gunther Schuller, 'there were ten lesser or no talents who sought refuge in the anarchy and permissiveness of the avant garde.'[3]

In the face of what George Russell called 'the war on chords', audiences were faced with seemingly random notes against an abstract background and a disorder alien to their previous listening experiences. How they might have come to terms with the challenges posed by free jazz became a moot point by the mid-sixties; the sudden and unexpected rise of rock music, while not exactly casting jazz as a whole into exterior darkness, did at least relegate it to the commercial twilight, and free jazz was particularly hard hit. Looking increasingly beleaguered at the barricades of socio/political issues, it turned inwards, into enclaves of its 'true be-lievers'.

Musicians collectives, such as the Jazz Composers Guild, formed in New York in 1964, the Association of Advancement of Creative Musicians (AACM) in Chicago and the Underground Musicians Artists Association (UMMA) on the West Coast—both formed in 1965—the Black Artists' Group in St. Louis, formed in 1968, and similar, though less influential, organizations emerged as forums for the avant garde. Here, like-minded musicians exchanged ideas and created playing situations, and member musicians gave classes and tutored young musicians. They emphasized pride in the whole black music tradition and helped sustain a cultural identity through jazz and improvised music.

During the 1970s several leading musicians from these groups gravitated towards New York, as ever *the* place to establish a reputation in jazz, and for several years the city's vibrant loft scene became the centre of a free jazz blood-letting that in the end confronted the dual reality that free jazz musicians had lost touch with any public but themselves and that total freedom, in the end, could in itself be limiting. 'It all started sounding the same—it wasn't free anymore,' said Steve Lacy.

By the beginning of the 1980s many musicians associated with free jazz began seeking areas of common ground with the jazz mainstream, seeking restraint after the reactionary tedium of extended solos and hedonistic free jazz gang-bangs. Having spent 20 years levelling the site the time had come for building. Musicians adept at playing 'outside' the harmonic changes began creeping 'inside', anticipating the eighties' stylistic regroupings. From within the ranks of the avant garde, playing 'in the tradition' set the tone for the 1980s; 'Maybe only in a period of national tumult are people willing to listen to music for the pleasure of being battered and tested', wrote Gary Giddins,[4] as the proselytizing message of free jazz receded in importance.

But this rapprochement with the mainstream was not, as some critics suggested, a rejection of the lessons of the sixties' avant garde, more a realization that freedom *per se* was only one part of a broader canvas, 'We started to structure the free, started to put limits on it,' said Steve Lacy, 'controlling what we learned in the '60s revolution. We use that material as an ingredient—but with fences all around it.' The either-or conflict between free and structured jazz was no longer at issue; musicians from both sides of the divide utilized methods of construction and de-construction, often in a single performance. Structure, it seemed, provided the obstacle inspiration needed.

THE MUSIC AND INFLUENCE OF ORNETTE COLEMAN

By the 1980s it was difficult to imagine how alto saxophonist **Ornette Coleman's** (b.1930) modest experiments with free jazz in 1959 excited so much controversy, something that highlighted how conservative many of his critics were at the time. Displaying an almost naive innocence, his early records were emotional, affecting and occasionally goofy. Coleman created a context that allowed licence for his strong, linear, melodic playing to follow his impulses; his melodic ideas had a definite tonal centre and with each new idea he might reach into a new key at will, like a series of modal interludes. From such beginnings free jazz was launched.

For a while Coleman held the centre stage, the *enfant terrible* of jazz; Leonard Bernstein and Dorothy Kilgallen said 'yes' and Kenneth Tynan said 'no'. But after the intoxication came the hangover; suspicious of being ripped-off by the white musical establishment, Coleman had virtually dropped out of sight by 1962, rarely working in New York clubs thereafter and giving about ten concerts there until 1982.[5] He made no records

Ornette Coleman: The man once accused of standing on the throat of jazz was welcomed back to the touring circuits in the '80s with a mixture of curiosity and affection.

between 1961 and 1965, at the height of free jazz, and only three between 1969 and 1975.

In 1975 Coleman formed Prime Time, recording 'Dancing In Your Head' (Artists House/A&M) in December 1976, a session that also produced 'Body Meta' (Artists House/A&M). It heralded a radical departure from his acoustic groups, consisting of two electric guitars, electric bass (later increased to two) and a drummer (again later augmented by another drummer and/or percussionist). But Coleman's playing remained unaltered; he had simply changed the backdrop.

Prime Time played what Coleman called 'harmolodics'—presumably a corruption of harmony, motion and melodic—although the effect was that of a schismatic 'free-fusion', a coalition of dissonance and a heavy backbeat. Coleman's definition, however, was so inscrutable as to be meaningless, 'Harmolodics is the use of the physical and mental of one's own logic made into expression of sound to bring about the musical sensation of unison executed by a single person or with a group . . . .'[6]

In 1979 he recorded 'Of Human Feelings' (Antilles) with Prime Time, which according to Coleman was the first digital jazz album to be recorded in the States. His management sold the tapes to Island Records in 1981, but Coleman fell out with both parties over a disagreement on funding a follow-up recording. 'Of Human Feelings' defined Coleman's electronic/harmolodic manifesto and remained the best representation of Prime Time on record throughout the 1980's; essentially polymodal, the several simultaneous tonal centres once again allowed Coleman's melodic gift free licence, his playing being in accord with some of the centres most of the time.

By delegating the management of his career to his son Denardo, also a Prime Time drummer, Coleman overcame his reticence of public performance during the 1980s, which had been as much to do with his old suspicions of negotiating with the white music establishment as anything, and the man once accused of standing on the throat of jazz was welcomed back to the touring circuits with both curiosity and affection. In 1983 the film 'Ornette: Made In America' was released and included extracts from his magnum opus, the puzzling 'The Skies Of America' for a symphony orchestra, during its second public performance. Subsequently re-orchestrated by John Giordano integrating Prime Time, it was performed in Verona in 1987 and London in 1988. In 1986 he collaborated with Pat Metheny on 'Song X' (Geffen), 'One of *the* events of the 1980s', according to *The Illustrated Encyclopaedia Of Jazz*, 'practically unlistenable', said *The Times*.

The live set with Prime Time from the 'Opening The Caravan Of Dreams' (Caravan Of Dreams) continued his harmolodic power-game that on record was becoming boxed in by the monotony of unrelieved ostinatos that no amount of simultaneous soloing could relieve; live, however, it was a functional, pumping body music. Prime Time also shared half of 'In All Languages' (Caravan Of Dreams) with the 1987 reunion of Cherry, Higgins, Haden and Coleman, who had launched free jazz in 1959. Coleman's combined troupe, acoustic quartet plus Prime Time, toured internationally in 1987 to the sort of acclaim that years before had been visited on Jazz At the Philharmonic. Such applause seemed to have prompted thoughts of broader commercial acceptance; Prime Time's 1988 'Virgin Beauty' (CBS Portrait) had a rock album mix and smacked of commercial acquiescence.

Ultimately Coleman's gift was to rationalize his limitations into a context where he was able to sound profound. He succeeded in 1959 and with Prime Time he succeeded again. Schoppenhauer called style the 'physiognomy of the soul' and Coleman bared his soul every time he played. It was the liberating factor in his music; exposed were the blues and the lonely cry of a revolutionary.

Trumpeter **Don Cherry** (b.1936) began to expand his vision of jazz to include pan-ethnic music when the original Ornette Coleman quartet broke up in 1961. Away from Coleman, Cherry persisted in the use of an eccentric pocket size trumpet, which by conventional standards produced an emaciated tone and made clean articulation difficult. Cherry's style, however, did not depend on the long quaver and semiquaver sequences of bop; instead they contained more variety in rhythm and phrasing that recalled Coleman's style.

An extensive traveller, he co-opted a variety of influences into a 'World Music' concept, often part musical, part sociological, involving his family and those of his collaborators. However, they raise questions as to whether we are concerned with something other than jazz; the 1980s 'Codona' series of three albums on ECM, for example, his collaboration with Oregon's Collin Walcott (who died aged 39 in a car crash in 1985) on sitar and percussionist Nana Vasconcelos, prompted *Stereo Review* to call 'Codona 2', 'a surrealist collage of postcards from exotic places'.

Certainly in setting out to create a music beyond category Cherry anticipated 'New Age' even before the term was coined (Cherry once studied with LaMonte Young); his work with Nu and his collaborations with Tim Moran and Tony Vacca on 'City Spirits' (Philo), suggested a free-form folk

Don Cherry away from Coleman expanded his vision of jazz to include pan-ethnic music.

music with jazz just one element among many. He also appeared on the Rock circuit in support of Lou Reed and Ian Dury and 'Home Boy, Sister Out' (Barclay) from 1985, a reggae, funk and rappin' album seemed as equidistant from jazz in one direction as several of his world music offerings were in another.

But despite the ambivalence of his global viewpoint, Cherry did not abandon his jazz heritage; 'El Corazon' (ECM), was a series of duets with drummer Ed Blackwell from 1982 that revisted their 'Mu' collaborations in the 1970s. Occasionally involved with the Leaders, playing with them on their first tour in 1984 and again in 1986 he also toured and recorded with Charlie Haden's Liberation Music Orchestra and his own group Nu. The disarming gentility of his 1988 'Art Deco' (A&M) with James Clay (ts, f), received wide critical acclaim and represented Cherry's 'back to the tradition' with his careful, Miles Davis-like organization of ideas. But it was Old And New Dreams, alongside fellow Coleman alumni Charlie Haden, Billy Higgins and tenor saxophonist Dewey Redman, that prompted some of Cherry's best recorded work.

'Old And New Dreams' (Black Saint) from 1976 was recorded at a time when free jazz was not only out of vogue but when performances in the idiom were marked by solos of interminable length at the extremes of instrumental ranges. In contrast, Old And New Dreams were to the point, joyous, urgent, and swinging. Two years later the band went on tour and in August 1979 they recorded 'Old And New Dreams' (ECM), which prompted considerable interest in acoustic jazz when it was released in 1980.

On New Year's Eve 1979 they broadcast a critically acclaimed concert on NPR, and followed it with a tour of the States that included two sold-out concerts at the Public Theatre, New York. For a generation who had only experienced Ornette Coleman's music on record, 'Old And New Dreams' were a link to the past through the present. 'The adoring audience whooped with recognition at the themes,' wrote Gary Giddins.[7] The live 'Playing' (ECM), their strongest album, from a concert at Theater am Kornmarkt, Bregenz in June 1980, captured their sympathetic interaction and high level of *melodic* invention. 'We've been together for so long,' said Haden, 'and in so many situations, that we can always anticipate what the others will be doing at any given moment.'

Tenor saxophonist **Dewey Redman** (b.1931) played with Ornette Coleman's group from 1967 to late 1974, recording some seven albums with him. Although he admitted to not having fully developed his style during the first year with the band, he developed quickly and as a member of the Keith Jarrett Quartet between 1971-76 his playing was regarded as a welcome alternative to the omnipresent influence of John Coltrane. In 1976 he joined Old And New Dreams and in 1980 he featured alongside Mike Brecker on Pat Metheny's '80/81' (ECM), brilliantly contrasting Brecker's Coltrane-influenced style. Throughout the 1980s Redman was a regular member of Charlie Haden's Liberation Music Orchestra, featuring on the fine 'Ballad Of The Fallen' (ECM) from 1982. In 1987 he toured with Cherry's group Nu.

The live 'In Willisau' (Black Saint) from 1980 was a wild collaboration with drummer Ed Blackwell, while 'The Struggle Continues' (ECM), with his own group, was in contrast to the cerebral concepts of his work from the 1970s, comprising conventional material for the most part. Redman's decision to pursue a career with his own group was one reason why Old And New Dreams ceased to perform regularly, 'I told them to get a new tenor player for the band, but they didn't want to do that so the group went out of circulation,' he said. But his international exposure, even with major figures such as Coleman and Jarrett, seemed to count for very little when seeking bookings in his own right. Redman, a powerful, original and convincing artist who by the end of the 1980s failed to define his talent on record, paid the price in terms of public acclaim, finding the more easily acceptable offerings of younger men all too readily claiming the media's attention.

Cornettist **Bobby Bradford** (b.1934) replaced Don Cherry in Coleman's band in 1961, although his recordings with the band were not released for several years. When he moved to Los Angeles in 1964 he formed an enduring association with clarinettist John Carter, who had been a high school friend of Coleman's. While Carter and Bradford rehearsed often the few records they made between 1969-72 remain little known. In the 1980s Bradford appeared with David Murray, Charlie Haden's Liberation Music Orchestra and in 'a fruitful combination'[8] with John Stevens as well as with his own ensembles.

As with Cherry, Bradford's articulation was less important than ideas expressed, describing his maxim as, 'logic, musical good sense and reference to the thematic portion of the performance.' Both 'Lost In L.A.' (Soul Note) from 1983 with his Mo'tet and 'One Night Stand' (Soul Note) from 1986 with the Frank Sullivan Trio, a live date in Florida, reveal Bradford's careful craftsmanship and highly refined melodic logic that never appeared to leave anything to chance, even in abstract surroundings, to produce solos of great charm and elegance—'there is glory in Bobby Bradford's music', claimed John Litweiler.[9] But it was with John Carter that Bradford performed most regularly; an association that most perfectly realized Coleman's use of melodic and rhythmic freedom.

John Carter (b.1929), a scholastic prodigy, spent his life within the educational system until 1982, when he decided to pursue a more active career in jazz, forming the private Wind College in January 1983 with James Newton, Charles Owens and Red Callender. His epic cycle Roots And Folklore; *Episodes In The Development Of American Folk Music,* was spread over five albums, 'Dauwhe' (Black Saint), 'Castles Of Ghana' (described by *Downbeat* magazine as 'one of—if not *the*—most important recordings of 1986'), 'Dance Of The Love Ghosts', 'Fields' and 'Shadows On A Wall' (all Gramavision) was the most significant body of music to emerge in jazz during the 1980s. A striking balance of written and improvised music, Carter's Ellingtonian care to place his soloists in carefully

John Carter and Bobby Bradford: An association that most perfectly realized Coleman's use of melodic and rhythmic freedom.

structured settings created work of great cogency and unity that dramatically portrayed the odyssey of a slave from Africa to America.

In 1984 Bradford and Carter combined with Coleman's original soulmates Charlie Haden and Billy Higgins for an engagement at Hop Singh's in Marina Del Rey, California, an event that went sadly unrecorded. The 1988 'Comin' On' (Hathut) reconvened a Bradford/Carter ensemble for the first time on disc since the 1973 'Secrets' (Revelation). With Don Preston (k), Richard Davis (b) and Andrew Cyrille (d), all of whom collaborated on the *Roots And Folklore* cycle, the live set produced jazz of depth and profundity, demonstrating that great taste was the axiom of the 'freedom principle'.

Coleman's concepts were equally adapted by graduates of his electronic ensembles; **James 'Blood' Ulmer's** (b.1942) first album, 'Tales of Captain Black' (Artists House) from 1978, could well have been issued under Coleman's name such was his influence both as a soloist and producer. 'Ornette Coleman opened the way for a particular kind of jazz,' observed Robert Wyatt, 'and out of that Ulmer was able to use the [Jimi] Hendrix in himself. That's really where Hendrix enters jazz. The door was opened by Ornette's funny theories and by Blood being the kind of guitarist who could use the kind of information that Hendrix left behind.'[10]

Away from Coleman, Ulmer's work, dubbed 'No Wave', was not entirely unrelated to what was happening in rock music at the time, with punk music the then current craze. In fact, Ulmer's group played the Manhattan punk venues—one reviewer quipped he sounded 'like the Bar-Kays gone mad'—and although his style precluded broad acceptance there were elements of his music that had much in common with punk's dissolution of rock music's certainties.

When Ulmer signed with Columbia in 1981 his work did not rule out the possibility of crossover appeal. The 1981 'Free Lancing' (CBS), followed by 'Black Rock' (CBS) and 'Odyssey' (CBS) did not coalesce, Ulmer's desperate edge failing to sit well with female glee clubs and vocals. Far more satisfying were 'No Wave' (Moers Music) from June 1980 and the 1988 'Music Revelation Ensemble' (DIW) with David Murray, Amin Ali and Ronald Shannon Jackson in orbit around Ulmer's frightening guitar. In 1985 he appeared at the Moers Festival in West Germany with Phalanx, a group he co-led with tenor saxophonist George Adams with bassist Sirone and drummer Rashied Ali; their lusty power-drive was captured on 'Original Phalanx' (DIW) from 1987.

With his own group, 'Got Something For You' and 'Live At The Caravan Of Dreams' (both Caravan Of Dreams) from 1985 effectively portray the ferocity of a live concert and although not especially well recorded, have moments reminiscent of Miles Davis's 'Agharta' and 'Pangaea'. But on the 1987 'America—Do You Remember The Love?' (Blue Note), Bill Laswell (b) and Ronald Shannon Jackson (d) seemed well-behaved in comparison; Ulmer's vocals—not a strong point—dissipated the instrumental intensity. Once again the suspicion lurked, as with the Columbia albums, of one eye on the cross-over charts. Ulmer as sideman, however, on Grant Calvin Weston's 'Dance Romance' (One + Out) is an exuberant harmolodic workout with backbone that offers as good a view of Ulmer in the '80s as any.

Ulmer's avant-funk-metal amalgam was adapted by Defunkt, led by Lester Bowie's younger brother and trombonist Joe—'Avoid The Funk—An Anthology' (Hannibal), and Kelvyn Bell's Kelvynator—'Funk It Up' (Blue Heron), where Bell attempts to 'bring the avant garde back through funk.'

Ronald Shannon Jackson (b.1940) came of age during the 1980s and, like Ulmer, harnessed the coruscating effect of ugliness as an aspect of authenticity, the legacy of both punk and free jazz on their respective mainstreams. A drummer with impeccable bebop credentials—he once played for Betty Carter, Joe Henderson, Jackie McLean and Kenny Dorham amongst others—he went on to work with both Ornette Coleman *and* Cecil Taylor.

In the 1980s his vision was further sharpened in James 'Blood' Ulmer's band, but when he came to form his own group he brought a sense of *party* to the harmolodic rainbow. Playing his own compositions and arrangements, he underpinned them with a hyperactive rhythmic complexity—part avant, part disco, part funk. The 1980 'Eye On You' (About Time) introduced his Decoding Society, an octet mixing acoustic and electric instruments, 'his vision is simultaneously enticing (the rocking patterns) and alarming (the disparities),' wrote John Litweiler.[11] No matter how angular or on the edge his compositions, Jackson's attention to detail ensured shimmering textures that were concerned as much with musicmaking as overall effect.

'Nasty' (Moers Music) did not fare so well, the cauterizing effect of shorter tracks giving way to rambling discourse, recorded after only two weeks rehearsal. Subsequent albums were more focussed; 'Street Priest' (Moers Music) was cut after the band had shaken down on the road at the end of their summer '81 European tour and 'Mandance' (Antilles) returned to more tightly structured compositions, a series of short-sharp-shocks plus a bit of hip-hop street-cred.

'Barbeque Dog' (Antilles) seemed to catch breath with time for Vernon Reid on banjo to emerge and submerge, like a passenger from the *Titanic;* less frantic, it blended control and adventure with harmolodic counterpoint and rhythmic energy in equal measures. 'Decode Yourself' (Antilles) was the first album to contain a non-Jackson composition, 49 seconds of Dizzy Gillespie's 'Be-Bop' that in its brevity captured the essence of what the band was about. Jackson's subsequent output from 1986 on the The Caravan Of Dreams label, 'Live At The Caravan Of Dreams' with the African singer Twins Seven Seven, 'When Colours Play' and 'Texas' (perhaps his best album since 'Barbeque Dog') and the 1990 'Taboo' (Virgin) continued his coded power-play and despite a shifting lineup the ensemble sound retained its unity, the whole more important than the sum of its parts.

The headlong march of Jackson's drums were the energizing force behind Last Exit and Power Tools, a quartet and trio respectively that pared down the dizzying multi-textured layers of Prime Time and the Decoding Society to establish a more elemental, one-to-one expressionism that in the instance of Last Exit realized the most exciting merger of the crude and the complex in the 1980s. Last Exit's appeal was based firmly on the 'Godzilla Principle', the appeal of the strong and ugly.

Combining saxophonist Peter Brotzmann, guitarist Sonny Sharrock and bassist Bill Laswell in front of Jackson's drums, Last Exit re-established the avant garde in jazz as a revitalizing force, 'This is a rebirth of energy,' explained Sonny Sharrock, '. . . back to high energy freedom combined with a highly melodic thing.' 'Last Exit', recorded in Paris, 'The Noise Of Trouble/Live In Tokyo' (all Enemy) and 'Iron Path' (Virgin) could be numbered among the most original and radical albums of the decade, 'We'd just crank it up and take it out,' explained Sharrock.

'Strange Meeting' (Antilles) by Power Tools combined Jackson with De-coding Society bassist Melvin Gibbs and guitarist Bill Frisell, who while not attempting the aural vandalism of Last Exit, created instead craftily wrought heavy metal textures that refused to collide with Jackson's cav-alry charges; 'Playing with Frisell—who has spacious sense—allows rhyth-mic ideas I'm already working on to work,' said Jackson. 'Playing with Last Exit allows me to play with the energy and the expression the drums are capable of.' In 1989 guitarist Pete Cosey had replaced Frisell in the Power Tools lineup.

THE PROPHET UNHEARD: CECIL TAYLOR

If Ornette Coleman's work and that of his disciples had been largely digested and disseminated by the end of the 1980s, then the work of pianist Cecil Taylor (b.1933) remained solidly in the vanguard of the avant garde. A lone pioneer, his music was never accessible or even par-ticularly attractive; he spoke in dense non-harmonic tongues and multi-note cascades that made it difficult to digest his artistic aesthetic, critic Benny Green once going as far to say he doubted what Taylor played was music, let alone jazz!

It was not until the 1980s that Taylor began to enjoy the sort of job security his visionary virtuosic odyssey deserved, and even then his playing remained as recondite as ever; 'Is it possible,' wondered Whitney Balliett, 'decade after decade, to appreciate a music that isn't fully comprehensible, that is boring and exhilarating, overweening and lyrical, ponderous and fleet—the music, in short, of Cecil Taylor?'[12]

In 1979 Taylor recorded two highly regarded albums, '3 Phasis' (New World) with a group that included Ronald Shannon Jackson and a duet with Max Roach, 'Historic Concerts' (Soul Note). Taylor's playing on the latter included 'some of the most tumultuous, yet immaculately controlled

Cecil Taylor: Made specific demands that even in the '80s few people were able to meet.

playing he has recorded,'[13] but it took until December 1989 to reconvene this remarkably sympathetic liaison in a concert at New York's Town Hall. The solo 1980 'Fly! Fly! Fly! Fly! Fly!' (Pausa) was an excellent continuum of Taylor's crusade to exile cliche, critically acclaimed it was among his best work but the 1981 twofer 'Garden' (Hat Art), commencing with a wail, as disconcerting on record as in live performance, floundered. 'Praxis' (Praxis) from 1984 fared much better.

'It Is In The Brewing Luminous' (Hat Art), with his Unit, was an excellent 1980 live date in New York. In 1982 he experimented with a larger ensemble called the 'Expanded Unit' that included many of New York's young lions for a short residency at New York's Lush Life. 'The Eighth' (Hat Art) is the complete 1982 Freiburger Jazztage performance (an edited version appeared in 1983 as 'Calling It The Eighth' [Hat Musics]). It was by a particularly commanding, but under-recorded, version of Taylor's Unit and revealed Taylor's long-time collaborator, Jimmy Lyons at close to his best (Lyons died suddenly in 1986). The 1984 'Winged Serpent (Sliding Quadrants)' (Soul Note) was by an international all-star version of the Expanded Unit. 'What's New' (Black Lion) was from 1985

while 'From Olim' (Soul Note) was his sixth solo album, described by
Cadence magazine as his best.

'Live In Bologna', 'Live In Vienna' and 'Tzotzil Mummers Tzotzil'—live
in Paris—(all Leo), were from his 1987 European tour with Carlos Ward
taking over the demanding role of the 'second voice' in Taylor's updated
Unit that included Leroy Jenkins (vn) and Thurman Baker (d). However,
only 500 copies of 'Chinampas' (Leo) were pressed, in anticipation of an
underwhelming demand for Taylor's recitation of six of his poems. In
1988/9 Taylor found perhaps his most sympathetic and, within the context
of his music, most able drummer in Englishman Tony Oxley, with whom
he toured internationally including a week's residency at New York's
Sweet Basil in 1989.

Taylor was arguably the greatest piano technician since Art Tatum, but
whereas Tatum's technique was harnessed in service of conventional harmony, Taylor played by his own conventions to create an intensely personal
language, a major alternative to anything else in jazz. In the final analysis,
however, Taylor's music has always been uncompromising and pitched
well over the head of the casual jazz follower and for the greater part of
his career more the province of critical acuity than public patronage.

By the end of the 1970s his reputation as 'a performance artist' at last
began to attract a following so that during the 1980s he was more than
able to achieve his own modest goal of drawing a salary equivalent to
that of 'a chamber music player'. It was not that his music was dense,
cerebral and demanding, but that it made specific demands that even in
the 1980s few people were able to meet, 'All you can do is to do your
work the best you can and through your work reach as many people as
you can,' he said in 1987.

Unlike every other major stylistic innovator on the piano, Taylor is alone
in that his playing, while touching many players, has not directly influenced other musicians in the way that Earl Hines, Art Tatum, Bud Powell,
Bill Evans and McCoy Tyner have done. But during the 1980s it was
clear that **Marilyn Crispell** (b.1947) was one of the few pianists who had
used Taylor's playing as an inspiration to develop her own individual
voice. 'It wasn't until I heard Cecil that I realized it was OK to play that
music . . . Before I made that connection, I guess I hadn't the confidence
or maybe the vision to do it myself,' she explained.

But beyond her speed of execution and the sheer physical involvement
of her playing, Crispell had clearly evolved her own style that also took
account of the Arnold Schoenberg/Alban Berg school. Of her several al-

bums on the Leo label, 'Gaia', with a trio, shows her dense, intense style at its most impressive, 'Two-fisted pounding, repetition of percussive clusters and rapid jumping from one phrase to another.'[14] Her solo 'Labyrinths' (Victo) is more ferocious and close to Taylor's style, while as a member of Anthony Braxton's Quartet, 'Six Compositions (Quartet) 1984' (Black Saint) concentrated her playing in a way that her work on the Leo label does not.

Cecil Taylor, as catalyst, was responsible for soprano saxophonist **Steve Lacy's** (b.1934) odyssey from dixieland revivalist in the early 1950s to perhaps *the* key figure in European free jazz movement in the 1980s. Lacy spent most of the 1950s with Taylor's experimental group and immersing himself in the work of Thelonious Monk (including a 16-week stint with him); legend has it his work on soprano sax was such it inspired John Coltrane to take up the instrument.

In 1967 he moved to Europe and soon established a reputation as an improviser who paid meticulous attention to his craft, a mixture of the sawtooth intervals of Thelonious Monk, controlled abandon and a patient lapidarian minimalism that chipped away at a phrase until perfectly shaped. One of jazz's master improvisers, more poet than polemicist, he appeared determined to leave posterity with plenty to sift through by ensuring his discography, over 80 albums by the end of the 1980s, grew at a remarkably prolific rate. Throughout Lacy's playing is a model of consistency, so the relative merits of individual albums hinge on both the context of his performances and the quality of his collaborators.

Lacy's best work tended to be with an inner circle of musicians that included Steve Potts (saxes), Kent Carter (b), Oliver Jackson (b) and his wife Irene Aebi on vocals, violin and cello, an ensemble that by the end of the 1980s was well over a decade old. The astonishing variety of his 1980s output, on a myriad of poorly distributed and often hard to obtain European labels, included 'art' music, the 'virtuous boredom' of solo recitals, duos with fellow ex-pat and minimalist Mal Waldron, and albums with British musicians Derek Bailey Evan Parker and Steve Arguelles. His two 'In The Tradition' albums, 'Regeneration' (Soul Note), with Roswell Rudd that revisited Monk and Herbie Nichols compositions, and 'Change Of Season' (Soul Note), with Misha Mengelberg and George Lewis, comprising Nichols compositions, deserve a place in any contemporary music collection.

In 1987 he signed with Novus, ensuring international distribution, and 'Momentum' (Novus) was his first album on a Stateside label for ten years. 'The Door' (Novus) from 1988 specifically excluded vocals at the producer's request but nevertheless both albums provide an ideal entree to his work; sympathetically produced, well recorded and a shrewd sum-

Steve Lacy: An improviser who paid meticulous attention to his craft.

mation of Lacy's art. Although 'Momentum' included some disconcertingly 'arty' *Sprechstimme* by Aebi of poetry by Giulia Niccolai, Herman
Melville and Brion Gysin, Lacy's group was fresh, original and free from
precedent. In terms of encapsulating his improvising skill, 'The Door'
illustrated a variety of performing situations by splitting his 'inner circle'
into varying permutations in what was virtually an anthology of his work.

The 1990 'Anthem' (Novus), included 'Prelude And Anthem' commissioned by the Ministry of Culture on behalf of the Government of France,
in honour of the 200th Anniversary of the French Revolution. Juxtaposing
an extract of 'Le Crépuscule De La Liberté' by Osip Mandelstam into the
proceedings, Lacy's tribute had an undercurrent of irony (all those heads)
but the *Sprechstimme* interlude seemed to present an unnecessary obstacle;
'Number One', 'The Rent' and 'The Mantle' sparkled.

COLTRANE: TWO 'FREE' DISCIPLES

Although Ornette Coleman and Cecil Taylor had come to personify free
jazz by the 1980s, it was John Coltrane (1926-67), particularly in his
final years (1965-67), who emerged as the most commanding figure during the free jazz revolution and in terms of freedom at least, his most
enduring legacy was energy music. By the 1980s Coltrane's influence had
touched practically every saxophonist performing in jazz through the variety of concepts he brought to improvisation, but Archie Shepp and
Pharoah Sanders could claim the distinction of performing alongside him
during his free period, somewhat enhancing their reputations in reflected
glory.

Archie Shepp's (b.1937) descent from Jackson Pollack-frenzy in the
'60s to his exploration in the early 1980s of what he described as jazz's
'Afro-Christian' past marked a profound stylistic realignment for the one
time self-appointed spokesman of the 'New Thing'. His move into the
jazz tradition revealed, however, a musician both fumble-fingered and
prone to intonational lapses.

Curiously these vices became virtues when the perspicacious owner/pro-
ducer of Steeplechase Records, Nils Winther suggested Shepp approach
the traditional blues and spirituals repertoire with pianist Horace Parlan.
'Goin' Home' (Steeplechase) explored spirituals while the more successful
'Trouble In Mind' (Steeplechase) the blues and was voted 'Album Of The
year' by the influential *Downbeat* magazine in 1980.

Numbers such as 'See See Rider' dated from a desperate time in America's past for their black population, and it was clear that the injustices

they suffered loomed large on the protagonist's mind when recording. It was a moving statement from Shepp, who had progressed from revolution to working within the system as a professor at the University of Massachusetts. Subsequent albums on the Denon, Enja and Soul Note labels revealed an unconvincing improviser, who in live performance completed the *volte-face* from poet-musician articulating the black tradition to a modest journeyman held afloat by his reputation, working out on numbers such as 'Girl From Ipanema' and 'Danny Boy'.

Once an heir-apparent in the Coltrane dynasty, **Pharoah Sanders'** (b.1940) post-Coltrane output was a disappointment, blurred by extra-curricular activities such as chants of peace and religious invocations. He made no recordings under his own name between 1974 and 1980 and when he finally resurfaced it was clear he had reconciled energy playing with his search for inner tranquility. He emerged with one of the most hauntingly rich tenor saxophone tones in jazz and his ballad performances were often compelling, a mixture of elegance and modest adventure, such as 'Kazuko' from the 1980 'Journey To The One' (Theresa).

The excellent 'Live' (Theresa), recorded during a 1982 West Coast tour, had a nonpareil rhythm section of John Hicks, Walter Booker and Idris Muhammad. Lifted by a responsive audience, the group ignite with some inspired playing, Sanders evoking middle-period Coltrane, not through technical excess but by paring down his style to a series of inspired, starkly defined abbreviations that evoked his *spirit*. His ability to capture the essence of Coltrane was again captured on the 1987 'Blues For Coltrane' (Impulse) with McCoy Tyner and David Murray, a reminder of how undervalued his talent had become.

'Heart Is A Melody' (Theresa) from 1982 was another live performance with a version of 'Ole' that in its primal ruggedness might have benefited from editing. A choral backing was added later to two other tracks, including the African 'hi-life' number, 'Going To Africa'. In fact, Sanders' hi-life numbers, ('Rejoice' (Theresa), for example, included 'Hilife' and 'Nigerian Juju Highlife') were infectious and exuberant and showed Sanders in a totally different light. A commanding player when the mood took him, with a unique control of 'multiphonics', 'Live' nevertheless remained his most exciting work. Elsewhere he presented himself in a variety of contexts that inevitably palled in comparison.

Pharoah Sanders: One of the most hauntingly rich tenor saxophone tones in jazz.

FROM UNDERGROUND TO RECONCILIATION

The musician's collectives—the AACM, BAG, etc—had a profound influence in shaping the conception of the musicians who emerged from
their ranks. Quite apart from encouraging the need to develop individual

instrumental technique, tone and compositional abilities, they emphasized the need for a musician to create a context in which to perform. It was to have a profound effect in shaping jazz during the 1980s. Conceptualization beyond the basic tenets of bop structures and instrumentation was rare; few seemed to have the desire to evolve their own repertoire and develop it within a set working ensemble, the key to memorable jazz. It was no coincidence, therefore, that some of the most influential and innovative ensembles were organized by alumni of the musicians' collectives.

Chicago's AACM trio **Air** comprised Henry Threadgill (b.1944) saxophones, Fred Hopkins (b) and Steve McCall (d). A balance of ensemble intimacy and free exchange, their collective improvisations achieved a unity through the direction of Threadgill. Their sixth album, 'Air Lore' (BMG/RCA) recorded in May 1979, is justifiably their most well-known work. A collection of Scott Joplin rags and Jelly Roll Morton tunes plus a Threadgill original, it is a unique statement reconciling the apparent opposites of classicism and experimentation that was influential in redirecting many musicians back to the jazz tradition as a method of expanding their expressionism.

After over ten years together, 'Air Mail' (Black Saint) from 1980 was a consolidation rather than an exploration of the mutual understanding the group had developed. '80 Degrees Below '82' (Antilles) was justly praised in 1982 and is the last group collaboration before Steve McCall departed (he died on 25 May 1989). 'New Air' (Black Saint), recorded live at the 1983 Montreux Festival, has Pharoeen akLaff in the demanding percussion chair as the group continue with barely a missed stride. 'Air Show No. 1' (Black Saint) included Cassandra Wilson, a young vocalist of great potential on three numbers, a relationship that was to end in acrimony over the ownership of a song.

Threadgill's prowess as an orchestrator was revealed on 'X-75 Volume 1' (Arista Novus) from 1979, with a drumless band of four basses and a saxophone choir that impressed with an arrangement of 'Celebration'. By 1982 he had slimmed down and revised this unusual ensemble to what he called his 'sextet' (a septet with two drummers, two basses, saxophone, trumpet and trombone). With the 1982 'When Was That?' (About Time) he introduced his penchant for the underlying theme of death in his compositions, a thread that runs through much of his 'sextet' work. Threadgill's 'funeral ballads', strong if sombre melodies with unusual voicings, were a sensitive issue. 'I DON'T WRITE NO DAMN DIRGES' he asserted in 1989.

Be that as it may, 'Just The Facts And Pass The Bucket' (About Time) from 1983 created the ambience of a New Orleans funeral with suitably gloomy music, often with unpretentious diatonic writing and chord-free soloing. Full of wry twists and turns, irony, pathos and humour it returned to the tradition to articulate and personalize predefined conventions through creative distortion.

'Subject To Change' (About Time) introduced the strong individual playing of Ray Anderson in place of Craig Harris's rugged fundamentalism, broadening the expressive range of the band in another strong album. In 1987 Threadgill signed with RCA/Novus and 'You Know The Number' (RCA/Novus), perhaps their most powerful statement, at times was in danger of sounding jubilant.

By the end of the 1980s Threadgill had gone on record as saying new advances in jazz may come from strings, percussion and voices[15] and 'Run Silent, Run Deep, Run Loud, Run High,' premiered at Brooklyn Academy of Music in 1987, experimented in bringing these elements together in an ambitious work that met with mixed acclaim. Threadgill's writing, simultaneously simple yet 'dangerous', multi-textured and stark, was, by the end of the 1980s, applied to a television documentary about the Panama Canal—'Diggers'—and a cantata—'Thomas Cole'—while his strong instrumental skills were in demand deputizing in the World Saxophone Quartet.

'Easily Slip Into Another World' (RCA/Novus) and the December 1988 'Rag, Bush and All' (RCA/Novus) continued the thread of Threadgill's exequies and his backwards march into the future, the moods less sombre, his vision more eclectic. But if the ends to which his two drummers were deployed seemed scarcely to justify the means, and Bill Lowe (tb) and Ted Daniels (t) appeared more as reliable journeymen, then the success of the 'sextet' lay not in individual strengths and weaknesses of the musicians but the totality of Threadgill's individualism that did not rely on the then current stylistic convention. In critical terms at least, Threadgill was celebrated as one of the major creative forces of the 1980s, even making a Dewar's profile. In a decade when the trickle towards the bop mainstream ended in a flood, when experimentation for its own sake had been overtaken by repetition, Threadgill's distraint appeared as a rural truth among urban conformity.

Anthony Braxton's (b.1945) tireless pursuit of the marginal embraced a great variety of projects, some whose elephantine labours yielded a mouse, while others, such as his groundbreaking album 'For Alto Saxophone (Delmark) from 1968, created a secure place for him in jazz and improvised music. As Whitney Balliet pointed out, Braxton had a 'curious, almost arithmetical way of phrasing'[16] which he applied to a whole range of projects, sometimes perverse, sometimes bogged down in the minutia of minimalism, sometimes garrulously spinning countless motivic permutations but always in hot pursuit of secret truths. Braxton was the darling of the European free jazz improvisers and their dedicated followers, and his discography numbered over 50 albums by the end of the 1980s, many on small, difficult to obtain independent labels.

However, 'Six Compositions: Quartet' (Antilles) was a satisfying collaboration with Anthony Davis (p), Mark Helias (b) and Ed Blackwell (d) from 1981, despite Braxton's unconventional approach to swing. In contrast, an outward-bound collaboration with arch-freedom guitarist Derek Bailey, 'Moment Precieux' (Victo), is a dialogue in free, spontaneous 'interaction'. But wilful indeterminacy, although brandished as the liberating factor of 'instant composing', confronted Montale's observation that, 'An art which destroys form while claiming to refine it denies itself a second and longer life: the life of memory and everyday circulation',[17] one reason, perhaps, why this area of the music remained on the margins.

But Braxton was at his best when working with pre-determined structures; 'Rova Saxophone Quartet with Anthony Braxton' (sound aspects) and the traditional quartet setting - Braxton plus piano, bass, and drums—on 'Six Compositions (Quartet) 1984' (Black Saint) both presented detailed organizational schemes that yielded tension within familiar instrumentation.

A lot of Braxton's music went far beyond the jazz idiom and if some performances included moments when he seemed to have perfected the art of playing over the heads of his audience it was because he was not concerned with conveying emotion, 'I never talk about feeling or haven't—up to 1983 or so—tried to address the emotional aspects of the music', he said. And while lack of emotion might be rationalized as an aspect of post-modernism, Professor Mark Gridley pointed out that, 'Very little of his music swings in the jazz sense.'[18] These two aspects helped create an aura of autism around Braxton's music, a fragile expressionism balanced between jazz and European models whose shifting allegiance, what Braxton called 'conceptual grafting', satisfied as many as it frustrated.

His compositions, each assigned a symbol like an architect's cartoon, were hailed for their scale or their ambition or both but rarely was direction the basis for assessment. Indeed, most critics have been so awed at Braxton's (sometimes Quixotic) ambition - a piece-for 100 orchestras,

Anthony Braxton: His compositions were hailed for their scale or their ambition or both. An extract of his music from 1985 forms the background.

each in a different city, for example, to be linked by satellite, ultimately stretching to orchestras on other planets in several galaxies . . .—and his sizeable body of work, that few have asked what are his great achievements, his masterpieces and, considering Braxton's relatively high profile, why so much has been largely passed by unacknowledged, save by his 'true believers'.

Perhaps the most famous product of the AACM, however, was the **Art Ensemble of Chicago**. Using silence, variations in timbre and tone and subtle diminuendo and crescendo effects on a variety of instruments that could be blown, banged, scraped or sucked, they approached modernism not by attacking the roots and structures of jazz but by creating compositional collages of sound that refracted the whole black music tradition, their maxim 'Great Black Music—Ancient To The Future.'

A group of great importance in free jazz, they were among the first, in the late 1960s, to realize that the great energy of players such as Ayler, Coltrane and Shepp was self-limiting and ultimately destructive. With a mixture of parody and the obtuse, humour and intuition they combined their considerable skills to common cause and emerged as perhaps *the* most innovative group of the 1970s. 'Nice Guys' (ECM) was a touch of ironic humour from 1979 and an attempt to show that they were not as inaccessible as their reputation might suggest. Lester Bowie (t), Joseph Jarman and Roscoe Mitchell (saxes), Malachi Favors (b) and Don Moye (d) stated a convincing case; and the reggae 'Ja' and the disarming straight-ahead swing of 'The Master' were able to confound most expectations of 'free jazz.'

'Full Force' (ECM), winner of several Record Of The Year awards in 1980/81, was washed with their incredible eclectism while 'Urban Bushman' (ECM), a live concert from 1980 at the Amerika Haus in Munich, had a depth that revealed a little more of itself each time; a suffocating urban summer evening is portrayed in 'Warm Night Blues Stroll' while 'Ancestral Meditation' is a compelling piece of group interaction. A reminder that they had been around, well a long time, if not 30 years by 1984, came with 'Third Decade' (ECM); their methodology unaltered, their vision intent on refining their use of form and structure.

Towards the end of the 1980s the AEC toured less frequently after internationally promoting 'Third Decade' in 1985 because of Lester Bowie's decision to pursue his own projects—as always laced with irony, humour and surrealism such as his 59-piece 'Sho' Nuff Orchestra' dismantling 'I Got Rhythm' or his 'Roots To The Source' serio-comic 'Let The Good Times Roll.'

For **Lester Bowie** (b.1941), the long arm of jazz tradition was an asset. A trumpet player of narrow technical range but unlimited emotional re-

Lester Bowie: A trumpet player of narrow technical range but unlimited emotional resources.

sources that included a heady melange of sweet and sour phrases, glissandos, smears, raspberries, growls and bronchial wheezes, he was a throwback to the early days of jazz when musicians such as Joe 'Tricky Sam' Nanton and James 'Bubber' Miley explored tonal distortion to increase their range of expression. Although his fleet solo on Little Milton's 1966 version of 'Who's Cheating Who' might have suggested otherwise, Bowie was never at home among fast moving patterns; reflecting on jazz-wunderkind Wynton Marsalis, he said 'with his chops [technique] and my brains, I could have been one of the greatest.'

In 1984 he formed his Brass Fantasy with fellow trumpeter Malachi Thompson as an outgrowth of the New York Hot Repertory Company (with whom Marsalis had performed). Their 1985 debut album 'I Only Have Eyes For You' (ECM) lacked focus, but the comically seductive title track was a summation of the group's style and leader's personality. 'Avante Pop' (ECM) from 1986 importuned an unlikely collection of songs as a basis for jazz improvisation, including Whitney Houston's hit 'Saving All My Love For You' and Patsy Cline's 'Crazy', creating a demand for the band that encouraged him to take it out on the road. His signature tune, 'The Great Pretender', the title track of his 1981 'Roots To The Source' album on ECM, announced a hyper Bowie, cheer leader, soloist, conductor and Master of Ceremonies whose visual trademark of a white laboratory coat had become institutionalized in sequins.

The 1987 'Twilight Dreams' (Virgin) and the 1988 'Serious Fun' (DIW), continued his ability to focus competing fantasies that for all their apparent iconoclasm and comical subversion succeeded in their own right. Brass Fantasy emerged as an ensemble of warmth and cleverly shifting tone colours, all too easy to overlook with Bowie's cheerful correlative of vaudevillian ham.

At the beginning of the 1980s **Arthur Blythe** (b.1940) seemed like the man to lead jazz out of commercial exile, 'the one unanimously praised soloist to emerge in jazz during the pluralistic 1970s'.[19] Blythe was a member of the Los Angeles collective UGMAA before moving to New York in 1974 where he gained attention with Chico Hamilton, Gil Evans and his own groups in the loft scene. One of the most lucid, passionate and accessible players to emerge from the avant garde, his work at the beginning of the decade was split between two bands, In The Tradition, a standard saxophone, piano, bass and drums quartet and his 'Guitar' band. 'In The Tradition' symbolized the trend towards reconciliation with the mainstream, and for a time Blythe was a central figure, 'My purpose is to rekindle old thoughts and feelings with modern ones,' he said.[20]

In contrast, the 'Guitar' band retained the uncompromising edge of the group he recorded for India Navigation between 1977 and 1979 ('The Grip' and 'Metamorphosis'), which applying the similar logic might have been dubbed the 'trumpet' band through the work of Ahmed Abdullah. The 'Guitar' band was a powerful, declamatory ensemble of contrasting textures that achieved a remarkable degree of stylistic unity. Balancing the twin realities of introversion—Abdul Wadud on cello, Bob Stewart on tuba—and extroversion—Blythe plus Bobby Battle drums and Kelvyn Bell or 'Blood' Ulmer on guitar, Blythe explained, 'I'm not one-faceted, I try not to be put in one area of expression.'

Blythe's debut for CBS, the 1979 'Lenox Avenue Breakdown' (CBS) included a mix 'n' match ensemble of Jack DeJohnette, with whom he was currently appearing as a member of Special Edition, James Newton, 'Blood' Ulmer and Cecil McBee; strongly rhythmical, it had what Blythe called 'that boody thang'.[21] Sadly, 'In The Tradition' (CBS), that followed was the only album given over exclusively to the standard quartet and was marred by a bizarre sound mix. However, the quartet did appear on

Arthur Blythe: 'The one unanimously praised soloist to emerge during the pluralistic 1970s'.

'Blythe Spirit' (CBS), 'Pa-Pa' (CBS) and 'Illusions' (CBS), greatly enhanced by the presence of John Hicks (p); their three tracks on the latter album are among the most exciting and dramatic moments of jazz from the early 1980s.

But it was the 'Guitar' band that received prominence and on albums such as 'Elaborations' and 'Light Blue' (both CBS) there were moments of avant garde rawness that raise the question of whether Blythe's career with a major recording company might have been more profitably fulfilled by pursuing the direction only glimpsed at with 'In The Tradition'. A tacit admission that this may have been the best way ahead came with 'Basic Blythe' (CBS) in 1988, a return to the quartet, albeit plus string quartet. But by then his career with CBS had long been eclipsed by the signing of Wynton Marsalis to the label in 1981, who soon achieved the breakthrough predicted for Blythe.

Blythe was among the finest alto saxophonists in jazz, with that most valuable of possessions, a highly individual and instantly recognizable tone whose heartbeat was the blues. Equally at home at the fastest tempos of bop, he appeared alongside Phil Woods and Paquito D'Rivera in a Jazz

At The Philharmonic-type cutting session recorded at the 1981 Kool Jazz Festival—'The New York/Montreux Connection' (CBS)—and was by no means bested, refusing to submit to garrulity or long streams of quavers. Blythe was also a member of The Leaders, formed 1984, a group that included AACM musicians Lester Bowie, Chico Freeman and Don Moye plus Cecil McBee and Kirk Lightsey, assembled for occasional tours and albums. 'Mudfoot' (Blackhawk) from 1986 seemed to pull in diverse directions, a problem unresolved with the 1987 'Out Here Like This' and 1989 'Unforeseen Blessings' (both Black Saint) that failed to realize the strength of the group lay in combining their strong, individual voices.

Blythe's frequent collaborator, **Bob Stewart** (b.1945) played an influential role in putting the tuba back on the map, 'I'm playing the tuba as a contemporary brass instrument,' he explained. Throughout the 1980s he could be heard in a variety of contexts: Blythe's minor classic 'Just A Closer Walk With Thee' from 'Blythe Spirit' (CBS); underpinning Bowie's Brass Fantasy, Carla Bley's Band, Gil Evans' orchestra and Charlie Haden's Liberation Music Orchestra; and soloing on Henry Butler's 'The Village' (Impulse) or the memorable 'Duet For Big Band' with David Murray on 'Big Band Live At Sweet Basil Vols. 1 & 2' (Black Saint). His own unheralded ensemble, the Bob Stewart Band, debuted in 1988 with 'Front Line', followed in 1989 by 'Goin' Home' (both JMT) that included a medley that went from dixieland to hard-bop, using 'Sweet Georgia Brown', Kenny Dorham's 'Windmill' and Jackie McLean's 'Donna', all with a common harmonic base.

A student of Muhal Richard Abrams at the AACM school, multi-reed man **Chico Freeman** (b.1949) worked in Chicago with Junior Wells, Memphis Slim and his own band Thunderfunk Symphony while studying mathematics at Northwestern University. On becoming a graduate student in composition at Governors State University he joined the GSU Jazz Ensemble and won two awards at the 1976 Notre Dame Jazz Festival as best soloist and best saxist. Within a year he had made his debut album, 'Morning Prayer' (Why Not/Trio) with Henry Threadgill, a mixture of experimental and accessible, a balance that was sustained through to his fourth album 'Kings of Mali' (India Navigation) a synthesis of African music and avant garde, hailed by Chris Albertson in *Stereo Review* as 'one of the most significant releases' of 1978. Freeman's act of reconciliation with the jazz mainstream was the 1979 'Spirit Sensitive' (India Navigation), a restrained but elegant reading of six ballads with John

Hicks (p) and long-time collaborator Cecil McBee (b) (who appears on most of his acoustic work). The breadth of Freeman's style resulted in his being touted as one of the coming greats of the 1980s. In fact what seemed like a transitional step was a move to a more serene approach to improvisation. The 1980 'Peaceful Heart, Gentle Spirit' (Contemporary) was richly textured and exotic, although 1981's 'Destiny's Dance' (Contemporary), an exciting post-bop collaboration with Wynton Marsalis and Bobby Hutcherson, was perhaps his best album of the 1980s. Marsalis in particular sounds far more relaxed than on his then current jazz projects for CBS, and shines with a bubbling, energetic solo on 'Wilpan's Walk'.

Freeman was a member of Jack DeJohnette's Special Edition from 1980 to 1982 and the drummer appears on his walk on the wild side, 'The Outside Within' (India Navigation) and the excellent 1982 'Tradition In Transition' (Elektra Musician), that included Wallace Roney (t). 'The transitional music of today will be the tradition of tomorrow,' said Freeman,[22] intending the remark to refer to his own playing, but in fact it seemed to have more relevance to the musicians around him.

Freeman's subsequent recorded work was framed in a series of concepts, but none had a really gripping quality; as the decade progressed the best from this talented musician always seemed ahead of him. By the end of the 1980s, he had gone full circle, touring and again recording with his father, tenor saxophonist Von Freeman, as he had in 1979 and 1980. The 1988 'Chico Freeman feat. Von Freeman: You'll Know When You Get There' (Black Saint) introduced electronic tone colours but overall the effect was no more than an exchange of pleasantries. Equally, as a member of the group Brainstorm he kept excess in check on the 1989 'The Mystical Dreamer' (In + Out). In contrast, a blowing date recorded at Ronnie Scott's club in London with Arthur Blythe, 'Luminous' (Jazz House) from February 1989, was his most revealing album as a soloist since 'Tradition In Transition'.

THE RECONCILIATOR: DAVID MURRAY

By the end of the 1980s, **David Murray** (b.1955) had established himself as possibly the most important of the young musicians engaged in reconciling the so-called avante-garde with the jazz mainstream. A tenor saxophonist and bass clarinettist, his kamikaze, Albert Ayler-influenced approach to improvisation began to bottom-out towards the end of the seventies when he began directing his energies into expanding his emotional and technical control of the saxophone and creating a context for his playing instead of the *ad hoc* blowing dates and solo recitals that had characterized his work to that point.

Initially he wanted to form a big band along the lines of the ensemble he presented at a series of concerts at New York's Public Theatre and Howard University in 1978, but was thwarted by economics. What emerged was the David Murray Octet which succeeded in creating a series of emotionally mature, enduring statements that are among the finest albums of the decade. Un-selfconsciously re-creating images of Duke Ellington and Ellington-through-Mingus, his glorious lop-sided ensemble had all the rough edges of a Mingus brawl, yet the depth and detail of Ellington's instrument.

The Octet recordings on Black Saint included a roll-call of major jazz improvisers. The first three albums were built around the nucleus of the group Air, plus Butch Morris, Olu Dara and George Lewis (brass) and Anthony Davis (p). Later albums included Bobby Bradford, Craig Harris, John Purcell, Baikida Carroll and Ralph Peterson Jr. The 1980 'Ming' included 'Dewey's Circle', an irresistible 'instant' classic while the 1981 'Home' included some of Murray's earliest compositions, 'Last Of The Hipmen' and '3-D Family', that had served him well in a variety of performing contexts.

The 1983 'Murray's Steps' was recorded after a European tour and had sensitive readings of 'Sweet Lovely' and 'Flowers For Albert'. 'New Life' from 1985, with a revamped lineup, had a quaintly indigestible version of the title song and succeeds in getting close to the spirit of Ellington with 'Train Whistle', a programmatic piece in the mould of 'Lightnin' ', 'Daybreak Express', 'Track 360' and 'Happy-Go-Lucky-Local'.

Persisting with the big band concept, Murray finally managed to secure occasional dates for a larger ensemble, including an appearance at the 1985 Kool Jazz Festival. Part of his big band's success lay with Butch Morris, who acted as conductor and *agent provocateur* using a system of gestures and expressions to spontaneously organize and re-organize melodies, counter-melodies, motifs and riffs, 'If I hear something that you play that I want you to repeat or develop, I have a gesture I'll give you for that,' explained Morris, 'If I want someone to do or emulate something that you're doing I have a gesture for that. It continues to grow, my vocabulary for improvisers.' His unique methodology is at work throughout the 'David Murray Big Band Live At Sweet Basil, Vols. 1 & 2' (Black Saint) from August 1984.

Murray's Quartet—John Hicks (p), Ray Drummond (b) and Ed Blackwell (d)—a group that the leader asserted 'will stand up to anybody's', produced 'Morning Song' in 1983 and on it a version of 'Body And Soul' that saw him move effortlessly alongside the great tenor saxophone masters. His ability to flex and relax the speed of his phrases, his control of notes an octave (and beyond) the normal range of his instrument, his lucidity and architechtonic conception marked him as a major voice on his instrument. Equally imposing was his command of the bass clarinet, extending the tradition of Eric Dolphy on Fats Waller's 'Jitterbug Waltz'. Although Ed Blackwell continued to be a regular member of the quartet, Ralph Peterson took over for the March 1986 'I Want To Talk About You' (Black Saint) recorded live at Charlie's Top, Boston, MA. 1988's 'Ming's Samba' (CBS/Portrait)—with Blackwell—was a powerful assertion of Murray's formidable improvising talent and, surprisingly, his first album for a major U.S. label.

Murray continued to work and record in diverse surroundings. 'The Hill' (Black Saint) was a 1986 trio collaboration with Richard Davis (b) and Joe Chambers (d) while 1987's 'The Healers' (Black Saint) was a dramatic encounter with pianist Randy Weston. However, the expected sparks failed to materialize on 'Children' (Black Saint), a collaboration that included pianist Don Pullen and 'Blood' Ulmer.

Seemingly never at a loss for ideas, in 1986 Murray performed a tribute to the saxophone greats, with a series of his compositions dedicated to Ben Webster and Lester Young that was broadcast on National Public Radio. One of the highlights was his orchestration of the 27 blues choruses played by Paul Gonsalves at the 1956 Newport Jazz Festival that expanded into a 45-minute extravaganza under the direction of Butch Morris.

Murray was in demand as a sideman on several albums during the 1980s but his most significant contributions were to Jack DeJohnette's Special Edition appearing on the group's debut album in 1979 alongside Arthur Blythe and the memorable 1984 'Album Album'. He was also a member, as bass clarinettist, of the occasional 'Clarinet Summit', with John Carter, Jimmy Hamilton and Alvin Batiste, appearing on 'Clarinet Summit Vols. 1 & 2' (India Navigation)—a live performance at New York's Public Theatre—and 'Southern Belles' (Black Saint). But it was with the World Saxophone Quartet, a group that quickly became something of an institution during the 1980s, that he was primarily associated when away from his own projects.

A MAJOR NEW GROUP: THE WORLD SAXOPHONE QUARTET

The **World Saxophone Quartet** was formed in 1977, comprising three members of the Black Artists Group of St. Louis: Hamiet Bluiett, baritone sax, Oliver Lake and Julius Hemphill alto saxophones, plus Murray tenor sax—but all doubled on other saxes, woodwinds and flutes. They were brought together at the invitation of Southern University in New Orleans for a performance with a local rhythm section but afterwards decided to organize themselves into a group *sans* rhythm, in so doing becoming a logical extension of the solo saxophone recital that had proliferated during the 1970s loft scene.

By the 1980s, virtually unanimous critical acclaim had established them as the foremost chamber group in jazz and their very tangible influence could be felt through the number of similar ensembles springing up throughout the world, such as Sweden's Position Alpha, Britain's Horn-web and Itchy Fingers, Germany's Manfred Schulze's Blaster Quintett and Kolner Saxophon Mafia and the Dutch De Zes Winden.

Not unnaturally, parallels were drawn with the chamber group of bop, the Modern Jazz Quartet. But the WSQ's role in reconciling and rethinking the role of improvisation and structure within a small group was not only more influential than the MJQ's at any time in its two lifetimes, but WSQ were closest to the 'pure' definition of a chamber group in that they were a quartet of soloists who are presented on equal terms (the MJQ have two leading voices and two supporting roles).

By dispensing with a rhythm section they frequently functioned more rhythmically, improvised or annotated, collectively and individually. Firmly rooted in the tradition of the black big band saxophone sections, they touched base with rich Ellingtonian harmonies yet were able to dissolve into an 'ensemble of perplexity' in their contemporary re-cycling of the Afro-American musical heritage. Their well-crafted repertoire—much of it the work of Julius Hemphill on the earlier albums—never loses sight of humour, which often took the form of deflationary irony, while their harmonic and ensemble resourcefulness suggested the past while looking into the future.

Often the distinction between written and improvised sections was impossible to discern as pre-arranged sections were seamlessly joined to passages of collective improvisation, a contemporary update of that long postponed ideal of New Orleans jazz. Aspects of their work suggest an awareness of the modern string quartet repertoire and it is perhaps no coincidence that references to Bartok, a master of the form, surfaced in their writing, particularly on the earlier albums.

'Steppin'' marked their debut on the Black Saint label dating from 1978. A sense of breakthrough washed the album with each track seeming like a celebration of their virtuosity. 'R&B' was a masterpiece: no wonder

David Murray: A conceptualist of great imagination, who created a variety of diverse ensembles in which to perform and record.

producer Giacomo Pellicciotti left in the groups' excited conversation towards the end.

'World Saxophone Quartet' from 1980 charted the group's growing sophistication, with the writing duties spread more evenly—the best coming from Bluiett whose 'Hattie's Wall' became a favourite, with insistent, compulsive riffs reminiscent of the 1940s' 'Jump' bands and was adopted as a signature tune. It introduced 'Live In Zurich' as the group emerged from stage left, playing the tune in the manner of a marching band. Quite how far the group had developed could be measured by comparing the 1978 version of 'Steppin' ' with the live 1981 update. The difference is not simply exuberance, familiarity through rehearsal and performance was beginning to develop a firm mutual understanding that was most impressive during solo exchanges and group interaction.

'Live At Brooklyn Academy Of Music' from 1986 continued their ascendance that reached a peak with 'Plays Duke Ellington' (Nonesuch), from 1986, which in terms of conceptual consistency was their 1980s' masterpiece, the whole group playing with superb control, especially during the *dolce* and *cantabile* sections. The 1987 'Dances And Ballads' (Nonesuch), comprised original compositions—including the irrepressible 'Hattie's Wall'—with Murray, Hemphill and Lake sharing the balance of compositions: 'When Duke Ellington first recorded his pieces, they had to be played for 20 years before they became standards. Maybe someday people will go back and play standards from "Dances And Ballads",' said Oliver Lake. Surprisingly, 'Rhythm And Blues' (Nonesuch) from 1989, disappointed, simply because their collective standards of execution and conception were less consistent. In late autumn 1989 Hemphill left the group to pursue his own projects and was replaced by Arthur Blythe.

Individually, the remaining members of the WSQ found their collective achievements overshadowing their work away from the group, 'The WSQ has been stronger than any one of us individually, so it helps our individual things,' said **Oliver Lake** (b.1944). 'When I do anything it says "of the World Saxophone Quartet" under my name. I don't have any problem with that.' Lake's commercial 'Jump Up' band featuring a funk/reggae amalgam emphasized rhythm with little room for the leader's powerful saxophone. Records like 'Jump Up' and 'Plug It' (both Gramavision) were exuberant but little else; Lake's solos paling in comparison to the real thing by Jamaicans Tommy McCook and Roland Alphonso.

His tribute to Eric Dolphy, the 1980 'Prophet' (Black Saint) and the subsequent 'Expandable Language' (Soul Note) were another matter however, but it was not until the 1987 'Gallery' and the subsequent 'Impala' (both Gramavision) in a standard quartet configuration with new young piano star Geri Allen that Lake presented the long overdue confirmation of his status as a major instrumentalist. The 1988 'Otherside' (Gramavision) was split between a quintet and a big band, the latter comprising another Dolphy tribute 'Dedicated to Dolphy' and 'Weave Song II' that veered between counterpoint and cacophony in an exhilarating game of disorderly conduct, suggesting Sun Ra's glorious confusions.

Julius Hemphill (b.1940) also had a commercial side with his JAH band, but 'Georgia Blue' (Minor Music) was only partly successful. Hemphill, however, was an inventive writer and conceptualizer; his 'Long Tongues: A Saxophone Opera' with a six-man sax section debuted at the Duke Ellington School of Arts in Washington DC in 1987, an ambitious attempt to trace the development of jazz and American society. His 1988 'Big Band' (Elektra/Musician) (including an equally ambitious 'Drunk On God', a poetry/jazz amalgam courageously indulged by producer Artie Moorhead, who made sure the rest of the album was one to be remembered), was described by *Musician* magazine as, 'What the music of the '90s will sound like'.

Hamiet Bluiett (b.1940) emerged as the leading baritone saxophonist of the 1980s. After working with a diverse cross-section of musicians that included Sam Rivers, Stevie Wonder, Gil Evans and Aretha Franklin plus two years on the road with Charles Mingus, the WSQ provided an ideal context for his playing. His remarkable technique extended the range of the baritone saxophone up into soprano sax territory, but albums under his own name, such as 'Birthright' and 'Dangerously Suite' (India Navigation and Soul Note) were not entirely successful. Ironically, his best album, 'Clarinet Family' (Black Saint) was made without the baritone and demonstrated his compositional and arranging skills that had not been used to their full extent with WSQ.

COMPOSITIONAL EXPERIMENTS

By taking the return to structure and form to its logical conclusion, some musicians whose sensibilities embraced modernist composers such as Cage, Bartók, Schoenberg and latterly Steve Reich, pursued a common meeting ground between classical compositional devices and improvisation. They sought to shape and control their experimentalism within their own carefully structured compositions. It was an old ideal still to be conquered that went back to ragtime, to create a new music, a new tradition that did not sacrifice the Afro-American experience but sought to channel improvisational rhetoric into a new direction of expressionism. By the '80s it was not simply the European tradition and jazz that shaped the content of their compositional form, world music also suggested new lines of development.

Perhaps more than any other musician during the 1980s, **Anthony Davis** (b.1951) reawakened the vexed question of the validity of combining jazz and classical music in general and improvised music and European and Asian traditions in particular. A leading pianist in the avant garde during the 1970s, he began channelling his virtuoso technique into exploring ways of combining improvised music within formal pre-set structures. Distancing himself from jazz, claiming the term limiting, he sought a less parochial audience with whom he could communicate on his own terms. His goal was to channel performers' creative impulses within pre-determined compositional devices. They embroidered turn-of-the-century impressionism, contemporary minimalism and pan-ethnic music that embraced Balinese gamelan music with the legacy of musicians such as Duke Ellington, Thelonious Monk and Cecil Taylor.

The result was a seamless whole that provoked a guessing game of where notation ended and improvisation began and albums such as the 1981 'Episteme' (Gramavision), the 1982 'Variations In Dreamtime' (India Navigation), the 1983 'Hemispheres', the solo 1984 'Middle Passage' and the minimalist gamelan groove of the 1988 'The Ghost Factory' (Gramavision) chart his progress and his ongoing 'Wayang' series. 'The improviser is required to work his way through the written composition to find moments of personal expression,' explained Davis.

Unconcerned with popularity, Davis created a unique and highly specialized niche in 20th-century music. It could be that outside the environment of private and public subsidized art its delicate beauties could perish, as in devising a radical realignment of structure and improvisation his success depended on a highly sympathetic ensemble—often his group Episteme—in much the same way as Cecil Taylor, Charles Mingus, Duke Ellington and Jelly Roll Morton relied on theirs. That the essence of their performances could not effectively be reproduced by other ensembles did not, however, lessen their achievements.

Davis has also written works for orchestras, including pieces commissioned and performed by the Brooklyn and New York Philharmonics and the Houston Symphony Orchestra. His opera, 'Opera X', based on the life of Malcolm X, with a libretto by his cousin Thulani Davis, debuted in Philadelphia in 1984 and received its grand premiere by the New York Opera in 1986. Davis was also a member of the David Murray Octet, appearing on the group's first two albums, and was not beyond a raunchy blues-based outing on Ray Anderson's 1988 'Blues Bred In The Bone' (Enja).

Jay Hoggard (b.1954) first played with Anthony Davis when they were students at Wesleyan and Yale respectively during the mid-1970s. Hoggard was an ethnomusicology major and travelled to Tanzania to study East African xylophone music. His vibes playing earned him a reputation as the most adventurous player on this instrument since the 1960s, although his collaborations with Anthony Davis on the 1980 duo 'Under The Double Moon' (Pausa) and 'Song For The Old World' (India Navigation) he is suitably careful and considered.

He made his name opening a concert for Joseph Jarman in November 1978, which was broadcast on National Public Radio and subsequently issued as 'Solo Vibraphone' (India Navigation). The track 'May Those Who Believe In Apartheid Burn In Hell' was a classic title and performance with a whole new outlook to vibes. However, Hoggard dabbled in 'soft-option' jazz, initially with the GRP label and on albums such as 'Riverside Dance' (India Navigation) that failed to live up to his reputation.

His composition 'Pleasant Memories' was featured in the 1982 'Young Lions' concert that reflected his African experiences, 'The Young Lions' (Elektra Musician), although his work with Chico Freeman, including 'Peaceful Heart, Gentle Spirit' (Contemporary) and frequent collaborations with James Newton, suggested the adaptability of a follower rather than a leader—his own albums were amiable and ingratiating rather than riveting. However, the 1989 'Overview' (Muse) with Geri Allen, Ed Rozie and Freddie Waits, suggested a more mature and defined vision of the real Jay Hoggard.

A flute virtuoso, **James Newton** (b.1953) was a frequent collaborator with Anthony Davis, pursuing similar goals of minimizing the distinction between improvisation and composition with his own chamber-like groups. Newton played flute exclusively, his tone owing a lot to classical models, but perfected the use of microtones and multiphonics, a technique that was featured extensively on the solo 'Axum' (ECM). Using multi-tracking and an extensive cross-section of the flute family 'Axum' was described by *Coda* magazine as 'a memorable listening experience'.

However, Newton seemed to be at his best when not preoccupied with Third stream puzzles; albums such as the 1982 'James Newton' (Gramavision) that included Jay Hoggard, Anthony Davis and John Blake, the brilliant 1985 'African Flowers' (Blue Note) a collection of Ellington and Strayhorn pieces interpreted by the likes of Arthur Blythe, Jay Hoggard and John Blake, and the 1986 'Romance and Revolution' (Blue Note), a homage to Charles Mingus, with Abdul Wadud, Geri Allen and Robin Eubanks, managed to elude the acclaim they deserved. In fact, in the context of the 1980s neo-classical mainstream they demonstrated a sophisticated grasp of jazz tradition that was far in advance of so many of his contemporaries locked in the hard-bop groove.

During the 1980s **John Blake** (b.1948) was hailed as 'the best new violinist of the decade'. After a stint with Grover Washington, Blake joined the McCoy Tyner Group in 1979 and stayed for six years, appearing on albums like 'Horizon' (Milestone), and 'Dimensions' (Elektra Musician). His own 'Maiden Dance' (Gramavision) from 1984 included former boss McCoy Tyner, a testament to his abilities but nevertheless a surprisingly low-key affair. The subsequent 'Twinkling Of An Eye' (Gramavision) from 1986 equally aimed more for elegance than urgency. A strong melodist, his traditionalist approach somehow mitigated his efforts to create a context for his playing.

In 1986 he became one-third of Rhythm and Blu, a violin trio with Didier Lockwood and Michal Urbaniak, originally appearing at the Blue Note in New York in 1986 followed by a short tour and the album 'Rhythm and BLU' (Gramavision). The group reformed in early 1987 for a further tour. Throughout, Blake maintained his association with James Newton, moving between his Third Stream experimentation to albums such as 'African Flowers' (Blue Note).

After two years in the Army, including a year in Vietnam, **Billy Bang** (b.1947), returned from his tour of duties 'completely spaced out'. His entry into music came through his involvement with politics, 'I wanted to play music again because we would somehow associate music with politics and the whole thing at the time,' he said. Emerging from the 1970s loft scene as an avant gardist with a strong, unique voice who was capable of moments of profound clarity and exciting deconstruction, he joined the New York String Trio in 1977, with whom some of his best work is to be found, such as 'Common Goal' and 'Rebirth Of Feeling' (Black Saint).

In 1983 he combined with Frank Lowe (tenor), Rafael Garrett (bass) and Dennis Charles (drums) (later Thurman Baker) to form The Jazz Doctors that refracted the mainstream through the prism of post-Ornette Coleman freedom, 'Intensive Care' (Cadillac). Bang's own work as a leader varies from the unorthodox swing of 'Rainbow Gladiator' (Soul Note) and 'Invitation' (Soul Note) with its strong memorable themes, possibly his best album of the '80s, to 'Outline No. 12' (Celluloid), influenced by post-modern classicism, which, unlike the work of Anthony Davis, left room for the improviser to breathe.

5
Miles and the Fusion Junta

WHEN MILES DAVIS'S electronic bandwagon started up in the late-1960s, it seemed the most logical direction for jazz to take. Such had been the impact of rock music, jazz simply could not expect to get away unscathed and for a while, quite a long while in fact, rock music had a significant effect on the outlook of jazz musicians. Pillars of the jazz community such as Duke Ellington and Count Basie recorded Beatles numbers, Sonny Stitt and Clark Terry experimented with electrifying their instruments with a device known as the Varitone while Gerry Mulligan summed up the rush to be trendy with an album entitled 'If You Can't Beat Them, Join Them'.

By 1965 rock was dominating the music business. In a two-week period in November that year *Billboard* received 281 singles to review and during the same period eight albums hit gold by groups such as The Rolling Stones, The Dave Clark Five, The Animals and, of course, The Beatles. In 1967 rock reached its high water-mark at a weekend festival at Monterey and demonstrated the grip the music had on the consciousness of a young generation. Eleven hundred media men alone turned out to cover the event and one hundred thousand orchids were flown in from Hawaii and scattered among the crowds at what was the greatest rock extravaganza ever.

Significantly, Clive Davis, the newly appointed head of Columbia Records was there, 'I realized this was the time for me to sign up some of these wonderful new stars,' he said.[1] Among the artists he signed were Janis Joplin, Laura Nyro and The Byrds, which represented a *volte face* for a label that had formerly relied on a middle-of-the-road philosophy dictated since the mid-1950s by Mitch Miller. But Columbia were not alone in reacting to the prevailing market forces; the hunt was on by all record companies to sign up new rock talent. A new musical aristocracy had arrived whose audience was measured in millions and fed by its own media machine.

Jazz, in the face of such competition, was not unnaturally undergoing something of an identity crisis. Record companies, clubs and concert halls soon realized they could make more money from rock than jazz. 'Jazz music seemed to be withering on the vine, in record sales and live performance,' said Miles Davis. '. . . in the United States we played to a lot of half-empty clubs . . . that told me something. Compared to what my records used to sell, when you put them against what Bob Dylan or Sly Stone sold, it was no contest.'[2]

At this time, during the mid-1960s, Davis was at the top of his profession in jazz, as was John Coltrane; 'One treacherous night,' recalled writer Gordon Kopulous, 'John Coltrane played Chicago's "Birdhouse" . . . He played to an audience which numbered ten at its height. I counted. As if to underscore the whole scene in living theatre, another group appeared on the south west side: Kenny Klopke Fantastics, a rock group . . . They packed in 600 kids . . . and turned away 300.'[3] And these were the headliners in jazz; for lesser mortals their plight was even more serious.

For a while it seemed as if the future of jazz itself was in question; 'Requiem for a jazz we knew and loved well', said the 2 September 1967 edition of Melody Maker. 'Jazz is dead . . . Folk is dead . . . long live Rock', said the October 1967 *Rouge* magazine and the cover of the 5 October 1967 *Downbeat* heralded: 'Jazz as we know it is dead.' In December 1967, Jim Morrissey wrote, 'My complaint is that too many of the jazz greats are producing noncommunicating music. They get deeper and deeper into their own bag where fewer of their fans hang out. There must be a wedding between some of the solid contemporary sounds that are evolving out of early rock and roll garbage. Twenty years ago jazz was pop music, today it has only a small proportion of the public on its side.'[4] In such a climate, survival became a function of commercial reality, the misery that acquainted jazz with a strange bedfellow, rock.

As the seventies approached Miles Davis was clearly under pressure from Clive Davis, the head of Columbia, because his records were not selling in the quantities rock was achieving. '50,000 albums barely takes you out of the red ink,' said the then Columbia boss. 'We began to give Miles additional money each time he recorded an album; we weren't making any money at all.'[5] And the head of the biggest recording company in the world was not backward in coming forward, 'He started talking to me about this younger market and about changing,' confirmed Miles

Davis.[6] By 1968 Leonard Feather was able to write that on visiting Davis he was surprised to find him surrounded by pop and rock records, 'Not a single jazz instrumental', he said.

Viewed from both sides of the fence, jazz certainly had much to offer rock in terms of technique and harmonic sophistication, plus a new angle to extend its shelf-life after folk-rock, acid-rock and country-rock had run their course. Rock, on the other hand, offered jazz a way of enhancing its diminished commercial standing. Although groups like Electric Flag, Blood Sweat And Tears and The Chicago Transit Authority adopted jazz devices and were, in the eyes of the public, the first of the 'jazz-rock' bands, they did not provide the answer jazz was seeking, as trumpeter Randy Brecker pointed out when he left Blood, Sweat And Tears in 1968, 'Ultimately,' he said, 'I was more interested in playing jazz, that's why I left to join Horace Silver's group.'

Among the first jazz musicians to experiment in merging the two genres were Free Spirits, including guitarist Larry Coryell and saxophonist Jim Pepper, Gary Burton's quartet (again with Coryell), the group Dreams with the Brecker Brothers and Billy Cobham and Jeremy and the Satyrs, a band run by the nervous young flautist Jeremy Stieg, although none could claim a breakthrough. Perhaps one of the most successful early attempts on record was the neglected 'Detroit' (Atlantic) by Yusef Lateef that actually mixed jazz with rock musicians in the studio to produce what was considered by many a key album at the time. Finally, in 1969 Miles Davis demonstrated the artistic feasibility of fusion with 'In A Silent Way' (CBS) and commercial potential with 'Bitches Brew' (CBS). 'I had seen the way to the future with my music,' he said, 'and I was going for it like I had always done.'[7]

The jazz-rock fusion became an extremely popular concept, resulting in the biggest audience for a jazz-based music since the swing era. It also gave jazz in general a much-needed infusion of popularity and a higher profile that enabled a wide popular audience to enjoy at least some elements of it—not least improvisation. No doubt the fact rock music was popular some 15 years prior to 'In A Silent Way' provided a ready-made audience for the new style. When jazz adopted the electronic instruments associated with rock, together with a prominent role for the drums and frequently repeating rhythmic section patterns it became a marketable commodity in a world that judged success by the number of units sold.

'Bitches Brew' (CBS) from 1969 was Davis' highest selling album; soon after several of his sidemen went on to form their own bands and while their level of improvisation and musicianship set them apart from the main thrust of rock music, the effect in volume was similar. Davis himself had moved significantly from his jazz base towards the music of Sly Stone, Jimi Hendrix and Billy Preston and his later albums had more relevance against a background of black pop than jazz or rock. Indeed, the bio of Davis hardly rates a mention in the *Encyclopedia Of Rock* but gets the full treatment in *The Encyclopedia Of Black Music.*

Artistically, the successes in the fusion field were initially almost solely confined to ex-Davis sidemen. Weather Report, a collaboration between Joe Zawinul and Wayne Shorter, was the most enduring and substantial of all the fusion groups—Davis included. The high-energy approach was represented by the rawness of the Tony Williams Lifetime, the gothic by John McLaughlin's Mahavishnu Orchestra and the mystic by Chick Corea's Return To Forever. Their styles depended on breathtaking runs and discursive harmonic play that operated on one emotional level, excitement, which after only moderate exposure assumed a curious monochrome quality.

In the end this virtuosity took on a strained, dandyish quality that suggested the style had entered a narcissistic cul-de-sac, 'In short,' wrote Charles Shaar Murray, 'fusion was undone by its humourlessness and by its weakness for corn-ball monumentalism.'[8] It was, nevertheless, a vein that was mined by a second generation during the '70s whose reputations rested more on technique than jazz credentials, such as Al Dimeola or Lee Ritenour. Compared to jazz, the commercial rewards were high and many accomplished jazz musicians 'crossed over' with varying degrees of success. But by the end of the '70s as fusion floundered they were left looking slightly foolish amid a legacy of highly stylized music fixed in time, like a lark tongue in aspic, just like the swing era 30 years before.

THE SECOND COMING—THE RETURN OF MILES DAVIS

More than any other musician during the 1980s, **Miles Davis** (b.1926) was a man tied to the weight of his past. During the 1940s his gauche trumpet played straight-man to Charlie Parker's sweeping virtuosity, in the '50s and early '60s his well-pared lyricism was focussed in a series of mood poems underwritten by Gil Evans while his acoustic quintets and sextets set lessons in group interaction that were still being echoed during the '80s. But it was his endorsement of what for many was the unthinkable that really stood the jazz world on its head when in the late '60s he acted as front man to a series of gradually evolving groups that led jazz into the realms of rock music.

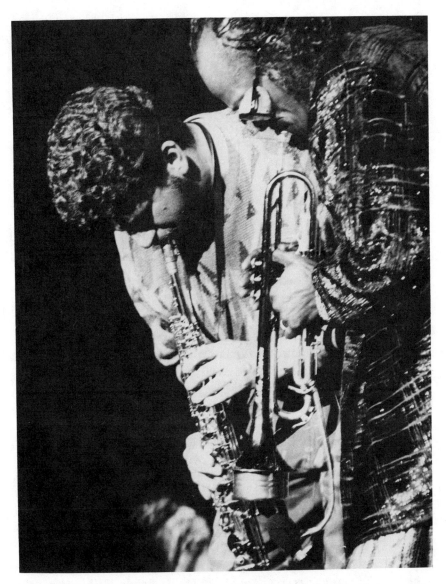

Miles Davis with Bob Berg: Davis was greeted like the prodigal son on his return to jazz in 1981, but by the end of the decade was accused of 'trading on credit for far too long.'

In 1975 he retired, initially planning a layoff of around six months, 'I felt artistically drained, tired,' he said, 'I didn't have anything else to say musically.'[9] By then his vision of fusion had become austere and by no means attractive; indeed his two pre-retirement albums, 'Agharta' and

'Pangaea' (both CBS), were heavily amplified electronic gang-bangs that led nowhere. 'The music from 1972-75 is self-contained and hard to grasp,' wrote Jack Chambers. 'It is probably the most forbidding and least accessible music that Davis ever made.'[10]

For the next five years rumour and speculation abounded about a return to active performance. Jazz, by the end of the '70s, seemed to have lost direction and Davis, who had more than once changed its history, was being looked upon to make a return and assert his role as musical path-finder.

But it wasn't just jazz that had lost its direction as the '80s approached; during the years of his layoff, Davis pursued what can only be described as an unsavoury lifestyle, a mixture of sex and cocaine.[11] Music played but a small part in his life during this period, although he did sit in with the Thad Jones-Mel Lewis band in 1978 and, in February-March, laid down some tracks for CBS with Larry Coryell and Al Foster of arrange-ments by Bobby Scott, but without liking the results. Finally in 1980, the blandishments of Dr George Butler, Head of A&R for CBS Records, prompted realistic thoughts of an attempt to rebuild his career.

His decision to make a comeback was finally prompted by a tape of a group led by his nephew, the drummer Vincent Wilburn Jr.. It led to rehearsals with the Chicago based band, plus Bill Evans (ts) and players recommended by producer Teo Macero, in New York in May 1980 when they recorded two numbers that appeared on his comeback album, 'The Man With The Horn' (CBS). The date was interrupted by a session un-issued in the '80s with Karlheinz Stockhausen and Paul Buckmaster, and quite probably Wayne Shorter and Joe Zawinul.

In early 1981 he completed the album with a group of musicians who would become the nucleus of a working band later in the year, including Evans, Al Foster (d), the thumbed bass of Marcus Miller and Mike Stern (g). Released in 1981, 'Man With The Horn' (CBS) was a disappointment; the title track was a eulogy to the leader that was both awkward and not a little embarrassing, and the track 'Shout' was issued as a single aimed at the pop charts. Guitarist and vocalist Randy Hall, one of Wil-burn's group who appeared on the album said, 'Some tunes are, like, pop.'[12]

When George Wein announced that Miles Davis was to play Avery Fisher Hall in Lincoln Centre on 5 July 1981 as part of the Kool Jazz Festival, it became the most publicized event in jazz history. Virtually every newspaper in the world made some reference to the event. In fact, Davis had debuted with his band the month before in an obscure Boston club called Kix. CBS, mindful of his health, had dispatched a remote to record the event, which together with an excerpt from 'Back Seat Betty' from his appearance at Avery Fisher Hall and 'Jean Pierre' from a Tokyo concert the following October (issued in both edited and unedited form), comprised the Grammy winning 'We Want Miles' (CBS) released in late summer 1982. Of his highly publicized Avery Fisher Hall appearance, Contat magazine wrote, 'Five years of silence from one of the four or five great creators of jazz, when all the others are dead and the music is stagnating, creates a mythology: the myth of the Messiah. Miles Davis, and this should be good enough to give us joy for the time being, is back.'[13]

At the end of 1982 he began working on 'Star People' (CBS) collaborating with Gil Evans on the cut 'Star On Cicely'. Davis also added John Scofield (g) to the band and his powerful improvisations encouraged him to adapt his repertoire in favour of Scofield's style, 'I felt comfortable playing the blues with him,' he said.[14] 'Star People', released in June 1983, was by far the best of Davis's work since his return; at last his faltering lyricism was cast aside in focussed understatement on both the title track and 'It Gets Better', each a slow blues. However, by the end of 1983 Davis was forced to let Stern, who by then was dabbling in drugs and alcohol, go.

In July the band began recording for 'Decoy' (CBS) with 'What It Is' and 'That's What Happened' from the Festival International de Jazz at Montreal and the remaining tracks from August-September in New York, with Branford Marsalis on four of them. 'It was pretty much the stuff I played in high school,' said a disappointed Marsalis. 'It was, you know, vamp music.'[15]

In November 1983 Davis was celebrated in a gala at New York's Radio City Music Hall, 'Miles Ahead: A Tribute To An American Legend', 'It was a beautiful night and I'm happy they honoured me the way they did,' he said.[16] It preceded a long layoff and an operation on his hip and a bout of pneumonia. 'Decoy' (CBS) was released in May 1984 to coincide with his return to live performance with a concert in Los Angeles on 2 June. By the time he had started recording 'You're Under Arrest' (CBS) at the end of 1984, Bob Berg had come in on tenor sax for Bill Evans who had left after their European tour; 'Davis's reluctance to let Evans prove his ability with fully elaborated solos or anything close to an equal share of the solo space baffled jazz fans and frustrated Evans,' wrote Jack Chambers.[17]

'You're Under Arrest' (CBS) had pop vocalist Sting as the policeman's voice and Davis' nephew Vince Wilburn Jr. on some tracks in place of Al Foster. It included D Train's 'Something's On Your Mind', Cyndi Lauper's 'Time After Time' and Michael Jackson's 'Human Nature'. All became de rigeur in live performance, with 'Time After Time' Davis' big ballad feature where he seemed to dwell as long on each passing chord as he wanted to. When the album was released in 1985, critic Francis Davis said: 'This is party music for stay-at-homes: it might be good dance music, but it's hardly likely to get anybody up on the dance floor . . . he's been trading on credit for far too long.'[18]

In November 1984 Davis was awarded the Sonning Award for his lifetime's achievement in music, and in February and March 1985 he recorded Palle Mikkelborg's 'Aura' (CBS), written in honour of the event, at the Easy Sound Studio in Copenhagen. Not released until 1989 when it won a Grammy, it had John McLaughlin (g), Vince Wilburn (d) and a distinguished cast of musicians from the Danish Radio Big Band, including Niels-Henning Orsted Pedersen on acoustic bass. Refracting elements of Davis' past, it inevitably brought to mind his orchestral collaborations with Gil Evans, albeit at a bleak and unsentimental remove. His best album of the 1980s, his playing was assured and the project adventuresome, key ingredients absent from so much of '80s discography.

The dramatic Irving Penn photographs of Davis on 'Tutu' (Warner Bros), dedicated to the South African bishop, heralded a change of record label in 1986. A Grammy winner, it created the illusion of a large ensemble with multi-tracked synths and again there were echos of Gil Evans, but the move to a big ensemble sound was this time perhaps inspired by 'Aura'. Now Marcus Miller was Davis's studio guru, writing the music and playing on a variety of instruments, building up ensembles through patient multi-tracking. 'I've found that taking my working band into the studio is too much trouble these days,' said Davis.'[19]

Miller received joint billing for their 1987 collaboration 'Siesta' (Warner Bros), his electronic Andalusian backdrop consciously evoking 'Sketches Of Spain' (CBS) from 1958, 'The music was to be a little like what Gil Evans and I had done on "Sketches Of Spain",' said Davis, 'so I asked Marcus Miller to try work up some music with some of that feeling.'[20]

'Siesta', however, was for the soundtrack for the Lorimar film of the same name and like Davis's previous film soundtrack albums—'Ascenseur pour l'échafaud' (Mercury) and 'Jack Johnson' (CBS)—there were moments that were subservient to visual rather than musical logic. Davis is a 'featured soloist', his highly individual trumpet laments one of several elements that Miller drew upon, including guitarists John Scofield and Earl Klugh, flautist James Walker and Miller himself on a variety of instruments.

Despite reaching out to 'Sketches Of Spain', particularly in the composition 'Loz Feliz' and the way the title track evoked Evans' 'Solea' in its suggestion of flamenco, an important element of 'Sketches Of Spain' was that it moved away from the notion of note-perfect orchestral interpretation. It emphasized feeling at the expense of precision and the result was an earthy power that suggested spontaneity for both soloist and ensemble. 'Siesta', and indeed 'Tutu', reversed this principle; each orchestration was built up by painstaking multi-tracking, creating instead the superficial gloss of functional consumerism.

'Amandla' (Warner Bros) was released in 1989, again mid-wifed by the highly talented Marcus Miller, and included appearances by current band members Joseph Foley McCreary (g), Kenny Garrett (as), Ricky Wellman (d) and ringers such as Joe Sample, Omar Hakim and George Duke. Davis's reliance on an unsubtle 'funky' backbeat was again in evidence but the overall impression was one of monotony of tone. In live performance his electronic jamming band, whatever description might be attached to the music it played, remained stuck in a formula groove, see-sawing between ostinatos and modal vamps often topped with the vicarious excitement of a heavy-metal jam. The band traded heavily on Davis' persona and charismatic trumpet sound, *The Times* observing that 'The actual quality of the music now seems to come a distant second to the emotional need to cling to his membership of the hipster elite.'[21]

Measured in terms of his illustrious past, Davis's music was neither stimulating nor innovative. It had bottomed out in the marketplace of Adult Oriented Rock, try as you might to look over the leader's shoulder to hookup with past triumphs. The value he placed on listening to jazz recordings was negative and his sources of inspiration remained remote from the music. 'In 1987 I was really getting into the music of Prince and the music of Cameo and Larry Blackmon and the Caribbean group called Kassav. But I really love Prince,' he said, referring to Hendrix's spiritual successor in the 1980s. '. . . I think Prince's music is pointing toward the future.'[22] It was perhaps not surprising that there was little to chew on for a jazz audience.

Once Davis remarked that he could put together a better rock band than Jimi Hendrix; it was as much macho challenge as statement of fact. Ever since Sly Stone and James Brown, Davis sought to be a cult figure for black audiences. Instead, there were more blacks at a Republican convention than a Davis concert; he had become a cult figure for white audiences, who, conscious of his innovative past, expanded their definition of jazz to accommodate him.

MILES DAVIS SIDEMEN—CLASS OF '81-89

Bill Evans (b.1958) was recommended to Miles Davis in April 1980 while still a student at William Patterson College in New Jersey. It was fair to say that Evans never really impressed Davis, indeed, towards the end of his stay with him suffered the indignity of his solos being cut short by a peremptory blast on the trumpet. Evans' debut as a leader, 'Living In The Crest Of The Wave' did nothing to rectify the image of Miles's 'man who never was'.

Evans joined John McLaughlin's relaunched Mahavishnu Orchestra in 1983; 'Mahavishnu' (Warner Bros) included Mitch Forman (k) Jonas Hellborg (b) and Billy Cobham (d) but like the subsequent 'Adventures In Radioland' (Sound Service) from 1986, with Danny Gottlieb's synthidrums injecting a criminally insensitive back-beat, the band disappointed. If expectations had been raised by the resurrection of the name Mahavishnu, evoking one of the great fusion bands of the '70s, it was soon dashed in both style and content, which offered the quick fix of superficial flash and coy hooks.

The 1985 'Alternative Man' (Blue Note), Evans' second album under his own name, covered many bases but mastered none. He was also a member of Gottlieb and Egan's band Elements, an inoffensive New Age/Fusion band,[23] performing and recording with them frequently as well as artists including Danny Gottlieb, Dave Sanborn and Gil Evans' Monday Night Orchestra. But by the end of the 1980s Evans remained mesmerized by fusion, his most interesting work appearing on the 1988 fusion party 'Echoes Of Ellington' (Verve), but his ability remained undefined, as firmly in the shadow of the decade as he had been on stage with Miles Davis.

Mike Stern (b.c1954) was recommended to Davis by Bill Evans to help complete 'Man With The Horn' (CBS) and was later invited to join the band in 1981. He had studied guitar with Pat Metheny at Berklee College Of Music, where he gained a reputation as a formidable and inveterate sitter-in. He joined Blood, Sweat And Tears in 1976, on the recommendation of Metheny, playing on their album 'Brand New Day' (CBS) and was briefly with Billy Cobham in 1978.

Stern made three albums with Davis and during his stay became the guitarist critics loved to hate. Although influenced by Wes Montgomery and Jim Hall he was told by Davis, 'Play some Hendrix, turn it up or turn it off!'[24] Davis was unequivocal in his requirements, even turning Stern's amp up if the decibel rate was not wound-up. 'Miles wants me to fill a certain role with this band, so I'm playing loud,'[25] explained Stern. However, during his stay with Davis, he fell prey to drug addiction. 'I was getting too high and he said . . . cool it out,' said Stern, 'But it took me another year to realize it for myself.' After Davis let him go he joined the Jaco Pastorius band, hardly helping his plight as the late bassist was also an addict—the stories of his excess almost legendary.

In 1986 he debuted as a leader with 'Upside, Downside' (Atlantic), sharing the front line with tenor saxophonist Bob Berg, who would figure on all his albums, on an album of originals. Full of high-tech runs and a heavy backbeat, it was genial, high-energy, foot-tapping stuff but with the emphasis on slickness rather than depth. By 1987 he had rehabilitated himself, after playing in Dave Sanborn's band and another spell with Davis in 1985.

In March '87 he appeared on Bob Berg's 'Short Stories' (Denon) and in the December he returned the favour with his own 'Time In Place' (Atlantic). All seven tracks are Stern compositions and some, including 'Chromazone', found their way into the repertoire of the Mike Brecker Band whom he joined in 1987 after impressing the year before when both he and Brecker toured as members of Steps Ahead. Some of his compositions also appeared on the excellent 'Mike Brecker' (Impulse) and the fragmented follow-up 'Don't Try This At Home' (Impulse). Stern's compositions uncoiled, both melodically and harmonically, in interesting and original ways. On the 1988 'Cycles' (Denon), under Bob Berg's name, he played a self-effacing role (as he had done on 'Short Stories') in a band that might have otherwise been a mirror image of his own in both conception and outlook.

His own 'Jigsaw' (Atlantic) from 1989 included Dennis Chambers (d) and was again slick, but, like all his albums, rose above run-of-the-mill fusion with his well thought out compositions and deft, albeit glossy solos. The band toured briefly in 1989, under the nominal leadership of Bob Berg, later recording 'In The Shadows' (Denon). Stern's best playing on record, however, features on Harvie Swartz's 1985 'Urban Earth' and 1986 'Smart Moves' (both Gramavision) where he is totally unrecognizable as the head-banger from the Miles Davis band. His playing on tracks like 'Pyramid', 'The Duke' and 'Mothership' on the former and 'Equinox',

'Mexico' and 'My Romance' on the latter are a revelation, and suggest a talent that was badly directed in terms of artistic content during the 1980s: Stern is a lucid, rhythmically secure and articulate musician, but his playing with Berg in an ephemerally slick, gee-whiz style seldom suggested the inner man.

John Scofield, (b.1951), a Berklee graduate who had studied with Gary Burton, already had a sound reputation in jazz when he joined Miles Davis in 1982. Scofield's recording debut was as a short-notice replacement for guitarist Mick Goodrick at the 1974 reunion of Gerry Mulligan and Chet Baker (CTI) at Carnegie Hall. Two weeks later he was with the Billy Cobham/George Duke band for a two-year gig followed by a year with Gary Burton and a profusion of jobs including recording with Charles Mingus and as a regular with the Dave Liebman band. In 1979 he formed his own trio with Steve Swallow (b) and Adam Nassbaum (d)—'Bar Talk' (Arista), 'Shinola' and 'Out Like A Light' (both Enja)— that saw him returning to his Jim Hall-orientated roots.

In 1982 he joined Davis, and his impact was such that of the band's albums during the 1980s, by far the most distinguished were the three

John Scofield quietly developed into one of the major instrumentalists to emerge in the 1980s.

Scofield was involved in, although Davis said, 'John had a tendency to play behind the beat, I had to bring him up,'[26]

In 1984 he featured on a powerful jamming session recorded live at the Club Bazillus, Zurich with George Adams—'More Sightings' (Enja)—and in 1985 toured Europe with the George Adams/Don Pullen Quartet, recording live at the Jazzhus, Montmarte in April—'Live At Montmarte' (Timeless). In 1984 he also signed with Gramavision and 'Electric Outlet' had a pick-up band including Ray Anderson (tmb) and David Sanborn (as) in a homage to bluesmen B.B. King and Albert King; included was a superb example of utilizing Phrygian voicings on his 'Best Western' solo. The 1985 'Still Warm' with Daryl Jones (b) and Omar Hakim (d), another pick-up group, was confirmation that he had accelerated up the learning curve at a remarkably fast rate of knots while with Davis.

In 1986 he formed a touring group comprising Marc Cohen (k), ex-Pockets bassist Gary Grainger and Ricky Sebastian (d), by which time his playing had assumed a highly individual rhythmic sense, a readily identifiable use of unusual intervals and rhythmic sequences and fluid, polytonal harmonies; Scofield had quietly developed into one of the major instrumentalists to emerge in the 1980s.

Later in the year the ex-Parliament/Funkadelic drummer Dennis Chambers replaced Sebastian in time for 'Blue Matter' (Gramavision), released in 1987. One of the decade's best albums, Grainger and Chambers combined with astonishing cohesion. The title track (with a Scofield trademark, a sinister, walking bass line à la Miles Davis), the soaring 'Heaven Hill' and a lesson in funk, 'The Nag', were album highlights that were frequently performed live. 'Pick Hits', a concert at Hitomi Memorial Hall, Japan from October 1987, now with Robert Aires (k), and the December '87 'Loud Jazz' (all Gramavision) collectively jumped into a groove and stayed there; this was neither cop-out, sell-out or cross-over, but solid creative musicianship of integrity and depth.

After almost three years of touring Scofield disbanded in 1988, and 'Flat Out' from the December, by a pick-up group including Terri Lyn Carrington (d), was less funk driven. However, in 1989 Scofield signed with Blue Note records and 'Time On My Hands' brought together Joe Lovano (ts), Charlie Haden (b) and Jack DeJohnette (d) in yet another important album. Scofield as both guitarist and composer bonded the group with unity of purpose while allowing sufficient latitude within the compositional structures for individual expression. Scofield subsequently toured with a quartet, but with Anthony Cox (b) and John Riley (d). The band still projected the same remarkable internal cohesion without sacrificing individualism and confirmed Scofield as a major figure in contemporary jazz. An original instrumentalist, he was able to create challenging and wholly successful contexts to focus his playing, 'What I really want to do is get better, somehow,' said he, 'You know, keep moving on.

Bob Berg (b.1951), a Julliard graduate, had acquired a modest reputation as a hard-blowing, Coltrane influenced tenor saxophonist when he joined Davis in 1984. By then he had come up through the hard-bop school with long stints in the bands of Horace Silver (1973-76) and Cedar Walton (1977-83).

Berg's work with Walton can be heard on albums like 'First Set' (Steeplechase), live at Montmartre shortly after he joined the band, the 1979 'Eastern Rebellion 3' (Timeless) and the 1980 'The Maestro' (Muse) that show a mastery and technical proficiency that was just a couple of years too early to earn the acclaim accorded to equally young and not necessarily greater talents later in the decade. In 1982 Berg toured Europe and 'Steppin' ' (Red Records) catches his ebullient, cascading style shortly before he took the plunge into fusion with Davis.

Berg appeared on just one album with Davis and left in 1987, according to Davis, 'Because he didn't like the fact that I had brought in a saxophonist named Gary Thomas to share duties with him.'[27] But Thomas didn't want to join the band so perhaps Berg was already on his way, as in March 1987 he was in the RPM Studios, New York to record 'Short Stories' (Denon). Berg had already collaborated on two Stern albums (Atlantic), but the guitarist remained largely under wraps to project a different group identity, although 'Friday Night At The Cadillac Club' was very much in the image of their Atlantic incarnation under Stern's leadership.

In March 1988 Berg's 'Cycles' (Denon) was perhaps undeservedly put in the shade by Mike Brecker's almost simultaneous release 'Don't Try This At Home' (Impulse); even down to the folksy 'Itsbynne Reel' on the latter and 'Pipes' on the former—comparisons however odious, were inevitable. The 1990 'In The Shadows' (Denon) deferred to Davis on the title track, but is the best focussed of all the Berg/Stern collaborations. Significantly Berg as hard-bopper rather than quick-please-artist was re-emerging; in December 1988 he recorded as a member of Randy Brecker's post-bop quintet on 'Live At Sweet Basil' (Sonet)—his playing fluent and assured, technically and conceptually nonchalant and sideslipping with ease, he was comfortable in an idiom in which he seemed to have much to contribute.

OUTLOOK—GOOD TO CLOUDY: WEATHER REPORT

Weather Report was launched in 1971 to wild enthusiasm from the CBS press department, show-biz brouhaha and even a lengthy encomium on the sleeve of their first release by the then president of CBS, Clive Davis. Their early albums were masterpieces of collective improvisation; spurts of melody might come from any instrument and there was little difference between soloist and accompanist—although one player might briefly stand out he would suddenly be re-absorbed into the overall sound texture. On their third album, the 1973 'Sweetnighter' (CBS), texture was integrated into sweeping orchestral tone poems, featuring the compositions of the two co-leaders, **Joe Zawinul** (b.1932) on keyboards and **Wayne Shorter** (b.1933) on tenor and soprano saxophones.

Weather Report developed into one of the most accomplished jazz units of the 1970s. Its existence continued into the 1980s—the only band from the beginnings of jazz-rock to do so—managing to sustain a level of artistic integrity unusual in the genre. All the band's albums charted in the top 200 in the USA, making them the most successful fusion group of all, the benchmark by which other groups in the idiom were judged.

Weather Report, one of the most accomplished jazz units of the 1970s continued until 1985. (L to R) Joe Zawinul, Jose Rossy, Wayne Shorter, Omar Hakim and Victor Bailey.

Zawinul was a master of electronic keyboards, although it was not until 1973's 'Sweetnighter' (CBS), their third album, that he first used a synthesizer on record; one of the first musicians to successively master the ring modulator, Arp, Prophet and Oberheim Polyphonic synthesizers, the sheer variety electronic tones and textures he created were neither artifice nor veneer but ensemble colours of depth and resource. But his virtuosity had, by the end of the '70s, increasingly marginalized the rest of the band—including co-leader Shorter.

'Night Passage' (CBS), the band's tenth album from 1980, included a variety of approaches; neo-classical (Ellington's 'Rockin' In Rhythm'), post-bop ('Night Passage' and 'Fast City'), world music ('Port Of Entry' and 'Madagascar') and tone poems ('Three Views Of A Secret', 'Forlorn' and 'Dream Clock'). It scripted the band's manifesto for the 1980s, a pace only forced by past achievements. The stunning electric bass virtuoso Jaco Pastorius played a less dominant role than in the '70s while Peter Erskine (d) was never less than a model of good taste. 1982's 'Weather Report' (CBS) suggested a slackening of momentum and creative tension; even the exuberant Pastorius was sidelined by Zawinul synths. After a ten-month lay-off the co-leaders re-emerged with a re-vamped line-up.

In June 1982 the band introduced Victor Bailey (b), Omar Hakim (d) and Jose Rossy (perc) at the Playboy Jazz Festival at Hollywood. However, they were confronted with an artistic dilemma; their 1981 appearance was followed by what promoter George Wein described as, 'one of the greatest ovations I have ever witnessed in my many years of presenting concerts.'[28] What to do in 1982? The group found the answer by bringing on unannounced and unexpected Manhattan Transfer, who had turned 'Birdland' from 'Heavy Weather' (CBS) into an unexpected '80s hit, for a one-off collaboration. Together with 'Volcano For Hire', a welcome expose of Shorter's talent, they form part of 'In Performance At The Playboy Jazz Festival' (Elektra Musician).

The 1983 'Procession' (CBS) featured a backdrop of World Music, with a minor latterday WR classic in 'The Peasant'. Zawinul's introduction of a vocoder, another tonal dimension in the electronic soundscape, became a novelty item that cropped up on all his subsequent albums. The 1984 'Domino Theory' (CBS) charts the ascendance of Hakim whose dominant personality fed Zawinul in the same way as Pastorius used to in the '70s, his influence apparent on the driving 'D flat Waltz'. A brilliant technician, Hakim's verve went some way to compensating for the increasingly mysterious humility of Wayne Shorter. Paradoxically, a concert highlight at this time was a duo performance by Zawinul and Shorter of indeterminate length, a model of empathy and spontaneous improvisation, highlighting just how close musically and spiritually they were.

'Sportin' Life' (CBS) from 1985 saw a small renaissance in Shorter's involvement, co-producing and contributing two compositions. Zawinul's continuing love affair with the vocoder resulted in a small vocal contingent headed by Bobby McFerrin being drafted in to bolster his Martian-sounding vocal efforts. Rossy's replacement, percussionist, guitarist, accordion player and vocalist Mino Cinelu, performed 'Confians'.

But by then the partnership that had lasted 15 albums and almost 15 years ended, 'We shook hands and agreed to go our separate ways for a while,' said Shorter. 'He [Zawinul] wanted to work on a one-man-band approach.' But their contract with CBS called for one more album. Due to schedule conflicts, Peter Erskine returned at the end of 1985 to replace Omar Hakim and ended up co-producing 'This Is This' (CBS). With Shorter absent for most of side one, Carlos Santana (g) was called in to overdub. By then the most successful fusion band of all had run its course.

Zawinul's attempt to become his own Weather Report came with the 1985 'Dia-a-lects' (CBS), with Bobby McFerrin heading up yet another vocal group, but it lacked the economy and compositional wisdom of the 1971 'Zawinul' (Atlantic), the previous album under his own name. Zawinul toured in the summer of that year as a single, but in 1986 continued as 'Weather Update', a group with guitarist Steve Khan in place of Shorter. 'My experience with Weather Update . . . ended up being Maiden Voyage and Farewell Tour all at once,' said Khan. '. . . There was no new music, no Weather Update music. There was just whatever Joe [Zawinul] selected, which was not exactly the richest material from Weather Report.'

In 1988 the formation of The Zawinul Syndicate, with the formidable guitar technician Scott Henderson, a faculty member of the Guitar Institute of Technology in Los Angeles, marked a more commercial approach. 1988's 'The Immigrants' (CBS) and the 1989 'Black Water', both with pop vocals, continued a direction begun with 'Can't Be Done', a dreary pop vocal by Willie Tee from 'The Domino Theory' (CBS), where Zawinul's skill in manipulating sounds seemed more important than content, with every instrumental sound coming from the keyboard. With the Syndicate, Zawinul's music moved into the orbit of MOR and FM airplay, the leader consumed with electronic gadgetry.

The assertion that Shorter was one of the finest tenor/soprano saxophonists in jazz would be difficult to argue from his recorded output during the 1980s, since when he came to perform and record under his own name, the results were a disappointment. His first album since the 1975 'Native Dancer' (CBS) was 1985's 'Atlantis' (CBS), with classical flautist Jim Walker, who played with both the group Free Flight and the Los Angeles Philharmonic, plus a female glee club.

By 1986 Shorter's touring group included Mitch Forman (k), Gary Willis (b) and Tom Brechtlein (d), later replaced by Terri Lyn Carrington, but failed to convince. Equally, 1987's 'Phantom Navigator' (CBS) and 1988's 'Joy Ryder' (CBS) were a disappointment, their shadowy exoticism an eliptical excursion into New Age-isms.

Shorter, it seemed, was not so much a leader as a follower. His most creative work came in the shadow of strong leaders to whom he committed himself for long periods. From 1959-63 he was a member of Art Blakey's Jazz Messengers, from 1964-70 he was with Miles Davis, from 1971-85 he seemed in the shadow of Joe Zawinul and in 1988 he toured and recorded with another strong leader, guitarist Carlos Santana. But during the '80s his profound melodic sense and involuted logic were best framed not in fusion but with Michel Petrucciani on his 'The Power Of Three' (Blue Note), Buster Williams's 1989 evocation of the Miles Davis '60's acoustic quintet, 'Something More' (In + Out) and the excellent 'Tribute To Coltrane' (Paddlewheel). Here, challenged by Dave Liebman (ss), he responded with his finest and most emotionally committed playing of the decade.

STEPS AND STEPS AHEAD

Steps was formed in 1979 by the vibraphonist Mike Mainieri (b.1938), initially an acoustic band with Mike Brecker (ts), Don Grolnick (p), Eddie Gomez (b) and Steve Gadd (d). Billed as the Mike Mainieri Quintet their performances at 'Seventh Avenue South', New York attracted considerable public interest, 'Once the word got out, you couldn't get into the place,' said Mainieri. 'These record executives from Japan came down, checked us out and offered us a contract to record in Japan.'

Assuming the name Steps they recorded 'Step By Step' at Nippon Columbia Studios on 8-10 December 1980 and 'Smokin' In The Pit' (both Better Days), a live double album, at Roppongi Pit Inn four days later. At the time the band were playing largely straight ahead jazz, but their integrated performances and ability to handle tension and release created moments of genuine excitement and creative drama. Brecker's work, sympathetically backed by Gadd, placed these albums in the top quartile of the early '80s jazz recordings.

When the band returned home, 'That was basically the end of the band,' said Mainieri. 'We came back to New York and everybody went their own way.'[29] Four months later they returned for a successful engagement at Seventh Avenue South and were again invited to Japan to tour and to produce another record. Gadd, unable to tour, was replaced by Peter Erskine, who had just emerged from the revolving rhythm section door of Weather Report. 'Paradox' (Better Days), recorded live at Seventh Avenue in 1981, had less highs than their previous work, the emphasis on careful ensemble dynamics, structure and form, with Grolnick's atmospheric Prophet synthesizer integrating well on 'Four Chords'.

During their tour in Japan the group decided to stay together on a permanent basis, and arranged for dates through Hawaii, the Coast and the Middle West to take them back to New York. 'But that didn't really count,' said Eddie Gomez, 'we had no record out, no road manager . . .' and each member was responsible for setting up and transporting his own equipment. On their return they enlarged their repertoire and completed further tours, including Europe. Although still involved in session work, Brecker, one of the most in-demand of all studio musicians said: 'The advantage for me is expression. The ability to express things, emotions, things musically you can't just do any other way.'

Steps, sophisticated and progressive, as an acoustic band it was earmarked as a 'band of the '80s'. (L to R) Eddie Gomez, Mike Mainieri, Peter Erskine and Mike Brecker.

In 1982 Grolnick was replaced by the Brazilian pianist Eliane Elias and when the band finally secured a Stateside recording contract, after three years of trying, the name of the band had to be changed to Steps Ahead for copyright reasons—a bar-room group in the deep South had registered the name first. 'Steps Ahead' (Elektra Musician) was issued in 1983. The sound was clean-cut, sharply defined and scrupulously attentive to detail, with standout cuts on 'Pools', 'Islands' and 'Both Sides Of the Coin' that prompted critics to dub their music a 'new acoustic fusion'. The band had developed a wholly individual identity quite different to anything else in jazz; sophisticated and progressive it was earmarked as 'The band of the '80s.'

Much of the material from their eponymously titled album was featured on their subsequent tour to Europe in 1983, their Copenhagen concert videoed by Titania Television, 'Steps Ahead Live In Copenhagen'. However, the band continued to experience difficulty in obtaining regular work. 'Nobody took us seriously as a band,' said Mainieri. 'Even that first album on Elektra was only a rumour. It sold 20,000 copies worldwide. It was still difficult even when that was released to get bookings and find agents.'

A drastic change of musical direction came with 'Modern Times' (Elektra Musician) from early 1984. Warren Bernhardt came in on keyboards and Chuck Loeb guested on guitar as the band actively pursued an electronic fusion in the Weather Report idiom. It helped solve their identity problem, becoming a best-seller, but their unique acoustic poise was immediately sacrificed for an electronic fundamentalism that prompted the departure of Eddie Gomez after the album was released, 'Gomez left the band because he felt he couldn't contribute as much as we needed. That was his point of view, not ours,' said Mainieri. However, the integrity of the band largely remained intact, it was just that they were now operating several decibels higher, the energy level more immediate and in a climate of rock/world rhythms à la WR.

In 1985 they composed and arranged all the music on Jane Fonda's 'Prime Time Workout' album and video and by the time they recorded their 1986 release 'Magnetic' (Elektra) the transformation into an energetic electronic band was complete. Mainieri featured his synthi-vibes, Brecker his Steiner EWI and bassist Victor Bailey underpinned the ensemble with funk lines. On numbers like 'Trains', 'Beirut' and 'Sumo', Steps Ahead suggested that it was capable of taking over the mantle of electronic respectability that endeared Weather Report to jazz audiences. By summer 1986 the band included Brecker, Mike Stern, ex-Miles Davis

MILES AND THE FUSION JUNTA • 165

bassist Daryl Jones, ex-Journey drummer Steve Smith and Mainieri. 'The band is just so fiery now,' said Brecker, 'we're talking about doing a live album next because we want to capture that high-energy thing that happens on stage every night.'

Sadly, the live album did not materialize* and by 1987 the band had gone their separate ways. In 1989 Mainieri revived the concept, this time not as a co-operative but with himself as leader. 'N.Y.C.' (EMI/Intuition) had Steve Smith, ex-King Crimson bassist Tony Levin, Steve Khan (g) and Bendik Hofseth (t), and for touring had Smith and Hofseth with Rachel Nicalazzo (k), Jimi Tunnell (g) and Victor Bailey (b). Their approach was not too far removed from the music several electronic bands were producing on New Age albums, a world music/jazz/rock amalgam, and with less space for the soloists, who were capable but lacked the riveting power of a Brecker, the attraction of the band diminished.

Steps and Steps Ahead never really achieved their potential even though their recorded legacy, particularly their first four albums, suggested a band of considerable importance was about to emerge in the post-fusion confusion of the early '80s. It was not for lack of commitment on behalf of the members, who forsook safe studio work to tour, even humping their gear themselves. In an interview in 1984, Mainieri had definite views on why the band was not getting what he considered their just desserts, 'The critics pretty much ignore this band and these musicians. We've had no review or recognition in the *Village Voice* or the *New York Times*. We were in *Downbeat,* but the press has generally taken an offhand kind of attitude, because we're just problems. Mike Brecker is an example—he hardly ever gets reviewed. If he was black and playing the same thing, he'd be the new genius.'[30]

PAT METHENY

Pat Metheny (b.1954) arrived in 1978 when his album 'The Pat Metheny Group' became a jazz best-seller. Since then he staked out what was in jazz terms at least, a considerable popular following, something he was quick to put into perspective—'I went to see The Police, I think it was at Shea Stadium . . . I know how many people were there and I know how much they paid to get in, and I realized their gross for that one gig was probably more than we'll gross in maybe five years.'[31]

---

*'Live in Tokoyo 1986' (NYC Records), released in 1994, was a disappointment.

Metheny was a child prodigy, teaching guitar at the University of Miami at 17 and a faculty member at Berklee at 19. He joined the Gary Burton Quartet in 1974, and debuted as a leader with the trio 'Bright Size Life' (ECM) in 1976 while still with Burton. He formed The Pat Metheny Group in 1977 and despite the group's subsequent success remained ingenuously unaffected by popularity. In essence a collaboration with ex-Woody Herman keyboard player Lyle Mays, The Pat Metheny Group created a non-threatening, romantic, almost Brahmsian sound-scape interpolated with breezy, sometimes intricate, sometimes folksy good humour firmly based on a high standard of musicianship and group interplay.

The 1979 'American Garage' (ECM), *Cashbox's* Top Jazz Album of 1980, had Mays, Mark Egan (b) and Dan Gottlieb (d); dedicated to embryo groups getting it together in the family garage, the title track was intentionally biased in favour of rock rhythm patterns but the 'The Epic' purposefully strides out into blowing territory, even if the cadences are a little cute. '80/81' (ECM) recorded in 1980 is an excellent collaboration with saxophonists Dewey Redman and Mike Brecker, Charlie Haden (b) and Jack DeJohnette (d), and was awarded the Preis der Deutschen

Pat Metheny, his group created a non-threatening, romantic, almost Brahmsian soundscape interpolated with breezy sometimes intricate, sometimes folksy good humour, firmly based on a high standard of musicianship and group interplay.

Schallplatten Kritik in 1981. Although two tracks received FM airplay, 'Every Day' and 'Goin' Ahead', the album alluded to Metheny's love of Ornette Coleman, directly, through the Coleman composition 'Turnaround' and obliquely, through Metheny's own 'The Bat' and 'Pretty Scattered'; 'To me Ornette is one of the most melodic musicians ever,' he said. 'It's not the same kind of melodies that you would find from somebody like Chet Baker or Wes Montgomery or something, and it doesn't fall in the usual cadences, but what kills me about Ornette is that he can't play anything that isn't melodic.'[32]

Intentionally evocative, full of pastel moods and atmospheric episodes, 'As Falls Wichita, So Falls Wichita Falls' (ECM) from 1981 arrived at New Age symbolism at a time when the Windham Hill label was taking off, although Metheny rejected that handle being put on his music. 'We wanted to try something where the improvisation happened not so much in a linear sense as a textural sense,' he explained. The Grammy winning 'Offramp' (ECM), from October 1981, introduced bassist Steve Rodby and Metheny's first recorded use on record of the Roland GR300 Series guitar synthesizer and the Synclavier. His best-selling album, it rolled with the punches when critics accused him of a homogenized approach with the diversity of material that satisfied his more temperate listeners and yet managed to rattle the bars of a few cages with the title track.

Recorded live in July, October and November 1982, 'Travels' (ECM) presented concert versions of several of his popular favourites, demonstrating just why they had become popular favourites; free from sharp edges and strong on lilting melodicism they remained finely crafted for all that. It was balanced by 'Rejoicing' (ECM) from November 1983, a trio session with Haden and Billy Higgins (d) that included three Ornette Coleman tunes that recalled his debut album (with two Coleman originals) and looked forward to 1985's 'Song X' (Geffen) with an energized original 'The Calling'.

1984's 'First Circle' (ECM) with his Group, had Paul Wertico (d) and Pedro Aznar drafted in to create a suitably authentic Brazilian backdrop. A Grammy winner and Metheny's favourite album, it demonstrated his music was constantly being refined and moved forward, its compositional design remaining accessible whilst providing an effective context in which to focus his playing.

Metheny had previously provided the soundtrack for a low-budget movie 'Little Sister' when in 1985 he and Lyle Mays combined with David Bowie, a boys choir and the National Philharmonic to provide the music for the John Schlesinger film 'The Falcon And The Snowman' that included Bowie's Top 20 hit, 'This Is Not America'. Cries of sell-out were strangled at birth with the December 1985 'Song X' (Geffen) with Ornette Coleman, Charlie Haden, Jack DeJohnette and Denardo Coleman. 'It was a fantastic experience,' said Metheny, 'making the record and especially the tour afterwards.' Powerful, uncompromising and raw it left some of his audience shell-shocked and others crying for more, selling in the process over 200,000 copies,[33] amazing sales for an avant album.

The 1987 album 'Still Life Talking' (Geffen) continued Metheny's ability to mix electronic and acoustic instruments and come up with a homogenized whole that was able to surprise in its range and colour. Now drawing on the wordless vocals introduced earlier in the decade by Nana Vasconcelos, it evoked Brazilian soundscapes. 'I'm kind of becoming an honorary Brazilian,' Metheny said, 'I spend all my time there and I've had a Brazilian girlfriend for about a year or so.'[34] As with the Grammy winning 'Letter From Home' (Geffen) from 1989, his music remained relatively free from the shadow of commercial excess, succeeding in moving to higher grounds where his artistic integrity remained relatively intact.

As ever it was Metheny's playing that gave his romantic flights focus, soaring beyond the limitations of the material in a way the finest improvisers are able to do. Despite his technical mastery, Metheny sought to simplify, distilling his playing into the very essence of his style, although there were moments when the harder edge he brought to 'The Calling' and 'Song X' might have made him appear less the school know-it-all who got it right all the time.

CHICK COREA

Chick Corea (b.1941) was one of the most popular crossover artists of the 1970s. But before adopting an overtly commercial stance with his electronic version of 'Return To Forever', he had demonstrated, along with Keith Jarrett and Herbie Hancock, that he was among the leading pianists of his generation. His 1968 'Now He Sings, Now He Sobs', reissued in the 1980s by the reactivated Blue Note label, was in its time highly influential and studied closely by young musicians. However, his fusion bands with guitarists Bill Connors and Al DiMeola and bassist Stanley Clarke were prime movers in bringing a new meaning to the slick and vacuous. Several devices the band used became widely imitated by aspiring fusion groups, such as the bass doubling the melody line. When Corea and his sidemen went their separate ways it was to pursue careers as glossy improvisers on the fringes of rock, pop and jazz, their success based more on the promotion of personal style and virtuosity than content or meaning.

As fusion began collapsing under the weight of its own pretensions at the end of the '70s, Corea had become so associated with the genre that a free pardon back to the realms of acoustic jazz was impossible. Nevertheless, in tune with the times he involved himself in a variety of acoustic projects, including duets with Gary Burton and Herbie Hancock, solo recitals a la Keith Jarrett, a myriad of Mickey Mouse indulgences made possible by the ECM label, performances of Mozart and his own concerto in three movements for piano and orchestra.

Akoustic Bands

The October 1979 duet with Gary Burton, 'In Concert, Zurich' (ECM) showed Corea's acoustic playing could by no means be written off on the strength of his work as a fusion mercenary, while 'Three Quartets' (Warner Bros), from 1981 with Mike Brecker, Eddie Gomez and Steve Gadd in peak form, remains one of the most underrated albums of the early 1980s. 'Quartet No. 2, part 2', dedicated to John Coltrane, was the high spot of the album with a superb example of modern tenor saxophone playing by Brecker and Corea really *playing*.

The double album 'Trio Music' was a 1981 rematch of 'Now He Sings, Now He Sobs' lineup from 1969, with Miroslav Vitous and Roy Haynes. By any standards it was a spectacular reunion and a demonstration of Corea's piano aesthetic that had taken account of Bud Powell, Bill Evans and McCoy Tyner on the one hand and 20th-century modernists such as Bartok on the other. One album was devoted to spontaneous improvisation and group interaction and the second an exploration of several Monk compositions. 'Trio Music Live In Europe' (ECM) from 1984, was a further reminder that Corea's talent could not be denied, although his *art nouveau* noodlings on 'Prelude No. 2' was a reminder that his eclecticism often pulled in several directions at once, threatening to undermine his credibility.

Corea was also a member of the Griffith Park Band in the early '80s, which in the light of subsequent developments was just ahead of its time. A post-bop unit revolving around Freddie Hubbard (t), Joe Henderson (ts), Stanley Clarke (acoustic bass) and Lenny White (d), 'The Griffith Park Collection' (Elektra Musician) was a studio album, and as Lenny White pointed out, 'The first time in six years Stanley, Chick and I have played together on record . . . though we're noted for playing electric music.'[35] 'Griffith Park Collection 2: In Concert' (Elektra Musician) from 1982 had moments of excellence from all the participating musicians and had the project been sustained throughout the decade the group might have provided a touchstone for many emerging young musicians. 'Echoes Of An Era' with vocalist Chaka Khan and 'Echoes Of An Era 2' with Nancy Wilson (both Elektra Musician) falter through the well-meaning but inadequate vocalists.

The Grammy winning 'The Akoustic Band' (GRP) released in 1989 was a trio with Elektric band rhythm mates John Patitucci (acoustic bass) and Dave Weckl (ds). Again, Corea showed that with a sympathetic rhythm section he could create at a level few pianists in jazz could equal. The group slotted together well, Weckl and Patitucci sophisticated and contemporary, making Vitous and Haynes a little flat-footed in comparison. If, and only if, Corea was to decide to put his artistic imprimatur on the '90s in a way that he conspicuously failed to do in the '70s and '80s, it needed a sustained burst of creativity suggested by this album to restore his flagging credibility. Clearly, Corea and his musicians were equal to the task, but the leader seemed unaware of the artistic challenge that had begun to loom over a talent so gratuitously dilettantish.

Elektric Bands

Corea's formation of his Elektric Band in 1985 was presaged by something of a fusion revival. The return of Miles Davis encouraged Herbie Hancock, John McLaughlin, Joe Zawinul and Wayne Shorter to return to the flag; equally, countless sub-species of high-tech young musicians MIDI'd up to the hilt from Berklee and the Guitar Institute of Technology were signed by recording companies wanting an angle on this latest glossy variant.

'Again And Again' (Elektra Musician) was a wearying session recorded in South Africa that showed Corea merely dabbling. Encouraged by the success of Herbie Hancock's Rockit tour, Corea emerged with 'The Chick Corea Electrik Band' (GRP) in 1985 with guitar whizz Scott Henderson, John Patitucci (b) and Dave Weckl (d). Despite the technical expertise, catchy rhythms and thorough-going craftsmanship the feeling prevailed that once again Corea was creating a disposable product for a 'throwaway' culture. Nothing of lasting value seemed on offer, something reinforced by 'Light Years' (GRP) that followed, with Eric Marienthal (ts) in for Henderson. 'Light Years' entered the Billboard chart at 15. 'Chick really wanted to go for more radio play with this one,' said Weckl. A year later came 'Eye Of The Beholder' (GRP) and the introduction of a Midi piano into Corea's fusion soup, followed by the 1989 'Inside Out' (GRP). But as with the electronic 'Return To Forever' a decade earlier, his music appeared as a cynical manipulation of his talent, if not aimed at the lowest common denominator then certainly the widest possible catchment.

CONTINUUM: FUSION AS POPULARIZER

Towards the end of the '80s, fusion seemed to assume a life of its own. Gifted musicians and their product emerged to compete in a marketplace that seemed to put more and more emphasis on electronic flash than substance. The GRP label, for example, gradually signed up a whole stable of glossy practitioners, including the Rippingtons, Lee Ritenour, Tom Scott, Billy Cobham, Mark Egan and Dave Benoit all eager to accumulate rock-style capital gains, and that was just the tip of the iceberg. Small labels like Passport Jazz and Frog and majors like Atlantic, MCA and CBS joined the celebration of technical excess.

But nothing seemed to compare to the early fusion bands who had learnt from Jimi Hendrix and John Coltrane in the early '70s. The elemental power of the early Mahavishnu Orchestra or Tony Williams' Lifetime had been replaced by a jejune repetition of triplets, double-stops, unisons and a heavy handed use of the wang bar in sanitized digital perfection. Although Tony Williams' 'Emergency' (Verve) rivalled Plastic Ono's album for sound quality, there was no doubting that at the time it was at the cutting edge of the idiom. But in the '80s multi-tracking increasingly allowed for second-guessing and spontaneity seemed less important than an exposition of technique.

Jean-Luc Ponty (b.1942) was a formidable technician, his violin replacing Jerry Goodman's in the 1974 version of the Mahavishu Orchestra. Later Ponty became a regular member of Frank Zappa's cast, appearing on, amongst others, 'Hot Rats' (Reprise), a successful jazz-rock album whose mention still tends to be infra dig in jazz circles. Ponty was a supreme craftsman, and while none of his '80s albums suggested anything like the excitement he could generate in live performance, they nevertheless included glimpses of his lyrical and imaginative improvisations. Albums such as 'Individual Choice' (Atlantic) from 1983, 'Open Mind' (Atlantic), 'Fables' (Atlantic) and 1987's 'The Gift Of Time' (CBS) are controlled and exacting in their pursuit of relentless technical perfection. They were at odds with December 1978's 'Live' (Atlantic), with the muscle-flexing 'Egocentral Molecules' that raised the roof in the way Mahavishnu used to do—and Ponty

Jean-Luc Ponty, a formidable technician.

could still see his way clear to do live, even in 1988, with like-minded cohorts Wally Minko, Jamib Glasser, Baron Brown and Rayford Griffin.

Dave Sanborn (b.1945) was probably the most imitated alto saxophonist of the 1980s. His style was fashionable, including appearances on albums by The Rolling Stones, Stevie Wonder, James Taylor, Paul Simon, David

Bowie, Steely Dan, Bruce Springsteen and Gil Evans. But Sanborn did not consider himself a jazz musician, 'What experience I've had in playing jazz has been pretty sporadic; most of it was working with Gil Evans,' he said. Even so, his style was widely admired by jazz musicians for his fluency and expressivity.

Sanborn's tone was steeped in the blues and his solos could be ringing and passionate, particularly when soaring over a funky R&B background. His albums were careful not to over-expose this more potent side of his musical personality, so the extent of his soaring power live remained more promise deferred than selling feature. The 1981 Grammy winning 'Voyeur' (Warner Bros), along with 'Taking Off' (Warner Bros), are good examples of his work.

It is tempting to say his 1980s output was more of the same, but his playing continued to grow in complexity; 'Hideaway', 'As We Speak', among the dreaded synthi-drums on 'Backstreet', the live-in-the-studio 'Straight From The Heart' and 'A Change Of Heart' (all Warner Brothers) and the 1988 'Close-Up' (Reprise) all sold at least 250,000 copies with each new release, reflecting Sanborn's wide appeal, 'I'm a romanticist,' confessed bebop master James Moody, 'I love David's sound . . . I like his vibrato.'

Spyro Gyra continued throughout the '80s quietly expanding their following and, with the demise of Weather Report became the longest established of the regular touring fusion bands. Originally members of the musical collective The Buffalo Jazz Ensemble, they put themselves on the map with 'The Shaker Song' from 'Spyro Gyra' (Amherst) in 1978 followed by 'Morning Dance' (Infinity) in 1979. By the mid-1980s saxophonist Jay Beckstein had assumed leadership and in 1983 vibeist Dave Samuels, after a couple of album appearances, joined the band to tour, which the band did extensively throughout the '80s.

Spyro Gyra's attraction was the easy virtuosity of Beckstein and Samuels but their albums often sacrificed a true group identity by importing studio musicians. At times they rather desperately sought sales by working their jazz-rock-Latin formula ruthlessly; 'Carnival', 'Freetime', 'Incognito', 'City Kids' 'Access All Areas', 'Alternating Currents' and 'Breakout' (all MCA) failed to have the depth and emotional clout of some of the best Weather Report albums, but live, their particular forte, they almost appeared to be one of the better fusion bands of the '80s.

The Yellowjackets had power guitarist Robben Ford in their early days but he left after appearing on the group's first two albums, their 1981 debut 'Yellowjackets' (Warner Bros) and the 1983 Grammy nominated 'Mirage A Trois' (Warner Bros). After the demise of Weather Report, their style, a rhythm and blues-jazz amalgam, pushed them to the fore-front of fusion groups and by the end of the 1980s could be counted among the most successful.

Bassist Jimmy Haslip (b.1951) and Russell Ferrante (b.1952) were foun-der members and were joined by Sanborn sound-alike, ex-Tower Of Power altoist Marc Russo (b.1957) for 'Samurai Samba' (Warner Bros). The 1986 'Shades' (MCA), perhaps their 'jazziest' album with the Sanborn feel up-front, was mostly recorded live and saw their original drummer Ricky Lawson replaced by Will Kennedy (b.1960). Later in the year the group were added to the soundtrack 'Star Trek IV'. 1987's 'Four Corners' (MCA) was their best album of the decade; integrated, professional with their own group sound, a wry balance of commercialism and friction. The Grammy winning 'Politics' (MCA) from 1988 did not sit in any specific groove, but was sure footed without being sensational, optimistic without being pretentious, perhaps the key to the best fusion. However, 1989's 'The Spin' (MCA) aimed for an acoustic groove underpinned by their love of jazz, and seemed honest if not wholly successful.

Drummer **Steve Gadd** (b.1945) was, like Dave Sanborn, one of the most imitated players of the decade. Gadd was perhaps the ultimate session musician, and such was the regard he was held in by his peers that any average radio station in the Western world included several numbers with his drumming on a daily basis.

His own albums, however, were disappointing, particularly 'Gaddabout' (Projazz). The Gadd Gang, formed in 1985, was a group that from time to time appeared in New York and appeared on the festival circuits in Japan and Europe. Including Richard Tee (k), Cornell Dupree (g), Eddie Gomez (b) and Ronnie Cuber (bs), the 1986 'Gadd Gang' (CBS) did include some successful tracks, particularly the Bob Dylan number 'Watching The River Flow', with a groove reminiscent of the group Stuff, which had included Gadd, Tee and Dupree during the late '70s and early '80s. The 'groove' was a speciality of Stuff, and Gadd's gang were drafted in *in toto* on albums such as Carla Bley's 'Dinner Music' (Watt) and Dianne Schuur's 'Talkin' 'Bout You' (GRP) to create that 'feel' to order. However an album of soul tunes, 'Here & Now' (Epic) from 1988 was dire, and with the exception of the 'groove' track 'Things Ain't What They Used To Be' unintentionally comic, particularly a version of 'Them Changes' which sounded like a hotel band.

Grover Washington (b.1943) was asked by Creed Taylor to overdub Hank Crawford's solos on 'Inner City Blues' (Motown) in 1973. The album was released under Washington's name and was a huge success. From then on the die was cast, soul-jazz and Washington became synonymous and with five gold albums (sales of 500,000 plus) that topped the jazz, R&B and pop charts and his 1980 'Winelight', a double Grammy winner, going platinum with sales of over a million, Washington was the best-selling jazz-based musician of the 1980s.

For many, Washington's albums were a first step into jazz; his playing, equally adept on flute, soprano, alto, tenor and baritone, has, within the carefully circumscribed commercial boundaries of his work, always maintained a quiet integrity. 'Everything, regardless of whether its a hook or not should be creative,' he said. 'We just try to maintain our personal standards through whatever we have to do. Sometimes you can't do what you want to do.'

Washington was an accomplished musician, something that was more apparent in live performance than record; his 1982 performance of 'Winelight' on 'In Performance At The Playboy Jazz Festival' (Elektra Musician) was a good example of how, within the constrictions of his commercial style, he could be both creative and convincing. His large discography was remarkably consistent; the CTI/Kudu albums from the 1970s were reissued by Motown in the '80s, while his 1980s' work appeared on Elektra and the CBS label.

Although his work was biased towards easy listening and FM airplay, he did take time out to appear in a jazz setting with 'Togethering' (Blue Note) from 1985 with Kenny Burrell (g) and sidemen Jack DeJohnette, Ron Carter and Ralph McDonald. It was the first time Washington had appeared in a straight-ahead environment for years.

Stanley Jordan's (b.1959) big break came in the summer of 1984 when unannounced he opened for Wynton Marsalis at Avery Fisher Hall during the Kool Jazz Festival and caused a sensation with his guitar playing. He was soon booked into the Village Vanguard and was signed up by Blue Note records, with the subsequent 'Magic Touch' (Blue Note) leaping to the top of Billboard's jazz and pop charts, where it remained for almost a year.

The reason was Jordan's unique 'hammering-on' technique whereby the fingers of both hands were used to strike the strings on the fretboard of his retuned Travis Bean guitar to produce the sound of two and three guitars in dialogue. It allowed him to simultaneously cover a bass line while comping *and* soloing. Hence the solemn pronouncements on the liner of 'Magic Touch' denying any musical legerdemain, and affirmations from the likes of Quincy Jones and George Benson that Jordan was the best thing to happen to the jazz guitar since the batch was pushed through the bacon slicer.

However, as with his self-produced debut album, 'Touch Sensitive' (Tangent), 'Magic Touch' was hampered by Jordan's choice of material, his rather mundane original compositions and numbers such as 'Eleanor Rigby' which gave the impression of a demo disc. Live, his style was initially mesmerizing but having created a style, Jordan used it to the full. While the complexity of what he was achieving meant occasional mis-struck notes he filled his lines to overflowing, cramming in as many notes in the manner of one of his main influences, Art Tatum, occasionally upsetting his tempo in the process. By playing on the guitar's fretboard and thus away from the pick-ups his tone was thin and metallic, and his fast runs irresistibly brought to mind Les Paul's 'Lover' (Capitol), with its guitar recorded at double speed.

The 1986 *a cappella* 'Standards Vol. 1' (Blue Note) was revealing in Jordan's choice of material, suggesting his sensibilities extended well beyond jazz with numbers such as 'Sound Of Silence', 'Sunny', 'Moon River'

George Benson, whose vocals took over from his brilliant guitar playing, 'a master musician content to let a prodigious talent languish in the service of commercial ends'.

and 'Guitar Man'. 1988's 'Flying Home' (Manhattan) was pure pop-jazz; Jordan, it seemed, promised much and delivered little.

George Benson's (b.1943) commercial success effectively removed him from the consciousness of jazz audiences and media, but the fact remained he was probably one of the finest guitarists in jazz during the '80s. But with the 1976 'Breezin'' (Warner Bros) everything changed and, like Wes Montgomery before him, left the orbit of jazz for the secure lifestyle his accessible, jazz-influenced, MOR style brought. His jazz legacy, albums such as 'It's Uptown', 'Cookbook' and 'Blue Benson', receded into the past as his popularity increased.

Jazz, however, still exerted a powerful pull on Benson, [it's] my favourite music because it gives me more freedom than anything else,' he said. 'But me recording jazz wouldn't make any sense to radio programmers. I know what they're thinking. That's why I'm alive and other cats ain't . . . .'[36] Benson, however, often took his red Mercedes convertible into New York to check the scene and sit in; playing with Jimmy Raney at Bradley's, jamming at the Blue Note with Bobby McFerrin, Jon Hendricks and Al Jarreau, sitting in at Salt Peanuts in the Bronx and jamming at Duke's Place in Harlem with his former boss Jack McDuff, whom he had join him on his 1988 touring schedule for a miniature jazz set among the commercial offerings.

On record, Benson's forays into jazz were few; among the best were two superb tracks on Dexter Gordon's 1981 'Gotham City' (CBS) and a more subdued session with Jimmy Smith 'Keep On Comin'' (Elektra Musician). In 1985 he appeared in a tribute to John Hammond at Avery Fisher Hall and in 1989 he joined in the Benny Goodman Tribute at Carnegie Hall—he had appeared on several television programmes with Goodman and BG's 1975 album 'Seven Come Eleven' (CBS).

Benson's commercial albums, the 1979 'Livin' Inside Your Love', 1983's 'In Your Eyes', 1985's '20/20' with the popular Bobby Darin hit 'Beyond The Sea', 1986's 'When The City Sleeps', the Grammy nominated 'Collaboration' with Earl Klugh from 1987 and the 1988 'Twice The Love' (all Warner Bros) all have brief moments of his guitar, tantalizing glimpses of a profound talent amid the commercial niceties. 'It served only to confirm the impression of a master musician content to let a prodigous talent languish in the service of commercial ends,' rued *The Times*.[37]

Kenny Gorelick (b.1957) grew up in Seattle, listening to Grover Washington albums and learning tenor sax. While in high school he played with Barry White's Love Unlimited Orchestra and was with Jeff Lorber's Fusion from 1979-82. As Kenny G he debuted on Arista in 1982 with an eponymously titled album, and with the follow up, 'G Force' (Arista) he sold 200,000 copies. An uncomplicated R&B based fusion, Kenny G's style on tracks like 'Wanna be Young' was tight and created a firm groove ideal for FM airplay. But both albums, and the subsequent 'Gravity' (Arista) were not served well by the vocal tracks. 'This wasn't working, trying to get a vocal hit on an instrumental record,' said Gorelick.

With 'Duotones' (Arista) Kenny G entered the bigtime, an album hit and success for the single off it, 'Songbird', which demonstrated the fluid, melodic qualities that made his style popular, and surprise, surprise, on a commercial cut, sheets of sound and circular breathing! 'On "Songbird" . . . there's a solo inside the context of the song that's as legitimate as anything anybody's done in the bebop bag,' he said. 'Same kind of licks but they happen to flow in a contemporary situation. I don't want to repeat the past licks of John Coltrane and Charlie Parker. That's all that is, when you hear a young guy playing today, playing bebop . . . technically it might be unbelievable, but what's he contributing?' The same question might well be asked, however, of Kenny G.

During the 1970's the fusion between jazz-rock, or perhaps more accurately jazz and R&B, was the most commonly performed variant of jazz. By the 1980s countless established greats in jazz had recorded in the idiom, from Dizzy Gillespie to Buddy Rich and from Stan Getz to Freddie Hubbard. Much was eminently forgettable, aristically superficial and emotionally one-dimensional. But it revolutionized rhythm section playing; even on the elementary chord sequences not uncommon in fusion, drummers, and more particularly bass players, created increasingly complex rhythmic patterns and there was an obvious carry-over into the jazz mainstream.

Established acoustic bassists such as Ray Brown and Ron Carter became adept at playing an electric bass and for drummers, independent co-ordination was an essential discipline more than ever hard earned. The best young drummers that emerged during the 1980s were just as proficient in straight ahead playing as laying down the funk, indeed, paradoxically, the appeal of fusion was often the exemplary playing of the rhythm sections rather than the front lines. And, as with the swing era, the most popular artists and albums were those with simple, repeating riffs and catchy hooks.

Fusion, although scorned by the purists, in that it seemed to be transforming an art back into a commodity by responding to commercial logic, nevertheless remained what many people commonly perceived to be jazz. It undoubtedly continued to play an important part in bringing elements of jazz to a wide audience and while it could occasionally be creative it often was tiresome, glossy, predictable and ephemeral, 'It's not intellectually intensive music,' said Jay Beckstein of Spyro Gyra, 'For me it's music from the heart. We dance around and smile. We feel good, We're not pensive black men who have suffered. We're happy white kids. We don't have a heavy cosmic message that we're trying to get across.'

6
Post-Bop and Beyond: The Expansion of the Mainstream

THE TERM POST-BOP is a wonderful catch-all, used not so much to describe what a style of music is, more what it isn't. Post-bop isn't free or fusion or hard-bop or mainstream; the very term seems to imply something that reaches beyond category. Post-bop, more label than definition, attaches itself more readily to musicians who have gone through the gateways of knowledge and learning to arrive at a high level of execution and understanding of the jazz improvisationary process. Generally, it was those musicians whose styles emerged from 'pre-Ascension' John Coltrane and 1960s acoustic Miles Davis territory.

Curiously there didn't seem to be such a thing as a convincing *young* post-bop musician; either the generic lineage of their playing seemed directly traceable to other areas of the music or they appeared more as post-modernists rather than post-boppers, with neither individual tone or technique. Post-bop rested most easily with the thirty-somethings; as Dave Liebman, the respected saxophonist and educator pointed out, 'By the mid-30s, by and large, the average serious [jazz] artist in our culture has had approximately ten to 15 years of experience. He is finally technically equipped to be freely creative and truly express his own vision.'[1]

In a decade of the young-and-praised it was often forgotten that many great jazz milestones were not recorded by the new kid on the block; for example, Duke Ellington was 40 when he recorded 'Ko-Ko', Coleman Hawkins was 38 when he recorded 'Body and Soul', Lester Young 30 when he recorded 'Lester Leaps In', John Coltrane 33 when he recorded 'Giant Steps', Miles Davis 33 when he recorded 'Kind of Blue' and so on. Acquiring skill *and* a personal voice took time. It was almost exclusively achieved by assiduous study, practice, assimilation of a variety of performing experiences and, finally, a little inspiration; 'I don't think you really mature, consolidate your ideas, until your 30s,' said Dave Holland, a faculty member of The New England Conservatory and instigator of the renowned Summer Jazz Programme at Banff.

But the time factor involved in a musician reaching artistic maturity often involved the risk of his being regarded as passe by the time he finally cracked it. Jazz audiences, after all, had, until the '80s, been brought up on a series of unrelenting shocks announcing the new. It had become embedded in jazz mythology and for a while during the decade unreasonable expectation was raised with the arrival of each new whizz-kid. The magazine *Record* was almost a lone voice when it pointed out in 1984 that, 'The promising jazz musician becomes a great jazz musician when he finds his own voice, his soul. As Charlie Parker put it, "You can't join the throng 'til you play your own song.' "

Many post-bop musicians were working definitions of what it meant 'to play your own song'; some were celebrated during the 1980s and some were not. Jazz had still to come fully to terms with the fact that by wooing the future it was in danger of overlooking the present. But beyond bop and hard-bop, on the fringes of freedom yet drawing on any number of advanced improvisational devices that extended the boundaries of harmony and rhythm, post-bop included many musicians who flirted with greatness. If it became more apparent during the '80s that collectively their work represented an important and significant area of jazz, it was because others had provided the context.

The bracing aural therapy of **McCoy Tyner's** (b.1938) piano was one of the exhilarating experiences of jazz. Focusing on the epicentre of a Tyner solo could be a hypnotic experience; the percussive, high-tensile attack full of densely layered sound-sheet arpeggios, fast side-slipping runs and thunderous pedal-points with Tyner's hands pounding the keyboard from shoulder height represented one of the great pillars on which the contemporary jazz piano was built. His 1972 'Echoes Of A Friend' (Milestone), for example, was described as 'one of the great solo piano achievements of the seventies.'[2] But Tyner was equally at home organizing ensembles of all sizes, from trios through orchestral works to the orthodox big band of '13th House' from 1980 (Milestone).

During the 1980s however, Tyner's playing seemed to reach a plateau; his style maintaining a series of holding patterns, with some albums less inspired than others. In 1981 he signed with CBS records and, as it not entirely unknown with jazz artists joining that label, saw the quality of his work fall away on the subsequent two albums. His sleeve note on 'Dimensions' (Elektra Musician) from 1984, his first album for almost two years since leaving CBS, was one of relief and gratitude. With a quintet including John Blake (vn) and Gary Bartz (as), Tyner was back on course, but it was a stunning solo performance of 'Prelude To A Kiss' and a powerfully grooving trio version of 'Just In Time' that were the album highlights. Shortly afterwards Tyner reduced his working group to a trio for the first time in his career, with Avery Sharpe (b) and Louis Hayes (d), a group that remained together until 1989.

'Just Feelin'' (Palo Alto) from 1985 was Tyner's first and best trio album of the decade; 'I Didn't Know What Time It Was', a number that had been in his repertoire since the 1968 'Time For Tyner' (Blue Note), opens with a jaunty stride that evoked James P. Johnson before rapidly shifting into gear with Tyner's assault on the changes. The high spot was a commanding version of 'Blues For Basie' with intimidating, rolling chords and surging pedal points that were the hallmarks of his style.

In 1985 Tyner appeared on 'One Night With Blue Note Vol. 2' (Blue Note), a concert celebrating the reactivation of the historic Blue Note label at New York's Town Hall. Tyner performed solo and with a group including Jackie McLean and Woody Shaw. It prompted 'It's About Time' (Blue Note) eight weeks later with McLean, but the results were disappointing. Similarly a reunion with Elvin Jones plus Pharoah Sanders, 'Re-United' (Blackhawk), never seemed to take flight; yet the earlier 'Love and Peace' (Trio), a quintet Jones and Tyner co-led briefly in the early 1980s, was far more successful.

Among the remainder of Tyner's output during the decade was the 1986 'Double Trios' (Denon) that included the 'Latino Suite', a feature during his live performances, in an otherwise lacklustre album. After a rather subdued 1987 'Bon Voyage' (Timeless) things were back on course with 'Live At The Musician's Exchange' (Kingdom) and the 1989 'Live At The Sweet Basil Vols. 1 & 2' (Paddle Wheel) with Aaron Scott (d) replacing Hayes.

'Uptown/Downtown' (Milestone), from 1988, returned to the big band format. 'I wanted to do some traditional stuff without sounding traditional,' said Tyner.[3] Brass heavy—'I . . . liked the sound of french horn and tuba with trombones and trumpets'[4]—'Uptown/Downtown' was a welcome contrast to Tyner's trio output that seemed to be in danger of becoming stuck-in-the-groove. Indeed Tyner relished appearing with the band on its occasional dates and in early 1990 he briefly toured California using West Coast musicians.

However, in 1988 Tyner recorded 'Revelations' (Blue Note), only his second solo album since 'Echoes Of A Friend' (Milestone). He revealed playing of composure, insight and historical perspective, drawing on the bravura Tatum and the flashing runs of Powell, in what was essentially an examination of the standards repertoire. Tyner's playing, with his profound respect for form and structure, was a masterpiece of manipulating the rising line and contrasting it with jarring release. While towards the end of the decade an aspect of post-modern critique was to view Tyner's technique and resounding emotionalism as excessive,[5] it avoided a basic truth that Tyner was perhaps the pre-eminent pianist in jazz, albeit tragically undervalued. At his finest Tyner could be spiritually moving, 'exultant, affirmative and life-enhancing'.[6]

Freddie Hubbard (b.1938) had, since he rose to fame in the early '60s, always had it within him to be the major trumpet voice in jazz. The fact that he continued to suggest this potential throughout the '80s, but yet again failed to make any progress towards achieving what was patently within his grasp was as frustrating as it was mysterious. Somehow Hubbard had become the greatest exponent of the artistic own goal in jazz.

By the 1980s, Hubbard's technical skills remained most assuredly in place, if anything with a fuller, more pleasing tone, but he often fell back on a comfort factor in his playing, a stock of well-worn cliches—albeit his *own* cliches—which overstepped occasional trademarks and became all-pervading architectural points in a number of his solos. But worse, Hubbard loved cross-over music; it is difficult to think of any other major jazz artist who made an album as dire as 'Splash' (CBS), for example. But at least in the '80s he began to play more straight-ahead jazz. 'Freddie Hubbard Live' (Pablo) from 1980 was recorded at the North Sea Jazz Festival and stands up well; Hubbard plays with great assurance and his regular band, if rather closely following the group VSOP, at least focused Hubbard's skills in a no-nonsense situation.

Hubbard's close association with Joe Henderson (ts) usually made him step up a gear from manual dexterity to the creative higher ground; 'Keystone Bop' (Fantasy), a live session from November 1981, and his recordings with the Griffith Park Band also that year—'Collection' and 'Collection 2' (Elektra Musician)—left no room for coasting. On the live 'Collection 2' he had to fight for his share of the laurels; once through the pain barrier anything seemed possible.

The recording quality on the 1983 'Back To Birdland' (Realtime) was the only drawback on a West Coast session that included Richie Cole (as); ironically the two clown princes of jazz stood toe-to-toe, neither giving an inch in their playing. While most of Hubbard's work for the Pablo label during the decade seemed complacent, the June 1983 'Sweet Return' (Atlantic) proved he was still a force to be reckoned with. Alongside Lew Tabackin (ts), Joanne Brackeen (p), Eddie Gomez (b) and Roy Haynes (d), assembled by George Wein for the festival circuit of 1983, it provided just the sort of peer pressure that brought out his best playing. But despite appearing to retrieve some of his lost credibility, Hubbard was still prone to commercial foible; 'Ride Like The Wind' (Elektra Musician) had more than a little fat-cat complacency and was for cross-over ears only.

In 1985 Hubbard returned to Blue Note Records and the two collaborations with Woody Shaw (t)—the 1985 'Double Take' and the 1987 'Eternal Triangle'—work well, but the 1987 'Stardust' (Denon), with an all star cast including Benny Golson (ts), Mulgrew Miller (p), Ron Carter (b) and Marvin 'Smitty' Smith (d), was only modestly successful considering the talent brought to bear on the subject. However, by the end of the decade sophistifunk beckoned and 'Life's Flight' (Blue Note), with a cast including George Benson (g), Stanley Turrentine and Ralph Moore (ts), and the 1989 'Times Are Changing' once again militated against Hubbard's artistic credentials.

That Hubbard could still turn it on was evidenced on the incredibly perverse 'The Satchmo Legacy Band—Vol. 1' (Soul Note), with an unusual job-lot of players assembled to tour the European festival circuit in 1987. In an otherwise plodding reading of Armstrong classics, Hubbard steps out of character from a role he had been terribly miscast with a contemporary reading of 'Stardust' that was a reminder of how he had enriched the jazz world with his beautiful ballad performances.

Tenor saxophonist **Joe Henderson** (b.1937) had long occupied a seat on the saxophone's Board of Governors; perhaps the only major post-bop saxophonist whose style showed little allegiance to John Coltrane, Henderson's style emphasized melodic, rather than harmonic delineation. By the 1980s he had moved to the West Coast, where throughout the decade he was involved in teaching. His freelance appearances included albums as diverse as JoAnne Brackeen's 'Ancient Dynasty' (Columbia), The Paris Reunion Band's 'For Klook' (Sonnet), George Gruntz's 'Happenin' Now' (Hat Art) and Freddie Hubbard's 'Keystone Bop' (Fantasy), the latter showing him in impressive form.

Joe Henderson: 'The slate of the tenor?'

In 1982 Henderson was a key figure in the Griffith Park sessions with Freddie Hubbard (t), Chick Corea (p), Stanley Clarke (b) and Lenny White (d). The two vocal albums, 'Echoes Of An Era' and 'Echoes Of An Era 2' (both Elektra Musician) were of peripheral interest. However, the instrumental albums, 'Collection' and 'Collection 2' (both Elektra Musician) contain some excellent Henderson solos; 'Collection', the studio session, has Henderson taking the laurels for his work on 'October Ballade', 'Why Wait' and 'Guernica'. The live 'Collection 2' fares better overall, although it didn't have the best sound quality, recorded onto a cassette by the sound-mixer. On the two ballad features, 'Here's That Rainy Day' and 'October Ballade' and on Thelonious Monk's 'I Mean You', his cutting, incisive phrasing and lyrical ingenuity were album highlights, despite the spotty mix.

Towards the end of the decade Henderson toured with an all-female rhythm section, that from time to time included pianists Rene Rosnes and Aki Takase. In 1986 he joined trumpeter Randy Brecker on 'In The Idiom' (Denon), a well worked back-to-Blue Note-blow. But his major work of the decade was 'The State Of The Tenor Vols. 1 & 2' (Blue Note), recorded live over three days in November 1985 at New York's Village Vanguard. With just Ron Carter (b) and Al Foster (d), Henderson's melodic ideas were developed incrementally using space and dynamics and the patience and experience of a master craftsman. Critically hailed as a masterpiece and described as one of the most important albums in the history of Blue Note records at the time of release, it certainly numbered among the decade's finest albums. The product of assiduous craftsmanship and carefully focused inspiration, there is a low-key intensity that is in equal parts gripping and compelling; but perhaps not the state of the tenor as much as the state of Joe Henderson's art.

One of the great tragedies in jazz during the 1980s was the gradual demise of the career of trumpeter **Woody Shaw** (1944-89). During the 1970s, very lean years indeed for jazz, he succeeded in building a career for himself to the extent that he was signed by CBS towards the end of the decade. By then Shaw's ability was widely acknowledged by his peers, including both Miles Davis and Dizzy Gillespie, for his originality, his precise, clearly thought-out solos and integration of elements of freedom in his playing, 'Woody is still the last in the line of trumpet players that really added something new to trumpet jazz' said Randy Brecker in 1986.

Shaw's playing was similar in conception to Freddie Hubbard's in that he favoured unusual intervals—often McCoy Tyner-ish descending arpeg-

gios full of notes that did not easily fall under the fingers of brass musicians—and, like Hubbard, he was influenced by saxophone players including Coltrane and Dolphy. But there was less element of risk-taking
in a Shaw solo; some of his work stood as a complete, unified statement
where the ideas he advanced seemed to be more the result of careful
deliberation than emotional exuberance.

From 1980-83 Shaw led one of the few regular touring groups in jazz
at that time, an exceptionally able group with Steve Turre (tb), Mulgrew
Miller (p), Stafford James (b) and Tony Reedus (d). The group debuted
on 'United' (CBS) from 1981 and the unusual all-brass front-line immediately gave the band a unique tonal identity (although Gary Bartz [as]
guests on two tracks).

The 1982 'Lotus Flower' (Enja) was the best example of the quintet's
work, in choice of material, solo, ensemble playing *and* in recording quality. It revealed a group whose identity had reached that optimum point
where the sum of the band had become greater than its component parts.
'Rahsaan's Run' contains a dashing Shaw solo that grows organically from
his striking original composition while 'Songs Of Songs', another Shaw
original, is a reminder of what an excellent, albeit underrated, group this
was. However, 'Live In Europe—Time Is Right' (Red) recorded during
what Shaw described as, 'a tedious six-week European tour',[7] was lacklustre *in extremis.*

On their return they went straight into New York's Jazz Forum to cut
'Master Of The Art' and 'Night Music' (both Elektra Musician). Bobby
Hutcherson guests on vibes and taken together these live sessions have
that spark so often missing from studio recordings. 'It went down so
smoothly and was so enjoyable that I forgot it was a recording session'
said Shaw later. However, leading a band did not come easily to him,
'He hated being a bandleader and all its attendant responsibilities,' said
record producer Michael Cuscuna. 'His avoidance of responsibility caused
his career to dip on many occasions.'

Following the breakup of his quintet in 1983, 'Setting Standards'
(Muse) was with a pick-up rhythm section with Shaw on flugelhorn for
four of the six numbers, mainly standards. The contrast to his set, working
group, however, was all too apparent. The remainder of Shaw's work on
the Muse label was competent but a little tame in the context of jazz
during the decade. The 1986 'Solid' with Kenny Garrett (as) or the 1987
'Imagination', a reunion with Steve Turre, for example, were simply hum-
drum.

Woody Shaw, one of the great tragedies of '80s jazz.

However, a live session at the Village Vanguard from September 1986 with a Mal Waldron group, 'The Git Go' (Soul Note), sees him working out with great imagination on the single chord, A minor, that represented the harmonic base of the title track. This, together with his work on the reconstituted Blue Note label—a performance alongside Jackie McLean at the Blue Note Town Hall concert, 'One Night With Blue Note Preserved Vol. 2' and the two meetings with Freddie Hubbard—contain his best work from the latter half of the decade.

Although Shaw formed *ad hoc* groups from time to time to tour, personal demons were at work in his life. 'Because he was a perfectionist, was subject to profound mood swings, Woody was never really happy unless he was making great music,' said Michael Cuscuna. Shaw found a kind of escape in drug addiction that forced his career into rapid decline at the end of the decade. 'Troubled, living like a nomad and indulging too many chemicals, Woody slipped away to Switzerland . . . but eventually he ended up in Holland where the vices from which he fled New York were in plentiful supply,' recalled Cuscuna.

While performing in Europe during the summer of 1988 it was clear that he had serious problems. Just how serious was revealed by Cuscuna after his death, 'His eyesight, which had always been horrible, began deteriorating rapidly . . . and he was found to be an AIDS carrier. Finally he was brought back to the home of his parents . . . where they took care of him with love and diligence.'[8] In January 1989 he attended the Village Vanguard but slipped away from the company. At 7am the following day he fell in front of a subway train; he lost his left arm, and hospitalized and in a coma, he died on 9 May 1989.

The Modern Jazz Quartet excepted, few ensembles lasted longer in jazz without making any changes in personnel than **The George Adams/Don Pullen Quartet.** Formed in 1979 it was a band that consistently delivered, a perfect reconciliation of inside/outside playing. Adams (b.1940) and Pullen (b.1941) graduated through blues bands and the cut and thrust of the New York jazz scene until they came together in Charles Mingus' group in the mid-1970s. After the death of Mingus in 1979 they reformed to tour Europe as a Mingus alumni group together with Dannie Richmond (d), Mingus' long time associate, and Cameron Brown on bass.

Three albums resulted, all recorded within 48 hours at the beginning of November in Milan. The studio 'Don't Lose Control' (Soul Note) and the live 'All That Funk' and 'More Funk' (both Palcoscenico), both from a concert at Milan's CIAK, rely almost exclusively on original material that contains all the hallmarks of the band's style: 'Intentions' and 'Big Alice' from the Palcoscenico set and 'Don't Lose Control' staples of their repertoire in live performance throughout the '80s.

Even on their first album the band displayed the unity of purpose and common vision few ensembles achieve, let alone on their debut recordings. Brown and Richmond's expansive, swinging foundation moved with heartwarming energy, allowing Adams and Pullen to superimpose the uncompromising grit of their hard-earned experience. Pullen's swinging 'horn-like' lines that suddenly launched into jagged, rubber-wristed knuckling of the piano keys, where the outline of his improvisation blurred and shimmered in the heat of the creative moment, were a perfect contrast for Adams' wholesome tenor. Shaped by rugged, on-the-job experience in the school of hard knocks, including organ combos where he 'walked the bar' for tips, his blues inflected lyricism could move into 'vertical', multi-noted Coltrane chord consumption or whoop and cry like Albert Ayler.

From 1980 to 1986 the band recorded a series of excellent albums for Wim Wigt's Timeless label in Holland,[9] their entire recorded output had so far been confined to European independent labels. It was a body of recorded work that was mature, inventive and unfailingly consistent and set high standards for jazz during the 1980s. But distribution problems failed to capitalize on the commonly held belief of those who saw the group live that it was one of the major *groups* of the decade.

The George Adams/Don Pullen Quartet: Mature, inventive and unfailingly consistent, it set high standards for jazz during the 1980s. (L to R) Don Pullen, Cameron Brown, Lewis Nash (who replaced the late Dannie Richmond, who featured on all the band's albums) and George Adams.

When the band were finally signed for Blue Note records in 1986 there was more than a little ironic humour on their first U.S. album 'Breakthrough' (Blue Note) from 1986, with the track 'We've Been Here All The Time', which was followed by the 1987 'Song Everlasting' (Blue Note). At the time of their release there was disappointment expressed because the full force of their controlled abandon was sacrificed in the studio. However, with the passage of time the albums stand up well, even if they do err on the side of caution.

On 16 March 1988 Dannie Richmond, who always asserted he 'led the group from the drums', died. He had played for Mingus, 'off and on for about 20 years,' his tight, energetic drumming as vital a part of the chemistry for Mingus as it was in the Adams/Pullen ensemble. Lewis Nash (d) was invited to join the group, but both Pullen and Adams began to think of life beyond the band, recording albums of their own for Blue Note during 1988; George Adams with 'Nightingale' and Don Pullen with 'New Directions'. In September 1988 Pullen made a decision to leave and the band fulfilled several final engagements before disbanding in early 1989. 'It was a fiery band,' said Pullen, 'fire was its middle name 'cause we had Dannie there, and Dannie was Dannie.'   .

Dave Liebman (b.1946) quietly began to assume the mantle of one of the giants of the saxophone during the 1980s. Although initially a tenor saxophonist, he switched exclusively to soprano saxophone in 1980, claiming 'depth requires mastery'. Since then he continued to develop and confine his virtuoso technique, initially inspired by John Coltrane, but by the '80s, firmly shaped by his own concepualism to the extent that he emerged as not only one of the major voices on his instrument, but also one of the major instrumental voices in jazz.

Liebman had studied with Lennie Tristano and Charles Lloyd in the '60s before working with Pete LaRoca, Ten Wheel Drive, Elvin Jones and Miles Davis. His own group Lookout Farm marked the beginning of a collaboration with pianist Richie Beirach. In 1979 he made one of the few artistically successful excursions into fusion with 'What It Is' (CBS) that included stars of the future such as Kenny Kirkland (p), John Scofield (g) and Marcus Miller (b). However, in 1978 he took a quintet into the Village Vanguard, with Randy Brecker (t), Beirach, Frank Tusa (b) and Al Foster (d); the result was 'Pendulum' (Artists House) and marked what Liebman called, 'the beginnings of Quest'.[10]

Quest, in essence a collaboration between Beirach (b.1947) and Liebman, underpinned the saxophonist's basic musical direction in the

Dave Liebman, high artistic purpose and integrity.

1980s, even though by the end of the decade he had appeared on a total of some 100 albums and as leader on about 25 per cent of them. Quest eventually consolidated into a quartet, and 'Quest' (Palo Alto), from 1981 was to be their only U.S. album of the decade. Quest was at once a highly interactive group, and whatever the tempo, there was constant dialogue among the musicians without ever impeding the role of the soloist. The constant sway of collective improvisation acted so as to thrust the music forward. 'Softly As In A Morning Sunrise' was brought alive by probing deep into the harmonies; Quest did not simply play the changes, they explored them, chromaticized them and discovered new implications in old assertions.

In 1984, Liebman and Beirach recorded two notable duo albums, 'Double Edge', an album of standards, and 'The Duo Live', an album of originals, (both Storyville). 'Quest takes the duet a step further to include the power of the bass and drums,' said Liebman, 'but still dealing with the language of the duet.'[11] The 1986 'Quest II' and the live 1987 'Midpoint—Quest III' (both Storyville) substitute Ron McLure (b) and Billy Hart (d) and refine the group's improvisational processes further. Here the original compositions are more angular, the challenges greater while the group respond with fluidity, rapport and an intensity of purpose that only musicianship at the highest level brings.

In March 1988 the group recorded an album of standards, 'N.Y. Nites' (Pan Music), that placed in sharp focus the highly sophisticated style and sound they had evolved, 'Standards helped form the roots of our early years of training,' said Liebman. 'To periodically return to them represents a way of measuring one's own growth, or as in our case the evolution of a group sound. The supreme challenge is to musically manipulate the melodies, harmonies, rhythms and formats of the known standard in such a way as to keep its integrity, but somehow cause it to sound like one of the group's original compositions.'[12]

'Natural Selection' (Pathfinder), from June 1988, was augmented on two or three tracks by oboe, percussion and synth, expanding the expressive palette without detracting from the internal balance of the group. Here, as on the other albums, it was Liebman's effect on those around him that seems to lift and transform the group with his inspirational and emotionally honest playing; his tone was direct, round and strongly focused, and, laser-like, seemed to expose inner meaning and truth.

Among the many albums Liebman recorded during the 1980s away from Quest, 'Tribute To John Coltrane' (Paddlewheel) and 'Homage To John Coltrane' (Owl) from 1987 and the 1989 'Time Line' (Owl) underlined his status as one of the major improvising musicians of the 1980s. The Coltrane albums were far from clone-like genuflexions. 'Tribute' placed Liebman alongside Wayne Shorter (ss) in a million-dollar combination that contrasted honest homilies with veiled indulgences. The rhythm section of Beirach, Eddie Gomez (b) and Jack DeJohnette (d) collectively kicked ass in the common cause of creativity in one of the decade's hottest albums, earning a Swing Journal 'Seal Of Approval'. 'Homage' served to demonstrate how Liebman used Coltrane's inspiration to form a highly personal voice of his own. On 'Crescent' a theme based on recurring II-V-I patterns, Liebman's sustained creativity over a recurring harmonic background was as imaginative as it was profound.

'Time Line' (Owl), inspired by the Booker Little albums 'Out Front' (Candid) and 'Victory And Sorrow' (Bethlehem), featured Liebman's intricate small group writing, a more formal challenge in what he described as a 'consistently evolving artistic path in which change and refinements are constants.'[13] Throughout the 1980s Liebman continued to impress with work of high artistic purpose and integrity but remarkably was forced to hustle for work. Unable to bring Quest together as often as he would have liked, he was forced to tour as a single, working with pick-up groups and giving clinics. 'This was a financial necessity because of the difficulty of steady work for a set group,' he said.[14]

Pianist **Steve Kuhn** (b.1938) could identify jazz recordings as a babe in arms, a feat that was recorded in H. Allen Smith's book *Low Man On The Totem Pole*.[15] After a period of intensive study of the piano, Kuhn moved to New York in 1959 and was almost immediately working with the big names in '60s jazz including Kenny Dorham's Quintet, the John Coltrane Quartet, the Art Farmer group and the Stan Getz Quartet. But an *affaire de coeur* took him to Sweden for a few years and when he returned in 1971 he found the scene dominated by fusion and worse, he discovered that in terms of his reputation, out of sight meant out of mind.

Kuhn's career never really got back in gear after that. It was a source of great frustration, and forced to take commercial work he went through something of a mid-life crisis in the 1980s. The child prodigy with a 'photographic memory', the musician schooled by Margaret Chaloff, one of the finest teachers in the Boston Conservatory, the Harvard graduate and the pianist who preceded McCoy Tyner into the John Coltrane Quartet found that after a lifetime's dedication to the piano, his position in jazz had gone full circle. He still remained very much a low man on the totem pole.

Kuhn's playing was one of subtlety and nuance. His touch had remarkable projection across the whole dynamic range, moving from impressionistic reveries to an 'orchestral' approach often using dissonance and unusual time signatures. Arthur Moorhead, who produced Kuhn's 1986 'Life's Magic' (Blackhawk) observed, 'There are many players who play standards well, but they play every standard with the same approach. If you snip off the head at either end, all they do is just deal with a set of chord changes. But Kuhn deals with the *song*, rather than changes. The guys who play with Kuhn's depth are, believe me, few and far between.'[16]

In 1979 Kuhn began augmenting his regular quartet of Steve Slagel (as,ss) Harvie Swartz (b) and Bob Moses (d) with vocalist Sheila Jordan, 'We worked together as a quintet for a while,' said Kuhn, 'and it seemed it worked just as well with just Sheila and no saxophone so we became a quartet.'[17] The 1979 'Playground' (ECM) saw Jordan totally in sympathy with Kuhn's labyrinthine lyrics in what was in essence an inspired integration of voice and piano. Her ability to pare a song to its emotional core yet retain its musical momentum brought Kuhn's word-heavy complexes alive.

A session at Fat Tuesday's, New York from April 1981 produced 'Last Year's Waltz' (ECM) but it was Kuhn's playing on two trio numbers, 'Mexico', and 'The Fruit Fly' that impressed, full of subtle harmonic and rhythmic shifts and 'orchestral' flourishes. But shortly afterwards, Kuhn recalled, 'The guy who was booking us left the agency and from that point on it was difficult to get good representation, so the work started to diminish and we began to drift.'[18]

Disillusioned, Kuhn withdrew into commercial work, largely playing for private functions, where his photographic memory stood him in good stead (he knew some 5,000 songs). 'I was expecting a lot and it wasn't happening,' he said, 'I was getting bent out of shape about it . . . it was not the best of times emotionally,' he said, 'but I came out of it in '85 and decided I wanted to work with a trio.'[19] For the rest of the decade his jazz work usually involved Al Foster (d) and bassists Ron Carter, Buster Williams or Eddie Gomez.

'Mostly Ballads' (New World Records) from 1984 and 'Life's Magic' (Blackhawk), live at the Village Vanguard from 1986, showed Kuhn to be the natural heir to much the same area of musical territory occupied by the late Bill Evans, albeit with a more explicit rhythmic pulse. By the end of the decade, Kuhn's persistence began to bear fruit; the 1988 'Porgy' (Jazz City) with Gomez or Williams (b) and Foster (d) with Laura-Ann Taylor (v) on two numbers was a deft, straight-ahead exploration of the standard repertoire. The 1989 'Oceans In The Sky' (Owl) continued his renaissance with Miroslav Vitous (b) and Aldo Romano (d) on another batch of sophisticated standards; controlled, unruffled, witty and urbane, Kuhn's playing was a model of taste and lyrical imagination.

By the 1980s, pianist **JoAnne Brackeen** (b.1938) was widely acknowledged to be one of the major contemporary pianists in jazz, despite a minimal recorded output and the problems of raising four children, several cats and a couple of dogs. The only female to have been a member of Art Blakey's Jazz Messengers (1969-72), appearing on 'Jazz Messengers '70' (Catalyst) recorded during a tour of Japan, she was with Joe Henderson before joining Stan Getz (1975-77), where her exposure with the group, particularly her performance on the Grammy winning 'Stan Getz Gold' (Inner City) brought her both critical acclaim and the attention of a wide audience.

By 1980 the respected jazz commentator Leonard Feather had gone on record to say that Brackeen's playing would be as important to the 1980s as Herbie Hancock's and Bill Evans' to the 1960s or McCoy Tyner's and Keith Jarrett's to the 1970s. Technically, Brackeen was a flawless player; her highly percussive touch, her impeccable articulation, her use of the foot pedals (something few jazz pianists have used to optimum effect) and her totally independent co-ordination that could sometimes sound like two pianists in dialogue, instantly set her apart. Her style had obvious antecedents in McCoy Tyner's percussiveness and polyrhythms and Bill Evans' harmonic vocabulary, but there could be no mistaking her sometimes jarring melodicism and expansive, almost athletic, keyboard derring-do. 'Her music breathes and it sings' said Robert Palmer in the *New York Times.*

At the end of the 1970s she signed with Bob James' Tappan Zee label. A live performance at New York's Town Hall in 1979, appeared as part of Bob James' 'All Around The Town' (Tappan Zee). However, the 1979 'Keyed In' (Tappan Zee) was a superlative trio album with Eddie Gomez (b) and Jack DeJohnette (d). Featuring Brackeen's inscrutable originals, her life teeming playing and the high level of sympathetic interaction from Gomez and DeJohnette, she brought colour and dimension to the traditional and most basic musical configuration in jazz. 'When I played with JoAnne I found I had an incredible understanding,' observed Gomez, 'Her use of rhythms is the most highly developed component of her play.'

The 1980 'Ancient Dynasty' (Tappan Zee) with the addition of Joe Henderson (ts) placed Brackeen's rigorous compositions in a broader context, and gave Henderson plenty to chew on, particularly 'Beagle's Boogie'. Together they produced jazz of a high order; uncompromising, powerful and with plenty of sharp edges. The 1981 'Special Identity' (Antilles) reverted to the trio line-up for another set of originals that were both quirky and slightly beyond comprehension. 'All I'm thinking about when I play is expressing life,' said Brackeen, '. . . you get a sense of really being alive when playing.'[20]

In 1983 George Wein assembled a band to tour the festival circuits under the leadership of Freddie Hubbard; 'Sweet Return' (Atlantic) sees Brackeen playing a significant role in forcing Hubbard down from what Gary Giddins called 'cloud cuckoo-land'[21] with her no-nonsense, uncompromising style.

When in 1985 she signed with the Concord label she found history repeating itself; Thelonious Monk's debut with Riverside Records in the early '50s was with an album of standards, rather than his own compositions which had acquired a daunting reputation with record producers and public alike. Equally, 'Havin' Fun' (Concord) attempted to place Brackeen's playing in a more accessible context. It succeeded. 'Some people think I can only play far-out,' she said, 'but I play a lot of different ways, including standards.'[22]

The 1986 'Fi-Fi Goes To Heaven' (Concord) was with the addition of Terence Blanchard (t) and Branford Marsalis (as, ss) with the title track commemorating Brackeen's Yorkie, who was first celebrated on her 1977 album 'Tring-A-Ling' (Choice)—both numbers rock-rhythm based, coincidentally. The front line just about manage to hold their own in the face of the pianist's strong playing in an outstanding album that moves from a sublime 'Stardust' to the haywire riffs of 'Cosmonaut'. The eloquent 'Live At Maybeck Recital Hall Vol. 1' (Concord) from June 1989 is an unaccompanied mixture of originals and standards that demonstrated the enormous breadth of Brackeen's talent. 'A person's consciousness produces their economics,' she said, 'I could feel like a quintet, or solo piano or even an orchestra—or all three instead of either/or.'

Bennie Wallace's (b.1946) robust tenor saxophone style moved from loft anarchy to Southern R&B during the course of the 1980s. It was an odyssey he managed to achieve with the minimum of stylistic concession so that his playing, inspired by Sonny Rollins, Coleman Hawkins and Eric Dolphy retained its integrity and hands-on intensity. Wallace's restless, relentless arpeggiated style used the entire range of the saxophone, from low A (muffling the sax bell against his leg) to the stratosphere in one breath, which he underpinned with a massive sense of swing. A player of great authority and maturity whose live performances could be devastating essays in saxophone mastery, Wallace never seemed to reap the critical approbation his talent warranted during the 1980s.

Wallace debuted as a leader in 1978 with 'Fourteen-Bar Blues' (Enja) that immediately won the Deutscher Schallplattenpreis; a trio album with Eddie Gomez (b) and Eddie Moore (d), it was a rigorous workout, daring and full of chances that seemed to take him to the limit of his technique and imagination. That swashbuckling, seat-of-the-pants recklessness featured on 'Live At The Public Theater' (Enja), this time with regular collaborator, Dannie Richmond in on drums. Tommy Flanagan (p) was added for 'Free Will' (Enja) from 1980 and his poise and old world charm was the perfect foil for Wallace's tenor madness, awash with ideas that arrived in stream-of-consciousness torrents.

The 1981 'Plays Monk' (Enja) substituted Jimmy Knepper (tb) for Flanagan, and confirmed Wallace's stature as a major talent. Monk's compositions have long been the Waterloo of many an aspiring improvisor, a daunting litany that demands getting 'inside' the composers intentions, but Wallace handled the structural nuances with the grit and bite the composer intended. Even powering through 'Straight-No-Chaser' Wallace was able to defer to Monk's gravity yet spell out his own equally angular fare. Wallace continued his impressive output when Chick Corea (p) guested on 'Mystic Bridge' (Enja) from 1982 in a no-quarter-asked, no-quarter-given session of gratifying conviction.

'Big Jim's Tango' (Enja), also from 1982, was something of an anti-climax in comparison, a trio with Dave Holland (b) and Elvin Jones (d). 'Sweeping Through The City' (Enja) from 1984 included The Wings Of Song gospel group and Ray Anderson (tb) and John Scofield (g) as The Blues Ensemble Of Biloxi. Imaginative, expansive and with no little humour, Wallace's continually evolving music seemed to be looking to broaden the base of its appeal. He succeeded with typical gusto. Scofield returned together with Wallace's regular trio on 'The Art Of The Saxophone' (Denon) from 1987 that introduced a series of guest saxophonists, but somehow Wallace got enmeshed in the personality of each, so the concept faltered.

In 1985 he signed with Blue Note records, appearing on their Town Hall gala in a trio with Cecil McBee (b) and Jack DeJohnette (d), 'One Night With Blue Note Vol. 2' (Blue Note). 'Twilight Time' (Blue Note), from later in the year, however, represented a radical departure from his tried and tested trio format. Crammed full of guests including DeJohnette, Ray Anderson (tb), John Scofield, Stevie Ray Vaughan (g) and Dr. John (p), Wallace went back to his Tennessee roots for a down-South

Ray Anderson: One of the most refreshing soloists to reach maturity during the '80s.

gumbo. The surprise record of the decade, a Saturday Night Function feel permeates the whole album that was a daring mixture of artistic licence and fun. The follow-up, the 1987 'Bordertown' (Blue Note) fares almost as well. This deft change of backdrop highlighted Wallace's maturity into one of the finest soloists in jazz. 'The more you learn about harmony,' he said, 'the closer you get to where you can use all 12 tones in any situation. It's just a matter of being able to know what you're doing and letting your taste allow it.'

One of the most refreshing soloists to reach maturity during the 1980s was **Ray Anderson** (b.1952), who championed the return of the trombone to the bass clef after years of flugelhorn-like dexterity by musicians such as Bill Watrous and Frank Rosolino. Anderson unselfconsciously plumbed the unfashionable depths of the instrument that had hitherto been the province of the Dixielanders and free musicians to reinvestigate the instrument's emotional spectrum; at the same time he used his technical clout to keep the upper range very much in view.

Anderson paid his dues in a wide diversity of performing contexts; a student of Frank Tirro, during the '70s he performed in blues bands, funk groups, regularly sat in with Charles Mingus, big band work and later in the decade became involved with the circle of musicians centered around Anthony Davis. In 1977 he began an association with Anthony Braxton and Barry Altschul whose influence was reflected on his 1980 debut as a leader on record, 'Harrisburg Half Life' (Moers).

As the '80s progressed, Anderson's originality was in demand in a variety of ensembles but it was as a member of the co-operative group Slickaphonics his playing came to the attention of a wider audience. Formed in 1981 with Steve Elson (ts) sharing the front line, their avant-funk albums were clever, sardonic and witty with Anderson's parched vocals to the fore, but also tedious and one-directional.[23]

Anderson's own work continued with 'Right Down Your Alley' (Soul Note), a trio with Helias and Mark Hemmingway (d). Moving from free ('Stomping') through multiphonics ('Portrait Of Mark Dresser') to the Caribbean ('Paucartambo'), Anderson laid on a virtuoso performance that had absorbed the whole tradition of the trombone in jazz. The 1985 'Old Bottles—New Wine' (Enja) was a magnificent workout on standards with Kenny Barron (p), Cecil McBee (b) and Dannie Richmond (d) that revealed yet another facet to his character; his vocal on 'Wine' moves from a jaunty singing-in-the-bath tenor through several shades of intensity culminating in a unique vocal-multiphonic cadenza that simultaneously recalled Louis Armstrong and Albert Mangelsdorff.

'You Be' (Minor Music) and the 1987 'Bass Drum Bone' (Soul Note) were trio albums with Helias and Hemmingway that touched base with new-music experimentalism with Anderson blowing himself red on some numbers while reverting to off-the-wall lyricism, sermonizing like the late Lawrence Brown on others. The 1987 'It Just So Happens' (Enja) with a small brass ensemble was concerned with texture, but Anderson's writing falls just short of its objectives in both style and content. However, with the 1988 'Blues Bred In The Bone' (Enja) and 'What Because' (Gramavision) from 1989 he created two minor masterpieces of trombone jazz. Like the late Vic Dickenson, Anderson's jaunty authority and high technical skill was never flaunted but used to produce the clever and the unexpected and showed that lack of critical acclaim was no impediment to producing memorable jazz.

Tenor saxophonist **Mike Brecker** (b.1949) was, by the '80s, the most influential saxophonist since John Coltrane; any aspiring saxophonist was forced to take account of his tone, technique, energy and his harmonic methodology. But Brecker, the most recorded saxophonist of his generation, with recording credits as diverse as Frank Sinatra, Dire Straits, P-

Mike Brecker, the most influential saxophonist since John Coltrane, enjoying the guitar playing of Mike Stern.

Funk and Pat Metheny, surprisingly did not make a record under his own name until 1987.

Brecker's jazz career gave best to commercial session work as early as 1970. However, he did play in the early jazz-rock band Dreams and the Horace Silver Quintet before forming the Brecker Brothers Band with Randy that was active until 1982. 'The Brecker Bros. Collection Vol. 1' (Novus) a 1990 re-release, included 'Funky Sea, Funky Dew' from 1977, an excellent example of his widely influential jazz-rock style. Brecker's best straight-ahead work was, however, to be found on other people's albums; the 1977 'You Can't Live With Out It' (Chiaroscuro) by Jack Wilkens, the 'Steps' albums on the Better Days label and a stunning outing with Chick Corea from 1981, 'Three Quartets' (Warner Brothers).

His 1987 debut as leader, 'Michael Brecker' (Impulse), was a long over-due *tour de force* by a saxophone master. 'I tried to make a record with some mystery,' he said later. 'One that bears more than one listening.'[24]

His tone ('Sea Glass'), his technique ('Syzygy') and his harmonic sophistication, fluent chromaticism and trade-mark alternate fingering were all dealt in a powerful hand that numbered among the best albums of the decade.

Also featured was Brecker's Akai EWI, an electronic wind instrument that triggered sampled sounds. Featured on Steps Ahead 'Magnetic' (Elektra), it was one synthesized sound among many, but on 'Original Ray's' from his Impulse album he used it to remarkable effect, 'It gave me the sensation of being in a sax section in a big band,' he said, 'kind of a big band on Mars.'

By the time the 1988 'Don't Try This At Home' (Impulse) was recorded, Brecker had toured extensively with his group of Mike Stern (g), Joey Calderazzo (p), Jeff Andrews (b) and Adam Nussbaum (d). Unfortunately the group only appear together on one track; recording the group live was an opportunity missed. The band had shaken down into a powerful unit with whom Brecker clearly derived great pleasure from playing and would surely have translated into a memorable album.

Unfortunately, 'Don't Try This At Home' (Impulse) did not succeed in the same way as his powerful, focused debut. There were highlights, 'Itsbynne Reel' and 'Suspone' that featured the EWI and 'The Gentleman & Hizcaine' that was pure tenor sax, but it lacked direction, and with sidemen coming and going on every track appeared exactly what it was, a jumbled series of sessions. In 1987-88 he also played with the John Abercrombie Trio and featured on 'Getting There' (ECM) with the group, contributing two memorable solos on 'Furs On Ice' and 'Sidekicks'.

Randy Brecker (b.1945), like his brother, seemed to find cutting the ties with fusion difficult. Since the days of their modest hit 'Sneaking Up Behind You' (Arista) both have succumbed to the sirens of the fusion camp with varying degrees of success. In 1982 he toured and recorded with Jaco Pastorius's 'Word Of Mouth' sextet and big band, appearing on 'Word Of Mouth', the small band album, and 'Twins I' and 'Twins II' live with the big band (all Warner Bros).

However, on the 1986 'Amanda' (Sonet) he joined forces with Mrs Randal E. Brecker—Eliane Elias—in an album of such high gloss that even a hairdresser and make-up girl were credited. But a fusion tribute to Duke Ellington, 'Echoes Of Ellington' (Verve) from 1988 alongside Bill Evans, Tom Scott and Robben Ford was surprisingly successful. Fortunately, he did take time to play pure jazz, appearing on albums as diverse as Loren Schoenberg's 'Solid Ground' (Music Masters) to a Mingus tribute, 'Big Band Charlie Mingus' (Soul Note).

In October 1986 Brecker recorded 'In The Idiom' (Denon) with Joe Henderson (ts), David Kikoski (p), Ron Carter (b) and Al Foster (d); 'There isn't much that Brecker can't do on trumpet and the demise of fusion seems to have restored him to the ranks of class jazz bands,' said Gary Giddins. 'His compositions are challenging but what stays with you is his glowing sound.'[25] In 1988 he took a quintet into Sweet Basil in Greenwich Village, New York and 'Live At Sweet Basil' (Sonnet) opens up the 'In The Idiom' style with looser, open-ended compositions with Bob Berg (ts) thriving in the post-bop environment and Joey Baron (d) a tower of strength in the rhythm section.

The group made several short tours—including a State Department tour of Eastern Europe - with Dennis Chambers (d) and appeared from time to time in New York, and Brecker also appeared with Stanley Clarke's Jazz Explosion Super Band. But even so the 1989 'Toe To Toe' (MCA) returned again to fusion. What was clear was that both brothers could cut it with ease, but were becoming unique as two hugely gifted musicians devoid of any aspiration to build a serious body of recorded work.

When **Marc Johnson** (b.1953) entered North Texas State University at 19, he was already playing the bass professionally with the Fort Worth Symphony Orchestra. On graduation he joined Woody Herman and appeared on three albums with him before joining the Bill Evans Trio in 1978, recording the critically acclaimed 'Paris Concert Vols. 1 & 2' (Elektra Musician) in November 1979. After working with the Monday Night Mel Lewis band he joined Stan Getz in 1981 for two years; 'After I left Stan . . . I wanted to play with guitars,' he said.

In 1985 he formed Bass Desires with Bill Frisell (g), John Scofield (g) and Peter Erskine (d) and their eponymously titled debut album on the ECM label from the same year marked the debut of a strikingly original and exciting new group. Johnson's original 'Samurai Hee-Haw' was among the album's highlights, contrasting the styles of Frisell and Scofield, two of the decades most exciting musicians, in shimmering solos and ensemble colours. 'I'm a leader in quotation marks,' said Johnson. 'I see myself as a co-ordinator, just getting everybody together and coming up with a few tunes.'

However, the ensemble remained on an occasional basis. 'The idea was to have a band, get an album and go on the road a few weeks every year,' said Johnson. The 1987 'Second Sight' (ECM) continued the high level of conception and execution; Scofield's 'Twister', a parody of the Beatles 'Twist And Shout' and his 'Thrill Seekers' were in contrast to a more reflective album of considerable depth, with Erskine's slow, laid-back groove on 'Sweet Soul' a model of control and disciplined ensemble playing.

Guitarist **John Abercrombie** (b.1944), a sought after session player and, together with Scofield and Frisell, one of the key contemporary guitarists in jazz, had been a regular on the ECM label since he debuted with the memorable and impetuously driven 'Timeless' (ECM) in 1974. Ten years later he gathered together the same personnel—Jan Hammer (k), Jack DeJohnette (d)—and together with Mike Brecker (ts) cut 'Night' (ECM) which won the Preis Deutscher Schallplatten Kritik that year. Among the decade's best albums it projected focus and definition, with every musician creating at the peak of their form; the dramatic, tight 'Ethereggae' contrasting the loose extemporizations of 'Four In One' and the muscular 'Believe You Me', the album's keenest track.

Marc Johnson's Bass Desires, a strikingly original and exciting group. (L to R) Bill Frisell, Marc Johnson, John Scofield and Peter Erskine.

In 1985 he formed a trio with Marc Johnson (b) and Peter Erskine (d) and their debut album, 'Current Events' (ECM) moved from standards like 'Alice In Wonderland' that evoked the Bill Evans trio, to contemporary blowing vehicles like 'Killing Time'. From 1986 the trio were joined occasionally by Mike Brecker (ts), who credited Abercrombie with 'freeing' his own musical concepts. He appeared on the 1987 'Getting There' (ECM) and the video of their Village Vanguard performance that year (Parkfield).

A live performance by the trio at Boston's Nightstage from 1988 was released as 'John Abercrombie/Marc Johnson/Peter Erskine' (ECM) and balances the standard repertoire with the Bass Desires' 'Samurai Hee-Haw' and the powerful 'Furs On Ice' from 'Getting There' (ECM). But it was Abercrombie's approach to standard repertoire that attracted attention; 'There's things I can do on a standard tune that I can't do on other material,' said Abercrombie, 'and because I know them so well, I'm very free with them. I'm just as free as when I'm playing with no chords at all.'

Peter Erskine (b.1954) was once the drummer in the big bands of Stan Kenton and Maynard Ferguson before joining Weather Report from 1978-82, a quantum leap into the then most popular jazz group in the world that announced the arrival of a major new drum star. Erskine appeared on four albums with the group and soon developed a reputation as one of the first call session musicians in both New York and Los Angeles. In 1982 he replaced Steve Gadd in the group Steps before joining Abercrombie's trio/quartet and Bass Desires in New York in 1985.

Erskine's recording debut as a leader, the 1982 'Peter Erskine' (Contemporary), recorded while he was resident on the West Coast, included the Brecker Brothers, Mike Mainieri (v) and Eddie Gomez (b)—essentially the Steps lineup with whom he was currently involved—augmented by Kenny Kirkland (p). It was a modest beginning; most of the compositions and arrangements were Erskine's with 'Leroy Street' and 'Change Of Mind' well thought out, and, mercifully, only one drum solo.

The 1986 'Transition' (Denon), recorded after his move to New York included an inner circle of Johnson, Abercrombie and Joe Lovano (ts) in an octet that blended electronic and acoustic instruments in an ensemble of considerable textural depth. From the empathetic interaction of 'Music Plays', the bop-influenced 'Transition' and the urban soundscape of 'Smart Shoppers', Erskine emerged as a leader of considerable potential. The Abercrombie trio also got a feature on 'My Foolish Heart', 'John was certainly influenced by Bill Evans' and Jim Hall's trios,' said Erskine.

'Motion Poet' (Denon) from 1988 reaffirmed Erskine's ability to conceptualize; here he returned to his formative influence of the big band, paring the larger ensemble to redefine it in a contemporary, Brecker Brothers-influenced setting. One delight was 'New Regalia', a rethink inspired by Frank Zappa's 'Peaches En Regalia' from 'Hot Rats'. A powerful 'Hero With A Thousand Faces' featured the Abercrombie trio plus Mike Brecker with horn accompaniment, while the trio featured on an intimate 'In Walked Maya'. Erskine and Johnson also appeared together on Gary Burton's 'Times Like These' (GRP) from 1988.

Even on the 1967 Woody Herman performance of 'Woody's Whistle' (incorrectly shown as 'Jumpin' Blue') on Woody Herman's 'Live In Seattle' (Moon), **John Hicks**, (b.1941) style had taken shape. By then he was a veteran of Art Blakey's and Betty Carter's groups. In the '70s he attained a Professorship at Southern Illinois University and went on to play with Blakey and Betty Carter again. His memorable support on Carter's 'The Audience' (Bet Car), from 1979, was an important contribution to making the album one of the finest jazz vocal albums of all time.

'When I left Betty [in 1980],' said Hicks, 'all kind of stuff had started happening. There was a backlog of people I'd been promising—or threatening—to play with.' Among the first was Pharoah Sanders, and of the three albums he made with the tenorman, 'Live' (Theresa), from 1982, stands out for his energized performance. While Hicks' playing exuded a confident strength that referred to the power of McCoy Tyner, it was equally identifiable. His solo on 'Miss Nancy' from Arthur Blythe's 1980 'Illusions' (CBS), for example, was wholly individual and remains one of the most exciting tracks the alto saxophonist has cut. 'He brings a lot of creative input to the music,' said Blythe.

Hicks was one of the most in-demand musicians of the 1980s, his most frequent calls coming from Arthur Blythe or David Murray to play inside/outside the changes or from Bobby Watson to play straight-ahead bebop. Somehow Hicks could make the transition with minimum alteration to his style, which incorporated the priceless gift of being able to *swing*. His first album in the '80s under his own name, the 1981 'Some Other Time' (Theresa), was with Walter Booker (b) and Idris Muhammad (d), at a time when they comprised the rhythm section for Pharoah Sanders. Containing Hicks' own 'Naima's Love Song', with its intriguing melody and counter-melody, the emphasis is on quiet, reflective moods, demonstrating Hicks' wide dynamic range that was equally effective interpreting ballads. That mood was sustained with the 1984 'John Hicks' (Theresa) although the 1985 'Sketches Of Tokyo' (DIW) with David Murray broadens the range from the tenor saxophonist's lusty 'New Life' to 'God Bless The Child'. Also from 1985, 'Inc. 1' (DIW), with Booker and Muhammad, is wholly forthright and more in character.

No recording date is given for 'Two Of A Kind' (Theresa), a duo with Ray Drummond (b) who frequently played with Hicks in David Murray's quartet. An excellent reading from the standard repertoire, Hicks' time and touch and precise articulation mark him as a pianist's pianist, 'For all that bundle of energy that I know and love about John Hicks' music there is this incredible romantic balladeer that John occasionally lets out into the fresh air,' said Drummond. 'John is one of a handful of pianists who can play ballads all night long and pull it off beautifully.'[26]

The 1987 'I'll Give You Something To Remember Me By . . .' (Limetree), this time with Curtis Lundy (b) and Muhammad, returns to Hicks' refreshingly contemporary swing. 'Naima's Love Song' (DIW) from 1988 has Bobby Watson (as) uninhibited by the burden of leadership and despite a self-conscious 'On The One', the session clicks. Hicks, as always, is unfailingly swinging and creative. 'Hicks' energy level and his ability to retain so much for so long makes me feel he's one of the best piano players around,' said Betty Carter, 'Especially the energy level. He never lets the audience down, he never lets himself down, and he never let me down.'

One of the welcome comebacks to jazz during the 1980s was the return of **Charles Lloyd** (b.1938). Lloyd had enjoyed huge success in the 1960s with a quartet that included Keith Jarrett (p), Cecil McBee or Ron McClure (b) and Jack DeJohnette (d) that suffered the fate of being overrated at the time and underrated thereafter. At the time Lloyd was accused of being a Coltrane copyist, but as subsequent events revealed he was merely the tip of the iceberg.

During the '70s Lloyd retired and moved to Big Sur, giving his life to spiritual pursuits and becoming a teacher in trancendental meditation, 'As far as he was concerned, music was something he wasn't going to do anymore.'[27] However, in 1982 the young French pianist Michel Petrucciani visited him at the invitation of a friend, 'I didn't even know who Charles Lloyd was,' said Petrucciani. 'In fact Charles didn't even want me at his house . . . One day he said, what do you do? So I said I try to play the piano. Well, why don't you play something? I played and he left. I looked around and said, Oh man, I must have bored him to death. And he went down to the *cave* to get his saxophone and he came out playing and we played all night. He said, OK, I really want to go back out on the scene, but I want you to be in the band.'

Lloyd, Petrucciani, Palle Danielsson (b) and Son Ship Theus (d) toured Europe in 1982, and their appearance at the 16th Montreux Jazz Festival appeared on 'Montreux 82' (Elektra Musician). Included was 'Forest Flower' that revealed his ravishing tone and a more serene approach to improvising than had characterized his '60s work. Part of their perform-ance at the July 1982 Le Festival International du Jazz d'Antibes appeared on the Jean-Christophe Averty video which captured Lloyd's obvious de-light at returning to jazz.

In Europe the following year, their performance at the 1983 Copenha-gen Jazz Festival was recorded by Danish Radio and subsequently ap-peared as 'A Night In Copenhagen' (Blue Note) in 1985. This is an altogether more impressive performance despite a brief guest appearance by Bobby McFerrin. While Lloyd evoked shades of Coltrane, on oboe on 'Lotus Land' and with an inspirational solo on 'Night Blooming Jasmine', there were sharp differences in approach; Lloyd was a far more patient

Charles Lloyd, a fluid melodicism that sought not to compete but to communicate inner peace and tranquility.

musician who favoured melodic, sometimes rhapsodic improvisations that allowed his beautiful tone to shine through.

For the Blue Note concert at Town Hall in 1985, Lloyd's '60s group was all but reassembled with Cecil McBee (b) and Jack DeJohnette (d) together with Petrucciani (p). Their set appeared in its entirety on 'One Night With Blue Note Vol. 4' (Blue Note), with Lloyd creating a ravishing solo on 'Lady Day'. In 1988 he again toured Europe, this time with Bobo Stenson (p), Palle Danielsson (b) and Jon Christensen (d), and on his return in 1989 they recorded 'Fish Out Of Water' (ECM). Here Lloyd's performance was a noncombative exposition of his saxophone tone reconciling his peaceful, spiritual concerns with a fluid melodicism that sought not to compete but to communicate inner peace and tranquility.

Creating A Context

In the same way that Elvin Jones was the most imitated drummer of the '60s and Billy Cobham of the '70s, **Jack DeJohnette** (b.1942) was *the* drummer of the 1980s. Throughout the decade he kept cropping up on class albums; but DeJohnette was more than just a drummer, he was a bandleader, conceptualist, arranger, pianist—a total musician.

At the end of the 1970s he was leading New Directions, a group comprising Lester Bowie (t), Eddie Gomez (b) and John Abercrombie (g) whose loose, highly sophisticated interaction earned them the Prix Du Jazz Contemporain for the 1979 'New Directions' (ECM), a studio album from 1978. Their live 'In Europe' (ECM) from 1979 was an equally riveting, compelling album that captured the magic of the improvisational moment.

However, also in 1979 DeJohnette formed Special Edition, homing-in on Arthur Blythe (as) and David Murray (ts) who were then emerging as significant new voices on their respective instruments. 'Special Edition' (ECM) from March 1979, with Peter Warren (b, clo), was an impressive reconciliation of swinging inside/outside expression, 'The session has all the hallmarks of a classic,' said Gary Giddins. 'It astutely assimilates two of the most individual contemporary saxophonists [and] registers the current revival of swing rhythms and sonorities.'[28]

Although Murray and Blythe left after touring with the group to pursue their own projects, they were replaced by John Purcell (bs, as) and Chico Freeman (ts, f) for 'Tin Can Alley' (ECM) from 1980. Once again DeJohnette's arrangements created sympathetic contexts for his band to function that simultaneously projected individuality and group identity. DeJohnette's compositions ranged from Ellingtonian hues ('Pastel Rhapsody') to collective improvisation ('Riff Raff'); 'There's a fine line between balance and imbalance,' said DeJohnette. 'There are times when everything should be totally in balance, controlled. There's a time when there should be space.'

'Inflation Blues' (ECM) from 1982 substituted Rufus Reid (b) and included special guest Baikida Carroll (t). Although DeJohnette presided over greater group improvisation than the previous Special Edition albums, the intensity of his soloists were directed as much through the mediation of his drumming as the sense of underlying form in his compositions. But the looseness was also contrasted by control; the title track was a loping reggae with a DeJohnette vocal while 'Ebony' evoked Ellingtonian grandeur.

In June 1984 he recorded 'Album Album' (ECM) with a powerful lineup of David Murray (ts), John Purcell (as), Rufus Reid (b) and Howard Johnson (bs, tu). One of the finest albums of the decade, DeJohnette reins-in his soloists to fit the compositional texture of the moment. 'An audience's attention span isn't what it was when Coltrane was playing,' he said, 'Now we're almost back to when Parker and Gillespie had to record two and three minute cuts. It makes you concentrate, consolidate yourself—and sometimes you get more out of that.' The band's range was wide, 'Ahmed The Terrible' included an expansive DeJohnette piano solo, 'New Orleans Strut' captured the essence of the Gulf City's marching bands and 'Third World Anthem' had Johnson on tuba, doubling Reid's lines to give the band a depth that previous—and indeed subsequent—Editions lacked.

In 1985 DeJohnette made his debut album as a pianist on 'The Jack DeJohnette Piano Album' (Landmark) with Eddie Gomez (b) and Freddie Waits (d); it was not well received by critics at the time. However, as the decade progressed it seemed to stand up well against the work of several young piano debutants celebrated for technique rather than content. Although uncharacteristically fragmented in concept, from Cyndi Lauper's 'Time After Time' to Coltrane's 'Countdown' (with only one DeJohnette original 'Lydia'), it might have survived such harsh critical glare if he had narrowed his focus and moderated his impulse to show-off his technique at the expense of developing ideas.

The 1987 'Irresistible Forces' (Impulse) introduced a new lineup, with Greg Osby (as), Gary Thomas (ts), Mike Goodrick (g), Lonnie Plaxico (b) and guest Nana Vasconcelos (perc, v). Once again DeJohnette's tonal palette shifted. What was missed at the time the album was released was that DeJohnette was moving his music towards the Lower Downtown sounds of Steve Coleman's M-Base while keeping Ornette Coleman's har-molodics under review. On the title track and '47th Groove' the alignment was at its clearest; the latter composition captured Duke Ellington's vivid verbal description of a 'Harlem Air Shaft'[29] in vivid, '80s urban realism. The remaining tracks were a paradox: apart from the post-bop-main-stream blow-out on 'Oesthetics', they were imbued with the spirit of ECM. However, by the 1988 'Audio Visualscapes' (Impulse) the M-Base idealism and moments of multi-key harmolodicism had been absorbed into DeJohnette's music. Even so, the conceptualism remained firmly in DeJohnette's grip; it was his personality that controlled the destiny of the music, as ever 'multi-directional', moving from within the jazz tradi-tion to explore the future.

In 1968 bassist **Dave Holland** (b.1946) was spotted in London by Miles Davis who promptly extended an invitation to join his ensemble. On leaving Davis, Holland's most frequent musical companions were Anthony Braxton and Sam Rivers who subsequently collaborated on his definitive 1972 album 'Conference Of The Birds' (ECM). Although seriously ill with endocarditis in the early 1980s, Holland emerged in 1983 with a talented band that combined the ethos of the swinging free expression that made 'Conference Of The Birds' so memorable with the spirited ensembles of the late Charles Mingus.

Exhilarating and intense, Holland's quintet combined the Canadian trumpeter **Kenny Wheeler** (b.1930), an outstanding ECM artist in his own right,[30] Julian Priester (tb), the fast emerging talent of Steve Cole-man (as) and Steve Ellington (d); 'My thing is to create a setting—and I learned this from Miles Davis,' said Holland. 'During the time I played with him he would create the environment for the music, then let the musicians deal with it. That's what I tried to do.'

A solo cello recital, 'Life Cycle' (ECM) preceded the 1983 'Jumpin' In' (ECM) with the group and it immediately delivered the postponed prom-ise of 'Conference Of The Birds' (ECM); the three-way conversational exchanges among the front line suggest the polyphony of New Orleans jazz transplanted into the declamatory, urban stress of Charles Mingus's ensembles. Holland's bass playing was resonant and purposeful, under-pinning the acoustic swirl of invention and re-invention, from communal interface to the fragmentary commentary of trumpet and saxophone be-hind Priester's trombone on the spirited 'You I Love'.

The 1984 'Seeds Of Time' (ECM) brought in the talented young Marvin 'Smitty' Smith (d); Holland later reflected on the influence of both Coleman and Smith on his playing, pointing to their, 'extraordinary new ideas in rhythm—I've had to develop new skills to play the music. There are some songs . . . where I've had to relearn certain things . . . like Steve Coleman's "Uhren" from "Seeds Of Time": it's got a very unusual rhythmic structure which was challenging for me to learn. It's a cycle of nine, the bar is in nine and the nine is divided up into two different ways.'

But Holland's Quintet balanced new ideas with old, most notably his sensitive, subtle adaption of the think-on-your-feet interaction that characterized the work of Charles Mingus; indeed, former Mingus sideman Doug Hammond contributed two powerful numbers including 'World Protection Blues' à la 'Boogie Stop Shuffle' while the jive-speak intro to Steve Coleman's 'Gridlock' recalled the theatre of 'Scenes In The City'.

'Razor's Edge' (ECM), from 1987, with Robin Eubanks now on trombone, was probably the best realized of the three albums; no open-ended blowing, the flexible charts allowed the piano-less ensemble to shape and mould both solo and texture to the mood of the moment. The 1988 'Triplicate' (ECM), with just Holland, Coleman and Jack DeJohnette (d), pared the ensemble down to the minimum for Holland's group interaction to catch fire. Coleman emerged as a profound, lyrical alto saxophonist with that 'dangerous' edge to his playing that so often sets the great jazz instrumentalists apart; indeed, Holland's group provided a context in which he could flourish and his best work during the '80s was to be found on these albums.

After studying trumpet at Berklee, **Jack Walrath** (b.1946) worked in rhythm and blues bands, with Gary Peacock, Glenn Ferris and Ray Charles before joining Charles Mingus between 1974 and 1978, contributing his own 'Black Bats And Poles' to 'Changes Two' (Atlantic). Since then his imagination has never lacked for ideas; throughout the 1980s he created a series of ensembles that worked out of the hard-bop tradition but always offered something more. Walrath used unusual instrumental combinations, challenging and oddly constructed original compositions, crafty voicings and ventured to the limits of inside/outside playing yet barely achieved the critical recognition that was showered on countless young players whose music had no pretence toward progress and experimentation.

His debut as a leader, 'Demons In Pursuit' (Gatemouth) from 1979, was with a group of then unknowns including John Scofield (g), Jim McNeely (p, k), Ray Drummond (b) plus his former Mingus associate Dannie Richmond (d). The album teems with ideas. 'The music was an attempt to show jazz could be emotional, free and knowledgeable at the same,' he said.[31] 'King Duke', for example, envisages a card game between Ellington, Mingus, Mozart and Beethoven. Walrath's compositions never said too much, were quirky, clever and carried, if not a knock-out punch, then a pretty good righthook. Soloists got to breathe but didn't hog the limelight and Walrath emerged as an artistically mature, streetwise trumpeter.

His 1981 'Revenge Of The Fat People' (Stash) had another stellar cast of musicians; Ricky Ford (ts), Michael Cochrane (p), Cameron Brown (b) and Mike Clark (d). 'This music wasn't learned, it was earned,' wrote Chip Stern.[32] The title track, 'Beer' and 'Blues In The Guts'—despite their unromantic titles—were powerful, committed performances. Walrath's own playing had a keen rough edge, his technique able to execute his imaginative ideas, full of unusual note choices, rhythmic hopscotch and harmonic savvy. The 1982 'Plea For Sanity' (Stash), a trio with Michael Cochrane (p) and Anthony Cox (b), simply boiled down the group concept down to its very essence, Walrath's technique and expressivity clear and cogent.

Later in 1982 he toured Europe with former West Coast blowing buddy Glenn Ferris (tb), Michael Cochrane (p), Cox (b) and Jimmy Maddison (d); 'In Europe' (Steeplechase) revealed a freer bop style live at the Montmartre, 'My music is not background music nor is it programmatic,' he explained. 'I don't attempt to describe waterfalls or walks on city streets, but try to produce exhilaration through purely musical means—such as melody, harmony and rhythm.'[33] In 1983 his group again toured Europe, and 'At The Umbria Jazz Festival Vol. 1 & Vol. 2' (Red Records) are looser still. Walrath especially likes his own playing on these albums.[34] 'You may hear bebop, Latin music, funk, blues, classical, near-eastern influences, tempo changes, metre changes, ragtime, no-time, happy music, sad music—at any time, without warning,' he said.[35]

In March/April 1986 he undertook the challenge of another trio setting, this time with Chip Jackson (b) and Jimmy Madison (d) on 'Wholly Trinity' (Muse) that stemmed from rehearsal sessions in Madison's basement studio. Playing with such spartan accompaniment is something most horn players choose to avoid, but Walrath succeeded by the strength of his musicianship and imagination in his searching investigation of his trumpet skills. A testament to his ability was '(The Last Remake Of) I Can't Get Started' where his range, tone and articulation marked him as one of the unsung trumpet stars of the '80s.

The following month he returned to hard bop with a vengeance with the British group Spirit Level. He'd sat in with them in France in 1985 and hooked up again for 'Killer Bunnies' (Spotlight); the whole band sustained a throaty roar throughout, pianist Tim Richards dwells in Tynerland while Paul Dunmall, who had played with Alice Coltrane and Johnny 'Guitar' Watson, sprays febrile Coltraneisms at anything that moves. Stark moments of free, 'outside' playing illuminate yet another facet of Walrath's musical personality.

In 1987 he signed with Blue Note Records and 'Master Of Suspense' (Blue Note) included another impressive roster: Kenny Garrett (as), Carter Jefferson (ts), Steve Turre (tb), James Williams (p), Anthony Cox (b) and Ronnie Burrage (d). Mingus sweeps 'A Study In Porcupine' while Walrath's off-the-wall humour included the Country-and-Western singer Willie Nelson on two tracks. They worked, with 'I'm So Lonesome I Could Cry' receiving a Grammy nomination! 'Meat', 'Children' and 'A Hymn For The Disconcerted' moved the music forward in the shadow of the tradition, never settling for the predictable, one of Walrath's hallmarks. With the exception of Garrett and Turre, he managed to keep the nucleus of the group together and the results showed on 'Neohippus' (Blue Note) from August 1988.

Once again, Walrath's work is never short of clever ideas, different approaches and wit. The tensions in his music were created by continuing to beat different paths out of the hard-bop base; the delight in his music is in the ways that he tries to achieve this end. If occasionally he failed, the point was surely in the *doing*. Throughout the '80s Walrath's ability, both as innovative bandleader/arranger and trumpeter, was barely recognized. But Charles Mingus, so selective in his choice of musicians, must have known that talent in the end will out. In 1989 Walrath appeared with Mingus Dynasty, were his playing at Eastern Europe's Jazz Jamboree was described as 'phenomenal' by *Jazz Forum*.

More importantly, Walrath realized the importance of a set working ensemble to provide a context for his playing and the importance of conceptualization rather than virtuosic recapitulation, 'The most significant innovations come from the soloist's or composer's concepts as expressed through the medium of a steady group,' Walrath asserted. 'The trend in recent years seems to have moved away from the band and experimentation and innovation to attempts at "recreations" . . . "regurgitations" of . . . safe formulae. We are constantly being besieged by "the New Trane", "the next Miles" . . . or the "Coming Whatever" *ad nauseam*. Those who promote these fabrications should realize that the giants . . . were playing music relative to their times. In other words it is not only impossible but also boobish to try and capture the past unless one has a time machine.'[36]

Streams of Consciousness: Two Views.

In 1986 Sonny Rollins (b. 1929) was hailed as 'the greatest living improviser.'[37] There were few arguments. But the problem during the 1980s, as much as it had been since his return from a second furlough from jazz in 1972, was one of delivery. While Rollins was capable of stunning live performances 'so beyond the ken of most musicians that it might shame many into another line of work,'[38] the secret was being in the right place at the right time and that was something that neither Rollins or his audience ever knew in advance. Quite simply Rollins' great talent, both in live performance and on record, had become as elusive as a piece of soap in the bath—you knew it was there but so often it remained out of reach. Things were not helped by his touring group, which from 1983 to 1986 was marred by his choice of bass, drummer, trombonist and occasional guitar whose collective contribution was the worst a major jazz artist had assembled since the ensembles of Louis Armstrong in the 1930s.

A sensitive man[39] with an 'artistry-intensive inferiority complex',[40] Rollins was from time to time consumed with self-doubt as to whether he could live up to his formidable reputation, paradoxically refraining to read his reviews in case anything complimentary was said about him, thereby adding further straws to the camel's back. He also developed an inability to listen to his own recordings. 'Sonny finds it very difficult to listen to himself' explained his wife Lucille[41], and from the 1982 album 'No Problem' (Milestone) she assumed coproduction and co-mixing duties. In practice this meant removing control of all post-production, including mixing, selection of tracks and the opportunity for self-analysis and evaluation, an unusual step for a musician to take.

Rollins' music in the '80s, as much as it had been in the '70s, was a continuing wrestling match with crossover rhythm sections and insubstantial material that frequently militated against his freeflowing, often spirited and occasionally inspirational playing. 'Don't Ask' (Milestone), for example, virtually set the tone for the '80s; a 1979 performance with Larry Coryell (g) it was funk-bound and insubstantial, even though Rollins wrote all the numbers. The 1980 'Love At First Sight' (Milestone), with Stanley Clarke and George Duke, continued the flirtation with pop-rock which Rollins seemed to have convinced himself was where the future of jazz lay. In spring 1981 he appeared with Grover Washington in New

York City and in 1982 made an uncredited appearance on the Rolling Stones album 'Tattoo You' (CBS).

The 1982 'No Problem' (Milestone) included the Dolly Parton hit 'Here You Come Again', which along with 'Isn't She Lovely' from the 1977 'Easy Living' album (Milestone) regularly appeared in live performance. But such insubstantial material—both harmonically and rhythmically—scarcely measured up to the unusual vehicles for improvisation Rollins had used in the past like 'There's No Business Like Show Business' or 'I'm An Old Cowhand', whose more sophisticated structures had evoked brilliant performances.

'Reel Life' (Milestone), from 1983, with Jack DeJohnette, was no better—or indeed worse—than anything that had gone before, hardly qualifications to excite purchase. 'Sunny Days And Starry Nights' (Milestone), from January 1984, brought his then regular band into the studio for the first time, but again Rollins merely played. Although since 1972 Rollins's groups continually messed about with electronic tone colours and rock rhythms, the moment he finished soloing the proceedings became numbingly tedious, something this particular group brought to a kind of bizarre perfection.

The long awaited 'Solo Album' (Milestone), recorded live at the Museum of Modern Art, New York City in July 1985 was many things to many people. Rollins had long specialized in effusive cadenzas in live performance; stream of consciousness parabolas that often competed with what had gone before with their startling audacity. Taking the concept without the launching pad of a tune, jumping in cold hoping that inspiration would take over, was a bold step. It almost worked.

Interestingly, when Rollins had previously recorded at the Museum of Modern Art, the 1975 'There Will Never Be Another You' (Impulse), he used two drummers and the 1957 'A Night At The Village Vanguard' (Blue Note) with Elvin Jones suggested his self-inspirational brilliance might be ignited by good drumming. On 'G-Man' from 1986 he had exactly that with Marvin 'Smitty' Smith. The result could well have been his best album since the sixties, but fade-ins and fade-outs and, ironically, a long drum solo that should have been edited, spoil what should have been a memorable album.

During the same year Rollins premiered 'Concerto For Saxophone And Orchestra'[42] in Japan and in 1987 went into his customary studio shell with 'Dancing In The Dark' (Milestone), with most of the 'G-Man' group. Towards the end of the decade Rollins used the 'G-Man' group whenever possible; at the 1988 Chicago Jazz Festival 'Smitty' Smith continued his single-handed mission to prevent Rollins becoming inspirationally earth-bound. 'He and drummer Smitty Smith could have left the rest of the sextet home without losing any intensity,' said *Downbeat*. But with the 1989 'Falling In Love With Jazz' (Milestone), Rollins ran with Jack De-Johnette (d) and Branford Marsalis, who sounded 'mealy by compari-son.'[43] It was just another Rollins session for critics and fans to pick over looking for crumbs of comfort. 'Listening to him is rarely the unequivocal pleasure it ought to be,' observed Francis Davis.[44] And this was the co-nundrum.

All the great improvisers in jazz, except Rollins, created effective con-texts to project their playing: Louis Armstrong's Hot Five's and Hot Seven's, Goodman's big band, sextet, quartet and trio, Charlie Parker's Quintet, John Coltrane's Quartet, Bill Evans' Trio, Ornette Coleman's acoustic and electric combos, the evolving ensembles of Miles Davis and so on. What Rollins lacked was a challenge or threat from within his group in the way that, say, Hines spurred Armstrong or Elvin Jones spurred Coltrane. Instead Rollins sought inspiration from within and when it was not forthcoming there was no-one to fall back on to force him

Sonny Rollins: Hailed as the greatest living improviser.

through the block. Thus all too often he worked within himself, genius on hold.

Pianist **Keith Jarrett** (b.1945) encompassed a myriad of influences so diverse as to make the word eclectic appear narrow and limiting. During the 1970s no one did more to stimulate interest in acoustic jazz in general and piano jazz in particular, and he was the only jazz musician during the decade to capture a mass audience without selling out to commercialism. His popularity came through solo performances whose universal appeal extended beyond jazz to audiences customarily more fond of symphonic music. Demonstrating a creative imagination of enormous scope, his streams-of-consciousness bonded pan-impressionistic-romantic reveries with jazz, ethnic folk idioms, country and gospel.

Jarrett's concerts were seance-like incantations in order to receive the 'blazing forth of a Divine Will'.[45] Adding to the mystique of the creative artist at one with the Absolute were his incongrous orgiastic cries, whimpers, grunts and foot stomps. These extra-mural noises, captured all too plainly on his recordings, were attended by various gyrations at the key-

Keith Jarrett: Receiving the 'blazing forth of a divine will.'

board, prompting *Village Voice* critic Chip Stern to describe Jarrett wryly as the 'Elvis Presley of high art'. His popularity was assured when the solo 'Koln Concert' (ECM) from 1975 produced remarkable sales for a jazz album; it also proved to be a major factor in establishing the viability of Manfred Eicher's ECM label. By 1979 he commanded the highest fees in jazz, $10,000 for a 90-minute solo performance.[46]

However, Jarrett's small group work, both with American and Scandinavian sidemen brought a tighter definition to his jazz improvisation. 'Personal Mountains' (ECM), recorded live in Tokyo in April 1979 and 'Nude Ants' from the Village Vanguard, New York in May 1979 with Jan Garbarek (t), Palle Danielsson (b) and Jon Christensen (d), contrasts dark side of the moon musings with joyful exuberance. 'New Dance' and 'Sunshine Song' from 'Nude Ants' (ECM) contain some of Jarrett's most powerful and focus playing, suggesting a rhythm section helped the 'Divine Will' get to the point. 'Concerts' (ECM) from May and June 1981 returned to the solo concept for the first time since 1976 but the conduit seemed to have got a crossed line; his energy is shot with echo and allusion. However, 'Paris Concert' from 1988 walks the tightrope between success and failure; 'October 17th 1988' was almost 40 minutes of foraging among the recesses of his imagination while 'Blues', just over five minutes, made the point in modest humility.

Jarrett's most satisfactory work from the 1980s came from a collaboration with Gary Peacock (b) and Jack DeJohnette (d), known as his 'Standards' trio.[47] Their model was the Bill Evans trio, whose lessons in interaction were reexamined by all three musicians. However Evans' search for inner meaning within the structure of the song often gave way to Jarrett's vicarious pursuit of the 'moment', curiously leaving some performances unresolved. 'What was striking was the gulf between the grand gestures and the final product,' said *The Times*.[48]

Jarrett's path in search of deferred self-realization led to his becoming increasingly involved in the classical repertoire, in parallel to his other musical activities. Performing his own works and those of Bach, Bartok and Stravinsky culminated in a recording of Bach's 'Well Tempered Clavier', while an equal and opposite reaction produced the folkish simplicity of 'Spirits'. By the time he recorded 'Dark Intervals' (ECM) in 1988—his first solo concert since 1982—the genre had become crowded with New Age *music-meisters*.

Windham Hill's George Winstone, a Fats Waller devotee, tidied up Jarrett's *Angst* and emotional searching with a soothing inevitability. Copied and diluted, Jarrett's solo epics became devalued by the glassy sheen of his imitators. By the '80s his search for truth, courageous in the '70s, sounded willed rather than real. In contrast, his explorations of standards with DeJohnette and Peacock had a more enduring integrity, moving one reviewer to quote poet Richard Wilbur, that 'the strength of the genie comes of his being confined in a bottle.'

7
Neo Faces

WHILE THE 1980s saw a profound change in the direction of jazz, it was not the result of the sort of startling evolution that had periodically traumatized it in the past. This time there was no Louis Armstrong, Charlie Parker, John Coltrane, Ornette Coleman or Miles Davis to grab it by the scruff of the neck and send it hurtling in a new direction. Surprisingly, for the first few years of the decade, there was no extremism and little innovation; instead a number of young, highly talented musicians reasoned that for jazz to move forward, some sort of rapprochement with the past was necessary.

It was a trend that critic Gary Giddins called 'neo-classical' conservatism; a return to the basic principles of hard-bop championed by the Blue Note label of the '50s and the acoustic Miles Davis. There was to be no musicological trauma that heralded the arrival of bop or free or the artistic quandary posed by fusion. Instead developments would be measured in terms of individual interpretation and recombinations of existing knowledge.

Since the mid-1960s the techniques of hard-bop had been taught in colleges and universities and educators such as David Baker, Jamey Aebersold and Jerry Coker had, by the 1980s, written exhaustive text books based on its methodology that were *de rigeur* for the study of jazz improvisation. In place, therefore, was an underlying set of standards, a community of belief with shared ideas of good and bad.

However, in the face of a rampant avant garde during the '60s and the popularity of fusion during the '70s such notions seemed conservative and old-fashioned. Yet the methods of hard-bop remained the basis of contemporary jazz improvisation (even the best free jazz relied on its musicians knowing the rules first, *before* breaking them). Mastery of the tenets of bop had long become the basic requirement for a musician to participate in jazz, tangible evidence of his instrumental and theoretical proficiency; 'Bebop', said Dave Liebman, 'is the callisthenics of jazz improvisation'.[1]

The return to the hard-bop mainstream was therefore seen by many young musicians as both diagnosis and remedy to what they perceived as the problems that ailed jazz during the '60s and '70s. It was an assertion of implicit and quantifiable values—swing, melodic and harmonic ingenuity, structure and virtuosity—that were a function of formal jazz education. Free jazz was thus viewed with suspicion, the home charlatans, and fusion was seen as limiting, 'Which fusion musicians have developed . . . to the degree Louis Armstrong developed the trumpet 20 years after Buddy Bolden opened the way?' demanded Wynton Marsalis,[2] trumpet *Wunderkind* and self-appointed spokesman of the young neos who articulated the trend in terms of his own uncompromising but conservative values.

In terms of reclaiming an audience for jazz, the timing was all but perfect. Many fusion fans of the '70s were seeking more challenge and fulfilment in their music while many disenfranchized pop and rock fans, aware that the arbiters of musical taste were the six to 16-year-olds around whom the music business centred, clung to an interest in music on their enforced graduation from the youth culture. As a sop to the spending power of this large collective, record companies created Adult Orientated Rock, but the results were more often than not cynical exploitation. It left a gap in the market that was in part satisfied by the 'New Age' phenomena of the early '80s instigated by the Windham Hill record label, offering a soft-jazz/folk/classical music hybrid.

Adventurous listeners, however, who sought more rhythmic stimulation and harmonic sophistication, discovered jazz, which coincidentally was entering a phase when the main thrust of the music was at its most accessible for 30 years. By 1982, Wynton Marsalis had emerged as a cynosure without precedent in the music, a young hero equally at home in the European tradition and the first of many single-minded musicians with whom young audiences could identify. Wynton Marsalis had 'style', and his sartorial elegance became widely associated with the 'new jazz'. 'If you want to listen to music for enjoyment of your soul,' he said, 'to challenge you intellectually as well as emotionally, you want something that's a little more, especially since there's been a thousand years of great music played already: Bach, Beethoven, Stravinsky, Monk, Louis Armstrong, "Bird"—everybody—and I don't think the end result of all that is Boy George.'[3]

ART BLAKEY AND THE HARD-BOP RENAISSANCE

When Wynton Marsalis replaced Valery Ponomarev in **Art Blakey's** (b.1919) Jazz Messengers in 1980, the fortunes of the band, which sadly had been flagging during the 1970s were revived. Significantly, Marsalis and the other young musicians Blakey chose to surround himself with were uncompromising and professional; the band turned out in immaculate lounge suits (the 1970s had brought casual clothes) and just as the Modern Jazz Quartet had taken on the white musical establishment at their own game 25 years before with a combination of elegance and dignity, Blakey's young musicians were just as committed to similar ideals in exposing jazz as an art form.

Art Blakey's self-appointed mission to provide a forum for young musicians to hone their craft began in 1954, when on the classic Blue Note recording 'A Night At Birdland', the 34-year-old band leader declared, 'Yes Sir, I'm going to stay with the youngsters. When these get too old I'm going to get some younger ones. Keeps the mind active!'[4] Since then he provided jazz with an impressive roster of leaders and foot soldiers. 'I want to play the kind of music I like and see young guys come up through the band and make a reputation for themselves.'[5]

It was to be Blakey's maxim throughout his career. Young musicians were made aware of his policy of continual renewal on joining the band, 'We discussed it,' explained Robert Watson, a Messenger between 1977 and 1981. 'Then the day came when he said—"Hey man, I think it's time for you to go" . . . he is about giving as many young people as possible a chance, before he has to hang up his drums.'

Throughout the 1980s the roster of young talent that passed through Blakey's unique finishing school continued unabated. In tracing the key personnel and albums it is significant that many young musicians either came to the attention of the jazz world through Blakey's auspices or at least enhanced their reputation as a result of their tenure with him, most going on to shape the sound of mainstream bop on graduating from his ensemble—just as he intended.

Wynton Marsalis' first recording with the Messengers was alongside Ponomarev as part of an augmented Messengers lineup (that also included Messengers-to-be Branford Marsalis and Robin Eubanks) from July 1980, 'Live At Montreux And Northsea' (Timeless). By October 1980 he had replaced Ponomarev and 'Live At Bubba's' (Kingdom) was recorded when he was just a few days short of his 19th birthday. He featured on a version of 'My Funny Valentine' and was clearly a musician of great promise, but

Art Blakey: Quite apart from his evangelizing role, 'From the Creator to the artist to the audience—there's no other music like it', Blakey became a central figure in mainstream hard-bop during the '80s.

like so many young musicians seemed unable to bring the swagger of the worldly-wise to ballad interpretation.

By the following April he was more at ease in his new surroundings and contributed his best recorded work with the band on 'Album Of The Year' (Timeless) with James Williams, Robert Watson (musical director), Bill Pierce and Charles Fambrough in what was now one of Blakey's all-time great ensembles, although the subsequent 'Straight Ahead' (Concord) from June 1981 lacked the hard edged focus that characterized the previous album. By January 1982 Donald Brown (p) had replaced Williams and Branford Marsalis (as) had come in for Watson with the musical direction passing to Wynton Marsalis; 'Keystone 3' (Concord) continued Blakey's rejuvenation.

In March 1982 Wynton Marsalis left and recommended 19-year-old Terence Blanchard (t) as his replacement and the 21-year-old Donald Harrison in place of his brother. They feature, together with fellow newcomer Johnny O'Neal (p) on the tentative 'Oh—By The Way' (Timeless). However by 1984 this band had matured into what was Blakey's other great

NEO FACES • 225

Art Blakey and the Jazz Messengers: One of his great ensembles with (l to r): Bill Pierce, Wynton Marsalis, Charles Famborough, Branford Marsalis and Blakey.

ensemble of the 1980s with the inclusion of Mulgrew Miller (p), Lonnie Plaxico (b) and Jean Toussaint (ts).

'Live At Sweet Basil' (Paddlewheel) from March '84 has a reverberating version of 'Jodi' and breathed fresh life into 'Blues March' and 'Moanin''. But it was the Grammy winning 'New York Scene' (Concord) from May, with an update of 'Oh—By The Way' that illustrated just how far this band had developed their own identity. On a performance that numbers among Blakey's all time best, the whole ensemble sounded dangerous, 'It's one of the best bands, if not *the* best, I've ever had,' said Blakey, whose drumming, even at 65, was simultaneously supportive and confrontational. The 1985 'Live At Kimball's' (Concord) continued the momentum; by September 1985 the lineup had been augmented by the enthusiastic bluster of Tim Williams (tb) but a rather lacklustre 'New Year's Eve At Sweet Basil' (Paddlewheel) from 31 December 1985 suggested a slackening of resolve. Changes were on their way.

When Blanchard and Harrison left in early 1986 they were replaced by Wallace Roney and Kenny Garrett; other changes included Peter Washington (b) and the return of Donald Brown (p), with Jean Toussaint taking over from Blanchard as musical director on 'Feelin' Good' (Delos), recorded just after Blakey's 67th birthday.

From this point changes in the Messenger lineups came thick and fast, none staying together long enough to create an identity in quite the same way as those headed by Wynton Marsalis and Blanchard. The rush of young players to enhance their cv's was understandable, for clearly Blakey could not go on forever. 'The notoriety you get from playing in his band was something I could definitely use,' explained Robin Eubanks, a Messenger between 1987-9, 'also he's not getting any younger and I wanted to play with him in the sextet setting.'

By 1987 Tim Williams had gone and Javon Jackson (ts) had come in with Benny Green (p) and Philip Harper (t), 'Hard Champion' (ProJazz). The March 1988 lineup had Robin Eubanks (tb) and MD, replacing Kenny Garrett, 'Not Yet' (Soul Note) and 'Standards' (Paddlewheel). In September Freddie Hubbard (t), a Messenger from 1961-64, sat in for a successful set, 'Feel The Wind' (Timeless), and Javon Jackson sounded not in the least fazed by the heavy company.

By the end of the decade the lineup included former Horace Silver trumpeter Brian Lynch, returnee Donald Harrison (as), Javon Jackson (ts), the John Hammond discovery Frank Lacy (tb) and MD, Geoff Keezer (p) and the Nebraska-born bass player Essiet Okon Essiet. Originals by band members featured less than Blakey classics, but it was yet another exciting ensemble.

In October 1989 Blakey celebrated his 70th birthday in Leverkusen, West Germany when Messengers past and present assembled to honour him, including Freddie Hubbard, Curtis Fuller, Benny Golson, Jackie McLean, Walter Davis Jr. and Terence Blanchard. Horace Silver, unable to be present sent a new composition, Roy Haynes sat in on drums and Blakey promised to go on until he was 100. The whole spectacular was broadcast live by West German television.

Quite apart from his evangeling role—'From the Creator to the artist to the audience—there's no other music like it'—Blakey became a central figure in mainstream hard-bop during the 1980s. One of the master drummers of jazz—his style rationalized modern jazz drumming into a post-Kenny Clarke/Max Roach lingua franca—his presence on the bandstand validated the work of young jazz musicians seeking to consolidate their individual styles and reputation in the hard-bop mainstream. Since 1954, when his band included Clifford Brown and Horace Silver, Blakey's musicians always represented an investment in the future.

Blakey's Class of 1980-89

By the time he left the Messengers in 1981, **Robert Watson** (b.1953) had contributed over a dozen original compositions, and through the 1980s was a prolific composer. He continued his association with bass player Curtis Lundy (he was married to Lundy's sister) that began in 1973, forming their own label, New Note to distribute their product. Watson subsequently appeared in ensembles as diverse as Panama Francis' Savoy Sultans, Sam Rivers' Winds of Manhattan, Ray Mantilla's Space Station (Red Record), The Louis Hayes Quintet (Steeplechase) and his own tribute to the Ellington/Johnny Hodges small groups, 'The Year Of The Rabbit' (New Note).

In 1983 he toured Italy with the Italian trio Open Form, 'Perpetual Groove' (Red) and again in 1985, 'Round Trip' and 'Appointment In Milano' (both Red). Here Watson reconciled his bop roots with forays into freedom and endless streams of quavers, made possible by circular breathing, that gave a more realistic view of his playing than the polite 'Beatitudes' (New Note) or 'Jewel' (Amigo). The 1986 'Love Remains' (Red), with favourite accompanist John Hicks (p) plus Curtis Lundy and Marvin 'Smitty' Smith (d) is solid but did not quite ignite. Two years later Hicks returned the favour on *his* session (this time with Victor Lewis [d]) on 'Naima's Love Song' (DIW) and almost succeeded in re-creating the fire and abandon they generated in live performance.

In 1988 Watson signed with Blue Note and 'No Question About It' had Frank Lacy (tb), Roy Hargrove (t) and a Lundy/John Hicks/Kenny Washington rhythm section; the same frontline is used with the addition of Messenger Bill Pierce and Don Sickler (t) on 'Superblue' (Blue Note) from 1988. Both sessions, however had a self-consciousness that recording studios often brought.

Far better were the two follow-ups. Watson's 'The Inventor' (Blue Note) from June 1989 with Melton Mustafa (t) from The Count Basie Band and Benny Green (p) at last came alive with self-confidence in one of his best albums. Equally, 'Superblue 2' (Blue Note) from April 1989 benefited from the presence of Wallace Roney (t), Robin Eubanks (tb), Ralph Moore (ts) and a rhythm section of Rene Rosnes, Bob Hurst and Marvin 'Smitty' Smith. Again Watson overcame his tendency towards self-effacement while the remainder of the band capably re-invented the past without crossing the threshold of inspiration so necessary to resurrect numbers like 'Round Midnight', 'Autumn Leaves' and 'Blue Bossa'.

However, Watson's playing frequently seemed most at home with the 29th Street Saxophone Quartet formed in 1981 with Rich Rothenberg,

Jim Hartog and Ed Jackson. 'Pointillistic Groove' (Osmosis), 'Watch Your Step' (New Note) and 'The Real Deal' (New Note) provide a vision of the saxophone quartet from the bop perspective, a wholly convincing alternative to the WSQ; 'Even though the WSQ might have opened doors in terms of the saxophone quartet being accepted as a valid means of musical expression,' said Watson, 'I believe our music has influenced more groups to come into existence.' Whether or not it was because he felt less pressure as a team player with the group, Watson's playing took on a new dimension, as if to say 'look, this is the real me!' and it is perhaps in this context that Watson's undeniable talent and creativity should be acknowledged.

A Messenger between 1977-81, during which time he also acted as Musical Director, **James Williams** (b.1951) also taught at Berklee College of Music between 1975-85. His debut as a leader, 'Images' (Concord) from 1980, including then current Messengers Bill Pierce and Charles Famborough, and his two subsequent albums on the same label, announced the arrival of an important straight-ahead hard-bop pianist who had taken account of Bobby Timmons' soul and McCoy Tyner's strength, but with a personality, touch and fleetness of his own.

The 29th Street Saxophone Quartet, the context in which Robert Watson's playing seemed most at home. (L to R) Ed Jackson, Rich Rothenberg, Robert Watson, Jim Hartog.

In 1985 he left the Boston area to establish himself in New York and two albums for the Sunnyside label, featuring his straight ahead but subtly softer-bop band Progress Report followed, including Billy Pierce (ts)— now a Berklee faculty member; 'Progress Report' and 'Alter Ego' (both Sunnyside). The 1988 'Magical Trio Vol 1' (Emarcy/Polygram) was Art Blakey's first appearance as sideman in 17 years alongside bassist Ray Brown and together with 'Vol. 2' with its equally strong lineup—Brown plus drummer Elvin Jones—showed Williams' solid craftsmanship and impish originality. 'There was no egos involved,' he said of the sessions. 'They were there in support of me.'

Williams gradually established himself on the New York scene during the latter half of the 1980s as a talented and highly respected soloist and accompanist. 'He is fast becoming one of the most important voices on the piano,' said Art Farmer in 1988 with whom he regularly worked.[6] From 1986 he was a regular member of the Jack Walrath Group, an important band rooted in the hard-bop tradition that profited by Walrath's experience with Charles Mingus; Williams plays a significant role in the success of the 1986 'Master Of Suspense' and the 1988 'Neohippus' (both Blue Note).

As sideman he also performed with Sonny Stitt, Milt Jackson, The Thad Jones-Mel Lewis Orchestra, Tom Harrell and Emily Remler. Perhaps the most important pianist to emerge from the ranks of the Messengers in the 1980s, his solo piano recital at Carnegie Hall in 1989 received critical acclaim. Williams also encouraged and supported the careers of subsequent Messenger pianists, keeping a close interest in developing young talent and doing all he could to advance their careers.

Donald Brown (b.1954) began as a trumpet player and received a scholarship to attend Memphis State University where he switched to piano. Offers of studio work in Memphis tempted him into the rhythm and blues scene that is so much a part of the town, including work with Rufus Thomas and Ann Peebles. In 1981 James Williams recommended Brown to Art Blakey, with whom he stayed for ten months before returning to Memphis where his talents were again in demand for session work for Hi Records and backing artists such as Jesse Winchester and Al Green.

Between 1983-88 he joined the faculty of Berklee College of Music in Boston as well as performing with Bobby Hutcherson, Jon Faddis and The Louis Hayes Group. During this time he was a member of Freddie Hubbard's group for a year, the Eddie Lockjaw Davis/Johnny Griffin

Donald Brown: Profound melodicism and a prolific composer.

Quintet for three months and again with Blakey for a year between 1987-88. He then joined the Donald Byrd Quintet with whom he worked regularly into the 1990s, appearing on 'Getting Down To Business' (Landmark). Brown's wholesome, energetic playing and profound melodicism rooted in the blues soon became appreciated by his peers; he is also a prolific composer and his compositions were used by, amongst others, Blakey, Ralph Moore, James Williams, Ralph Peterson Jr, Art Farmer, Donald Byrd, Rene Rosnes and Wynton Marsalis (on 'J-Mood' [CBS]).

As well as appearing on albums by drummer Carl Allen and vibeist Steve Nelson, Brown debuted on record as a leader with the sensitive 'Early Bird' (Sunnyside) from 1987 which included six of his compositions with a group that included Donald Harrison (as), the Wynton Marsalis rhythm team of Jeff Watts (d) and Bob Hurst (b) with Bill Mobley (t) and Steve Nelson (v). It was followed by a trio, 'The Sweetest Sounds' (Jazz City) from 1988 with Charnett Moffett (b) and Alan Dawson (d) and the 1989 'Sources Of Inspiration' (Muse), a quintet that included Eddie Henderson (t) and Gary Bartz (as). In 1988 he joined the faculty of the University of Tennessee as an Assistant Professor of Music from where he frequently emerged working with Donald Byrd, Jack Walrath and his own group, which toured France in 1989.

Along with James Williams, Memphis-born **Mulgrew Miller** (b.1955) was generally considered to be among the foremost pianists to emerge during the decade from the hard-bop mainstream. After studying with Margaret Chaloff (mother of jazz legend Serge) and James Williams in Boston, he played with the Duke Ellington Orchestra directed by Mercer Ellington (1977-79), Betty Carter (1980), Woody Shaw (1980-83), Johnny Griffin (1983), Art Blakey (1983-86), and the Tony Williams Quintet from 1986.

A sympathetic accompanist and a convincing and unhurried soloist, he appeared on albums by Branford Marsalis, Freddie Hubbard, Bobby Hutcherson, Terence Blanchard/Donald Harrison, John Stubblefield, Frank Morgan, Donald Byrd, Kenny Garrett, Steve Turre, Superblue, Wallace Roney and Marvin 'Smitty' Smith. His own albums, the trio 'Keys To The City' and 'Work' and the quintet 'Wingspan' (all Landmark) bear his carefully considered style in the tradition of Herbie Nichols. 'Music has many rewards to be found beyond its shock value and obviousness,' he said, 'We must also appreciate its subtlety,' the key to his piano style.[7] Never one to grandstand, Miller's quiet authority was deceptive; calm and logical, his playing had a surprisingly delicate touch that concealed a sound technique that always retained plenty in reserve. In August 1987 he fronted his own quintet at the Village Vanguard to critical acclaim.

After playing with Eddie Henderson on the West Coast, **Benny Green** (b.1963) moved to New York in 1982, and worked with Bobby Watson, who introduced him to James Williams who 'was very supportive'. Between 1983-87 he was with the Betty Carter trio and from 1987-89 with Art Blakey's Jazz Messengers. Appearing on Ralph Moore's 'Images' (Landmark), his own debut as a leader, 'Prelude' (Criss Cross) was with an equally hard-bop quintet, followed by the trio 'In This Direction' (Criss Cross), that touched base with Monk and Bud Powell in a very competent hard-bop work-out. 'The future of jazz is in good hands,' observed Ira Gitler.

In 1989 **Geoff Keezer** (b.1970) made his New York debut at Bradley's with Walter Booker (b) and Jimmy Cobb (d) after studying under the guidance of James Williams, who produced his debut album 'Waiting In The Wings' (Sunnyside). It was recorded in 1988 when the young pianist was still 17 and studying at Berklee College of Music under ex-Messenger Bill Pierce and Herb Pomeroy. During the summer of 1989 he toured with the Generations Sextet, his Bradley's trio plus Roy Hargrove (t) and Ralph Moore (ts), and in the autumn joined the Jazz Messengers on James Williams' recommendation. Keezer's astonishingly mature conception, his clear touch, together with the obvious inroads he was making into developing his own individual style, marked him as a major talent in the making as the 1980s drew to a close.

Kenny Garrett (b.1961) began a three year stay with the Duke Ellington Orchestra directed by Mercer Ellington in 1978. Graduating through Mel Lewis (he is on the Band's video in the Jazz at Smithsonian series) and Lionel Hampton, he debuted as a leader on 'Introducing Kenny Garrett' (Criss Cross) and successfully auditioned for the Blue Note records bop creation 'Out Of The Blue' in 1985. He appeared on 'OTB', the 1986 'Inside Track' and 'Live At Mt. Fuji' (all Blue Note). In 1986 he joined Art Blakey and in 1987 was invited to join Miles Davis on the recommendation of tenor saxophonist Gary Thomas. 'Playing with strong leaders makes you a strong person,' explained Garrett. 'It helps you determine what you want to do and what you don't.' His playing with Davis still retained the patois of bop, however, and his soulful licks appeared on the 1989 Davis album 'Amandla' (WEA).

A powerful alto saxophonist in the bop axis, his fast, scurrying lines and unusual note choices—'Nathan Jones' from 'Live At Mt. Fuji' is a good example—are featured on his own 'Garrett 5' (Paddlewheel) from 1988 that remained in the OTB groove, but was curiously disappointing. With his 1989 'Prisoner Of Love' (Atlantic) Garrett's solid craftsmanship attempted to cover all bases with mixed results. 'Big 'Ol Head' had Miles Davis guesting on the altoist's new but undistinguished electronic groove. Garrett was also in demand by several established leaders including Dizzy Gillespie, Tom Harrell, Freddie Hubbard, Woody Shaw, Jack Walrath and Donald Byrd.

Wallace Roney (b.1960) is a trumpeter whose use of space in his solos gave his work a calm assurance; he made his recording debut on Blakey's 1981 'Killer Joe' (storyville). His playing on Chico Freeman's 1982 'Tradition in Transition' (Elektra Musician) and Ricky Ford's 1983 'Interpretations' added to a reputation that was enhanced with another period with Art Blakey in 1986. Later that year he moved to Tony Williams' Quintet and remained with him throughout the decade, appearing on

Kenny Garrett: 'Playing with strong leaders makes you a strong person'.

'Foreign Intrigue', 'Civilisation', 'Angel Street' and 'Native Heart' (all Blue Note), distinguishing himself on every album. He also appeared on Marvin 'Smitty' Smith's 'Keeper Of The Drums' and 'The Road Less Travelled' (both Concord), Kenny Barron's 'What If' (Enja) and Kenny Garrett's 'Garrett 5'.

His debut as a leader with 'Versus' (Muse) was locked into the hard-bop groove, but the 1988 'Intuition' (Muse) attempted to move away from the prevailing trend of bop re-invention to experimentation with polychords and polyharmonies. His appearance on Christopher Hollyday's 1989 debut album for Novus contrasted the young alto saxophonist's rush of ideas with the calm poise of a now mature artist. His appearance later in the year at Carnegie Hall with the Tony Williams Quintet saw his melodic invention, articulation and lucid imagination mark him at the forefront of the young trumpet players who emerged during the 1980s.

Robin Eubanks (b.1955) studied trombone at the Philadelphia College of Performing Arts and joined Slide Hampton's World Of Trombones in 1978. Through Hampton he moved to New York City in 1980, sharing a flat with his brother Kevin Eubanks the guitarist and tenor saxophonist Ralph Moore. His first experience of the Messengers came as a member of Art Blakey's Big Band in 1980, 'Live At Montreux And North Sea' (Timeless). With such an unfashionable instrument he took a while to establish himself on the New York scene, deputizing in the Mel Lewis Jazz Orchestra and playing with Bobby Watson.

An association with Steve Coleman led to a continuing involvement in the altoist's M-Base music throughout the 1980s. An introduction led to Broadway and pit band work, another continuing avenue of work during the decade. In 1986 he joined Dave Holland's ensemble, toured with Abdullah Ibrahim and in 1987 joined Art Blakey's Jazz Messengers as musical director. 'Since Robin has been with Art he has really blossomed, come into his own with something to say,' said fellow trombonist Steve Turre.

Throughout his career Eubanks consciously avoided attempts at pigeon-holing, being equally at home in hard-bop, such as Alvin Queen's excellent 'Jammin' Uptown' (Nilva) or the harmolodic power-game of Ronald Shannon Jackson's Decoding Society 'Decode Yourself' (Island). Other album appearances included James Newton's 'Romance And Revolution' (Blue Note), Marvin 'Smitty' Smith's Concord albums, Steve Coleman's Five Elements, Branford Marsalis's 'Scenes In The City' (CBS), Geri Allen's 'Open On All Sides' (Minor Music), Mark Helias's 'Current Set'

(Enja), his brother Kevin's 'Guitarist' (GRP), Herb Robertson's 'Shades Of Bud Powell' (JMT) as well as commercial dates with Talking Heads and Patti LaBelle. His own recording debut as a leader, the June 1988 'Different Perspectives' (JMT), reflected this eclecticism, but failed to do his talent justice.

Brian Lynch (b.1956) studied trumpet at the Wisconsin School of Music and moved to New York in 1981, where he worked in the bands of Toshiko Akiyoshi/Lew Tabackin, Mel Lewis, George Russell and Bill Kirchner. From 1983-85 he was featured in the Horace Silver Quintet on the recommendation of Tom Harrell. His debut as a leader was the 1986 'Peer Pressure' (criss cross) followed by 1989's 'Back Room Blues' (criss cross).

A featured soloist with the Toshiko Akiyoshi Jazz Orchestra, Lynch has also worked with Eddie Palmieri and appeared on albums by Dave Stahl, vocalist Mark Murphy and alto saxophonist Jim Snidero. 'I never set my sights on the studio scene,' he said, 'I just came to New York to learn more about the music . . . I don't think there's a higher calling than a jazz musician.' Towards the end of 1989 he joined the Messengers, becoming one of the very few musicians in jazz who have worked in the ensembles of both Horace Silver and Art Blakey, a testament to his growing talent.

'We never thought of stardom. We were thinking about music and how to learn more, because we wanted to be as great as the rest of them,' said Donald Harrison in 1985. He was speaking at the first live appearance of the **Blanchard/Harrison Quintet,** a group that seemed permanently in the shadow of the Marsalis brothers. Their initial albums were recorded while still with Art Blakey, the 1983 'New York Second Line', the 1984 'Discernment' (both Concord) and the 1986 'Nascence' (CBS). Reflecting their determination not to put a foot wrong they melded their New Orleans heritage with bop. Equally, a live 1986 date at the Sweet Basil for the Japanese Paddlewheel label, celebrating the music of Booker Little and Eric Dolphy, continued their calculated voyage into reinvention.

Both Terence Blanchard (b.1962) and Donald Harrison (b.1960) were graduates of the New Orleans Centre for the Creative Arts, although Harrison subsequently went to Southern University and Berklee, Blanchard continued his music studies at Rutgers University. Reunited in the Blakey Band at the recommendation of Wynton Marsalis in 1981, they remained until early 1986. With the 1987 'Crystal Stair' and the

1988 'Black Pearl' (both CBS) they continued firmly 'in the tradition', a mixture of careful pre-planning and, well, careful pre-planning. However, Harrison's alto lept with out-of-school abandon on Don Pullen's 1985 'Sixth Sense' (Black Saint) and Terence Blanchard's trumpet had such fluent authority on Alvin Queen's 1985 'Jammin' Uptown' (Nilva)—positively propelled upwards by John Hicks (p) and Ray Drummond (b)—that suggested a little more urban rawness rather than collegiate control might have taken them out of the shadow of the brothers Marsalis.

The Brothers Marsalis Plus One

Wynton Marsalis (b.1961) had developed a formidable trumpet technique before entering jazz; by the age of 14, for example, he was performing Haydn's Trumpet Concerto. At 18 he took leave of absence from Julliard School of Music to join Art Blakey's Jazz Messengers and his prodigious talent was such that he played a key role in reviving Blakey's fortunes. It is no exaggeration to say that the considerable media interest he attracted helped create a climate for acoustic jazz to flourish in the early 1980s and his youth personified an image of jazz with whom a new, younger audience for the music could identify.

In 1981 he left the Jazz Messengers and joined the old Miles Davis rhythm section of Herbie Hancock, Ron Carter and Tony Williams to tour Japan. On their return they recorded 'Herbie Hancock: Quartet' (CBS), a double album that included some particularly arresting work from the young trumpeter. As a direct result Marsalis was immediately signed as a soloist to the label in his own right, creating a historic precedent as the first artist to be simultaneously signed by a major recording label in both jazz and classical fields. His first album, the 1982 'Wynton Marsalis' (CBS), was rush-released when he had no set, working group. That emerged later in the year and comprised his brother Branford Marsalis (ts), Kenny Kirkland (p), Jeff Watts (d) and a revolving cast of bass players.

A unique first came in 1983 when his second album 'Think Of One' (CBS) and his CBS Masterworks collection of trumpet concertos by Haydn, Hummel and Leopold Mozart were awarded Grammies by the National Academy of Recording arts—the first time in their history this had happened simultaneously for a jazz and classical album by the same artist.

In late 1983 a further tour with Herbie Hancock, Carter and Williams, together with his brother, billed as VSOP II, underlined both brothers' exceptionally close affinity with the music of the mid-'60s acoustic Miles

Davis—indeed on 'Wynton Marsalis' they had recorded 'RJ', a Ron Carter composition that had appeared on the renowned 1965 Davis album 'ESP' (CBS). Sadly VSOP II never recorded, (although tapes do exist of their London concert, owned by Capital Radio); significantly Wynton Marsalis was extended by his peers to a degree of adventure he kept under wraps with his own work. Indeed, with his own band his playing erred towards a humourless mastery of the idiom, albeit running parallel to, but not ahead of, Davis's experiments.

The 1984 'Hot House Flowers' (CBS), was an album with strings arranged by Robert Freedman, a risky undertaking in the world of jazz—even Clifford Brown's album in similar ilk was not wholly successful—and duly received a unanimous thumbs down from the critics. He was back on course with the 1985 'Black Codes' (CBS) but the break-up of this talented band came in March that year with the defection of his brother and Kenny Kirkland to tour and record with the pop singer Sting; both were summarily red-carded by Marsalis, scornful of rock, pop, and fusion.

The Wynton Marsalis Quintet: The most talented of all the young neo-classical ensembles to emerge in the 1980s; (l to r) Delbert Felix, Wynton Marsalis, Jeff Watts and Branford Marsalis (pianist Kenny Kirkland is off camera).

The following three months were not happy ones for Marsalis but his road manager had sent pianist Marcus Roberts some tapes of the band. 'My life was kind of out,' said Marsalis.[8] 'My band had just broken up. Marcus came up to my apartment and man, he knew all the music better than I knew it! When I saw that, that gave me renewed faith just in the music, and a deep love for Marcus. From that point on he played in the band.' It was June 1985.

The new group, now a quartet, recorded in December that year with Roberts, Robert Hurst (b) and Watts (d)—'J Mood' (CBS). 'Marsalis Standard Time Vol. 1' (CBS) from September 1986 confirmed that this was his best ensemble of the decade; making brilliant use of shifting metres, Marsalis demonstrated lyrical, harmonic and rhythmic ingenuity, employing a subtle variety of tonal variations, particularly on 'Caravan'. But it was not until 1988 the best Marsalis on record appeared with 'Live At Blues Alley' (CBS), a date from the Washington DC jazz club from December 1986. Reconciling his virtuosity with an altogether more exuberant vision that didn't smack of the intricate, almost painstaking search for perfection that marked so much of his studio work, it was the first time on record that action spoke louder than hyperbole.

A feeling of risk-taking added a humanizing factor to his playing, particularly on 'Delfeayo's Dilemma' and 'Chambers Of Tain' (from the earlier 'Black Codes' album) that surged with spontaneity. It was balanced by 'Just Friends', where he avoided engulfing the listener with fluency, more content to develop his ideas, pacing his delivery and 'playing' his silences. But on 'Knozz-moeking' (from 'Think Of One'), he constructed a series of huge glissando loops that brought to the surface the question of how much the classical persona impinged on the jazz improviser.

A few weeks earlier he had recorded 'Carnival' (CBS Masterworks) featuring the Eastman Wind Ensemble under the direction of Donald Hunsberger. The press release boasted it contained 'the fastest version ever recorded!' of 'Flight Of The Bumble Bee', and there are moments when similar patterns emerge in Marsalis's solos. It is inevitable that in the improvisatory process a player will reach back into the subconscious, to habit and acquired patterns that can be applied within a solo while fresh ideas are being organized.

At the challenging tempo of 'Knozz-moe-king' there were those moments when patterns based on this cliche from the classical repertoire surfaced. Shortly afterwards he stopped performing classical music in public. 'I found there was not enough time for me to pay respects to the unarguable greatness of European music or jazz . . .' he said. 'The time

I spent bludgeoning Haydn could have been devoted to learning how to swing and reaching a functional appreciation of the blues.'

In 1988 he introduced tenor saxophonist Todd Williams to his line-up, and both appear on Roberts' debut album for BMG/Novus. In March 1989 Marsalis, ever conscious of the heritage of jazz, presented an Ellington Orchestra re-creation featuring high school musicians at the Music Educators National Conference in Boston. However, in 1988 he had been appointed to the chair of the Task Force to Perpetuate New Orleans Music, which resulted in a radical shift in his musical perspective.

The 1988 'Majesty Of The Blues' (CBS) explored jazz from the New Orleans perspective, complete with tailgate trombone, banjo et al. It almost seemed as if having mastered growls, smears and plunger effects Marsalis was confronted with the problem of finding a context in which to feature them. Certainly the return-to-the-roots modernistic/traditional settings provided the answer; but conceptually the title track and 'Hickory Dickory Dock' were only moderately successful. However, the suite 'The New Orleans Function' contained a sermon of such monumental boredom that it was difficult to know whether to laugh or cry. And although 'Oh, But On The Third Day' exuded great charm, it was impossible to determine to what ends and purpose his obdurate rationality within the tradition was leading.

In 1989 at New York's Town Hall he used his New Orleans band to explain patiently to an audience of children the basis of jazz and what is meant by jazz and improvisation. However, the 1989 Christmas album, 'Crescent City Christmas Card' (CBS), continued his odyssey within the jazz heritage, expanding the New Orleans vision to include Ellingtonian 'Jungle' effects in an album whose limited shelf-life detracted from the concepts at hand.

For Wynton Marsalis it seemed as if the past was more secure than the future and in 'exploring certainties he seemed unaware that uncertainty was a necessary pre-condition for adventure'. Widely admired for his virtuosity, he appeared to be heading for the same area of jazz occupied by the likes of Sarah Vaughan, Ella Fitzgerald and Oscar Peterson, artists who were beyond criticism for their technical excellence—although it was Miles Davis who once observed that Oscar Peterson 'had to learn to play the blues'.

Branford Marsalis (b.1960) began his career on alto saxophone, changing to tenor saxophone for the 1982 'Fathers And Sons' (CBS), 'Wynton had been urging me to play tenor since our time with Art Blakey,' he explained.⁹ An alumnus of the New Orleans Centre for the Creative Arts and Berklee College of Music, Marsalis joined the Clark Terry Big Band in 1980 and The Messengers in 1981. While with Blakey he came under the influence of fellow Messenger Bill Pierce who is said to have helped shape his developing style. He appeared on three albums with Blakey before joining his brother's quintet, making four albums with Wynton before CBS signed him as a jazz and classical artist.

In 1983 he toured with VSOP II and made his debut as a leader in his own right with 'Scenes In The City' (CBS). Although fragmented, it suggested an artist of great potential; the title track was a piece of Mingus theatre dating back to 1957 and set the tone of the album with a distinct sense of *deja vu*. However, unlike his brother he did not succeed, or apparently try very hard, to create a context for his playing other than fulfilling occasional personal appearances with a quartet comprising Larry Willis (p), Charnett Moffett (b) and Jeff Watts (d). Branford Marsalis gave notice early on that he seemed happy to settle for the role of a 'horn for hire'.

When he left his brother's band in 1985 it was to join the pop singer Sting to tour, record and film with the group 'The Dream Of The Blue Turtles' and 'Bring On The Night' (both A&M). The eight-month commitment had, by his own confession, a knock-on effect on his next album as a leader, 'Royal Garden Blues' (CBS). 'Looking back,' he said, 'My record would have been 100 per cent better if I'd waited six months, my jazz chops had fallen off, definitely.' Even so, he still maintained contact with Sting, appearing on the 1988 '. . . Nothing Like The Sun' (A&M).

In 1986 he toured with Herbie Hancock; this time his playing seemed possessed with the after-effects of 'Romances For Saxophone' (CBS Masterworks), a collection of light classics. The 1987 'Renaissance' (CBS), six quartet tracks and one incongruous trio, was a Blue Note workout, *circa* late '50s, early '60s, in the shadow of Joe Henderson, Wayne Shorter and Sonny Rollins. 1988's 'Random Abstract' (CBS) hints at directions beyond the mainstream of modern tenor saxophone (Ornette Coleman) but, like 'Renaissance', was a massively competent exercise in absorption and reinvention.

Marsalis continued to record in a variety of settings, notably with Miles Davis, Dizzy Gillespie, JoAnne Brackeen, Tina Turner, Roy Ayers, Kevin Eubanks, Bobby Hutcherson, Billy Hart, The Dirty Dozen Brass Band, Steve Coleman, The Duke Ellington Orchestra, Kent Jordan, Ray Drummond, Nancy Wilson, Carole King, Janis Seigal and The Neville Brothers. But by the end of the 1980s it was still by no means clear what artistic direction he proposed following, or to what ends he would direct his undeniable talent.

The 1989 'Trio Jeepy' (CBS), despite the efforts of veteran Milt Hinton (b) and Jeff Watts (d), was overlong and complacent, an endurance as he continued to indulge the foibles of his learning curve. 'My records don't sell worth a damn so they are really experimentation for me,' he said. 'The world has the benefit of watching me practise, basically.'[10] But why should the world be interested?

Delfeayo Marsalis (b.1965) toured as featured trombone soloist with the Ray Charles Orchestra in summer 1985 while studying Music Production and Engineering at Berklee College of Music. A producer and album jacket annotator on several of his elder brothers' albums and those of Marcus Roberts and his father, pianist Ellis Marsalis, he emerged as the leader of the Berklee Jazz Ensemble that won the 1989 Southern Comfort College Jazz Competition. Changing their name to 'No Corporate Rubbish', a Gold Award followed at the 1989 Musicfest finals; described by adjudicator Alex Acuna as 'the best **** young jazz band in the world', they were listed in Downbeat's 'Talent Deserving Wider Recognition' in the 1989 Critic's Poll. Other band members included Roy Hargrove (t), Chris Cheek (ts), Antonio Hart (as), Julian Joseph (p) and Masahiko Osaka (d).

Marcus Roberts (b.1963) was a graduate of Florida State University, and took first place in the River City Arts Festival Jazz Piano Competition in 1981, the Great American Jazz Piano Competition in 1982 and the Thelonious Monk International Jazz Piano Competition in 1987. A sightless person, Roberts joined Wynton Marsalis in 1985, a high visibility spot that led to his signing with BMG/Novus in 1988. The subsequent 'The Truth Is Spoken Here' charted on release in 1989; 'Roberts runs the gamut from stride to incredibly intricate knots,' wrote Leonard Feather.'. . . Derivative or not he is capable of original concepts . . . in this inspiring debut.'[11] The 1990 'Deep In The Shed' (Novus) remained equally conservative with musicians whose artistic immaturity was exposed in such calculated surroundings. More dramatic, however, was his work on 'Live At Blues Alley' (CBS) as a member of the Wynton Marsalis Quartet, which revealed a declamatory, adventurous talent poised to upstage his talented leader.

Neo-classicists II
The London-born tenor saxophonist Ralph Moore (b.1956) started out on trumpet at the age of 14, 'but my teacher had a tenor sax and I liked

Ralph Moore, secure with a growing mastery of ballad performances.

the way it looked', he said.[12] Emigrating to California at 15, he later studied for a couple of years at Berklee College of Music. His reputation was established with a stay with Roy Haynes and almost three years with the Horace Silver Quintet alongside Brian Lynch (t) before becoming active on the New York scene with Freddie Hubbard, the Mingus Dynasty, John Hicks and the big bands of Dizzy Gillespie and pianist Gene Harris.

His assured, solid playing was also featured on albums by Marvin 'Smitty' Smith (Concord), Brian Lynch (Criss Cross) and Joyce (Verve). His own debut as a leader came with '623 C Street' (Criss Cross) followed by the 1985 'Round Trip' (Reservoir) with Lynch and Benny Green (p). The 1988 'Rejuvenate!' (Criss Cross) with Steve Turre (tb) sharing the front line and 'Images' (Landmark), with Terence Blanchard (t) the new front line, showed just how firmly he was planted in the mainstream; secure, with a growing mastery of ballad performances, and on occasion, adventurous.

On 11 April 1987 **Roy Hargrove** (b.1971) won a $5000 scholarship at the 1987 Musicfest in Chicago, but despite his proficiency on the trumpet could not afford one of his own. One was soon supplied, courtesy of Doc Severinsen, and together with $4500 won from various *Downbeat* competitions he headed for Berklee College of Music on graduating from Arts Magnet High School in Dallas in 1988. By then he had traded solos with Wynton Marsalis and Freddie Hubbard in the Caravan Of Dreams, Fort Worth, Texas and appeared in Europe with Frank Morgan. In 1988 he appeared on Bobby Watson's 'No Question About It' (Blue Note) and Watson asserted: 'He's a thoughtful player, always phrasing. He doesn't go out for pyrotechnics even though he has the chops for that too.'[13]

Roy Hargrove. 'He's a thoughtful player,' said Bobby Watson, always phrasing. He doesn't go out for pyrotechnics, even though he has the chops for that too.'

In 1990 he debuted as a leader with 'Diamond In The Rough' (Novus), but like so many young neos the result was conservative and, well, remarkably unexciting. Other album appearances included 'Superblue' (Blue Note) and with David Fathead Newman. He also appeared with the Dallas Symphony Orchestra, Bobby Hutcherson, Herbie Hancock, John Hicks and the student band 'No Corporate Rubbish' that was acclaimed at the 1989 Musicfest finals. A calm, unruffled player, Hargrove seemed to be developing a style that was not dependent on speed of execution or range, more an ordered, vertical lyricism.

At the age of 12 **Christopher Hollyday** (b.1970) was learning Charlie Parker solos by heart on alto and developing an astonishing technique that led to his debut album, albeit on his home-produced label, at 15. In 1988 his album 'Reverence' (RBI) attracted considerable media attention as Hollyday rubbed shoulders with top pros Cedar Walton, Ron Carter and Billy Higgins. A tour with Maynard Ferguson and a week's engagement at the Village Vanguard—the youngest ever headliner—led to his major label debut with Novus records in 1989; 'Christopher Hollyday' (Novus). Throughout Hollyday continued his studies under Arnie Lawrence's music programme at the New School in New York City, and was a finalist in the 1989 Musicfest finals with his own quartet.

With 'On Course' (Novus) from 1990, Hollyday again flashed his excellent technique, albeit again prone to drop into a freefall of assimilated influences, the product of assiduous study and imitation; 'I think it is very important to know what the history is,' he said, 'and to be thankful it got us to where we are. I'm always going through different periods where I listen to certain masters and take what I can from them.'

By the time **Joey DeFrancesco** (b.1971) was eight he was performing on Hammond organ in Philadelphia jazz clubs encouraged by his keyboardist father. At ten he began study in earnest at the Settlement Music School and the High School for the Creative and Performing Arts. A Musicfest USA Jazz Combo All-Star in 1987,1988 and 1989 and a finalist in the 1988 International Thelonious Monk Piano Competition, DeFrancesco's first love continued to be the Hammond B3. Stylistically locked into the Jimmy Smith-Groove Holmes-Jimmy McGriff tradition, DeFrancesco learnt the B3 both inside and out, effecting his own repairs and stripping down his Hammond to modify it 'to make the sound cleaner'.

By 1987 he had opened for Wynton Marsalis, B.B. King and Bobby McFerrin and had appeared and recorded with Grover Washington Jr. In 1988 he was invited by Miles Davis to open during his autumn tour, subsequently appearing on his album 'Amandla' (WEA) and was signed by Dr George Butler of CBS, but his 1989 debut album, 'All Of Me' (CBS), attempted to cover too much ground—from funk to sentimental strings. However, the Jimmy Smith number 'Blues For J' showed his powerful swing, albeit undiluted Smith-Holmes-McGriff. The 1989 'Where Were You?' (CBS) with a cast of thousands including John Scofield, Wallace Roney, Illinois Jacquet and Milt Hinton celebrated his talent but originality of style still eluded him.

DeFrancesco's regular bassist, Christian McBride, a year his junior (in 1989 heading for Julliard) and drummer John Roberts, a year his senior, won chairs in the high school orchestra re-creating Duke Ellington directed by Wynton Marsalis in 1989. The trio appeared in New York's Mood Indigo and Avery Fisher Hall later that year together with Robert Langdon (as) when they appeared in danger of believing their own publicity; a lot of wild-eyed soloing concealed a sense of *deja vu,* unaware perhaps that in Germany the equally youthful Barbara Dennelain was making the B-3 speak with originality.

Ralph Peterson Jr. (b.1962) was introduced to drums by his father, also a drummer. He gained a music scholarship to Rutgers University and studied drums with Michael Cervin and trumpet with William Fielder. He was student director of the Rutgers Jazz Ensemble during his tenure as well as its drummer, and first began attracting attention as a member of the Terence Blanchard/Donald Harrison group, appearing on their albums for Concord and CBS between 1983-86. His performance with the group at the 1985 Kool Jazz Festival was one of the Festival highlights.

Peterson also appeared during the same period with the Jon Faddis Quintet. Earlier in the decade his first 'name' job had been with the Walter Bishop Trio, appearing on 'Scorpio Rising' (Steeplechase). In 1985 he auditioned for the Blue Note label's group Out Of The Blue, appearing on the group's first three albums between 1985 and 1986. However, he was capable of more adventurous powerplay as the 1985 'New Life' and the 1986 'I Want To Talk About You' (both Black Saint) with David Murray demonstrated.

His debut as a leader, the April 1988 'V' (Blue Note) contained five of his own compositions, with one by pianist Donald Brown, that showed a willingness to individualize and personalize his music beyond the self-

Ralph Peterson Jr: Showed a willingness to individualize and personalize both his playing and music beyond the self-imposed limitations of neo-classicism.

imposed limitations of neo-classicism. Using unusual time signatures and structures the quintet, which included Terence Blanchard (t) and Geri Allen (p), probed restlessly at the prevailing status quo.

His willingness to experiment was given freer rein on the August 1988 'Triangular' (Blue Note), a trio album featuring Geri Allen that included four more Peterson originals and imaginative recastings of 'Bemsha Swing', 'Move' and 'Just You, Just Me'. Peterson's work as a leader was among the more exciting to emerge from the decade's neo-classic bop orthodoxy, among the first to begin to move the music beyond assimilated influences, in his case Ed Blackwell, Elvin Jones and Andrew Cyrille, to the creative higher ground.

A major talent on tenor saxophone who was overlooked in the 1980s, **Ricky Ford** (b.1954) was fresh from the New England Conservatory when he joined The Duke Ellington Orchestra directed by Mercer Ellington in 1974. Eighteen months later he replaced George Adams in the Charles Mingus Ensemble, spending two years in what was the bassist's last regular working band and followed it with stints with Sam Rivers, Walter Bishop Jr, Mingus Dynasty, Jack Walrath and, in 1981, Lionel Hampton. Throughout the 1980s he appeared from time to time with Abdullah Ibrahim, appearing on albums such as 'Water From An Ancient Well' (Blackhawk) and 'Mindif' (Enja).

His 1977 debut as a leader, 'Loxodonta Africana' (New World), was a striking album in a world that was not quite ready for a return to the mainstream or to celebrate the young and talented. Ford's assured writing for six- and nine-piece ensembles was only equalled by what for a 23-year-old was playing of class and authority with a tone that had taken account of the 'Cotton Tail' Ben Webster. Then followed a series of albums on the Muse label—his 1987 'Saxotic Stomp' was his eighth—that were remarkable for their consistently high standard of conceptuality and execution. With a strong cast of musicians, including Jimmy Cobb (d), James Spaulding (as/f), Kirk Lightsey, John Hicks or Albert Dailey (p) and Rufus Reid and Ray Drummond (b), all Ford's albums had something original and profound to say within the context of the 'tradition'. His sure sense of direction, his reliance on his own original material together with his mature and exciting playing quite simply set him apart from his peers.

Among the highlights of his work on the Muse label was 'Flying Colours', a 1980 quartet with John Hicks (p); Ford playing with confidence and authority on a set of his ingeniously constructed compositions. 'Shorter Ideas', an album of four Wayne Shorter compositions, plus two originals and Ellington's 'Reunion Blues', scored by Ford for a six-piece ensemble in 1984, is an excellent example of his deft, original small-group writing and sure handling of form and structure. 'Looking Forward' took its inspiration from South Africa but also includes a highly original version of the Ellington/Tizol composition 'Conga Brava.'

1987's 'Saxotic Stomp' came from a period when Ford was Artist In Residence at Brandeis University exploring the music of Mary Lou Williams with a student big band. The arrangements, pared down from his big band charts, were described by Ford as 'the closest you'll get to my big band writing for now . . . I wanted to make something contrapuntally

Ricky Ford, a major talent overlooked in the '80s.

interesting but short—like in the 78 era, when you had to create a significant amount of music in a short time.'[14] It was a powerful lesson masters like Jelly Roll Morton, Ellington and Charlie Parker learnt well, but was obscured by the development of the LP when so many performances were guilty of expanding to the length of time available at the expense of content.

The Harper Brothers: Drummer Winard (b.1962) played with both Dexter Gordon and Johnny Griffin in 1982, before studying with Jackie McLean in 1983. After moving to New York he worked with Clifford Jordan, Walter Davis Jr, Shirley Horn, Abdullah Ibrahim, Brook Benton and Betty Carter, appearing on her 1988 'Look What I Got' (Verve). Later that year he appeared as a member of the Stan Getz Quartet.

Trumpet playing Philip (b.1965), worked with organist Jimmy McGriff for 18 months before studying with Jackie McLean in 1983. Encouraged and assisted by Wynton Marsalis and Terence Blanchard he joined Art Blakey between 1987-89 and appeared on 'Hard Champion' (Pro Jazz), 'Not Yet' (Soul Note) and 'Standards' (Paddlewheel).

The brothers formed their own band in 1985 after appearing at New York's Blue Note in a series of 'Young Lion' concerts where they played alongside the likes of Ralph Moore and Benny Green. Their hard-bop quintet debuted on record with the 1988 'The Harper Brothers' (Verve) with Betty Carter graduates Justin Robinson (alto), Stephen Scott (piano) and Michael Bowie (bass). Exuding a loose-limbed rawness, in contrast to the earnest efforts of many of the new guard, they showed they had absorbed Blakey's persuasive lessons in internal balance, dynamics and pacing a solo, and were sparked by Winard Harper's exceptionally mature and compulsive drumming. Philip Harper incorporated a modest growl technique in his tone that set him apart from his peers, and if his execution was not yet in place then his melodic construction was.

'Remembrance' (Verve), recorded live at the Village Vanguard in 1989 captured the snap and crackle of the band that more than any other of the young neos delighted in the thrill of discovery and risk-taking, contrasting the almost monotonous inevitability of po-faced virtuosity that had become the norm. The Harper Brothers' ingenious sparkle communicated; in an idiom of re-invention it was the key.

In 1985 producer JoAnne Jimenez came up with the idea of creating a young bop ensemble to celebrate the return of the Blue Note record label under the aegis of EMI. Out of 35 young hopefuls a sextet of young bop-orientated musicians, mainly from Rutgers University, were selected and launched as **Out Of The Blue**. The group, comprising Michael Philip Mossman (t), Kenny Garrett (as), Ralph Bowen (ts), Harry Pickens (p), Bob Hurst (b) and Ralph Peterson Jr. (d), debuted in 1985 with an eponymously titled album and not a little hype from their sponsors.

Their 1986 'Inside Track' (Blue Note) was powerful, direct and while derivative at least included several originals. Although exposure with a major recording label appeared slightly premature for Mossman and Bowen, the remainder of the band demonstrated the youthful accomplishment that, as in so many instances in the 1980s, deflected criticisms of unoriginality. It took the live album, 'Live At Mt. Fuji' to confirm that the band contained genuine talent, with Kenny Garrett's solo on 'Nathan Jones', Ralph Peterson's live-wire drumming and Harry Pickens' piano impressing.

However, by 1986 Bob Hurst had departed to Wynton Marsalis, where as Robert Hurst III he became a member of the trumpeter's new quartet, and Garrett left soon afterwards. With fewer bookings the band foundered but were picked up by the Japanese subsidiary in 1988 with Mossman and Bowen co-leading with Rene Rosnes (p), Billy Drummond (d), Steve Wilson (as) and the return of Hurst. 'Spiral Staircase' (Blue Note) from January 1989 was OTB's most advanced and sophisticated album; Mossman's conception matured sharply after a stint with Roscoe Mitchell's Sound Ensemble and moved the band from simply emulating the classic Blue Note albums of the past to a creative, contemporary post-bop climate. The maturity of material and of delivery, with four compositions by Mossman and one by Bowen, show the band, like that of the Harper Brothers, assuming a creative personality of its own.

Already a jazz legend by the 1980s for his ground-breaking drumming with the 1960s' Miles Davis acoustic quintet, **Tony Williams** (b.1945) was in imminent danger of having achieved too much too soon and losing direction at the beginning of the 1980s. His recorded work under his own name, 'Lifetime' and 'Spring' (Blue Note) from the '60s had moved into the avant garde, while his early 1970s group Lifetime produced a series of seminal jazz-rock albums that still impress with their confrontational virtuosity. His 1979 'The Joy Of Flying' (CBS) was also rock-orientated but bombed. Meanwhile, Williams had toured and recorded with the 'supergroup' VSOP but equally was touring and recording with rock musicians with no pretensions towards jazz, including Public Image Ltd.,

Yoko Ono, Portland, Johnny Rotten and Santana, as well as appearing on the soundtracks of movies such as 'Blade Runner' and 'Star Wars'.

In 1985 he appeared in the movie 'Round Midnight', both on screen and on the soundtrack, and ended a six-year break as a leader on album with 'Foreign Intrigue' (Blue Note). Perhaps surprisingly, Williams returned to the hard-bop mainstream with Wallace Roney (t), Donald Harrison (as), Mulgrew Miller (p) plus Ron Carter (b) and Bobby Hutcherson (v). Aside from the occasional clatter of a drum machine, the music—all originals by Williams—were set in the Blue Note groove; a return to the style from which Williams originally emerged as a teenager in Jackie McLean's band in the early 1960s.

More impressive was the 1986 'Civilization', with what was now his regular touring group with Billy Pierce (ts) instead of the alto and vibes and Charnett Moffett (b) in for Carter. Williams' drumming, very forward in the sound-mix, gave the music impact, particularly on 'The Slump' and 'Mutants On The Beach', and his choice of musicians gave the music poise and more than a touch of class. Williams was not beyond giving the drums a bit of welly, 'I do like that kind of drumming . . . where you have to hit the drum hard,' he said. In live performance he could appear to be overwhelming his group, but what he played fitted the moment and was frequently a staggering exhibition in playing time; Williams' independent co-ordination, his dramatic and imaginative fills, his continual commentary that formed a percussive counterpoint behind a solo and his ability to play behind, on top and in front of the beat had long been admired by drummers.

The 1988 'Angel Street' (Blue Note) reaffirmed that Williams' entry back into acoustic jazz was not merely a dabble. He had established a sure sense of direction and the group had long since shaken down into one of the most exciting within the neo-classic orbit, the leader's drumming was just one element in a group where Pierce, Roney and Miller's strength of purpose combined to give the group its character. Williams' compositions—he continued to study composition with Dr. Robert Greenberg of Berkeley throughout the '80s—were by no means simple heads. Several were well crafted lines whose modest development allowed soloists logical interludes of varying length before sweeping on, frequently lifting the music out of the clutches of *deja vu*.

In the summer of 1989 Williams appeared in Carnegie Hall with his group, now with Ira Coleman (b), playing with uncommon urgency and commitment his young musicians would need to sustain a career in jazz; nothing was forced but the group were now negotiating the transition from neo-classicism to post-bop with hard-core precision and respect for the tradition. The September 1989 'Native Heart' (Blue Note) captured those longer, rolling compositions with their melancholy sweeping lines; both bandleader and band had matured, able to tell old stories as new adventures.

THE SEDUCTION OF STYLE

Without a doubt the most heartening aspect of jazz during the 1980s was the steady emergence of young dedicated musicians who had developed sound instrumental techniques and fluency within the harmonic and rhythmic vocabulary of bop and hard-bop. The institutionalization of jazz education made advanced technical skills commonplace, with colleges producing young musicians well versed in the craft of improvisation who might have stunned the jazz world just 20 years before with their technical prowess. Effectively these young neo-classicists looked to role models who had defined bop and hard-bop from around 1948 to the mid-'60s, when the parameters of the music were codified and perfected by a handful of key musicians.

But with so many musicians supporting the same sources of stylistic inspiration, similarity in concept and execution was inevitable with their faith resting in such a narrow repository of the jazz repertoire. Consequently individuality became less important than shared values of craftsmanship—technique, familiarity with the harmonic and rhythmic conventions of the music, an orthodox tone and precise articulation. Being able to converse freely in the dialect of hard-bop at the youngest possible age—even if it was through the adopted voice of a role model such as a Jackie McLean, a Jimmy Smith or a Joe Henderson—seemed cause enough for celebration.

The intensive study required to achieve theoretical knowledge and technical skills so young created a kind of tunnel vision that in the end was bound to be limiting. Christopher Hollyday, for example, felt in 1989 that alto saxophonist Jackie McLean was, 'Right now . . . playing more music than anybody,' yet confessed, 'I haven't listened much to Arthur Blythe . . . I haven't checked him out that much.' 15 With their ears so close to the ground checking out hard-bop, the young neos were in danger of not glimpsing the horizon. When they did the result could be startling icon juggling; by the end of the decade Wynton Marsalis had moved from his previously intractable mid-1960s Miles Davis phase to discover pre-war idioms of New Orleans and Ellingtonian 'Jungle' music.

Criticism changed subtly to accommodate these values; in a musical culture shaped predominantly by recordings, critique referred less to cultural and social origins and more to subjective values evoked by the music. Jazz, as Roger Taylor observed, was now 'firmly within the grip of the aesthetics of Romanticism'.[16] Even musical excitement was solemnly learned; what had once been a music of protest and assertion for the musician and escapism for his audience had become a form of escapism for both listener *and* musician.

These changes were gradually reflected in the recording business. By the mid-1980s areas of the jazz record business were beginning to mirror aspects of the classical record business. In the classical field it had become *de rigeur* for each succeeding generation's celebrated virtuosi to record *their* versions of the classics, thus stimulating record sales with new versions of the established repertoire. 'If a marketing manager thinks the company wants a new Beethoven cycle, it is useless to protest that conductor X needs another ten years to mature his ideas on Beethoven, or that the company already has four Beethoven cycles in its back catalogue,' wrote critic Richard Morrison.[17] 'Corporate values mean two species of musician are favoured: photogenic stars and photogenic prodigies.'

Such thinking began to surface in jazz, producing new versions of old classics by the current generation for a new, younger audience unable to identify with past and often posthumous heros of the '50s and '60s—thus stimulating sales. The popularization of Wynton Marsalis, closely examining Miles Davis's work of the early '60s, became the most obvious manifestation of this trend, and he was by no means alone as the 1980s progressed; young neos wanted *their* versions of the standards on disc, often in advance of artistic maturity, just as young conductors and instrumentalists wanted *their* versions of the great classics on record. Trumpeter Brian Lynch's debut as a leader in 1986 was called, not without some irony, 'Peer Pressure' (Criss Cross).

As in classical music, these new young stars posed the inevitable question of whether they were as 'good' as the legendary names of the past; 'Early in their careers as conductors', wrote Hugh Canning, 'Bernard Haitink and Sir Colin Davis worked with many of the greatest violinists of the sixties and seventies . . . and while both agree that technical standards are as high as ever, neither seems convinced that young players have the musical insight or personality of their predecessors. "We live in a yuppie society" . . . [said] Haitink . . . "in which everything has to be made so quickly."[18] Once again the parallel in jazz was all too apparent.

But perhaps the most important question for posterity posed by the 1980s' neos was to what extent a music so remote from its origins retained its integrity and expressiveness when shaped by entirely different cultural and social values; technical mastery is one thing, individual *style* was another. When Branford Marsalis admitted his recordings were practising in public he was also admitting he had no idea of what direction to pursue in his music beyond listening to the 'tradition' to expand his vocabulary, 'I'd been listening to a lot of people . . . guys like Ben Webster and Gene Ammons. So when I'm playing . . . I'm not really thinking, "Who am I going to play like now?" though on a lot of songs I do.'[19]

With the exception of Art Blakey, Betty Carter and Horace Silver, or a Dave Holland and a Jack DeJohnette, the opportunities of learning at the side of an elder master had gone. Young musicians therefore absorbed the jazz tradition second-hand as they searched for an identity. Thus a Christopher Hollyday or a Joey DeFrancesco or a Benny Green became a reflection of this month's assimilated influences, influences that stemmed from similar sources—from educational programmes in colleges such as Berklee or North Texas State, and from the bop/hard-bop albums of the '50s and '60s. Where the breeding ground of bop had once been the clubs and after-hours joints in Harlem, the sound of the neo-classicists in the 1980s was shaped by young musicians who practised their licks in the bedrooms of middle-class suburbia.

8
Village Voices and Downtown Sounds

BY THE END of the 1980s, the broad generic term jazz was being stretched to accommodate what the *New York Times* described as music that flew 'past the pigeonholes'.[1] The increasing institutionalization of jazz education in schools and colleges meant that instrumental technique and improvisational skills of a high order were becoming more and more commonplace among young musicians, who, like the new gunslinger in town, arrived on the scene expecting to kill off the opposition on pure firepower alone. But to establish a reputation in jazz, the emphasis was increasingly shifting to embrace compositional and organizational abilities as well as technical expertise. To have mastered your chosen instrument, even as a teenager, was becoming the rule rather than the exception; the challenge now was to create an effective context in which to function as a jazz musician.

It was a conundrum that even some of the great jazz musicians, not least Dizzy Gillespie and, since his comeback in 1972, Sonny Rollins, were unable to resolve satisfactorily. During the '80s, however, it gradually became the *sine qua non* that sorted the men from the boys, the inability of the Brothers Marsalis, for example, to create an original platform to focus their undeniable talents was a significant factor in the wane of their once seemingly impregnable reputations.

But the creation of a group to rehearse and develop original works and new ideas was not financially feasible in most cases, so the problem was often overcome by informal groupings of like-minded musicians who were prepared to work together without payment in each other's ensembles to prepare their ideas for the performance situation. The shared musical affinities of such groups tended to make for tight, hermetically sealed constituencies of style and approach, 'Once musicians are set with a certain type of musician they always play with them,' said trumpeter Herb

Robertson commenting on the New York scene in the 1980s. 'It was hard for me to break into . . . they already had their own circle of musicians who were familiar with their way of writing and playing music. I had to stay with the people I knew.'[2]

As the decade progressed, new bands began to emerge quicker than journalists could put tags on them; some musicians helpfully labelled their product, M-Base, for example, while others were invested with a broad generic description, such as free-bop. John Zorn described his music as 'jazz from hell', which although a publicist's dream was a dual-edged sword, tending to make the jazz public shrink from sampling the exciting, surprising new areas of music he was staking out.

Pianists, drummers, bass players, saxophonists, brass musicians, guitarists all wanted to be leaders in their own right. Many had new angles to frame their improvisational skills, often seeking ways in which the music could be moved beyond the domination of the trumpet/saxophone lineup to produce more contemporary ensemble textures by utilizing different instrumental combinations, 'new technology' electronic devices, pop music, rock, funk, disco, ethnic music and classical music.

Their playing was not only influenced by the great jazz master musicians of the past and the compositional and improvisational devices they used, but also the musical experiences they grew up with as a part of the youth culture phenomena of the '60s and '70s, 'I grew up in New York City as a media freak,' said alto saxophonist and conceptuaiist John Zorn, 'watching movies and TV and buying hundreds of records. There's a lot of jazz in me, but there's also a lot of rock, a lot of classical, a lot of ethnic music, a lot of blues, a lot of movie soundtracks, I'm a mixture of all those things.'[3] Equally, the talented alto saxophonist Greg Osby said, 'We grew up on Sly and the Jackson 5. That's going to be in the music too.' It was in stark contrast to the players of the late '40s, the '50s and '60s who remained totally immersed in jazz.

To make use of these diverse lines of input, compositional form assumed great importance, indeed, one of the most interesting things about the work of these new, young musicians was their writing as much as their improvisations, 'I believe that improvisation needs to be combined more with composition in order to create something new,' said Zorn. 'We should take advantage of all the great music and musicians in this world without fear of musical barriers, which are sometimes stronger than racial or religious ones.'

The key ingredient was that improvisation had to fit into the concept of the piece, 'I strive to put each soloist in a position where he has to respect the form,' explained the brilliant young drummer and composer Bobby Previte. 'I try to make them listen very deeply; each note is important to the structure. I like to obscure the improvisation within the form of the composition, to give the music the sense it continues on from somebody's solo; that' something I work very hard on.'[4]

The question these musicians posed was simply how long could it continue to be valid to rely on the 12-bar blues and the ternary form, the traditional AABA or ABA construction, as vehicles for improvisation. Arthur Moorhead, the young record producer who was behind albums like Wayne Horvitz' 'The President—Bring Yr Camera' (Nonesuch) and Tim Berne's 'Sanctified Dreams' (CBS), observed, 'I really think the most interesting things that are happening have as much to do with writing as with improvising. Improvisation continues to be the key, but not to the same extent as it did in the '40s and '50s with bebop and the '60s with free and the AACM stuff. Certainly my own feelings have changed to this way of thinking over the last few years, and I don't get any flack from musicians and critics over this. For the "most important young musicians" involved in the "Down Town" sound, the key ingredient is writing; improvisation has to fit the concept of the piece. It's no longer "run the head down, everybody take six choruses and out"; you write the piece first, *then* where it makes sense you put a tenor solo or a keyboard solo or whatever.'[5]

Since 1986, some of the most exciting, radical and unusual of these developments were primarily centered around Downtown Manhattan, finding outlets in places like the Roulette, and Tin Pan Alley. However, by far the most important venue became the Knitting Factory at 47 East Houston Street, just below Greenwich Village. Here two, three and even four groups nightly who might never have had performance opportunities were encouraged to present their music. Run by Michael Dorf, 'The Factory' was a unique success story of the 1980s jazz scene; 'So these guys from Wisconsin blow into town,' wrote Peter Watrous in *Village Voice*. 'Nobody tells them you can't start a club in New York, or that the scene is dead, that black improvised music and white improvised music don't belong together. What do these cornbiters go and do? Start a club. Three months later they are the scene, with performances daily, like it's no big deal.'

M-Base.

'I call my music M-Base because I figure I should have a right to name it,' said alto saxophonist **Steve Coleman** (b.1957). 'M-Base is just a name that means something to us—a whole group of us . . . what we're trying to do is form a common language. M stands for macro . . . Base is . . . for "basic array of structured extemporations", which is what most of us are doing. We're all involved with improvisation and it's usually structured.' But M-Base was something more, it was also a self-help organization. 'The musicians have to take control of the music,' said fellow M-Base member and drummer Marvin 'Smitty' Smith, 'to network with one another, with agents and booking agents, managements and with people at all levels of the business. They must control the product.'

Steve Coleman arrived in New York in May 1978 after hitch-hiking from his home town of Chicago. Within ten years he had established himself as one of the finest and most promising musicians of his generation. Initially he found work in big bands, including Monday nights with Mel Lewis and with Sam Rivers, recording with both, the Collective Black Artists band and from time to time with larger ensembles run by Cecil Taylor, Paul Jeffrey and Charles Sullivan. But during the daytime he played the New York streets with Graham Haynes (t), Billy Johnson (b) and Mark Johnson (d) who formed the nucleus of his band Five Elements, a forum for M-Base, the ideas he had been working on, that attempted to combine different elements and styles into one sound while still remaining jazz.

However, in 1983 he was invited by Dave Holland to join his ensemble, 'He said he was looking for the same kind of thing I was,' said Coleman, 'a freedom within structure combination. He wanted to hook me up with Kenny Wheeler, who I had never heard of, and later he brought in Julian Priester.' Coleman's subsequent exposure with the group, including three ECM albums with them plus his assured, inventive performance on 'Triplicate' (ECM) with just Holland (b) and Jack DeJohnette (d), revealed a powerful, imaginative new voice with that dangerous edge to his playing that seemed to be the province of the major jazz instrumentalists.

It was his work with Holland rather than, ironically, his own group Five Elements that consolidated his reputation in jazz. Although M-Base used elements from the jazz tradition, it also drew on funk and world music. 'I'd like to have all those elements in the music,' he said, 'something for people who want to dance, something for people who are intellectual and want to find some abstract meaning and something for people who just want to forget their troubles.' The group debuted with 'Motherland Pulse' (JMT) and included 'No Good Time Fairies' with an excellent vocal by Cassandra Wilson, a ballad ('On This') and powerful swing ('Irate Blues'), but at the core were chattering funk rhythms. '[It's]

Steve Coleman, I call my music M-Base because I figure I should have a right to name it'.

not a pop band,' Coleman asserted. 'There's so much improvisation in what we do you have to call it jazz.'

'On The Edge Of Tomorrow', 'World Expansion' (both JMT) and 'Sine Die' (Pangaea) followed but the impression was one of monotony of tone, of straining for effect, more of roccoco arty-funk than substance. The coruscating virtuoso of 'Triplicate' (ECM) seemed a far cry from the hip posturing on 'Sine Die'. But while M-Base was in 1988 'the jazz critics' flavour of the month for, well, months',[6] in retrospect it seemed a pre-emptive attempt to deflect any dismissive labels like 'cross-over', 'fusion' or 'jazz-rock' that might obscure its concerns with rhythm and the interchangeability of lead and rhythm instruments in the ensemble textures.

Perhaps the most sophisticated application of these principals was Strata Institute s C-l-P-H-E-R S-Y-N-T-A-X (JMT), with Coleman (as), Greg Osby (ss, as), David Gilmore (g), Bob Hurst (b) and Marvin 'Smitty' Smith (d). While at one level it proved the continuing good health of the one-chord-vamp and fulfilled Coleman's intention that M-Base should also be a dance music, on another level the musicianship and inventiveness of the players lifted it out of the ordinary. But equally it posed the question of a limiting formula—by the end of the album the approach began to wear thin and whether it could stand up to further scrutiny over yet more albums seemed doubtful.

Coleman recorded in a variety of contexts, from Branford Marsalis' 'Scenes In The City' (CBS) to David Murray's Big Band 'Live At Sweet Basil Vols. 1 & 2' (Black Saint), and in 1987 he toured with the pop singer Sting. However, he continued his association with Dave Holland, joining him on the faculty of Banff Centre For The Arts in 1990 as Artistic Head, along with Holland's group and fellow M-Base practitioners. But despite his ambitions for M-Base, that it might become synonymous with a specific style, just as Motown, for example, the fact remained that artistically, the best from this talented musician had come from other areas of jazz.

On graduation from Berklee in 1983, **Greg Osby** (b. 1960) immediately stepped into the Jon Faddis Quintet where he remained for 18 months. In 1985 he substituted for David Murray when Jack DeJohnette's Album Album band went on tour and from that point his reputation began to grow. He became a regular member of DeJohnette's Special Edition, appearing on the 1987 'Irresistible Forces' (MCA) and the 1988 'Audio-Visualscapes' (MCA) and quickly began making all the right career moves, appearing with David Murray, deputizing in the World Saxophone Quartet, jamming with Dizzy Gillespie and performing with John Scofield, John Abercrombie, McCoy Tyner, Pat Metheny and Herbie Hancock.

When he linked up with Steve Coleman, he was immediately attracted to the M-Base principles, and soon was regularly jamming with members of the Brooklyn-based co-operative, including Coleman ('My partner in crime'), Geri Allen, Graham Haynes, Jean-Paul Bourelly and Cassandra Wilson as well as linking up with pianist Michele Rosewoman, appearing on her 1987 'Quint-essence' and 1988 'Contrast High' (both Enja). In 1987 he debuted with as a leader on 'Greg Osby And Sound Theatre' (JMT) that reflected his love of the Japanese culture and included Rosewoman (p), Kevin McNeal (g), Lonnie Plaxico (b) and Paul Samuels (d). *Musician* described Osby as, 'Possibly the best ballad player of his generation . . . a measured soloist, but emotionally intense'—an excellent example of that ballad-playing ability can be found on drummer Cecil Brooks III's 'The Collective' (Muse). The 1988 'Mindgames' brought in Geri Allen and Edward Simon alternating on keyboard in a cerebral, carefully planned session that ultimately remained grounded through lack of momentum.

But like Coleman, Osby's best work seemed to be on other people's albums, with DeJohnette, with Rosewoman's post-Dolphy complexities and, following a week's preparation at the Knitting Factory, Andrew Hill's 'Eternal Spirit' (Blue Note) from 1989.

With DeJohnette, Osby shared the front line with tenor saxophonist **Gary Thomas**. A rugged individualist, he was invited to join Miles Davis in 1987. 'Miles asked me if I would consider playing some funk licks,' explained Thomas. 'I told him no, that's not the way I play'.[7] He left.

Thomas also performed with Michele Rosewoman, appearing on 'Contrast High' (Enja), and his playing was described by Kevin Whitehead as: 'The sound of an East Coast tenor is an urban shout, a citified roar'. Making his debut as a leader with the 1988 'Code Violations' (Enja), his sinister funk-based but rhythmically sophisticated charts seemed to have more depth than the M-Base experiments of Coleman and Osby. The 1989 'By Any Means Necessary' (JMT) included a strong line-up of John Scofield and Mike Goodrick (g), Geri Allen (k) and Greg Osby (as, k) alongside regulars such as Dennis Chambers (d) and Anthony Cox (b). Conceptually Thomas seemed to have struck a balance that eluded Coleman and Osby, his deep seriousness and darker tone colours projecting intensity, while his compositional forms had greater variety.

Geri Allen (b.1957) had, by the end of the decade, acquired a reputation as an uncompromising pianist as she struck out against over-hyped, over-produced directionless music. Allen began playing the piano at seven, influenced by her father's love of Charlie Parker and her own love of Motown and the Jackson 5, 'We have such a rich cultural experience to draw from and it's all part of who I am, so I've got a bear hug around it all.' After studying at Howard University and a period as a teaching assistant in the masters programme in ethnomusicology at the University of Pittsburgh, she moved to New York in 1982.

Through the drummer Pheeroan ak Laff she was introduced to Oliver Lake, with whom she made a number of albums, including 'Plug It', 'Impala', 'Gallery' and 'Otherside' (all Gramavision) and 'Expandable Language' (Black Saint). Gradually, her reputation grew and she was soon working with James Newton (appearing on his 'Romance and Revolution' [Blue Note]), Joseph Jarman, Lester Bowie, Roscoe Mitchell, Jay Hoggard as well as linking up with Steve Coleman's M-Base circle, appearing on his Five Elements albums.

In 1984 she debuted as a leader with the trio 'Printmakers' (Minor Music) with Anthony Cox (b) and Andrew Cyrille (d) that showed her mixing her European and Afro-American influences into exceptionally powerful music. The solo 'Homegrown' (Minor Music) that followed delivered on her early promise, with her ability to play inside/outside with great charm and precise elegance.

'Open On All Sides In The Middle' (Minor Music) from 1986 introduced her octet and electronic keyboards with an odyssey from traditionalism through Brazilian pop to Cecil Taylor. In 1989 the Verve label reissued 'Twylight' (previously released on the Minor Music label), a trio album with electronic and acoustic keyboards augmented by percussion and voice. It continued her wide-ranging eclecticism that reached back to 'The Printmakers', yet seemed to make allusions to other styles and influences. But the chances she took and the choices she made were all unerringly stamped with her own individualism.

In 1988 she appeared on 'Triangular' and 'V' (both Blue Note) with Ralph Peterson Jr., both important albums that attempted to move beyond the earnest reinvention of neo-classicism without cutting ties with the past. A European tour with Charlie Haden (b) and Paul Motian (d) produced 'Etudes' (Soul Note) and together with the 1989 'In The Year Of The Dragon' (JMT) and 'Segments' (DIW) evoked the three-way discourse of the Bill Evans trio albeit with more plain speaking. 'Segments' (DIW) earned the coveted Seal Of Approval from Japan's prestigious

Swing Journal; Allen's playing, a distillation of the whole spectrum of the jazz piano enriched by her advanced studies in ethnomusicology, was one of the unfolding delights of the late '80s, cutting through categories to create an individual voice of charm and steely strength.

Drummer **Marvin 'Smitty' Smith** (b.1961) had, by the end of the 1980s, been featured on more than 30 albums, including four with Steve Coleman's Five Elements, but his energetic style consistently refused to be limited by category. He featured on the soundtrack of Spike Lee's 'School Daze', pop singer Sting's 1987 '. . . Nothing Like The Sun' American tour and Robert Mugge's documentary on Sonny Rollins, 'Saxophone Colossus'. His album credits during the '80s included those by David Murray, George Shearing, Steve Coleman's Five Elements, the Art Farmer/Benny Golson Jazztet, Dave Holland, Branford Marsalis, Bobby Watson, Mulgrew Miller, Sonny Rollins, Donald Harrison/Terence Blanchard, Donald Byrd, Gunter Hampel and Jon Hendricks.

Smith completed his studies at Berklee and evidence of his well-rounded musical education came with his debut as a leader, the 1987 'Keeper Of The Drums' (Concord), where he composed and arranged all the selections. Although the music retreats into the hard-bop axis, it is one remove from father Blakey's vision, with Smith constantly shifting the role of lead instrument throughout the front line of Wallace Roney (t), Steve Coleman (as), Ralph Moore (ts) and Robin Eubanks (tb) to create a variety of ensemble textures that do not fall into the cliched trumpet lead of hard-bop.

His unusually concise writing allowed for little extended blowing, instead Smith imposed the challenge of forcing his players to sustain a logical, flowing line even though three or four players may share a single chorus. This was not something new, Horace Silver tried the idea with success on 'Blowin' The Blues Away' (Blue Note), for example, but it does indicate Smith's willingness to experiment. On the 1989 'The Road Less Travelled' (Concord) he continued in hard-bop mode, but this time he used the full four horn lineup twice, ringing the changes from quartet (with Ralph Moore) to septet. This time he leaned into post-bop with 'Gothic 17', and once again, while nothing new is being said, it is at least a statement of great promise. Towards the end of the decade Smith joined the faculty of the Banff Center and the Drummers Collective in New York.

Pianist **Michele Rosewoman** (b.1953) moved to New York from the West Coast in 1978. Her compositional and organizational abilities

Geri Allen with Charlie Haden: Their collaborations together with Paul Motian were an unfolding delight in the late '80s.

quickly surfaced in 1983 when she led her 14-piece New York-Uba ensemble, a synthesis of her jazz and Afro-Cuban influences, a result of years of playing Latin music as well as jazz. She made her recording debut as a leader in 1983 with 'The Source' (Soul Note), a quartet with Baikida Carroll (t). Rosewoman's rhythmic drive sweeps through the album, as does her firm structural control; inspired by hard-bop, it often moved to the subversive left with angular dissonance inspired by Cecil Taylor.

The 1987 'Quintessence' (Enja) introduced her regular ensemble with a front line of Steve Coleman and Greg Osby, with Anthony Cox (b) and Terri Lyn Carrington (d). Here she had refined the post-Dolphy/Braxton 'square' phrasing underpinned by a conventionally swinging rhythm section that dissolved into post-Taylor confusions such as 'Springular Springle'. With the 1988 'Contrast High' (Enja) Gary Thomas (ts) was in for Coleman, Lonnie Plaxico (b) for Cox and Cecil Brooks III for Carrington. On it Rosewoman debuts as a creditable vocalist ('Of All', 'Akomado'), while drawing on her Afro-Cuban influences on two tracks. Rosewoman's convoluted themes, her use of collective improvisation and abrupt rhythmic shifts contrasted her powerful straight ahead playing ('The Source' and the trio 'Panambula') and placed her at a unique confluence of ideas, at home with the electronic and funk ideals of M-Base but equally at home with free-bop and beyond.

FREEBOP AND BEYOND

Tim Berne (b.1955) recorded 'The Five-Year Plan' (Empire) in 1979. His intention was to give up his day job and concentrate on music full time. It took him seven years. The highly motivated alto saxophonist studied with Julius Hemphill from 1974 and by the time he was ready to record attracted players like John Carter (cl), Vinny Goila (as, ts) and Glenn Ferris (tb) to participate in his carefully organized suite-like compositions, 'If you're going to do a concert with six musicians', he said, 'you don't want it to be "solo city", you've really got to rack you're brains to make it work.'

More self-produced albums on his Empire label followed: '7X' with a heavy-handed Nels Cline (g), 'Spectres', a 1981 live date 'Songs And Rituals In Real Time', a two-album set with Mack Goldsbury (ts), Ed Schuller (b) and Paul Motian (d) and '. . . Theoretically', a duet with Bill Frisell (g) (later re-issued by Minor Music). Berne showed he was a talented composer and conceptualist, constantly trying new ideas and structural shifts while using ostinatos to underpin free episodes which frequently snapped back into time. 'I want to find a way of structuring things without resorting to cliches, and not to have improvisations that could sound like they're on any piece of music,' he said.[8]

'The Ancestors' (Soul Note) from 1983 introduced Berne's frequent playing companion, Herb Robertson (t) and guest Ray Anderson (tb) into the 'Songs And Rituals' lineup for another live date. Robertson's cadenza on 'Shirley's Song' revealed a mature, exciting player who would become a perfect foil for Berne's alto.

'Mutant Variations' (Soul Note), *sans* Anderson, continued the inside/outside duality and while Berne's work could not yet be described as great, his willingness to embody Ornette Coleman-like dirges, free-swinging vamps and post-bop-like heads in search of his own voice suggested his determined experimentalism would pay off. A move to CBS produced the 1987 'Fulton Street Maul' (CBS) with Bill Frisell (g), Hank Roberts (c) and Alex Cline (d), mix-and-matching urban clatter and pan-ethnic chants that confronted free and funk and art-hip struts. 'Sanctified Dreams' (CBS) pulled back from the electronic/harmolodic brink to return to his regular acoustic quintet with Robertson, Roberts, Mark Dresser (b) and Joey Baron (d) on well rehearsed arrangements that cut and ran as

Tim Berne. 'If you're going to do a concert with six musicians you don't want it to be "solo city", you've really got to rack your brains to make it work.'

soon as they took shape, mixing freebop and fanfares, metre changes and rhythmic gear shifts.

Suddenly CBS dropped him. 'The whole episode with Columbia was bizarre,' he said, 'totally *bizarre.*' In March 1988 he recorded a pared-down version of his quintet—himself, Baron and Roberts—as 'Miniature' (JMT); 'By turns wild and wooly, intimate and thoughtful, in about equal proportions,' said the *New York Times.* 'The idea of the group was to use a lot more electronics than, say, the quintet: to have this small group with a big sound,' said Berne, '. . . Miniature's also a little more spontaneous.' With 'Fractured Fairy Tales' (JMT), a quintet session from 1989, Berne's grip on form and content seemed better realized; his influences receded to become reference points glimpsed in the fog rather than illuminated signs flashing their source of origin. But fairy tales could be dark and threatening, and like the forbidding forests of the Brothers Grimm, Berne aspired to deep purpose. 'Fractured Fairy Tales' seemed to be the slightly overdue artistic culmination of that five-year plan.

Berne's right-hand man, pianist **Herb Robertson** (b.1951), was relatively late to emerge in jazz. After studying at Berklee he left in 1972 and worked in jazz-rock bands before hitting a personal crisis, which was finally resolved working in the tourist resorts in the Catskill Mountains. Determined to pursue a career in jazz, he arrived in New York in 1978/9, where he linked up with Tim Berne's circle, which included the bass player Mark Helias. After touring with Berne in Europe he formed his first band in 1983. His debut as a leader, the 1985 'Transparency' (JMT) including Berne, Bill Frisell (g) and Joey Baron (d) revealed Robertson's arranging talent that explored 'the potential of group improvisation and short solos that embodied the flavour of the composition'.[9]

The 1987 ' "X"-Cerpts: Live At Willisau' (JMT) with Berne, Gust Tsilis (vb), Lindsey Horner (b) and Baron (d) was a declamatory assertion of inside/outside playing, highly successful and, with the passage of time, underrated. Equally, his 1988 'Shades Of Bud Powell' (JMT) with a line-up of Robertson and Brian Lynch (t), Robin Eubanks (tb), Vincent Chancey (fh), Bob Stewart (tu) and Baron (d), represented an important contemporary exploration of the pianist's music.

Roberton's re-evaluation of Powell, taking his compositions out of their pianistic context and balancing both tradition and innovation, were described by *Cadence* magazine in 1988 as 'One of the best efforts of the past year'. Arthur Moorhead felt Robertson was, 'clearly working to offer new solutions to old music. By using Powell's legacy as a composer and improviser as only a point of departure, his statement is on two levels.

On the surface to create revitalised music for what may appear an unorthodox instrumentation . . . but on a deeper level to explore the compositional and harmonic implications of Powell's music, something more than just a series of furiously unfolding chord changes.'[10]

Pianist/composer **Wayne Horvitz** (b.1956), despite moving to Seattle, Washington towards the end of the '80s, was one of the mainstays of the downtown sound. Equally at home in John Zorn's jump-cut 'games', hard-bop, free, rock, blues and directing the big band he organized in 1986 with his wife Robin Holcomb (The New York Composers Orchestra), it seemed remarkable that he was a self-taught musician who hardly ever had any piano lessons.

Horvitz studied at the University of California, music courses, he asserted, not piano lessons. 'There was a whole other scene there, this whole New Music classical scene. I got a lot out of that, but I was really involved with avant garde jazz players. I was also listening to all sorts of rock, and improvised rock and psychedelic music.' He debuted on record in 1980 with the Cecil Taylor-influenced 'No Place Fast' (Theatre For Your Mother), attracted by Taylor's sense of form and 'unit structures'. When he moved to New York and linked up with John Zorn such variegated experience was invaluable. Initially they were involved together with free jazz, but gradually began drawing on a whole range of music that was a part of Zorn's grand conception.

Maintaining his involvement as a key member of Zorn's groups, Horvitz continued his interest in free jazz, with trumpeter Butch Morris, best known in the 80's as the downbeat for the David Murray big band. Together with Bobby Previte they formed a trio that John Rockwell of the *New York Times* described as, 'virtuosic, varied in texture, mood clever in sonorous combinations and far removed from the rave-up frenzy that can affect the less talented of these improvisational ensembles'. The high level of collective interaction and imagination featured on 'Nine Below Zero' and 'Todos Santos' (both Sound Aspects), the latter, featuring compositions by Horvitz' wife Robin Holcomb, was described by *Village Voice* as a 'quintessential New York album, an artistic retort to a polluted environment'.

Holcomb's own sextet, including Horvitz, Marty Ehrlich and Bobby Previte featured on the 1988 'Larks, They Crazy' (Sound Aspects), performing her compositions that were, 'oddly haunting . . . compelling . . . and [filled with] serene enigmas.'[11]

Yet Horvitz did an about face and came up with a memorable 'In the tradition' album; the 1985 'Voodoo' (Black Saint) by Horvitz' Sonny Clark Memorial Quartet was one of the great neo-classic albums of the 1980s. With John Zorn (as), Horvitz (p), Ray Drummond (b) and Bobby Previte (d) projecting both composure and individualism, it was neither a manifesto of technique or acquired influences; each player had found their voice and adapted it to the requirements at hand, Horvitz in particular was needle sharp and incisive. Together they swung, they said something and it served to underline the fact that while they could work comfortably and convincingly within the then fashionable status quo, their main musical endeavours were to expand the horizons of jazz.

One area of new ground Horvitz was exploring was demonstrated on 'This New Generation', released in 1987, a compilation of 15 tracks from the albums 'Dinner At Eight' and 'The President' (both Dossier) from 1985. A combination of jazz (phrases rather than solos), ethnic music (gamelan music) and electronic sounds, he plugged into a computer-like soundscape that evoked a mass of urban images; the bustle of grey-coated office workers, ghetto blasters and traffic jams. Inspired in part from gamelan music, one of his interests, the composer was firmly in control; solos emerged and submerged, part of the sound, texture and strong rhythmic undercurrent of the music. 'One of the best discs representing the lively East Village scene,' said the *New York Times*.

With the rock-influenced 'Bring Yr Camera' (Elektra Musician) by his group The President from 1988, Horvitz adapted the wheel-within-a-wheel gamelanism of 'New Generation' to hard-hitting, attention-demanding rock rhythms. 'Wayne is a guy who has very definite ideas of what he likes to do and how he orchestrates things,' said Arthur Moorhead, the album's producer, 'This is one of those typically downtown groups that's been together for about ten years, but only play a gig every few months or so, so the book is small. Here we tried to develop the tunes that had not been recorded on the European Dossier label; get a good sound in the studio and get that cohesion between the pieces they recorded.'[12] Sharply defined, Horvitz' subtly manipulated revolving patterns, with a slashing rhythmic undertow that imposed stylistic continuity on his improvisers; instrumental mastery was taken for granted, now they had to fit into the scheme of the composer.

Drummer **Bobby Previte** (b.1952) exuded joy when he played. He seemed to grow in stature behind the drums, a stunning technician who knew by instinct the most vital lesson in jazz, how to limit what he

Bobby Previte. 'The way playing is integrated into the theme is where I'm at, rather than the head-solo-head philosophy.'

played to the needs of the moment. Sensitive, sympathetic but above all with a perfect sense of time and timing, he was equally at home in free, rock, blues, straight ahead and any challenges the new music might throw at him. Previte learned his drumming through hard, practical experience in groups, bands, backing cabaret and shows and studied Western Percussion in college before finally deciding to try his luck in New York in 1980.

Initially he only knew Elliot Sharp, the experimental composer and guitarist, but gradually extended his circle of connections so that by 1984 he was giving his own concerts. Previte was working on two fronts, as a drummer and as a composer. As a composer he wrote for film, video, television, theatre and dance and was awarded grants by The National Endowment Of The Arts (twice), the New York State Council On The Arts and New York's Meet The Composer programme. In 1986 his soundtrack for the video production, 'Bought And Sold', a sinister, dark, all-engulfing musical fog, was issued as 'Dull Bang, Gushing Sound, Human Shriek' (Dossier). As a drummer, his controlled exuberance was in demand from players such as Elliot Sharp, John Zorn, The Lounge Lizards, bluesman Bobby Radcliffe, Wayne Horvitz' The President, Robin Holcomb's sextet, Tim Berne, Butch Morris and folk singer Bonnie Koloc.

His debut as composer/bandleader/drummer in his own right was 'Bump The Renaissance' (Sound Aspects) from 1985 with an unusual front line of Lenny Pickett (ts), Tom Varner (fh) with Richard Schulman (k), David Hofstra (b). Previte approached orchestration as if he was solving a vast musical acrostic; everything was based on logic and balance. Like a craftsman, each phrase was hand-polished and inserted into place so that the end result teemed with shining ideas that from wherever they were viewed showed no weak link or redundant phrase. Once the compositional whole was erected, Previte then slotted in the improvisers, who were charged with moving within the same concentric circles of his composition, yet without dulling their lustre. 'Untitled', exemplified Previte's preference for dark pastel shades while 'Short Of Breath' was patiently expanded over Previte's insistent, repeated drum rhythm.

The 1987 'Pushing The Envelope' (Gramavision) substituted Marty Ehrlich on tenor for Varner, in whose group Previte frequently played. As with his first album, the music was like chamber music of the film noir; 'Mirror, Mirror' was a composition taken from Previte's soundtrack for the motion picture 'Chain Letters', while the opening track, 'Open World' summed up his compositional style at this point. 'That tune is the kernel of my sensibility,' he said, 'It's very much composed, but there's a lot of playing on it. And it's the way the playing is integrated into the theme is where I'm at, rather than the head-solo-head philosophy'.

With 'Claude's Late Morning' (Gramavision) from 1988, Previte took the ambitious step of attempting to integrate disparate instruments within his compositions so that their individual sounds and textures actually became integral parts of the compositions; included was Wayne Horvitz on Hammond Organ, keyboards and harmonica, Ray Anderson on trombone and tuba, Bill Frisell on guitar and banjo, Josh Dubin on pedal steel guitar, Carol Emanuel on harp, Guy Klucevsek on accordion with additional percussive assistance from Joey Baron and Jim Mussen with Previte on keyboards, marimba, vocals, drum machine and drums.

'Look Both Ways', with its in-between pitches (trombone sliding and slide guitar), duality of rhythmic figures (5/4 over 4/4) and shifting tonal backgrounds revealed Previte's growing maturity and sure handling of form and content plus a deep involvement in balancing tempo, texture and mood. Among the best albums of the decade, Previte observed: 'It's intricate, but who cares? I really don't. It's for people who feel something, if they don't feel anything it's worthless to me.'[13] Like so many downtown experimenters, much of Previte's conceptualism never broke out of Manhattan like his 'Two-Man-Big-Band' or his sextet, a regular hard-bop lineup with a book of just seven compositions, each a startling refraction of tradition and Previte's remarkable imagination.

Guitarist **Bill Frisell** (b.1951) tried Berklee for a semester in 1970, didn't like it (too much rock) and studied for a while with guitarist Jim Hall

Bill Frisell (with Marc Johnson on bass); every few years a guitarist appears who manages to wring something new out of the most played instrument in the world.'

in 1971. He tried Berklee again in 1975, and this time found it more stimulating. Through faculty member Mike Gibbs he was recommended to bassist Eberhard Weber, subsequently appearing on his 'Fluid Rattle' (ECM). It opened the door to ECM and Jan Garbarek, touring and re-cording with him ('Wayfarer' and 'Paths, Prints' [both ECM]). But it was through Pat Metheny's recommendation that he joined **Paul Motian** (b.1931), an association that would last through the decade; 'Playing with Paul has been a great learning experience,' said Frisell, 'I have a lot of room in this band, as well as the freedom to try just about anything I want, which makes it a situation that encourages growth.'

Motian's drumming gained international recognition as a result of his sensitive interaction within the delicate piano trio of the late Bill Evans between 1959-64 where 'his style . . . became a model for drummers working within similar settings and contributed to the emancipation of the rhythm section'.[14] However, with his own groups he took a long stride from the airy persuasiveness with Evans to a rugged, bustling in-tensity that left nowhere for his musicians to hide. Frisell took on the role of interpreting the percussionist's vision by providing an incredible array of tonal sounds that could alternate between a Stuka dive-bomber plus air-raid warning with Motian pattern bombing in his wake to heav-enly-host chords that seemed suspended in the atmosphere; Frisell was quietly and modestly revolutionizing guitar playing by pulling together the opposing poles of Jim Hall and Jimi Hendrix under one roof.

Motian's group, formed in 1980 with Frisell, which became his main vehicle for expression (although he did play with Tim Berne, Geri Allen and Marylin Crispell). His quintet comprised Jim Pepper and Joe Lovano (ts), Ed Schuller (b) and Frisell which he pared down to a trio with just Frisell and Lovano; the trio and quintet's output was a deep and fasci-nating body of work in '80s' jazz, 'It Should Have Happened A Long Time Ago' and 'Psalm' (both ECM), 'The Story Of Maryam', 'Jack Of Clubs', 'The Paul Motian Quintet' and 'One Time Out' (all Soul Note) and 'Monk In Motian' and 'On Broadway Vol. 1' (both JMT).

Motian's honest playing and his angular, sometimes bleak conception created the challenging environment Frisell needed to develop his style, 'With Paul, 90 per cent of the material is his own. And each of the tunes is a world of its own. Some of them are conventional chords and melodies, played in time. But some are complicated harmonies, or involve harmony and melody but the time isn't strict . . . he's got tunes that are fast and loud, but not strict 4/4—the phrases breathe. And there are tunes we play as compositions, then go totally beserk on, that are based on a scale.'

Frisell debuted as a leader with 'In Line' (ECM) from 1982, with bassist Arilid Anderson, a quiet reflective 'ECM' album of his eerie originals. It was followed by the 1984 'Rambler' (ECM) with Motian, Kenny Wheeler (t), Bob Stewart (tu) and Jerome Harris (b) that was carefully orchestrated, but like Motian's music, remained challenging and surprising. 'Every few years a guitarist appears who manages to wring something new out of the most played instrument in the world,' said the *New York Times*. 'American guitar watchers now have a chance to discover Bill Frisell.'

The 1987 'Lookout For Hope' (ECM) from 1988, with his now regular band, Hank Roberts (clo), Kermitt Driscoll (b) and Joey Baron (d), saw him moving Downtown embracing the melange of influences that John Zorn was pioneering. 'Before We Were Born' (Elektra Musician) from 1988 was produced by John Zorn and his humour, jump-cut impatience and the restless energy feature on his arrangement of 'Hard Plains Drifter', with Frisell's serio-comic C&W guitar essaying the tune's subplot: 'Or: as I take my last breath and the noose grows tight, the incredible events of the past three days flash before my eyes.'

Once again, Frisell presents his quartet, augmented on one track by a horn trio including Julius Hemphill (as); again the emphasis is on struc-

John Zorn with part of Naked City (L to R: Wayne Horvitz, Zorn, Fred Frith)—a brilliant, iconoclastic mincing machine.

ture and form, despite the creative distortion that seems to shred moods and textures. By the end of the decade Frisell was rightly being hailed as one of the most innovative *and* creative (they don't always go together, witness Stanley Jordan) guitarists of the decade. His sheer range of expression, from heavy metal freelancing with Vernon Reid on 'Smash And Scatteration' (Minor Music) and Power Tools' 'Strange Meeting' (Antilles) to his work as a member of John Zorn's Naked City, Marc Johnson's Bass Desires and in-demand session work that included Marianne Faithful and Ambitious Lovers, Frisell emerged as one of the major new stars of jazz. 'I'm just beginning to realize that all these years I thought I was learning to play the guitar, I was really learning to play myself,' he said.[15]

After over a dozen years of struggle to establish himself as a professional musician, by the end of the 1980s **John Zorn** (b. 1954) could finally claim to be perhaps the most recognizable, prolific and far-ranging of the downtown musicians. It was by no means an easy ride; in 1984 he spoke of 'unspeakable abuse' from critics and audiences from the days when he experimented with duck calls on his saxophone. But there has always been a certain method in Zorn's apparent madness; a fan of cartoon music from an early age he completed his college thesis at Webster College in St. Louis on the cartoon music of Carl W. Stallings, who wrote for Warner Brothers in the 1940s. Zorn was also influenced in equal parts by Webern and Stravinsky—'Stravinsky's whole thing was working with blocks of sound and reordering them,' he said, 'his "Rite Of Spring" is a typical example of this . . . all's that's happening is, boom, boom, boom, these quick changes'—plus Cage, Stockhausen, Philip Glass and Varese.

He went on to study composition at the U.N. School in Manhattan under Leonardo Balada but meanwhile had come under the spell of the music of the Black Artists Group back in St. Louis, where Oliver Lake had taught at his college. On hearing Anthony Braxton's 'For Alto' (Delmark), 'It freaked me out,' he said; he switched from piano to alto and immersed himself into bebop. Then followed a transition from the 'soundmakers' of the '60s—Ayler, Coltrane and Pharoah Sanders—to duck calls and blowing sax mouthpieces in buckets of water. Meanwhile he began staging ambitious, large-scale avant garde productions at venues such as the Public Theatre, characterized by abrupt segues and solo recitals (many recorded on Zorn's own label Parachute Records).

As a record store clerk during this period of frantic experimentation, his already enormous knowledge of music grew to encyclopedic proportions and fragments of almost anything that caught his ear was excavated like a hidden treasure for future possible use. They surfaced in what he called his 'game' structures, ('Cobra', 'Archery', 'Track And Field' etc.) that decentred both the process of improvising and composition by abrupt segue. 'There's a lot of talking and eye contact and direct communication among musicians which has been taboo in improvising . . . I'm very interested in working with systems and communicating by word or eye contact or cue. My music is . . . really fast and changes from one world to the next, never staying on any one for a long period of time.' This effect was like zapping from channel to channel on television, a commonplace action for contemporary youth culture.

After a myriad of self-produced solo and concept albums on obscure and hard-to-obtain labels (Parachute, Nato, Rift, Zoar, Yukon, Lumina etc.) Zorn gained a kind of respectability with his contribution to Hal Willner's tribute albums to Thelonious Monk and Kurt Weill (A&M), 'In spite of all the flak I've gotten in the past,' he said, 'I feel like I've just touched the tip of the iceberg.'

With 'The Big Gundown' (Nonesuch) from 1985, the massed ranks of the downtown music scene assembled to give collective voice to the music of Ennio Morricone (famous for his work on the spaghetti westerns). Here Zorn fine tuned his diverse influences, from bebop to Looney Tunes to the BAG to Stravinsky, to create a brilliant iconoclastic mincing machine. It was new, radical and exciting, living up to its subtitle, 'Once Upon A Time In East—Village'. Zorn took incredible pains to ensure his music fitted the visual images. 'I looked at what he looked at when he came up with the melody, then I said, "This is what I'm going to come up with," and mixed it with what he came up with; so it works on the film, it works with the notes on the page and works with the people here in the studio.'

The October 1985 'Cobra' (Hat Art) returned to 'game' strategies both in the studio and in live concert in a two album set, again with his regular downtown cohorts creating fast-moving episodes of solo and ensemble improvisation, some perplexing, some humorous but all brilliantly interpreted by musicians such as Wayne Horvitz, Bobby Previte, Bill Frisell and Elliot Sharpe. With 'Voodoo' (Black Saint) from the following month and 'The Big Gundown' getting column inches in that bastion of respectibility, *Time Magazine,* Zorn's star was in the ascendance. On 'Voodoo', Zorn's solos threaten to veer 'outside' at any moment and create a unique tension that remains with repeated listening. It is this underlying current of danger that sets the album apart from the neatly expurgated solos of the neo-classicists; by showing he could play by the rules if he chose to,

Zorn surprised critics, audience and musicians alike, 'You really *can* play the saxophone,' Anthony Braxton told him after he heard the album.

'Spillane' (Nonesuch) from 1987 was a celebration of the film noir with its powerful, compulsively changing explicit imagery, relentlessly arousing the listener's curiosity by defying expectation; the title track, for example, had 60 jump-cuts in 25 minutes. 'Two Lane Highway' was a concerto for bluesman Albert Collins in the same way Duke Ellington wrote concertos for Cootie, Barney, Rex Stewart et al. Here Zorn creates 12 'moods' to expose the talents of Collins (rather than jump-cuts), framed after listening to 'almost every record Collins ever made',[16] to reveal the dynamic bluesman's personality. The result was an imaginative manipulation of the tradition, but stamped with Zorn's personality and authority that nevertheless allowed Collins full rein as a soloist.

The 1987 'New For Lulu' (Hat Art), recorded live at Jazzfestival Willisau, was another bebop homage, but imaginatively recast with Bill Frisell (g) and George Lewis (tb). Here Zorn plundered the compositions of Clark, Hank Mobley, Kenny Dorham and Freddy Redd and showed that the tradition could be energized by imagination far more strikingly than by imitation.

Since 1983 Zorn appeared from time to time with C and D, a band co-led by Tim Berne (as) that revisited Ornette Coleman compositions. The 1988 'Spy Vs Spy' (Elektra Musician) brought the group into the recording studio to, as one writer put it, 'impact as many Ornette Coleman compositions on to a pinhead as possible'. With a rhythm section of Mark Dresser (b) and Joey Baron and Mark Vatcher (d) it was hair-raising stuff; the effect was not so much that of a cold shower as a water cannon, as Zorn intended, '[by taking] that approach with the Ornette material, doing it faster and faster, shorter and shorter, to make it even more powerful and on the edge.' However, even if their armoured passion concealed a profound respect for form, the content was a series of unrelenting gales that, while sounding fun to do, was ultimately limiting in its one-dimensional emotionalism.

With his regular group Naked City, formed around 1987, Zorn was able to refine his compositional techniques within a set working ensemble. The 1989 'Naked City' (Nonesuch), with Wayne Horvitz (k), Fred Frith (b) and Joey Baron (d), pared Zorn's sweeping extravaganzas on 'The Big Gundown' and 'Spillane' to their very essence. Thirty-second jump-cuts of ferocious earslaughter were allowed to stand as compositions in their own right, while the jump-cut principle was applied to shorter compositions of between three to four minutes. This less-is-more principle gave

Zorn's music greater focus while still retaining the capacity to surprise and startle. 'Latin Quarter' was full of abruptly changing imagery, Ornette Coleman's 'Lonely Woman' was irreverently given a Peter Gunn-like bass-line while 'The James Bond Theme' and 'A Shot In The Dark' got accorded the full respect of Zorn the film freak.

The arrangements, all meticulously crafted to allow the band to bask in their magnificent iconoclasm, were powerful and dramatic; like all the best jazz, that sense of danger, that gnawing possibility of confrontation with the unexpected continually lurked beneath the surface, 'It's really the way music should be played today—exciting, on the edge . . .,' said Zorn. 'It's not just running changes the way Sonny Stitt or Bird did; there's no point in copying that, you can take out the record and play it if that's what you want to hear. It's tunes and changes and a certain tradition that needs to be updated to keep it alive. I think music is great today, and I'm trying to play it today.'

9
Voice

IN 1983, THE critic Francis Davis wrote, 'we seem to begrudge even exemplary singers the hosannas we lavish only too gratefully on the humblest instrumentalists'.[1] Remarkably, his was a lone voice raised in protest at the parlous state of the jazz vocal art that had succeeded, decade after decade, to remain remarkably under-appreciated, not only by many critics—something of a cardinal sin in itself—but by a large proportion of the jazz audience. In a minority music this automatically placed the jazz singer pretty low on the totem pole. For while an Ella Fitzgerald or a Sarah Vaughan might have enjoyed wide acclaim, there were countless jazz singers plying their craft in semi-obscurity.

It was a curious paradox. Of all the sounds of jazz, the vocal is the most accessible yet the most undervalued. It is also the most individual, but because the voice is the most familiar and immediate reflection of emotion, the vocalist has not acquired the mystery or romance of the instrumentalist because singing is something we imagine we can all do. Access to a song is as much through the *sound* of the voice as its lyrics—as Greil Marcus pointed out: 'Words are sounds we feel before they are statements to understand.'[2]

The sound of the voice also reveals nuance and once internalized and absorbed into our imagination, enjoys a 'second life', the life of memory. A good hook and an evocative delivery can make bathtub singers out of us all, a duality of fantasy and reality, where one becomes the other; Bing Crosby, for example, once suggested his success was due to the fact that the man in the street imagined he could sing equally well as he.[3]

But the vocal also implies adherence to melody and lyric in a way that the instrumental solo does not; the instrumentalist is able to cast himself free of such restraints but the vocalist remains shackled to the intentions of composer and lyricist. The sound of the voice, therefore, clearly presents a different sort of challenge in jazz from that of the instrumentalist.

Jazz criticism, however, has always placed great store on the voice-as-instrument notion, a colourful if vague metaphor that seems to imply that the criteria used to judge an instrumental performance should also be applied to the jazz vocal art. But since the majority of instrumentalists in jazz are male, hopelessly outnumbering the singers, most of whom are female, this does seem somewhat chauvinistic. The implication being that you do it our way, you sound like a horn, you scat, or it's not jazz.

But the voice simply does not have the fluidity or technical potential of a horn, and comparing the two simply highlights an inadequate aesthetic that although may take into account rhythmic and harmonic imagination, fails to acknowledge actual performance or musical setting, such as Betty Carter's intensely personal choreography that underlines her every song or the drama a singer can evoke, as in Billie Holiday's 'Strange Fruit'. As critic Howard Mandel pointed out, a jazz singer 'needn't scat, or freely improvise, so much as give real, personal meaning to words'.[4]

Some songs, particularly those from the 20th century American popular songbook—as much the property of jazz as popular culture—are a marriage of words and music that the best jazz singers could charge so as to reach an audience in a way that an instrumental solo could not. This carries with it the implication that the jazz vocal dispenses something of the common touch, which is probably quite true; it is difficult to imagine, for example, Louis Armstrong enjoying the extent of his popularity without his inimitable vocals. But the suggestion of jazz singing entering the domain of popular culture is, of course, bound to offend the elitists who are ever wary of anything that smacks of 'popular'. But the jazz vocal can be popular art, as in Billie Holiday's 1941 version of 'All Of Me', a favourite of countless homesick GI's in World War II, while in contrast, popular art could also be jazz, such as some performances by Bing Crosby, Fred Astaire and Frank Sinatra that undoubtedly qualified as jazz.

Precisely because the jazz singer's performance has always been likely to be more readily understood by a wider audience than their instrumental counterparts, most jazz vocalists have at some time or other either succumbed, or have been importuned, into a distinctly non-jazz environment using songs and arrangements intended for the widest possible appeal. But this does not devalue their work as a jazz vocalist; theirs has been a battle for survival, artistic *and* economic, in what is primarily an instrumental music.

The vocal performance in jazz, often viewed as an optional bolt-on extra, was initially purely functional; in pre-bop jazz as entertainment (Armstrong, Fats Waller), in the Swing Era as a touch of glamour on the bandstand, but rarely as a feature in its own right like the work of, say, Billie Holiday. With the emergence of bop, vocalists were jettisoned by the small combos and left to do their own thing. They survived the '40s and '50s but foundered when rock emerged in the '60s. Some worked in studios and in the hotels of Las Vegas and Miami until the dilution of rock and the disappearance of the ten per cent federal entertainment tax helped their renaissance, but few bands hired jazz singers and there was no longer a place for them on radio or television. The jazz singers home, therefore, became hospitable night clubs and an ambiguous existence cheek by jowl with popular culture in supper club entertainment.

It is inevitable, therefore, that a large grey area exists between popular vocal performances and jazz vocal performances in much the same way that Hegel's beach is neither land or sea. The modulation from one to the other is, on occasion, imperceptible so that to draw a definitive boundary is impossible. But that does not mean that beaches do not exist, or that the jazz vocal or the popular vocal are the same thing. However, the suggestion of popular culture impinging upon a jazz performance has often been sufficient cause for countless singers to be struck-off the register of jazz history as if some unwritten hippocratic oath had been violated.

Certainly there has been a lack of unanimity among critics as to the validity, let alone an aesthetic, of jazz singing beyond feeble rationalization. This usually takes the form of Billie Holiday, Ella Fitzgerald and Sarah Vaughan and en passant, Louis Armstrong and Jack Teagarden being placed end-to-end to form a potted history, albeit in instrumental terms, of the jazz vocal—Armstrong and Teagarden because their vocals were an extension of their instrumental personalities, Holiday's because she closely paralleled a Lester Young solo and the onomatopoeia of Fitzgerald and Vaughan's scat as the vocal equivalent of bop. If this rather simplistically aligned the jazz vocal within clearly proscribed limits of acceptability, then it also might explain Francis Davis' dismay at, 'the omission of the names Mildred Bailey, Connee Boswell, Lee Wiley, Maxine Sullivan, and Ethel Waters from the standard roll calls of great (jazz) singers',[5] a list that could be extended with each succeeding decade from the 1930s.

In reality, the jazz vocal has often absorbed influences beyond the terms of reference applied by most of its critics and audience, suggesting it has become rather tightly compartmentalized within conveniently partisan parameters. When Alec Wilder spoke of Cole Porter bringing, 'a certain theatrical elegance, as well as interest and sophistication, wit and musical complexity to the popular song form',[6] he implied a corollary value judge-

ment that might distinguish not only better songs but also better performances. It also inadvertently seemed as good a working definition of
a jazz singer as any.

FEMALE VOICES

The futility of erecting barricades between jazz and popular singing is
demonstrated by the work of Ella Fitzgerald and Sarah Vaughan. Both
have discographies which are biased in favour of material where jazz considerations are by no means paramount and both have long moved between jazz and popular modes with ease. **Ella Fitzgerald** (b.1917), under
the careful guidance of Norman Granz, became one of the best known
of all jazz performers but her reputation was made beyond jazz through
her many commercial recordings with Decca and her nonpareil 'songbook'
projects[7] dedicated to the major American songwriters that are now acknowledged to be among the finest examples of popular singing on record,
a jazz *lieder* of perfect pitch and diction.

The girlish timbre of her voice, however, did not guarantee universal
approbation. Fitzgerald was not a profound interpreter of lyrics, the cheerful disposition in her voice failing to sit well with tragedy, drama or
pathos. Instead, she responded to harmony and her infallible ear allowed
a scat singer par excellence to develop alongside her 'popular' personna.
Her zest for work continued through the 1980s; an excellent 1979 collaboration with the Count Basie Orchestra 'A Classy Pair', a 1982 big
band plus strings arranged by Nelson Riddle 'The Best Is Yet To Come',
the 'With the Tommy Flanagan Trio' from 1982, three sessions with Joe
Pass from 1983—'Take Love Easy Again', 'Speak Love' and 'Easy Living'—and an incongruous outing with Andre Previn on piano on an album
of Gershwin songs, 'Nice Work If You Can Get It', in 1984 (All Pablo).

The Pass collaborations are the best of her 1980s' albums; mature statements by a mature artist that perfectly reconcile the detached cool of her
popular singing with the natural exuberance of her jazz performances. In
1986 there was serious concern for her health when she was admitted
into intensive care for heart trouble and a long period of recuperation
followed. In 1988 she returned to active performance with a concert at
Hollywood Bowl and in June appeared at Carnegie Hall, thin and walking
stiffly, her voice lagging slightly behind her imagination. A year later she
returned with a concert that took her well known sobriquet 'Ella, First
Lady Of Song' as the theme, together with her trio and her special, inevitable guest Joe Pass, her voice slightly frayed but marvelously intact,

'I love giving concerts,' she said. 'Doesn't weaken me, strengthens me. I look out there at the audience, especially the young ones. I feel the love they give me and I try to give it back with my songs.'[8] In early 1990 she was again touring extensively.

If Ella Fitzgerald long ago transcended arguments about the 'popular' bias of many of her recordings, then **Sarah Vaughan** (1924-90) side-stepped the issue completely, claiming 'I'm not a jazz singer, I'm a singer'; certainly her recorded legacy showed no singular, exclusive commitment to jazz. But there was no denying that her enormous talent became all the more compelling when focussed in a jazz environment, which, it must be said, was the only area of music that allowed the enormous breadth of her abilities full rein. Although described by Gunther Schuller as 'the greatest vocal artist of our century,'[9] the mystery is why, as a creative artist, her choices of musical direction so often undermined the best which she had to offer.

In live performance, however, with just piano, bass and drums she could be riveting and if she didn't wish to be thought of as a jazz singer then so be it. Once inside the recording studios, however, her discography during the 1980s continued her bilateral affinity between jazz and popular ephemera that's been the despair of the jazz world since the days of 'Passing Strangers'.

If the 1980 two album set 'Duke Ellington Songbook' (Pablo) personalized Ellington's songs to an extent that Fitzgerald wisely refrained from 20 or so years earlier, then her treatment of Sondheim's 'Send In the Clowns' with the Basie band (Pablo) and 'Autumn Leaves' on 'Crazy And Mixed Up' (Pablo) needed her re-invention to be heard with fresh ears. Her flirtation with Brazilian music, however, responded to the law of diminishing returns, starting with 'I Love Brazil' (Pablo) and descending through 'Copacabana' (Pablo) to the 1987 Sergio Mendes production 'Brazilian Romance' (CBS), that was as disappointing as the 'Songs Of The Beatles' (Atlantic).

Other projects included 'South Pacific' (CBS) with Dame Kiri Te Kanawa and Jose Carreras, a duet with Barry Manilow on his album '2.00AM Paradise Café' (Arista), performances of Gershwin with Symphony Orchestras conducted by Michael Tilson Thomas that produced the Grammy winning 'Gershwin Live' (CBS), and a performance of the poetry of Pope John Paul II adapted by Gene Lees and set to music by Tito Fontana and Sante Palumbo—'The Planet Is Alive: Let It Live', a limited edition album. In 1989 she toured with her trio, guesting with various symphony orchestras presenting 'A Duke Ellington Songbook'. However, her artistic ambition was quelled forever on 3 April 1990 after undergoing operations for skin cancer. But even though she had reached further outward during the '80s, the definitive Vaughan on record had remained as elusive as ever.

Like Vaughan, **Carmen McRae** (b.1922) was part diva and part dramatist. But whereas the diva almost subsumed Vaughan, McRae made greater use of theatre, albeit subtly underplayed, and feminine irony to telling and profound effect. For years Sarah Vaughan introduced herself in concert, saying 'For those of you who don't know me, I'm Carmen McRae', an oblique compliment to a singer's singer. But Carmen McRae commercial singer almost buried Carmen McRae jazz artist, on record at least, until the 1980s when she signed with the Concord label; 'You're Looking At Me', the superb 'Two For The Road' with George Shearing and 'Fine And Mellow' recorded live at Birdland West, Longbeach, California. An album of duets with Betty Carter, 'Carmen McRae—Betty

Sarah Vaughan: 'I'm not a jazz singer, I'm a singer.' However, with just piano, bass and drums she could be riveting and if she didn't want to be known as a jazz singer, then so be it.

Carmen McRae. Used feminine irony to telling and profound effect.

Carter Duets' (Great American Music Hall) charted in Billboard's Top 20 in 1987.

While Fitzgerald, Vaughan and McRae had no qualms about tackling commercial projects, **Betty Carter** (b.1930) steadfastly remained true to her art. 'Betty Bebop is a jazz singer,' asserted Sarah Vaughan[10] and Carmen McRae said: 'There's really only one jazz singer—only one: Betty Carter.'[11] But sadly such an uncompromising stance meant that for years no record company was interested in recording her.

Undeterred by this gross miscarriage of justice, Carter formed her own record label and her third release, the Grammy nominated 'Audience With Betty Carter' (Bet Car), recorded in December 1979, produced one of the finest jazz vocal albums ever: a bravura, uncompromising statement with like-minded sidemen, John Hicks (p), Curtis Lundy (b) and Kenny Washington (d). 'An audience makes me *think,* makes me reach for things I'd never try in the studio,' she said later.

Carter imposed herself on her material in a way few singers manage with a unique process of creative distortion; like images glimpsed in a hall of mirrors, songs are bent this way and that by her astute musical imagination, creating an aural drama that in live performance was visually underlined with the additional dimension of 'theatrical elegance', so that song and performance reached out to touch her audience as a complete entity unique in jazz.

The Michele Parkenson film from the early 1980s, 'But Then, She's Betty Carter', although filmed on a budget, captured the essence of her live performances in a valuable record of this great singer. 'Whatever Happened To Love' (Bet Car), another Grammy nominee recorded live at N.Y.C.'s 'Bottom Line' in 1982, included a string section but is by no means a saccharine affair and was a worthy successor to 'The Audience'.

Carter's accompanying trios, like Art Blakey's Jazz Messengers, were proving grounds of excellence for young musicians: pianists such as John Hicks, Onaje Alan Gumbs, Mulgrew Miller, Benny Green and Stephen

Betty Carter created aural drama that in live performance was underlined by 'theatrical elegance'.

Scott were just a few who passed through her trio in the late 1970s and the 1980s. Carter studied music at the Detroit Conservatory of Music and joined Lionel Hampton as both vocalist and arranger in the early 1950s. Her arranging skills were much in evidence in the organization of her material, with dazzling tempo and metre changes, sudden segues and sophisticated modulations.

In 1987 she signed with the reconstituted Verve label and 'Look What I Got' (Verve), although recorded with her trio in transition plus the unnecessary Don Braden (ts), at last produced the elusive Grammy in 1989, but incredibly her record company refused to pay for her trip to the Award ceremony. 'They said it wasn't in the budget,' she wryly observed. But at least it meant coverage in the *Rolling Stone, USA Today* and *Christian Science Monitor* amongst others. TV spots followed, including appearances on the much vaunted 'Bill Cosby Show'. After over 40 years of singing pure jazz, Betty Carter was, by 1989, not only in danger of becoming an overnight success, but more importantly was being acknowledged by most critics as the premier singer in jazz.

Likewise, the indifference of record companies to the talent of **Anita O'Day** (b.1919) meant that she too was forced into self-production and, as with Betty Carter, jazz was the better for it. O'Day's style was not one of reinterpretation so much as quasi-instrumental expression. With a range of barely two octaves she organized her tonal material with an alluring, husky seen-it-all-before directness and a conspicuous use of melismatics that above all else swung. Her scat, legato and chromatic, was her own. Described by Leonard Feather as '*The* definitive jazz singer', her traumatic lifestyle[12] stood in the way of her realizing her full potential until the 1970s when she began to retrieve her career with exhaustive touring supported by releases on her own Emily label—including an excellent 1975 'Live In Tokyo' and two fine 1979 performances, 'Live At The City' and 'Second Set'.

The 1981 'Mello' Day' (GNP) continued a run of excellent albums: 'This one's got to be among her best', said *Downbeat*. In 1985 she celebrated her 50th year in jazz with a big band and quartet at Carnegie Hall—'A Song Is You' (Emily). 'S'Wonderful' (Emily), again with a big band was followed by the 'The Tokyo Big Band Video' (Emily Productions). In 1987, together with Buddy DeFranco, she fronted the Woody Herman Herd in place of its ailing leader for most of that year. The Grammy-nominated 'In A Mellow Tone' (DRG) from 1989 revisited some earlier material, including 'Anita's Blues' and 'On The Trail' with a nonpareil rhythm section of Pete Jolly, Brian Bromberg and Frank Capp in perhaps her finest album of the decade.

In 1988 she entered negotiations with the estate of the late Gene Krupa, with whom she rose to jazz stardom in the 1940s, to use the late drummer's arrangements and formed a mini-big-band called 'The Krupa Legend'. Held over at Michael's Pub in New York in the summer of 1989, the *Daily News* said: 'Go see Anita O'Day and the Krupa Legend musicians—YOU'LL NEVER SEE ANYTHING LIKE THIS AGAIN.'[13] Approaching 70, Anita O'Day was at last coming of age.

O'Day's unique style influenced several emerging singers during the early 1950s, including June Christy and Chris Connor. Christy (1925-90) had all but retired from music by the early '70s, and her 1980s appearances with Shorty Roger's Giants failed to recapture the magic. Not so **Chris Connor** (b.1927). Her 1983 'Love Is Here With You' (Stash) was warm and worldly-wise but it was her performances on the Contemporary label that impressed.

In 1970 Ran Blake described her live performance of 'Ten Cents A Dance' as, 'near-perfect and perhaps the definitive interpretation.'[14] Her 1986 album 'Classic' (Contemporary) included that very song and 16 years on the verdict was the same. The 1987 'New Again' (Contemporary) confirmed the impression that both albums were slightly overcooked by producer Helen Keane; Connor would have stood well with just a trio, re-creating the intimate one-to-one feel she projected live. But Keane, who had brought the best out of pianist Bill Evans, also drew some fine performances from Connor, who like so many other committed jazz singers, remained woefully under-appreciated during the '80s at a time when she seemed to be reaching the height of her powers.

Carol Sloane (b.1937) never achieved the recognition she deserved, often plucking defeat from the jaws of victory. 'Her career would just be getting off the ground, and then she would disappear with another beau,' explained Helen Keane[15] whose production skills are again apparent on the 1988 'Love You Madly' (Contemporary). 'She's been long known in musician's circles,' she explained. 'There are so many players who love working with her'.[16] Indeed Ella Fitzgerald included her in a short list of her favourite singers.[17] With musicians such as Art Farmer, Kenny Burrell, Clifford Jordan and Kenny Barron, 'Love You Madly' (Contemporary) takes its place alongside Connor's 'Classic' (Contemporary) as among the finest interpretative reinventions of American popular song for over 20 years.

Chicago based **Judy Roberts,** a pianist with a cute piping voice, like an adrenalized Blossom Dearie, seemed throughout the '80s on the verge of overnight success—despite almost 20 years in the business. *Cashbox* praised her 'breathy, velveteen voice' and while it did not move mountains it may well have made them go weak at the knees. Roberts' worldly, yet curiously vulnerable style, particularly her affinity for the work of Dave Frishberg, communicated a genuine sense of shared pleasure that simply did not convey itself through her recorded work.

She has always used top notch accompanists (bassist Brian Torff was one of her discoveries), so the fast company of Ray Brown and Jeff Hamilton on 'Trio' (Pausa) by no means intimidated her, the album getting high praise from Japan's *Swing Journal.* The earlier 'The Judy Roberts Band', 'The Other World' and 'Nights In Brazil' (all Inner City) show the after-effects of '70s fusion, but nevertheless had considerable FM airplay. Her trio, with Jim Cox (b) and Marc Wofley (d) recorded 'My Heart Belongs To Daddy' in 1988, and later in the year they cut a couple of albums in Amsterdam. 'Miss Roberts' crisp inventive keyboard work impresses; her singing seduces,' said the *Washington Times*—it just seemed a matter of time before recognition caught up with her talent.

Nina Simone (b.1933) returned to active performance in the 1980s to reassert her reputation as powerful pianist and singer when she returned from self-imposed exile in North Africa. After two unsuccessful personal relationships and a period as the adopted daughter of Mrs Antoinette Tubman, wife, niece and daughter of former presidents of Liberia, her career gradually regained momentum, her charisma as powerful as ever.

Once described as 'one of the richest and mature voices in the black search for identity',[18] personal problems appeared to conspire against her from time to time. A 1984 SRO engagement at Ronnie Scott's in London was rebooked for a return engagement a few weeks later; she failed to turn up. 'Nina's Back' (VPI Records) from 1985, intended to celebrate her return to active performance, showed her adjusting into an electrical environment.

In 1987 her recording of 'My Baby Just Cares For Me' (Charly), originally recorded in 1959 for Atlantic, became an unexpected hit after being used in a television advert for Chanel perfume and charted in the United Kingdom. Her 1987 album 'Let It Be Me' (Verve), recorded live with bass and drums at the Vine Street Bar & Grill, Hollywood, demonstrated what is meant by 'variable form,' but live, when the muse was upon her, she showed she had lost none of her intensity that gave artists such as Roberta Flack inspiration.

Sheila Jordan (b.1928) a typist by day and jazz musician by night during the bop era, sat-in with the very best, including Charlie Parker. A student of Lennie Tristano, she was forced to maintain her day job throughout her career but it did at least mean she did not have to compromise her art. 'I don't just have to take *any* kind of singing job,' she said. Her reputation was made by a powerfully emotional version of 'You Are My Sunshine' on the 1962 George Russell album 'The Outer View' (Riverside) and her 1963 album 'Portrait Of Sheila' (Blue Note), a welcome re-release in 1990.

But life was often difficult; her marriage to pianist Duke Jordan ended in failure leaving her as a single parent and for a while she struggled with alcohol. 'I knew that if I kept on going I wouldn't be able to sing',

Sheila Jordan, 'who demands much but is never less than absorbing'.

she said after pulling back from the brink. Throughout she persisted with her musical career and her underground reputation gradually spread so that by the 1980s she was generally recognized as one of the most original and diverse vocal stylists in jazz.

In 1979 she joined the sadly short-lived Steve Kuhn Quartet in a unique integration of voice with piano, bass and drums that produced 'Play-ground' (ECM) in 1979 and the live 'Last Years Waltz' (ECM) in 1981. Although the band drifted apart from lack of work, she maintained contact with bassist Harvie Swartz with whom she developed an intuitive rapport that is clearly apparent on 'Old Time Feeling' (Palo Alto). With the addition of Tom Harrell, Kenny Barron and Ben Riley on the 1984 album 'The Crossing' (Blackhawk) came 'Sheila Jordan's masterpiece—the album to make sceptics believe'. And sceptics there were; *The Times* appeared baffled by her performances, describing her as 'one of the most idiosyncratic contemporaries'.[19] But Jordan's up-front emotionalism was a triumph of the unexpected: 'A difficult singer,' wrote Richard Sudhalter, 'who demands much but is never less than absorbing.' In 1985 her 'Celebration' concert at New York's Public Theatre was as much a testament to her unswerving commitment to jazz as much as public thanksgiving. 'If it wasn't for hearing all these musicians, I wouldn't be alive today,' she sang.

Jordan's style, of varying dynamics, timbre and rhythmic displacement and her use of sawtooth intervals, was one of the last ports of call before casting-off into abstraction. **Jay Clayton** (b.1941) relinquished lyrics in favour of her own vocal sound-world of onomatopoeia, syllabification and a range of vocal effects that ranged from a rusty barn door to a screech owl; the 1987 'String Trio Of New York With Jay Clayton' (West Wind) and the 1988 'As Tears Go By' (ITM) with John Lindberg plus the Trio again. However, on 'All-Out' (Amina) she confined herself to voice-as-instrument improvisation alongside saxophonist Jane Ira Bloom. Clayton's experimentalism was taken a step further by **Urszula Dudziak** (b.1943), who used electronic gadgetry to duet with herself, creating a rising hubub of tape-loop mayhem and extending her range from godzilla-like roars into the realms of the dog-whistle; 'Future Talk' (Inner City) and an appearance with The Gil Evans Orchestra from 1988, 'Tribute To Gil' (Soul Note) essayed her space-age scat.

In 1982 Clayton and Dudziak formed the nucleus of an *a cappella* group 'Vocal Summit' together with Jeanne Lee, Lauren Newton and Bobby McFerrin. Their first performance was shown on European television to critical acclaim and they occasionally appeared with a revolving cast of players throughout the '80s. Their album 'Sorrow Is Not Forever, Love Is' (Moers Music) appeared in 1984.

Although it seemed as if McFerrin, Dudziak and Clayton were pushing the voice to the limits of invention by instrumental parody, onomatopoeia and abstract distortion, it was in fact a limitation of the voice's full potential. By frequently denying themselves the dimension of language, the results, although interesting and occasionally arresting, were, after repeated listening, irritating simply because in the literal sense they had nothing to say. When harnessed to the vision of a composer and lyricist, the voice can be as emotive and moving as the finest instrumentalist simply through its 'storytelling' privilege.

Equally, scat singing, even on a predetermined chord structure, could become wearying if used as a means in itself; rather it is but one aspect of the jazz singer's art, 'I don't think you have to scat sing to prove anything,' said Sheila Jordan.[20] 'If the feeling's strong and you do it and it's uniquely your own, it's great. But I don't think it's necessary to scat every number or scat at all unless you feel like it . . . scat singing doesn't necessarily make you a jazz singer.'

MALE VOICES

The re-birth of **Mel Torme** (b.1925), whose vocal equipment during the decade 'gleamed with new lustre and magnificence, greater ease and control',[21] began in the early 1980s with the remarkable *tour de force* 'Live At Marty's' (Finesse). However, as with another minor Torme masterpiece, the 1974 'Live At The Maisonette' (Atlantic), it passed almost unnoticed through poor distribution. The real breakthrough came when he signed with the Concord label to record with George Shearing. Together they produced a series of immaculate albums, with 'An Evening With' from 1982 and 'Top Drawer' from 1983 both earning Grammy Awards; but just as good were 'An Evening At Charlie's' (1983), 'An Elegant Evening' (1985) and 'A Vintage Year' (1987). His album with Rob McConnell's Boss Brass from 1986 was described by McConnell as among the 'great times'[22] had by the Band.

A long-awaited reunion with Marty Paich finally materialized in August 1988, 'Mel Torme And The Marty Paich Dek-Tette' (Concord), but was not wholly successful with the Dek-Tette playing a backing role for Torme rather than the integration of ensemble and voice that had characterized their 1950s collaborations plus Torme's fallible choice of material.

However, all was made good in December 1988 with 'In Concert Tokyo' (Concord), the first ever live performance by Torme and the Marty Paich Dek-Tette. The effect of an audience on Torme, as always, made him extend himself; his natural *joie de vivre* clearly communicating from the stunning tempo change in 'Sweet Georgia Brown' to his rumbustious drum solo on 'Cotton Tail', creating a rising spiral of excitement that was only diffused by 'The Christmas Song'.

Mel Torme's style was the epitome of cool perfection. On the 1946 recording of 'What Is This Thing Called Love' (Musicraft) he sang with an open bel canto style that was ahead of its time and not universally adopted by vernacular singers until the mid-1950s. Until then singers had been taught by Billie Holiday and Bing Crosby to become objects of the microphone, their message intended for intimate consumption in individual seclusion. In contrast, Torme wanted the world to hear his gift, which from the mid-1950s took account of Ella Fitzgerald, an influence that emerged clearly during his scatting.

But Torme was not without his detractors, perhaps because of the ease he made the musically complicated sound easy, aided by inch perfect intonation, clear diction, rhythmic and harmonic ingenuity and his ability to swing even the most recalcitrant rhythm section. Torme's range was wide, from A below middle C up through two octaves to B flat; what was often mistaken for a falsetto were in fact head-tones. 'When I sing the last part of 'New York State Of Mind' [on 'Live At Marty's],' he explained, 'I purposely sing the high note and slide down to a very low note so that you can hear there's no break in the voice.'[23] Some critics saw his occasional excesses of bravado as denoting an entertainer rather than a jazz musician, but during the '80s he answered them with some of his finest work on record. His performance of 'When The World Was Young' from 'Live At Marty's' (Finesse) lacks for no emotional commitment while 'In Concert Tokyo' (Concord) carried the stamp of a master.

The stylistic affinity between Torme and the work of **Mark Murphy** (b.1932), both in terms of diction and timbre, stopped at Torme's Swing Era roots; Murphy came from bop. Not well served on record, Murphy sounded twice as good live than on any of his recordings. In performance he used two bizarre vaporizers to help prevent his voice drying out, plus a shelf of medical preparations to thwart any throat infections lingering in the atmosphere. It was worth it; wildly under-appreciated, the occasionally affected hipness of some of his recordings seemed at odds with his whole-hearted commitment in person.

While it might be tempting to say Murphy wore his heart on his sleeve, it was in fact a total lack of inhibition which occasionally clouded his musical judgement; such hipness, as on the 1981 'Bop For Kerouac' (Muse), could be an irritation, but Murphy, when the poetry reading was over, was lifted by Bill Mays' arrangements and Richie Cole's alto to produce one of his best albums. But the 1983 'Viva Brazil' and 'Sings Nat's Choice Vols. 1 & 2' (both Muse) and the 1984 'Living Room' (Muse), confirmed that his recording company should have taken a remote to record a typical Murphy performance live. However, 'Beauty And The Beast' (Muse), recorded in 1985/6, taking its title from a composition on Wayne Shorter's 1975 'Native Dancer' (CBS), was recorded with class young musicians such as Brian Lynch (t) and Joey Baron (d) and confirmed that Murphy deserved wider recognition.

Joe Williams (b.1918), described by *Village Voice* as 'probably the best living male jazz singer', came to fame with a string of hits made with Count Basie in the 1950s, including 'Every Day' that sold 250,000 copies, something of a sensation in 1955. Williams' style was powerful and dramatic; not for nothing was a 1989 reissue of some of his '60s RCA material entitled 'The Overwhelming Joe Williams' (BMG). His risque blues performances often lasted over 20 minutes, crammed full of humorous sexual innuendo, but he was equally at home with the American Popular Song, albeit washed with spirit and feeling of the blues.

'Nothing But The Blues' (Delos) from 1983 shows no lack of energy from the surprisingly youthful 64-year-old, and is one of his best albums for years. The reconstituted Verve label recorded him live at Vine Street, Hollywood in 1987, 'Joe Williams' and again he is irrepressible, this time with Norman Simmons (p) with just guitar, bass and drums. All his favourites are revisited, including 'Everyday I Have The Blues' with a segue into 'All Blues', something he had been doing for years live but somehow never got on to record. It was followed by 'In Good Company' (Verve) from 1989, with Marlena Shaw, Shirley Horn and Supersax. His career enjoyed a welcome fillip during the '80s with his appearance as the fictional father of Bill Cosby on the 'Bill Cosby Show', and from time to time he revisited past glories with the Count Basie Band directed by Frank Foster on the festival circuits. In June 1989 he celebrated his 70th birthday in Carnegie Hall, in the 'good company' of Marlena Shaw and, inevitably, the Basie orchestra.

In the same way Mark Murphy related to Mel Torme, **Joe Lee Wilson** (b.1935) related to Joe Williams. A powerful baritone who worked with

Miles Davis, Sonny Rollins, Archie Shepp, Jackie McLean and Lee Morgan in the '60s, Wilson's relative anonymity, like that of Murphy, simply did not square with his manifest ability, described by Harvey Siders as 'a jazz singer in the true sense of the word'.[24] His repertoire was mostly his own, although mixed with obscure non-original songs, and an occasional blues.

SINGER/SONGWRITERS

Singer/songwriters have always been something of a rarity in jazz. But considering the radical change in pop music since early 1960s in favour of the singer/songwriter, it was surprising that this trend was not reflected more in jazz. Nevertheless, several singer/songwriters did emerge in jazz and their work was often shrewdly observed, bitingly satirical and frequently delightful.

Mose Allison (b.1927), a ubiquitous figure in the 1960s who recorded almost 20 albums, was by the end of the '70s an almost forgotten figure. His return to the club and Festival circuits in the 1980s was cause for minor celebration; his style, unaltered since his heyday—and still with an aversion to the hi-hat cymbals—was intended to convey the slow Southerner, a veneer that disguised a hip urban cynicism that has been mentioned in the same breath as William Faulkner. His bustling piano style, full of Bartokian rumblings that somehow suggested Bud Powell playing boogie, were as much part of his performances as his vocals.

The 1982 'Middle-Class White Boy' (Elektra Musician), his 19th album and first for eight years, was a bit of a culture shock for his fans; with Phil Upchurch (g) and Joe Farrell (ts), the intimacy of his trio had gone and his use of electric piano seemed to have been the last straw for some and was accordingly downrated. But his wry charm was in abundance; the backdrop had changed, Allison hadn't. The live 'Lessons In Living' (Elektra Musician) from the Montreux Jazz Festival had quite a mix of players, including Billy Cobham (d) and Lou Donaldson (as) and although less intimate had some memorable moments, including a magnificently ironic 'You Are My Sunshine.'

Allison resurfaced in 1987 with 'Ever Since The World Ended' (Blue Note), with guests Arthur Blythe (as), Benny Wallace (ts) and Kenny Burrell (g) some new originals and more superb irony. However his guests occasionally trod on his toes, something rectified with the wholly successful 'My Backyard' (Blue Note), recorded in New Orleans in 1989 with local musicians to capture his, 'uniquely southern flavour that [lent] a philosophical dimension to gallows humour.'[25]

Allison was a role model for both Ben Sidran and Dave Frishberg, who adapted his conversational delivery and astringent humour to different purposes. **Ben Sidran** (b.1944), who produced Allison's work on Blue Note, had smooth crossover FM appeal on albums such as 'Bop City' (Antilles), 'On The Live Side' (Magenta) and 'Too Hot To Touch' (Windham Hill Jazz). **Dave Frishberg** (b.1933), however, vocalized with the nostalgic appeal of Hoagy Carmichael mixed in almost equal parts with the non-appeal of Jimmy Rowles' vocal style. During the '80s he worked the European and American club circuits to increasing acclaim and his piano recital at the 1989 JVC New York Jazz Festival was warmly received by critics. 'Live At Vine Street' (Fantasy) and 'Can't Take You Nowhere' (Fantasy) chart his grisly charm and shrewd piano but Concord placed him in their usual Mainstream surroundings on the 1989 'Let's Eat Home' that detracted from his intimate style.

Frishberg's lyrics for 'I'm Hip' and 'Long Daddy Green' and 'Peel Me A Grape' were hits for **Blossom Dearie** (b. 1926), a like-minded po-faced humourist whose repertoire extended from her own *bons mots* such as 'My Attorney Bernie' through George Gershwin to Spike Milligan. 'Her piping voice is not to everyone's taste,' warned the *The Times,*[26] perhaps chauvinistically. 'Simply, Positively, Et Tu Bruce', 'Chez Wahlberg Part 1' and 'Songs Of Chelsea' (all on her own Daffodil label)—the latter inspired by her regular residencies at 'The Ballroom' in New York's Chelsea District during the 1980s—were somewhat one-dimensional but added the ingredient of whimsy, her own special property, to jazz.

Perhaps the most unlikely of all the singer/songwriters was bassist **Jay Leonhart** (b.1940). After establishing himself as a nonpareil bassist and a favourite of singers Mel Torme and Barbra Streisand, he began writing his own material that reflected his off-beat humour and sharp intellect. Extending the tradition of Allison and Frishberg with his cunning verse, his vocal style seemed perpetually surprised at his own wit. During the latter half of the '80s he formed a group comprising Roger Kellaway (p), George Young (ts, ss) and Grady Tate (d) that became a regular Sunday lunchtime feature at New York's 'Blue Note'.

While 'Salamander Pie' (DMP) was a duo with Mike Renzi (p), 'The Double Cross' (Sunnyside) featured his Blue Note group that after years of working together framed Leonhart's music to perfection. 'I wish I could take them on tour,' he said, adding, 'If only someone would ask me.'[27]

His delightfully eccentric titles such as 'Grady Tate In An Earthquake', 'They're Coming To Get Me', 'Do Not Nag' had lyrics to match; his clever, witty 'Robert Frost' from 'The Double Cross' appeared as an instrumental on Gary Burton's 1988 'Times Like These' (GRP) but the sting was in the lyrics. Leonhart pondered the problems of being a poet; could Robert Frost escape the washing-up by claiming the muse was upon him, or did he have 'dishpan hands?'

NEW VOICES

Bobby McFerrin's (b.1950) unique style made him the first young singer during the '80s to garner acclaim after a long period when very few young singers seemed willing to commit themselves to jazz. Restricting his tonal palette to a wordless vocalese that often sounded like acoustic and electronic instruments, his recording debut was with Pharoah Sanders on 'Journey To The One' (Theresa) from 1980. But it was his duet with Wynton Marsalis at Carnegie Hall in 1982, featured on 'The Young Lions' (Elektra Musician), that attracted attention to his extraordinary talents.

Albums under his own name, however, respected no stylistic limitations, their creative thrust divided between jazz and pop, the bias towards the latter growing progressively stronger—from 'Bobby McFerrin' and 'The Voice' (both Elektra Musician) the commercial overtones became more overt through 'Spontaneous Inventions' (Blue Note) until finally 'Simple Pleasures' appeared on the commercially slanted EMI/Mahhattan label that included his wonderfully ironic 1988 chart success, 'Don't Worry Be Happy', the first *a cappella* song to reach number one on *Billboard's* 'Hot 100'.

Cassandra Wilson (b.1963), debuted at The Galleon, NYC in 1982 and on record in 1985 with Steve Coleman and his Five Elements on 'Motherland Pulse' (JMT). By the time her own 'Point Of View' from 1986 and the 1987 'Days Aweigh' (both JMT) announced the arrival of a major new talent she had explored free singing on New Air's 'Air Show' (Black Saint) and mainstream on Jim DeAngelis and Tony Sigma's 'Straight From The Top' (Statiras).

Even though she had not fully cast off the influence of Betty Carter and to a lesser extent Abbey Lincoln—both acknowledged influences—her voice was described by *Downbeat* as 'the most strikingly sensual, warmly cunning set of vocal chords to hit the jazz world in years'.[28] Her 1988 'Blue Skies' (JMT) with a highly sympathetic trio comprising Mulgrew

Cassandra Wilson: 'The most strikingly sensual, warmly cunning set of vocal chords to hit the jazz world in years.'

Miller (p), Lonnie Plaxico (b) and Terri Lyne Carrington (d) was a sophisticated work-out on standards. 'One of the great vocal albums of recent years,' said *Village Voice.*[29] Wilson, like alto saxophonist Steve Coleman whose M-Base world she also inhabited, performed best from within the tradition. But the M-Base rule book insisted on the uphill task of wedding

jazz and funk and although the 1989 'Jumpworld' (JMT) featured Coleman and the M-Base first-team it was a disappointment, neither challenging nor stimulating.

Equally, **Dianne Schuur** showed that she had the potential to move
the tradition of Fitzgerald, Vaughan and Carter forward with craft and
originality and, like Wilson, seemed to dissipate her gifts instead of refining them; in Schuur's case by pursuing glossy endeavours. Enthusias-
tically encouraged by Stan Getz, ('She has the most passion and pathos
of any singer since Ella Fitzgerald and Sarah Vaughan'), Schuur came to
jazz via the gospel route. However, the glossy setting of her debut album
'Schuur Thing' (GRP) failed to do her justice. Her handling of American
Popular Songs on 'Timeless' (GRP) suggested a formidable talent as did
several tracks on the 1987 session with the Count Basie Orchestra (GRP)
under Frank Foster's direction. 'Take a singer who has the church and
gospel roots,' said Joe Williams, 'give them the training of a big band
and wow! There's a fully developed jazz singer.'

Her gospel roots were examined in the 1988 'Talkin' 'Bout You' (GRP)
with the Gadd Gang and the Edwin Hawkins Singers, a session that
proved the plagal cadence was still alive and well, but the feeling persisted
that GRP's packaging of their starlet did not present her at her best,
Dave Grusin describing GRP's philosophy as being 'comfortable in a type
of fusion jazz'. Live, however, she removed all misgivings; 'A superior
stylist with a hearty and soulful delivery,' said the *Washington Post*.
Dianne Reeves (b. 1956) was discovered by Clark Terry at a National
Association of Jazz Educators Festival in Chicago when she was 17. A
contralto with a $3\frac{1}{2}$-octave range, her demo-disc-like Blue Note album
'Dianne Reeves' covered all bases, not unlike her earlier 'Welcome To My
Love' (Palo Alto). 'It's like my stage show, as varied as I can make it,
with jazz as the thread holding it together,' she said.[30] Such stylistic
ambiguity assured appearances in the jazz charts, Black Music charts and
the Billboard pop chart. But the glossy production for Blue Note by
George Duke almost succeeded in concealing the fact that she had the
potential to become a powerful jazz singer if she could only focus her
talent more sharply within the jazz idiom; live she could be compelling.

Equally, **Carmen Lundy's** (b.1955) 'Good Morning Kiss' (Blackhawk),
with five of her own crossover appeal compositions, contained warmth,
precision and range; but why did such a talent avoid the jazz environment? **Susannah McCorkle**, however, remained firmly within the ambit
of the American Popular Song and her hard work on the poorly distributed
Inner City label showed elegance and sincerity. In 1988 she signed with

Concord Records, a good career move to a higher profile label. 'No More Blues' moved *Stereo Review* magazine to describe her as, 'the finest interpreter of sophisticated songs we have today'; such hyperbole can often kill an artist with kindness, but in McCorkle's instance it was not so far from the truth.

Patti Cathcart slipped into view towards the end of the 1980s as a singer of emotional depth and cunning resource as part of a duo with guitarist husband Tuck Andress. The 1988 'Tears Of Joy' and the 1989 'Love Warriors' (both Windham Hill) charted on *Billboard's* Jazz Chart and revealed two accomplished musicians of considerable warmth succeeding in the most searching of surroundings. Andress was described by the *Bay Guardian* as 'one of the most extraordinary guitarists to ever put ten fingers against six strings', while Cathcart was described by the *San Francisco Chronicle* as 'a sensational vocalist in her own right, with star potential'.

VOCAL GROUPS

The community aspect of gospel singing undoubtedly inspired many vocal groups within jazz, although by the 1940s a more direct line of influence came from orchestral and instrumental models. The duo of Jackie and Roy in the 1940s showed that sophisticated part singing could be adopted to modern jazz, which was being echoed in the 1980s by Kim Shaw and Marion Cowlings. In the 1950s, Lambert, Hendricks and Ross took the concept of vocalese, or lyrics set to a previously recorded instrumental solo (originally devised by King Pleasure and Eddie Jefferson), to a level of execution widely admired at the time.

Manhattan Transfer continued the tradition of Lambert Hendricks and Ross into the 1980s, their technical perfection and excellence often overlooked because of the MOR quotient in their repertoire. But Manhattan Transfer treated the jazz repertoire with immense respect, their hit single, 'Boy From New York City' (Atlantic), for example, had Charlie Parker's 'Confirmation' on the flip side. Every album they released contained at least one jazz number that attested to their love of the idiom: 'Body and Soul' and the two-Grammy-winner 'Birdland' came from the 1979 'Extensions' (Atlantic), 'Four Brothers' from the 1978 'Pastiche' (Atlantic), the gospel 'Operator' from the 1975 'Manhattan Transfer' (Atlantic) and 'Until I Met You (Corner Pocket)' and 'Confirmation' from the 1981 'Mecca For Moderns' (Atlantic).

Their surprise appearance at the 1982 Playboy Jazz Festival with Weather Report for a one-off performance of 'Birdland', a hit for WR in

1977 and for Manhattan Transfer in 1979, was both dramatic and appealing, an interesting direction unfulfilled by both groups on 'Live At The Playboy Jazz Festival' (Elektra Musician). The 1985 'Vocalese' (Atlantic) won three Grammy awards in 1986 and although it may not have been their most successful album financially, musically it was an assertion of their affinity with the jazz culture more then the leisure vanguard, an ambivalence that often remained unreconciled.

Collaborator Jon Hendricks, formerly of Lambert, Hendricks and Ross, wrote the lyrics for virtually all of 'Vocalese' (Atlantic); ' "Vocalese" is really the culmination of that love they have for Lambert, Hendricks and Ross,' said Hendricks, 'they are keeping the flame alive!' 'Live' (Atlantic) from 1987, recorded at the end of their '87 Japanese tour, was a live workout on much of the 'Vocalese' material that, despite some good-humoured MOR, showed just how far they had extended the territory originally opened up by LH&R.

Jon Hendricks: Keeping the flame of vocalese alive.

Jon Hendricks (b.1921) himself continued the vocalese tradition of Lambert, Hendricks and Ross with his own Jon Hendricks Company, comprising Hendricks, his wife Judith, daughter Aria and Kevin Burke but found the competition intense with groups such as Rare Silk (Palo Alto), The Ritz (Denon), New York Voices (GRP), Singers Unlimited and L.A. Voices (Capitol/EMI), all well received by the critics. But it was Manhattan Transfer, despite their MOR posturing, whose best work set the standard by which vocal groups were judged during the '80s.

GOSPEL

'Gospel singing is jazz gussied up and dressed in the clothes of a lamb,' wrote Whitney Balliett,[31] and certainly the secular tradition of gospel singing has had an important role in shaping the jazz vocal, not least through the influence of the church, a training ground for countless vocalists, from Sarah Vaughan to Dianne Schuur. The gospel sound also created a small but significant subculture within jazz, that of the 'testifying' style that can be heard in the work of such post-war singers as Mahalia Jackson, Dinah Washington, Aretha Franklin and, in the 1980s, Dianne Schuur.

Gospel singing never lost sight of jazz and vice versa; tangible evidence of its influence still lingered in jazz, whether it was the plagal cadences of Art Blakey's Jazz Messengers playing 'Moanin' ', the question and answer riffs of the big bands or in reminding jazz that the vocal need not be a solo affair. While in the '80s gospel groups such as the Sensational Nightingales still embodied 'pure' gospel roots, **Sweet Honey In The Rock** attracted attention, both for their carefully arranged *a cappella* singing and their presentation of feminist and black issues. Formed in 1973 by Bernice Johnson Reagon who became a director of black culture at the Smithsonian Institute, their 1985 'The Other Side' (Flying Fish) focussed on religious and political issues while the 1986 'Eyes On The Prize' (Flying Fish) highlighted the civil rights movement. 'Live At Carnegie Hall' (Flying Fish) demonstrated their captivating power which could evoke an African tribal chant or stir hearts in praise of the Lord.

Take 6, an *a cappella* group whose secular and jazz-based repertoire were the hit of the 1989 Monterey Jazz Festival, emerged from Oakwood College, Alabama where they had been known as Alliance. The group entered the big-time in 1989 after a tour with Al Jarreau and their album 'Take 6' (Reprise) was awarded two Grammys, four Dove awards (the gospel Grammys) and went gold. Comprising Claude McKnight, Mark

Kibble, Mervyn Warren, Cedric Dent, David Thomas and Alvin Chea, they surmounted the problem of performing gospel material to jazz-orientated audiences by evoking the sound of a jazz combo with their stunning vocal arrangements that at times simulated bass and brass sections. 'We present the message in an attractive package and hopefully the folks will leave the show humming a tune,' they said. 'We let the Holy Spirit take it from there.'

SHOUTING THE BLUES

Jimmy Witherspoon (b.1923) had a voice that was flexible enough to handle non-blues material convincingly, but always made the blues his adopted home, fitting the 'shouting' style of Kansas City and the Southwest, personified by Jimmy Rushing (1902-72), Walter Brown and Joe Turner into the demands of modern jazz. A brush with throat cancer temporarily sidelined him in 1982 but Witherspoon continued to make a number of excellent albums. On the 1980 'Sings The Blues with Panama Francis's Savoy Sultans' (Muse), his approach was 'faithful but not literal'[32] to the spirit of the Kansas City tradition; Rushing/Basie, Walter Brown/Jay McShann and Joe Williams/Basie. 'Live' (MCA) with guitarist Robben Ford reached out to the modern blues tradition.

Witherspoon was deeply influenced by **Big Joe Turner** (1911-1985), the legendary Kansas City blues singer who had several hits in the 1950s that were purloined by lesser (white) mortals as Rock 'n' Roll took off, including 'Shake Rattle And Roll', 'Corrine/Corrina', 'Lipstick, Powder and Paint' and 'Chains'. Turner remained true to jazz, however, and in the 1970s signed with Pablo and recorded with various permutations of the label's stable of stars, with its often unsatisfactory yet insistently incestuous recording policy. The best of Turner's latter-day albums turned out to be 'Big Joe Turner/Roomful Of Blues' (Muse). Crisp and rocking (without being rock), Roomful Of Blues was a compact little powerhouse of a band dedicated to re-creating that unique time when jump bands metamorphosed into R&B in the early 1950s; it provided the ideal backdrop for Turner's barnstorming style, rolling back the years and allowing him to relax and enjoy himself, despite his recent stroke.

Roomful Of Blues again recreated the magic with **Eddie 'Cleanhead' Vinson** (1917-1988), who like Turner recorded for Pablo; the 1981 'I Want A Little Girl' (Pablo) was a typical lukewarm Pablo jam. Vinson, a storyteller rather than a shouter and alto saxophonist who in his day inspired John Coltrane as well as composing 'Tune Up' and 'Four', part of the repertoire of the legendary Miles Davis Quintet of the 1960s, gets down to business on 'Eddie "Cleanhead" Vinson & Roomful Of Blues' (Muse) from 1982. **Roomful of Blues,** left to their own devices produced their irrepressible 'Live At Lupo's Heartbreak Hotel' (Rounder) recorded in 1986, unmatched for its raw, joyful excitement. Their collaboration with New Orleans bluesman **Earl King,** 'Glazed' (Rounder), again from 1986, manages to achieve similar results by slightly more sophisticated means.

THE BLUES

The Blues played a vital influence on jazz—'I don't really separate [Eric] Dolphy from [Sly] Stone from [Thelonious] Monk from [John] Coltrane because the common thing that links all those people together is the blues. The blues is what links [Ornette] Coleman to the Temptations or Hendrix to 'Trane,' said Vernon Reid in *Village Voice*.[33] The essence of the blues is feeling. 'The blues is more than a . . . bunch of chords licks and scales,' wrote Charles Shaar Murray, 'it is an index of the *quality* of expression that can be brought to bear with instrument or voice.'[34] Indeed, grappling with the *essence* of the blues was something that troubled many young instrumentalists, including Wynton Marsalis and the young neo-classical boppers, throughout the '80s.

Even before Bessie Smith sold 750,000 copies of 'Downhearted Blues' in 1923, the blues had a profound effect on the jazz vocal. The spirit of the blues touched base with social realism and could give a familiar song a lived-in feeling and emotional credibility that was not so much due to execution as to expression. It staked out the profound differences in interpretation between a Bessie Smith or a Mildred Bailey; one evoking life's sordid realities and the other an invitation to a bright and cheerful land.

The blues; once an urban expression of the black community that mirrored the ups and downs of life, was gradually replaced by more hip, contemporary trends; rock, soul, Motown, disco, reggae and rap. But although this meant a gradual erosion of its traditional listenership, the blues survived. Initially the 'British Invasion' in the 1960s introduced the Blues to a large, white, predominantly middle-class market when influential groups like the Stones and Beatles made it clear their underlying inspiration came from the 'subjective black man', artists like B.B. King, Muddy Waters and John Lee Hooker.

B. B. King, the most universally known of all the important Bluesmen.

Since then the blues have tended to revolve primarily, but by no means exclusively, around white audiences, often at colleges and universities, and changes towards their preconceptions and tastes have crept into the music. Instrumental prowess increased, a by-product of both jazz and rock's influence, but the essential message remained the same.

B. B. King (b.1925) was still performing 300 times a year in 1989, by which time he was the most universally known of all the important bluesmen. Live he still played his earlier material rather than pop/funk influenced offerings that had appeared on albums such as the 1985 'Six Silver Strings' (MCA). The 1980 'Now Appearing At Ole Miss' (MCA), a double album, gave a good idea of his stage show, always exciting, as demonstrated by the cool insistence of 'Rock Me Baby', while 'Blues n'Jazz' (MCA) was essentially the same B. B. but in a more acoustic environment.

Almost anything by John Lee Hooker (born 1917) on the old Bluesway sessions capture his dramatic, worldly-wise style, sometimes no more than just three tones chanted in constant pentatonicism. Once described as 'the greatest living bluesman', Hooker was sadly scantily recorded since the early 1970s and while 'Jealous' (Pausa) did the old man little justice, the 1988 re-release of the 1969 'Get Back Home' (Black and Blue) shows how powerful his singing style was, a folk-blues affair, just voice and six-string guitar.

However in 1989 Pete Townsend recruited Hooker to sing the lead in his musical 'The Iron Man', reflecting a renaissance of interest in his music. The esteem in which he was held was reflected on his 1989 'The Healer' (Silverstone) when he was able to call upon guest performers Santana, Bonnie Raitt, Robert Cray, Los Lobos, Canned Heat, George Thorogood and Charlie Musselwhite and show how their varied approaches to the blues all came from the same source.

Albert King (b.1923), an equally powerful performer, had from time to time in his career, succumbed to commercialism. 'San Francisco '83' (Fantasy) showed him at the top of his form, running the knife-edge between tension and release with his 'taciturn, menacing understatement'.[35]

Albert Collins, (b.1932), had a million-seller hit with the instrumental 'Frosty' in 1960. It was followed by a series of similarly titled blues instrumentals, including 'Frost Bite', 'Icy Blue' and 'Don't Loose Your Cool' and ever since allusions to the cold have continued, even down to the name of his group—'The Icebreakers'. His bluesy shuffles had a timeless appeal and his work justified recognition during the '80s as one of the major modern bluesmen, despite his diversions into rock and funk. 'Frozen Alive' (Sonnet) recorded live at The Union Bar, Minneapolis in 1981 captures the excitement and power he generated, but 'Live In Japan' (Sonnet) from 1982 showed the adjustments he made for broader based appeal. The 1986 'Cold Snap' (Sonnet) with Jimmy McGriff on organ quite simply cooks. In 1987 John Zorn featured Collins on his 'Two Lane Highway' from 'Spillane' (Nonesuch). It distilled the essence of his style in what was a remarkably sympathetic 'portrait' inspired by Ellington's instrumental features in the 1940s.

Otis Rush, one of the great Chicago bluesmen, (born 1934) was another sadly under-recorded musician. After a mysterious three year layoff from 1981-84, he returned to be recognized by the W. C. Handy Blues Awards Hall Of Fame in 1984. When his 1985 performance at The San Francisco Blues Festival with the Bobby Murray band was recorded, 'Tops' (Blind Pig Records), it was his first album to be issued since 1977. It contained some of his most reliable showcases, including 'Right Place, Wrong Time', and prompted writer Dick Shurman to observe that Rush, 'still had the creativity that has long enabled him to turn even the most familiar songs into exploratory and emotional revelations'.[36] Coincidentally, his classic 1971 'Right Place, Wrong Time' (Hightone), also recorded

Otis Rush: 'Still had the creativity that long enabled him to turn even the most familiar songs into exploratory and emotional revelations.'

in the Bay area, was re-released in 1986 and was equally indispensable. Live his music was almost evangelical in its power, showing how it influenced the early careers of Eric Clapton, Johnny Winter, Jeff Beck, Mike Bloomfield, Little Milton and a host of others.

NEW BLUES

Until the 1980s the blues remained pretty well in the shadow of its major artists. And although many younger bluesmen had begun using devices from rock—as jazz itself had done during the 1970s prompting claims of selling out from the purists who saw the music no longer addressing the interests of black audiences—it was also true that by the 1980s the blues were stagnating. Many of its younger artists remained true to the precepts of its older, respected players whose performances carried the authority that their younger imitators lacked.

The '80s saw this impasse being resolved. After 20 years of gigging in Texas blues joints, **Stevie Ray Vaughan** (b.1953) appeared at the Montreux Jazz Festival in 1982. A tape of his performance was heard by John Hammond, who had nursed the formative careers of Billie Holiday, Benny Goodman and Count Basie amongst countless others; Hammond promptly signed him to the Epic label and the two Grammy nominee 'Texas Flood' (Epic) took just a couple of days to complete. The title track was an instant modern blues classic; Vaughan's guitar playing drew on the influence of older bluesmen, his brother Jimmie of Fabulous Thunderbirds fame and Jimi Hendrix and was refracted through his often startling imagination. Vaughan effortlessly achieved the feat of singing and playing contrary lines against the beat, his earthy-cool voice neither plagiaristic nor hip.

Subsequent albums failed to capture the clarity of vision of his debut album, moving closer to the blues/rock of bands like The Fabulous Thunderbirds, but 'Couldn't Stand The Weather' (Epic), again with Hammond involved in the production, albeit with keyboards added, was a sort of 'Texas Flood' revisited with the bonus of what had become something of a legend in live performance, a hyperthyroid version of the Jimi Hendrix number 'Voodoo Chile'. In 1985 he appeared at Avery Fisher Hall in a tribute to John Hammond with his group, later jamming memorably with George Benson. He guested on Benny Wallace's 1985 'Twilight Time' (Blue Note), and again his playing was suitably on the money. By the time the 1989 'In Step' (Epic), in memory of John Hammond (died July 1987), was recorded Vaughan had fought a battle with alcoholism and drugs and it was perhaps no coincidence that it was his best album since 'Texas Flood'.

Robert Cray (b.1953) finally made a major breakthrough in the 1980s after years of gigging through the 1970s in semi-obscurity, including two years with Albert Collins. Drawing on rock and soul he did much to update the blues tradition, winning countless W. C. Handy National Blues Awards and the approbation of John Lee Hooker, who said he was 'way ahead of his time.'[37] His original repertoire, perhaps best described as bluesy soul tunes and soulful blues, was contemporary; his contribution was to bring the persona of the bluesman up-to-date.

Cray's singing was warm, reminiscent of the Stax soul singers who influenced his style, yet able to create the pathos so important to the blues. His guitar playing appeared effortless, the product of an impressive technique. 'Bad Influence' (Hightone), Cray's third album from 1982 effectively put him on the map; at the National Blues Awards ceremony at Memphis in 1985 it won an unprecedented four first-place awards, including one for 'Phone Booth', an original blues that Albert King went on to cover. The album charted in the United Kingdom and was followed by the equally impressive 'False Accusations' and the million-seller 'Strong Persuader' (both Hightone).

Jeff Healy (b.1966), was blind from the age of one. He developed an unusual guitar technique, playing it on his lap in the sitting position and his playing earned praise from both Stevie Ray Vaughan and B. B. King. Just 22 years old when his debut album 'See The Light' (Novus) was released, his singing and virtuoso guitar playing were remarkable for their authority and power. Prominently featured in the movie 'Roadhouse', Healy's band, formed in 1985, soon acquired an international following.

Healy's influences came from his huge collection of early jazz and blues on 78s and his style, although touching base with good, old-fashioned Rock 'n' Roll and Jimi Hendrix, had overtones of blues players from Robert Johnson to B. B. King as well as the lyricism of early Louis Armstrong, another personal favourite. 'See The Light' (Novus), pulled together these diverse influences and although underwritten by rock, was directed at the new, younger audience for the blues and showed how far the tradition had expanded in the 1980s.

10
European Dreams and the Global Democracy

LONG BEFORE THE '80s jazz acquired an international following. When the first ever jazz recording was being cut by The Original Dixieland Jazz Band, sheet music of jazz 'novelties' was already on sale in Europe, and that in an age when the fastest way for most people to get from A to B was by horse. With the rise of the phonograph record the methodology of jazz was painstakingly worked out by imitation, note by note, phrase by phrase by musicians in America and Europe eager to participate in the new craze. On 19 January 1919 *The Times* reported: 'A capital programme this week at the Coliseum is the effort of the orchestra to convert itself into a jazz band, one of the many American peculiarities that threaten to make life a nightmare.'[1] By the '30s the message had spread globally: Adi Rosner was leading The State Jazz Orchestra of the Byelorussian Republic in Stalin's Russia and Buck Clayton's Big Band was playing a residency in Shanghai, China.

Almost from the word go jazz went international and outside influences soon began to be felt in the music: in the 1920s Jelly Roll Morton introduced what he called 'The Spanish Tinge', in the 1940s Dizzy Gillespie experimented with 'Afro-Cuban' influences, in the '60s there was a rush to record Brazilian compositions while John Coltrane examined Indian ragas, and in the '80s Anthony Davis incorporated Balinese gamelan devices into his work.

But at its core, jazz remained an American music with an international audience. This has always been something of a bone of contention for non-Americans, who have gone to incredible lengths to prove the repository of performing talent was not an exclusive American preserve and anything they could do, we could do better. And while many non-American musicians have proved to be equal, or in some cases superior, to their American counterparts, it overlooked a basic truth that while there have always been countless good non-American jazz musicians, many excellent ones and several brilliant ones, most have basked in the reflected glare of the American stylistic innovators. The number of non-American players who have influenced the direction or styles of the home-grown product has been very small indeed.

In the 1930s Belgian guitarist Django Reinhardt and in contemporary times the British guitarist John McLaughlin and the Austrian electronic keyboard and synthesizer player Joseph Zawinul comprise a list that no doubt could be expanded by pleading extenuating circumstances in the case of some European free players, but nevertheless largely remain the sum total of non-American musicians who have had a casting vote on the way jazz has been shaped within the States. The American model has been the theme jazz musicians in Sydney, Tokyo, London and Warsaw have followed with only slight variations. The same historical sources that inspired a Wynton Marsalis or a Courtney Pine are pretty well the same throughout the globe: the process of assimilation and imitation with the ultimate goal of innovation, the hope of young jazz musicians from Berklee to the Guildhall College of Music in London.

The rapid global assimilation of jazz, however, posed problems of 'authenticity' at the hands of musicians more and more remote from the American source. Did an indigenous American music shaped by the Afro-American experience become less meaningful when played by non-Americans? The answer lay in how the music was perceived; it was given validity, suggested Simon Frith, by making 'the music a matter of feeling, expressive of personal not social identity, of sensual not cultural need'.[2] Within these European terms of reference, the ECM (Editions of Contemporary Music) label, for example, formed in Munich by Manfred Eicher in the early '70s, proposed a significant alternative vision to American stereotypes.

Eicher's auteurism certainly had its detractors, but what was more important was that at a time when major American recording companies were fulfilling their commitment to jazz by recording fusion, creative jazz musicians were being given a license to develop their careers without 'selling out'. Jan Garbarek, for example, one of the major ECM artists, saw a certain incongruity in a middle-class white boy from Oslo playing the blues. 'It's really not my tradition,' he said. 'The so called standards are not my standards. I don't feel a close attachment to that music.' Garbarek's personal expressionism, his 'sensual' saxophone tone framed in a context quite unlike anything to those of his American contemporaries, represented just one example of an equally valid, 'authentic' sound of jazz remote from the American tradition.

But it was the development of free jazz in Europe since the 1960s that represented the most significant area of jazz to be developed and extended beyond the borders of the States, 'The European circuit of clubs, festivals and recording sessions,' wrote John Litweiler, 'became an essential means of support for free musicians.'[3] As much through the work of ex-patriate musicians such as Anthony Braxton, The Art Ensemble Of Chicago and Steve Lacy as through European musicians, European free jazz gradually assumed a specific identity quite apart from the American scene.

European freedom, with its arcane preoccupation with the radical, and one might unkindly add, the marginal, undoubtedly offered the greatest scope to deviate and develop apart from American models. Indeed there was nothing inherently 'American' or 'European' within the subjective terms of reference applied to abstraction other than in how it was perceived; in Europe it was valued in terms of romanticism where its critique raged 'in a state of Bohemian disgust with the masses and the bourgeoisie alike in the name of the superiority of the avant garde.'[4]

Outside of free, improvisation based on rhythm, harmony and structure closely followed American models; having reached a threshold of excellence many musicians felt the need to match and test their talent alongside their American peers, which simultaneously had the effect of validating their work for the global audience. An Austrian version of Weather Report, for example, despite Joe Zawinul at the helm, would be difficult to imagine enjoying the same degree of acclaim as the Zawinul/Shorter collaboration. Universal acceptance in jazz for the non-American, despite protestations to the contrary, certainly benefited by a reputation built in the States.

Paradoxically, while it was generally accepted that in order to make it in jazz it was necessary to develop a reputation *inside* America, it was the global village, the audience *outside* America, that enabled the continued survival of jazz. Catering for this audience in the 1980s had a bearing on a musician's artistic choices; when the talented young trombonist Robin Eubanks made his recording debut in 1988 with 'Different Perspectives' (JMT) he said: 'I knew that Japan was really into standards, so I included "Walkin'" and "You Don't Know What Love Is"; and the US is more pop-orientated so I did a Stevie Wonder tune I really like . . . And then Europe is just wide open for anything. So I designed it so it would have some kind of appeal for those three markets.'

However, the global support system was more than simply providing an audience for the music; independent Japanese and European recording labels had sprung up since the early 1970s and were providing a more accurate summation of the state-of-the-art than record companies inside America. Labels such as Nils Winther's Steeplechase in Denmark, Switzerland's Hathut, France's Black and Blue and Owl, Holland's BVHAAST and Wim Wigt's Timeless, Japan's DIW, East Wind, Better Days and King and Germany's JMT and ECM each specialized in specific areas of jazz, from mainstream to avantgarde. But it was Giovanni Bonandrini's Italian Soul Note and Black Saint labels that represented some of the most exciting developments in contemporary jazz during the 1980s; by the end of the decade they had been voted number one jazz label for the sixth consecutive year by the *Downbeat* International Critics poll.

EUROPEAN DREAMS

European Traditional

Although Django Reinhardt died in 1953, his recorded work still remains one of the high water marks of European jazz. During his lifetime his skill as an improviser overshadowed that of his long-time associate in the Quintet Of The Hot Club Of France, **Stephane Grappelli** (b.1908). Grappelli's skill, long ignored in jazz, was due in part to the fact he was a non-American, but also because he played the violin, perhaps the most unfashionable instrument, other than Rufus Harley's bagpipes, in jazz.

After Reinhardt's death, Grappelli preferred to use a pianist in his group, avoiding working with guitars until he was persuaded by Djangophile Diz Disley to tour Britain in 1973 with two guitars and a bass. 'Diz Disley has the *perfume* of Django Reinhardt in his playing and we had another very good guitarist. So since 1973 I've played with the guitars,' he said. After the unexpected success of the tour, Grappelli's star was once more in the ascendant; in 1974 he played in Carnegie Hall to a standing ovation, and successful tour followed successful tour. Age seemed to have no bearing on Grappelli's career; he toured internationally, recorded prodigiously, including four albums with Yehudi Menuhin, and his playing, instead of slowing down, appeared revitalized and actually seemed to improve with each passing year.

Grappelli personified pre-bop swing, his style romantic but always ingenious, his rhythmic control and melodic development served by a virtuoso technique. Grappelli's recordings were remarkably consistent and represent a body of pre-bop work that by almost any definition can be called superior music. The excellent 'Young Django' (Pausa), from 1979 with Larry Coryell and Philip Catherine (g) and Niels-Henning Orsted Pedersen (b) lives up to the promise of *le jazz hot* with its all-star cast; a British-born Belgian, Catherine distinguished himself with playing that returned to his formative influence. Pedersen is also on hand for 'Tivoli Gardens, Copenhagen' (Pablo) which puts Grappelli's pre-bop swing alongside Joe Pass' post-bop guitar with the minimum of stylistic incongruity.

Grappelli's regular group, which in 1980 included two highly talented British guitarists in Martin Taylor and John Etheridge (formerly of the rock band Soft Machine) plus Jack Sewing (b) feature on 'At The Winery' (Concord), recorded live at the Paul Masson Mountain Winery, Saratoga in September 1980. Once again Grappelli's sheer swinging elan—which also included the mid-brown tone colours of an electric viola—instantly overcame his date-stamped style. Among the highlights of his 1980s output were 'Live In San Francisco' (Elektra Musician) and 'Live At Carnegie Hall' (Doctor Jazz), both with his regular group. The 1987 'Plays Jerome Kern' (GRP) had a string orchestra backing Grappelli's group, but the master's elegance shines through. The 1989 pairing with classical cellist Yo-Yo Ma, 'Anything Goes' (CBS), was clearly aimed at the non-jazz audience who made the Menuhin collaborations of the late '70s—early '80s best-sellers.

Throughout, Grappelli maintained the *spirit* of Reinhardt, without ever suggesting he was seeking to re-create past glories, 'Django is irreplaceable,' he said, 'And you will find that onstage, I always put a chair there. An empty chair, thinking of him . . . but you see, that's the chair for Django—because, after all, I started with him and I like his shadow to be there. Maybe I'm a bit funny. But I'm like that and it can't be changed now. It's too late.' Once Hal to Reinhardt's Hotspur, Grappelli gave conclusive proof during the '80s he too was one of jazz's great musicians and that his place in the jazz hegemony was in need of drastic revision.

After Reinhardt's death in 1953 it took almost 30 years for a school of players to emerge whose style directly drew from his inspiration. What can only be described as European traditional jazz, a tradition based on Reinhardt's style, seemed a reality by the end of the 1970s with the emergence of guitarists Philip Catherine (b.1942), Fapy Lafertin (b.1953) and the formidable Bireli Lagrene (b.1966). Meanwhile, the group Waso continued the acoustic swing of the Hot Club of France through the '80s while Boulou and Elois Ferre tried to adapt the Hot Club style to the modern jazz repertoire on their 1985 'Relax and Enjoy' (Steeplechase).

The Belgian group **Waso** had origins that could be traced to a contemporary of Reinhardt's, the violinist Piotto (Limberger), who formed the group in the early 1970s. Piotto's youngest son, Vivi Limberger continued to play rhythm guitar when the group was taken over by multi-

Waso, showing the small step it took to move from gypsy extemporization to the jazz style of Django Reinhardt.

instrumentalist Koen de Cauter when Piotto retired at the end of the decade. The group's strong Romany links were emphasized through their featured guitarist Fapy Lafertin, who came from the same Flemish gypsy heritage as Reinhardt himself. 'Gypsy Swing' (Munich) and 'Live In Laren' (Polydor) showed how the group maintained the Hot Club tradition into the '80s, closing all lines of input jazz has wrought since the 1930s.

What they made clear was the small step it took to move from gypsy extemporizations on flamencos, folk laments and tangos to the jazz style of Reinhardt. Throughout the '80s they appeared with great success at festivals throughout Europe; by the mid '80s Lafertin left to pursue a solo career, his style solidly in the Reinhardt mould, but with greater delicacy and fluidity.

The Belgian guitarist **Philip Catherine** (b.1942), who played with Jean-Luc Ponty and studied at Berklee in the 1970s, toured with Larry Coryell in the late 1970s. Charles Mingus dubbed him 'the Young Django' and he continued to tour Europe in the 1980s, with Jasper van't Hof and Charlie Mariano and in a group with emerging young Django superstar, Bireli Lagrene.

Bireli Lagrene (b.1966) first played the guitar as a child in the gypsy caravans of his family members of the Sinti tribe of Alsace. Taught by his father since the age of four, he was fluently imitating Reinhardt by the age of seven. He made his recording debut in 1980 with a 'Hot Club' group that included his brother Gaiti on 'Routes to Django' (Antilles); Lagrene was only 13 at the time. Even then he showed he was no mere copyist; all the tunes were originals and the speed of his execution, without sacrificing lyricism, surely would have impressed even Reinhardt himself.

His second album, 'Bireli Lagrene At 15' (Antilles) from 1982 moved beyond Django with thoughts of contemporary voicings on the solo tracks showing an astonishing maturity for his age. 'Bireli Swing '81' (Jazzpoint) is another perspective on Djangology and by 1984 he had sat in with Benny Carter in London and Benny Goodman in Antibes and made his Carnegie Hall debut during the Kool Jazz Festival in a 'Salute to Django' concert with Grappelli, Benny Carter and The Great Guitars. In 1985 he returned to New York for another Django tribute, this time with guitarists Larry Coryell and Vic Juris at Fat Tuesday's and succeeded in stunning all those present.

He guested on two tracks of 'Django's Music Vol.1' (Stash), an ensemble run by New York guitarist Mike Peters dedicated to Reinhardt's music. 'Live' (Jazzpoint) is from a live concert in France that succeeds in creating the rather club-footed swing of the original Hot Club with Diz Disley, Vic Juris and Gaiti Lagrene pounding out the crotchets with remorseless glee. By 1986 he began moving out of Reinhardt's shadow, 'I had been representing Django's tunes for so long that it didn't give me any room to represent myself,' he said.

'Bireli Lagrene' (Jazzpoint), with Coryell and Miroslav Vitous (b) began this process by using distinctly non-Reinhardt material; 'All Blues', 'All The Things You Are', a Bossa original 'Berga', a furious flamenco 'PSP NR.2' and a boppish 'Alibi.' In 1986 he appeared at the Nice Jazz Festival with two-thirds of the former rock group Cream, Jack Bruce and Ginger Baker, representing a radical break with his past. 'Stuttgart Aria' (Jazzpoint), from later in the year, goes the whole hog, cutting the umbilical to Reinhardt in no uncertain fashion in a disappointing fusion meeting with Jaco Pastorius (b), backed by a European rhythm section. In 1987 he signed with Blue Note records, but on the numbingly anonymous 'Inferno' (Blue Note) he became just another crossover guitar-whizz working out on below-average material. The 1988 'Foreign Affairs' (Blue Note) fared only slightly better; there was a sense of commercial detachment in his work that suggested technique alone is no substitute for artistic direction.

Europe: Two Young Keyboard Voices

One of the most important of the young jazz musicians to emerge during the 1980s was the young French pianist **Michel Petrucciani** (b.1962). His emergence as a piano virtuoso was remarkable, not just because it was unusual for a European player to make an impact on the American jazz scene, but because it was achieved in the face of terrible physical handicap. Discovered by the musician/critic Mike Zwerin, he toured France with Lee Konitz when he was 18. His recording debut, with Zwerin, the 1980 'Flash' (Bingo), was not entirely satisfactory but the 1981 'Michel Petrucciani' (Owl) revealed a startlingly self-composed musician; with J.F. Jenny Clark (b) and Aldo Romano (d) his percussive touch, contrasted by Bill Evans-like chord voicings and long linear runs reminiscent of Lennie Tristano plus his sheer authority instantly marked him as a major young musician. On 'Juste Un Moment', with the bass solo dispensed with right at the beginning of the composition, Petruc-

Michel Petrucciani. One of the most important musicians to emerge during the 1980s.

ciani's uninterrupted, bravura solo of building intensity, power and excitement announced the arrival of an important new talent in jazz.

In 1982 he won the Prix Django Reinhardt as French Jazz Musician of the Year and recorded 'Estate' (Riviera)—made in Rome with Romano and Furio Di Castri (d)—a duet with Lee Konitz 'Toot Suite' (Owl) and the solo 'Oracle's Destiny' (Owl). He moved to the U.S. later that year, and was taken under the wing of Charles Lloyd, whom he had met on a visit in 1980. His playing inspired Lloyd to make a comeback in jazz, 'For me, Michel is an avatar of the keyboard,' he said, 'It all comes through so lovingly clear.'[5] Petrucciani appeared with Lloyd on the 1982 'Live At Montreux' (Elektra Musician), the 1983 'A Night In Copenhagen' (Blue Note) and on the Claude Galloud film 'Le Festival International du Jazz d'Antibes' from July 1982.

His first Stateside album, the solo '100 Hearts' (Concord) from 1983, occasionally became weighed down by the plethora of ideas he tried to cram into each number. More successful was the March 1984 'Live At The Village Vanguard' (Concord) with Palle Danielsson (b) and Eliot Zigmund (d). Largely free of the compression of ideas that simultaneously impressed but ultimately detracted from some of his earlier work, there was an urgency that suggested every number he played may be his last. This underlying tension was further heightened by moving through a series of climaxes he seldom chose to resolve making his playing simultaneously appear driven yet emotionally demanding. 'Cleo' for example, was a *tour de force* in the stand-offish manner of a Tristano complex, 'Nardis' and 'To Erlinda' suggested Bill Evans' romanticism, while 'Say It Again' reflected the elliptical stream-of-consciousness of Keith Jarrett. However, he could be his own man too; playing apart from the basic pulse to create an angular feeling of tension, comping with dense, dissonant figures in polyrhythmic opposition to the bass and drums and articulating his unusual note choices with supreme lyricism.

'Notes N' Notes' (Owl) from October '84 was a solo performance that borrowed from the Bill Evans 'Conversations With Myself' sessions on Verve on two tracks. Given Petrucciani's tendency to embellishment, the result was an almost naive desire to simultaneously please and prove himself that resulted in aural indigestion. The January 1985 'Cold Blues' (Owl), a duet with former Charles Lloyd bassist Ron McClure, was perhaps his most mature statement to date, his playing less florid and more concentrated.

In 1985 Petrucciani signed with Blue Note records and 'Pianism' (Blue Note) was recorded just a few days after a six week international tour with Danielsson and Zigmund. Not only does the group sound relaxed and integrated, but Petrucciani seemed content to treat each number on its own merits rather than hijack them to reveal every facet of his technique. Later in the year he toured as a duo with Jim Hall (g), videotaping a session at the Village Vanguard; 'Live At The Village Vanguard Vol. 5' (Parkfield). 'Power Of Three' (Blue Note) was recorded live at the 1986 Montreux Jazz Festival with Petrucciani and Hall joined by Wayne Shorter for 'Limbo', 'Morning Blues' and 'Bimini' in a session that brought to mind the hushed intimacy of Hall's work with Jimmy Giuffre.

In 1987 Petrucciani's trio comprised Gary Peacock (b) and Roy Haynes (d), touring through 1988. They comprise one half of the 1987 'Michel Plays Petrucciani' (Blue Note), sharing the album with Eddie Gomez (b) and Al Foster (d) with John Abercrombie (g) sitting-in on two tracks. It's tempting to say that this was the best from the diminutive pianist during the '80s; a mature, self-assured statement that had at last shed the collision of ideas occasionally apparent in his earlier work which sometiems prevented him swinging. Now he was interacting with top-class rhythm sections; less garrulous, he nevertheless remained the bardic voice that never stopped storytelling.

Less rigorous was 'Music' (Blue Note) from 1989, that in comparison to his previous work almost suggested an 'off duty' feel; relaxed Petrucciani was less concerned with asserting his talent as letting the breeze flow through it. It was the work of a musician who was altogether more confident of his place in the jazz hegemony, moving from 'Lullaby' to 'My Bebop Tune', from 'O Nana Oye' with Tania Maria's vocals to 'Thinking Of Wayne' with Joe Lovano.

After an initial flurry of organ trios inspired by Jimmy Smith, Jimmy McGriff, Brother Jack McDuff and Richard 'Groove' Holmes during the late '50s, and early '60s, the Hammond B-3 organ became eclipsed by the rise of electronic keyboards—not least on the grounds of portability. With a return to the jazz of the 1950s by so many young musicians, it was perhaps surprising that there were few takers for the fiesty sounds the B-3 could generate.

In the States Joey DeFrancesco took up the challenge, but the most exciting talent to emerge during the 1980s on the instrument was **Barbara Dennerlein** (b.1964) from Munich. Dennerlein was given her first organ in 1975; by the age of 13 she was giving public performances and was playing the Munich jazz clubs by the time she was 15. Influenced by Jimmy Smith, she played alongside him when he was on tour in Germany and accompanied Al Porcino, Sonny Fortune and Benny Bailey amongst others. Her own self-produced albums 'Jazz Live At The Munich Domicile' and 'Bebab' both won coveted 'Preis der Deutschen Schallplattenkritik' awards and 'Tribute To Charlie Parker' was recorded with the Peter Herbolzheimer Orchestra. During the last few years of the decade she appeared as either a duo with Andreas White (d) or as a trio with the addition of Christoph Widmoser (g), appearing at most European festivals and making regular appearances on German radio and television.

Her 1988 'Straight Ahead' (Enja) was an impressive major label debut. Dennerlein swings powerfully, makes resourceful use of the organ's stops to get a personal sound that's both contemporary and funky and uses her foot pedals to drive the tempo faultlessly. Backed by Ray Anderson (tb), Mitch Watkins (g) and Ronnie Burrage (d) she emerged with an integrated group sound, rare for a pick-up band. Her organization of the group's resources, her choice of material—mostly her own compositions—her conceptualization, suggested an exciting talent was ready to emerge on the world stage.

European Mid-Bands

The Dutch saxophonist and composer Willem Breuker (b.1944) had played in what was virtually a Who's Who of the European free scene, including the Globe Unity Orchestra, the Instant Composers School and with musicians such as Hans Bennink, Peter Brotzmann and Alex Schlippenbach, when he formed his Kollektief in 1974. The Spike Jones of the avant garde, Breuker's elaborate jump-cut imagination made his compositions sound like soundtracks for crazy silent movies; in fact, Breuker, in a different incarnation, wrote award-winning music for the Dutch theatre and film industry.

But with his ten-piece Kollektief he took no prisoners; arrangements might flash through Kurt Weill, polkas, swing band cliches, the oompah of brass bands and end up powering through an arrangement at 196 beats per minute. In live performance the Kollektief sustained a devastating level of hyperkinetic energy for over two hours of non-stop music. During this time the whole band participated in a form of musical charades. 'Much of life is humorous if you look at it from a special side,' explained Breuker. 'You have to keep the music open enough to accept the unexpected. You can do something with it both intelligent and serious.'[6]

Breuker first toured in the U.S. in 1977, returning through the auspices of the Dutch Ministry of Culture in 1983 when they recorded 'Willem

Willem Breuker. 'You have to keep the music open enough to accept the unexpected. You can do something with it both intelligent and serious.

Breuker Collective' (About Time), their first album for an American label. Nothing was as it seemed; the scene was set only to dissolve in parody or contradiction. Humour was used as a stinging weapon or a polite rebuff, the pace breathless, the musicianship impeccable. 'Preparations And Farewell' began with a Music Hall fanfare and ends as a pastiche of 'Farewell Blues' with a stomping R&B tenor solo from Breuker himself. 'Kontrafunkt', military-band-meets-funk in 6/8, stayed serious but off-centre while 'Women's Voting Rights' in a sombre 3/4, was one of Breuker's many sideswipes at 'The Establishment'.

The rest of the Kollektief's albums were released on Breuker's own BVHAAST label, poorly distributed and totalling more than 15 by the end of the decade. 'It's limited, but people find it,' Breuker conceded. An excellent representative album from his BVHAAST output was the live 'Klap Op De Vuurpijl' (BVHAAST) from 1985 with the crazy cops imagery of 'The Little Ramblers' and the film noir-meets-Albert Ayler of 'Casablanca Suite'. But Breuker's reputation was built not so much on his recordings as on the strength of his performances, 'I'm more interested in performing for people and doing my work as good as I can . . . I'm not so interested in success,' he said.

He toured the U.S. again in 1985 and 1988, including a stopover at The Knitting Factory. At the 1989 North Sea Jazz Festival he received a 'Bird' award in recognition of his achievements; previous recipients had included Miles Davis and David Murray. Breuker was a genuine performance artist; when the major recording companies were spending not inconsiderable sums hyping their latest young signings, Breuker's reputation spread by word of mouth. Original, inventive and with a special cultural twist-in-the-tail, his ensemble was among the most exciting, original and stimulating of the decade.

While Breuker ransacked European culture and Tin Pan Alley to frame his viewpoint, **Pierre Dorge** (b.1946) embraced the global vision. The Danish guitarist formed his New Jungle Orchestra in 1980, and if Breuker's music was closer to the barrel-organs and brass bands of Amsterdam, Dorge's music refracted elements of Fletcher-Henderson-through-Sun-Ra, Gil Evans and George Russell as well as his highly distinctive ethnic borrowings. Dorge's compositions were framed in the classical Ellington manner of utilizing individual voices within his ensemble; his key soloist was tenor saxophonist and guru John Tchicai with whom he often collaborated on compositions.

The band featured regularly at European festivals and visited the States in 1986; more laid back than Breuker, the band debuted eponymously in 1982 on the Steeplechase label. Activity remained sporadic until the 1984 'Brikama' (Steeplechase) attracted the attention of European Festival producers and with more performance opportunities Dorge was able to integrate soloist and ensemble. 'It sounds much more organic when musicians develop their own approach, and I don't make a heavy distinction between what's written and what's improvised,' he said.

The 1985 'Even The Moon Is Dancing' (Steeplechase) included the band's strongest lineup; Africa met traditional on 'The Mooche' while contemporary Africa met America on 'Suho Ning Samo'; the band was loose, it swung, it handled the head-to-head free interludes with aplomb and the leader's guitar endorsed every move with shades of Wes Montgomery and Frank Zappa. 'Johnny Lives' (Steeplechase) from 1987 was another excellent album including evocative titles such as 'Waltz For Two Camels' and 'Root Eating Rag'. George Russell's influence peeps through, but so did contemporary Africa—Dorge visited Gambia four times during the '80s—and Ellington. 'For me,' said Dorge, 'music should be an adventure, it should tell a story if possible and express feelings you can't express in words.'

The Vienna Art Orchestra, formed in 1977 by the Swiss pianist **Mathias Ruegg** (b.1952) often applied the jump-cut versatility of Breuker, but without the Dutchman's manic humour. The VAO included in its ranks some strong soloists; Roman Schwaller (ts) played with Mal Waldron and Harry Sokal (ts) and Heiri Kanzig (b) performed with Art Farmer, appearing on his 1981 'Foolish Memories' (L+R). Ruegg's arranging inclination was not to write for instrumental combinations but for specific individuals, 'I can almost predict beforehand what they will play,' he said, 'and that is something I take into consideration when I write our music.'[7]

Simultaneously arty and impressionistic, obscure and bombastic, drawing from ragtime to Charles Mingus to early 1970s Miles Davis, Ruegg's arrangements have included imaginative recastings of compositions by Scott Joplin, Erik Satie, Ornette Coleman, Lennie Tristano, Anthony Braxton, Booker Little and Blood Ulmer. 'Concerto Piccolo' from 1980, 'Suite For The Green Eighties' from 1981, 'From No Time To Ragtime' from 1982, 'The Minimalism Of Erik Satie' from 1983/4, 'Tango From Obango' from 1985 and 'Perpetuum Mobile' from 1985, all on the Hat Art label, and 'Blues For Brahms' (Amadeo) represent an impressive body of work.

However, Ruegg's continual urge to segue created tensions and contradictions that occasionally exhausted the meaning of what he was trying to achieve. His musical complexes avoided the formula of the standard big bands but substituted another, that of theatrical surprise, that moved self-consciously away from those places where the American big bands had drawn their meaning, 'Certain of the sound combinations derive from the European classical tradition,' explained Ruegg, 'But it's American jazz in the sense that the writing is basically a vehicle to encourage individual expression from the soloists.'[8]

George Gruntz (b.1932), the Swiss pianist and composer began leading a series of all-star big bands in 1972. The director of the Berlin Jazzfest since 1973, he finally booked his own band in to the festival in 1988 to celebrate its 25th anniversary. Gruntz's all-star aggregations have included top American musicians such as Phil Woods, Dexter Gordon, Elvin Jones, Mark Egan, John Scofield, Woody Shaw and Europeans including Nils-Henning Orsted Pedersen, Jasper Van't Hof, Daniel Humair, Palle Mikkelborg and Franco Ambrosetti. For each season the band toured, Gruntz composed and arranged new material, which placed his stars in challenging performing situations.

Gruntz, who had written music for the cinema and was for a while the Musical Director of the Zurich State Theatre, also wrote opera. 'Money', written with poet Amiri Baraka was performed in New York in 1982 while his 'Cosmopolitan Dreams' was loosely inspired by Bessie Smith and ecology (!). His frequently adventurous compositions for the Concert Jazz Band, however, drew on classical and folk influences, and were well crafted but functional vehicles without being especially memorable. It was the soloists that gave his work lustre, 'The idea was to have friends come together,' he said, 'I wrote the charts custom-designed for the soloists.'

The Concert Jazz Band tour was an annual event, from which came the 1980 'Live At The Quartier Latin, Berlin' (MPS), 'The George Gruntz Concert Jazz Band '83: Theatre' (ECM) and perhaps his best representation on disc, the 1987 'Happening Now!' (Hat Art), recorded live at the Caravan Of Dreams, Fort Worth. With musicians such as Marvin Stamm, Kenny Wheeler, Ray Anderson, Lee Konitz, Joe Henderson, Howard Johnson, Bob Moses and Sheila Jordan, Gruntz's novel settings included a multi-themed 'Novelette' ending in a blowsy, tongue-in-cheek 'Falling In Love Again', an extract from his 'Cosmopolitan Dreams', 'Happening Now' (with Sheila Jordan deftly handling Allen Ginsberg's doom-laden lyrics) and a sprightly arrangement of Joe Henderson's 'Inner Urge'.

The 1989 'First Prize' (Enja) did not quite include the galaxy of stars Gruntz had assembled in the past, but his appearance in Tokyo that year included Stanton Davis, Larry Schneider and Adam Nussbaum and won the Japanese Association of Critics of Music and Audio 'First Prize' for their Tokyo concert, a testament to Gruntz's continuing standard of excellence as much as his love of the larger ensemble.

Sound Ideas: The ECM Label

The sound sculptures that comprise the majority of the ECM corpus were often studies in a hushed, intimate and etheral ambience that anticipated the New Age success of Will Ackerman's Windham Hill label by almost a decade. Manfred Eicher's dictum, 'The company records only musicians who share the company's musical philosophy', held sway for the best part of the 1970s and ensured the main thrust of the label carried the imprimatur of the 'house' style—although it did become more variegated as the 1980s progressed. However, certain artists seemed to epitomise Eicher's philosophy, of pastoral moods, of subdued rhythmic and linear events and a serene, frequently minimalistic approach to improvisation. 'I was raised on chamber music,' he said, 'and I want ECM to reflect this side of jazz rather than the rough and bombastic side . . . I'm interested in music that gets to you slowly not music that hits you first time.'[9]

Eicher, however, was only articulating a view prevalent in post-modernism that saw technical display and virtuosity as both excessive and in bad taste; for whilst his label certainly included artists whose work might be called 'rough and bombastic'—Sam River's 'Conference Of The Birds', the work of Jack De-Johnette's Special Edition, for example—these were always in considerable disproportion to the rest of the ECM catalogue.

Eicher's stance was in many ways the antithesis of the American jazz tradition. His concept was of a minimalist jazz, a European hybrid that emphasised quality of sound as much as content which he described as 'The most beautiful sound next to silence, a movement next to no movement'.[10] Eicher reached for the 'virtuous' boredom of minimalist composers such as Philip Glass and Steve Reich—indeed Reich was one of the label's artists. Bassist Eberhard Weber, another of the label's artists, called it, 'European improvisational music, which is based on jazz, but following our European roots'.

The oppositions set up here, of Afro-American versus European cultures, was simply the belief that jazz could be reinterpreted by a different culture and still remain 'authentic', 'You can apply any personal input coming from whatever part of the world, and it's possible to find a way that will work in the jazz idiom,' said Jan Garbarek, one of ECM's key artists, '. . . we have players from any part of the world now doing their own, shall we say, native version. They find their own direction, influenced by their culture, but still using the very strong basic elements of jazz.'

Jan Garbarek. 'You can apply any personal input coming from whatever part of the world, and it's possible to find a way that will work in the jazz idiom.'

The significance of the ECM label was that it actually gave momentum to these ideas; in 1970 **Jan Garbarek** (b.1947) was one of Eicher's first signings and became a central figure in defining the ECM image. His early 1970s group included Norwegian guitarist **Terje Rypdal** (b.1947), 'Terje wasn't playing improvisational music at the time. He was playing in rock groups,' said Garbarek, 'We asked him to join us.' Rypdal went on to become an important ECM artist in his own right, while Garbarek's association with the German bassist **Eberhard Weber** (b.1940) was based on firm, mutual respect for each other's work. Weber regularly appeared on Garbarek's recordings and Weber's own albums for ECM frequently included members of Garbarek's groups, and on 'Chorus' (ECM), Garbarek himself.

Garbarek exemplified what Eicher was trying to achieve; subsequent signings such as Azimuth, Egberto Gismonti, Jon Hassell, Keith Jarrett, Art Lande, Masqualero, Pat Metheny, Oregon, Shankar, Steve Tibbetts, Ralph Towner, Edward Vesala, Collin Walcott all employed jazz devices, cultural patching and folk forms spread over minimalistic soundscapes that established the ECM style. Garbarek himself created music that projected the stark imagery of nature near the Northern Lights. His work represented an ordered calm in the often frantic world of jazz; rigorous and highly disciplined, he had the ability to transport the subconscious to areas of thought that were mystically, even aesthetically beckoning. Working within a self-limited harmonic and rhythmic palette he created an evocative tranquility strongly rooted in European folk-forms that gave prominence to his saxophone *tone* as the main expressive force.

As the 1970s progressed, rhythmic motion became secondary as Garbarek's lone voice appeared to commune with nature, an effect he liked to heighten as on the album 'Dis' (ECM) recorded with a wind harp. 'Eventyr' (ECM), from 1980, actually evoked warmer climes with John Abercrombie (g) and Nana Vasconcelos (perc). 'Paths, Prints' (ECM) from December 1981 brought together Garbarek's frequent collaborator Eberhard Weber (b), with Bill Frisell (g) and Jon Christensen (d). Brooding and atmospheric, 'Paths, Prints' illustrated Garbarek's economy of purpose and singular tonal focus, a subtle tautology of the accessible and mild experimentalism. 'Wayfarer' (ECM) from March 1983 introduced Michael DiPasqua (d) and is slightly more industrious; the title track a three-part discourse with the leader's tenor sax.

'It's OK To Listen To The Gray Voice' (ECM) substituted David Torn (g) and continued Garbarek's impressionistic seances, this time inspired by poet Tomas Transtromer, but like Kant's 'thing-in-itself' the poems add nothing to our comprehension of the works in question. The 1986 'All Those Born With Wings' (ECM) was a solo album, Garbarek supplying a wide variety of effects from chants to sampled keyboard to frame his meditations. The 1988 'Legend Of Seven Dreams' (ECM) permutated Weber, Vasconcelos and Rainer Brunginhaus (k) to create a cloak of subjectivity around his playing in much the same way as he did for himself on his previous album, creating what *The Times* described as, 'a New Age ambience'.[11]

Taken together, Garbarek's albums were inescapably monotonous, often dwelling in a condition of evocative tranquility. However, the high status accorded minimalistic art during the 1980s consciously erred on the side of boredom—the ship of tyres and 'Equivalent VIII', a rectangle of bricks at the Royal Academy, Lisa Milroy's 'Handles', winner of the 1989 John Moore Liverpool Exhibition, or Richard Long's sculpture 'Halifax Circle', $14\frac{1}{2}$ tons of coal organized in a circle—all lacked variety and a sense of momentum. The question was, however, whether jazz could survive such rigorous pruning, with so many of its essential ingredients stripped away.

What's Nouveau: Jazz In Britain

As the mid-1980s approached, Britain began to enjoy a revival of interest in jazz. Not only were clubs beginning to play jazz for dancing, but several young talented musicians began to emerge with whom a wider, younger audience could identify. An optimistic new breeze blew through the British jazz scene as both the young musicians and, just as important, their young audience celebrated the thrill of discovering jazz. 'The new generation of British musicians is responsible for the healthiest complexion the London scene has worn since the end of the 'sixties,' wrote Richard Williams in *The Times,* 'banishing the dismal sallowness of older attitudes by liberal applications of youthful energy and optimism.'

Musicians such as Courtney Pine, Steve Williamson, Andy Sheppard and Tommy Smith were signed by major labels and appeared in Sunday colour supplements and glossy magazines. Jazz music—Thelonious Monk, no less—began to feature in television adverts as the media awoke to the kind of demographic jazz pulled. Jazz in Britain became synonymous with 'style' and dubbed 'The New Jazz' by the media, began to attract a considerable following. New clubs sprang up in London and the Provinces and between 1987-88, for example, the British Market Research Bureau for the Arts Council highlighted the increasing popularity of jazz nationwide, particularly among students, indicating a year on year increase of over ten per cent.

Harbinger of a Trend—Loose Tubes

Loose Tubes, a folly of 21 young British musicians emerged from a series of Creative Workshops run by Graham Collier in the early 1980s. The band gradually began to assume a personality of its own, expressed best in material actually written from within the band, and with Collier's blessing the band left his control to pursue their own destiny. Their first national recognition came with a 1984 *Guardian* review of a performance at Covent Garden's 'Seven Dials' but it was not until a booking at Ronnie Scott's in May 1985 that the British jazz establishment really sat up and took notice. 'Part of the band's secret—aside of immensely sophisticated ensemble writing bristling with fresh ideas—is its urge to surprise,' said the *Guardian*.[12] 'Loose Tubes have resurrected the freewheeling optimism that long evaporated from the British jazz scene,' declared *The Times*.[13]

Undeniably big, Loose Tubes avoided stage band cliches and frenzied assaults on the subjective and in their place substituted the sweeping imagination of their main arrangers, **Django Bates** (b.1960) (k) and **Steve Berry** (b) who remained uninhibited by category or boundary. Gospel, Latin, funk, ragtime, South African hi-life and rough and ready choral passages were threaded together to ambush the listener with a glorious noise that might be embellished by a referee's whistle, a dustbin lid or a heavy-metal tea tray.

'Loose Tubes' (Loose Tubes) recorded in 1984/5 was their powerful, self-produced debut; the roaring 'Descarga' and the scrambling ensemble passages of 'Rowing Boat Delineation Egg' arranged by Berry and 'Mister Zee' by Bates were cornerstones of the band's repertoire at this time and made full use of the resources the band's massive head count offered. The 1986 'Delightful Precipice' (Loose Tubes), better recorded, included 'Sad Afrika' by Bates, 'Shelly' by Berry with strong solos by Mark Lockheart and Iain Ballamy and two ambitious pieces, 'Sunny' and 'Hermeto's Giant Breakfast', that were both mature and deftly handled.

In 1987 the band performed a late-night Prom at the Royal Albert Hall, and a tape found its way to Teo Macero who had produced most of Miles Davis's best work on record. When the band signed with Virgin Records' EG subsidiary, Macero agreed to produce and direct the recording of 'Open Letter' (Editions EG), 'Most young players don't produce that sort of sound anymore. But these guys are interested in real composition, real melodies, not just being superhip,' he said, '. . . I haven't seen a young band in the U.S. that wants to do things like that.'[14] 'Open Letter' represented a peak for Loose Tubes; it was also numbered among the finest albums made by British jazz musicians.

Loose Tubes also split into a number of sub-cultures; Bates and Steve Arguelles (d, perc) formed Human Chain and their 1986 eponymously titled album (Loose Tubes) featured Bates's occasionally rambling electronic keyboards. Steve Berry's 1988 'Trio' (Loose Tubes) combined Mark Lockheart (saxophones) and Peter Fairclough (d) in a more intimate, but equally discursive album.

Courtney Pine and the Saxophonists

By the end of the '80s the bustling British jazz scene, within the international context, had come to be represented by three tenor players, with great things expected of a fourth. Courtney Pine (b. 1964) had, by almost unanimous consensus, become regarded the 'main man' of Britain's 'new' jazz scene; 'It's impossible to ascribe the same status which Pine enjoys to more senior players,' said *Wire* magazine in 1988, 'We aren't talking about relative values in the all-time Hall Of Fame for British jazz—we're talking about the moment, about today. It doesn't really matter if he's Number One or not: it is simply his time, his and his contemporaries'.'

Pine studied clarinet, but switched to tenor saxophone after hearing a Sonny Rollins record. In the early 1980s he participated in John Stevens' jazz workshops and by the mid-'80s formed his own workshop to help members of the black community to take more interest in jazz. From this project emerged The Jazz Warriors, a sprawling, enthusiastic workshop-in-progress that took elements of West Indian music—calypso, reggae and ska—to produce a dynamic imbroglio that preserved the musician's cultural identity; 'Out Of Many, One People' (Antilles). Pine's own playing, a highly disciplined examination of pre-Ascension Coltrane, offered emotional commitment in exchange for plagiarism and, like Wynton Marsalis, the deferred promise of innovation.

Like Marsalis, Pine became a darling of the media; he walked tall and created a profile for jazz in Britain that had barely existed before. He played with Elvin Jones, Art Blakey, George Russell and Rolling Stone Charlie Watts' Big Band. His 1986 recording debut, 'Journey To The Urge Within' (Island Records) enjoyed unparalleled media hype for a British jazz recording but, perhaps not surprisingly, when the dust settled, the album failed to live up to expectations. Pine suffered from intonational problems and 'Children Of The Ghetto' was a stab at popular appeal, although his technical assurance showed through, particularly on 'I Believe' and 'Peace'. More importantly, however, the album was bought by a wide audience, in excess of 70,000, some of whom were purchasing a jazz record for the first time.

The 1987 'Destiny's Song (& The Image Of Pursuance)' (Island) is better focused; a quartet session that reflected Pine's steely purpose to master his craft. The 1989 'The Vision's Tale' (Antilles) is altogether more relaxed. In the company of an American rhythm section, Ellis Marsalis (p), Delbert Felix (b) and Jeff Watts (d) he explored standards and sounded less stylistically hidebound by precedent. Paradoxically, Pine's recordings were less important than what he had come to represent. By the end of the decade he had appeared at several international jazz festivals that spoke of his growing reputation; all that was left was for him to deliver on his enormous promise.

Tommy Smith (b.1967) took up the tenor saxophone at 12 and by 15 had appeared on national television. His first albums, 'Giant Strides' (GFM) and 'Taking Off' (Head) were recorded prior to his leaving for Berklee when he was 16. There he formed his own band Forward Motion, which won an Outstanding Performance commendation, toured and performed throughout New England and recorded 'The Berklee Tapes' and 'Progressions' (both Hep). While in Berklee he became a member of The Gary Burton Quartet, touring with them during 1986/7, and appeared on the 1986 'Whizz Kids' (ECM). However, despite his American experience Smith's playing developed European' characteristics associated with Jan Garbarek: concern with tonal inflection rather than momentum.

In July 1987 he left Burton's group to develop his own career, which was celebrated by a BBC TV documentary and a brief series where he hosted and performed in a variety of playing situations. His debut on the Blue Note International label, the 1988 'Step By Step' (Blue Note) included musicians such as Jack DeJohnette, John Scofield and Eddie Gomez and was produced by Gary Burton but added up to less than the sum of the musicians taking part; laid back, it casually avoided the point. On the 1990 'Peeping Tom' (Blue Note), Smith surrounded himself with mere mortals, including former members of Forward Motion. His playing, polarized between Jan Garbarek and Coltrane, suggested artistic maturity lay ahead of the much praised, highly promising 22-year-old.

Andy Sheppard, described by *Wire* magazine as, 'the strongest and most imaginative of all the new British saxophone stars,' had not heard jazz until he was 19. Since then the West Country saxophonist learnt his craft, 'the old way, alongside better players'. Sheppard developed his career both in Paris, where he recorded with the 19-piece big band Lumiere and in the UK, where he recorded two albums with the group Sphere. He made his name when the 1986 Schlitz Jazz Sounds competition was televised on British television. Joe Zawinul, one of the panel of judges, described him as, 'a world-class saxophone player'. However, to the astonishment of all present, he came second.

The miscarriage of justice did him no harm at all: his moral victory launched his career. In 1987 he toured Europe with the George Russell Orchestra and in 1988 played and recorded with a French edition of the Gil Evans Orchestra. His 1987 debut as a leader, 'Andy Sheppard' (Antilles) included Randy Brecker in the cast list; 'Coming Second', an intentionally ironic title, was in powerful, post-Messengers vein, while 'Want A Toffee' had him jousting for honours alongside an excellent Brecker solo.

The 1989 'Introductions In The Dark' (Island) represented a conscious effort to create a context for his playing rather than the simple heads-down-and-blow quartet formula. Sheppard created accessible soundscapes that were contemplative rather than exploratory, with an emphasis on melodic involution rather than harmonic extensibility. He had moved from American 'hard' to European 'cool' with moments reminiscent of ECM's cultural patching and Jan Garbarek's caverns of ice. Even so, he showed that he was willing to confront the importance of placing his playing into an integrated group concept, a problem something both Smith and Pine had not, by the end of the 1980s, wholly reconciled.

Steve Williamson (b.1965), a fast and furious tenor saxophonist dubbed 'The Ginseng Man' when he sat in with Jazz Warriors in October 1988, did not leap immediately into recording, preferring instead to develop and refine his talent by assidious study and practice. By the time of his 1989 debut 'A Waltz For Grace' (Verve), Williamson had assumed the trappings of something of a cult figure on the London circuit. Produced by Steve Coleman and recorded in New York and London, it was a proud assertion of his talent; in interviews he pointed out the long-term nature of a jazz musician's development. With both tone and technique in place the next step was conceptualization.

European Free
Since the 1960s the European free jazz scene continued to celebrate its own unique variation of musical anarchy, 'Yes, this music disregards tradition,' wrote Mike Zwerin, 'but on the other hand the idea is to find

Steve Williamson pointed out the long-term nature of a jazz musician's development.

new forms or frameworks to replace the old. Trouble is 90 per cent of the free players disregard period. It is much harder to invent new forms than improvise over old ones.'[15] But if European freedom gloried in its non-specific terms of reference, by the '80s it appeared in a cul-de-sac, bypassed by developments elsewhere in the music. Once the cutting edge, their radical message had been blunted with the passage of time, seeming only to draw inspiration from their own techniques; even so, the European critical establishment was immensely proud of musicians such as Evan Parker, Derek Bailey, Han Bennink, Albert Mangelsdorff and Alex von Schlippenbach, who were regarded as equal of their American counterparts.

Perhaps the most significant events in European free jazz during the 1980s were the European free players who distinguished themselves on the world stage; the British drummer **Tony Oxley** (b.1938) toured with Cecil Taylor in 1988 and proved to be one of the most sensitive and imaginative accompanists the pianist had ever performed with. Equally, German saxophonist **Peter Brotzmann** (b.1941) became an essential component of Last Exit, perhaps the most vital and dangerous of all the post-Coleman groups.

THE GLOBAL DEMOCRACY

The Latin Connection

In 1977 the first, and only, jazz cruise from the U.S. to Cuba was organized including musicians such as Earl Hines, Dizzy Gillespie, Stan

Irakere: The dynamic Cuban ensemble that spawned Paquito D'Rivera and Arturo Sandoval at the beginning of the decade continued to tour through the 1980's.

Getz and David Amram with a much publicized stop-over in Havana. When the Cuban group **Irakere** were added to the bill they caused a sensation among the musicians and the jazz press with their concert at the Havana Libre Hotel. Word was passed back to Bruce Lundvall, then head of CBS, who arranged for the band to become the first Cuban band in over 20 years to be signed to a U.S. recording company. When the group appeared in America and Europe in 1978, their appearances at the Newport Jazz Festival, New York and the Montreux festivals that year were such that their performances prompted genuine speculation about establishing a mass crossover market for Latin jazz.

Quite apart from their Cuban traditions, the band blended jazz, rock and funk that was technically sophisticated and musically ambitious. At the time the band included two world-class virtuoso soloists in their ranks in altoist Paquito D'Rivera and trumpeter Arturo Sandoval, and their debut on CBS records, the Grammy winning 'Irakere' (CBS) held out a promise of great things to come. Recorded live at the Newport and Montreux Festivals in 1978 and released in 1979, the band delivers a powerful punch; the Afro-Cuban 'Junana Mil Ciento', 'Ilya' and 'Aguanile' contrasting an ambitious tone poem 'Misa Negra' ('The Black Mass'), with its frequent time changes, a typical element in Yoruba music.

After such a spectacular debut expectations were high, but 'Irakere 2' (CBS) was influenced strongly by disco music. In March 1979 CBS Records and Fidel Castro joined forces to produce 'The Havana Jam', three days of concerts featuring CBS and Cuban groups at the Karl Marx Stadium. One of the stars of the show, Irakere appeared on 'Havana Jam Vols. 1&2' (CBS) in a soaring festival romp. They toured the States shortly afterwards, opening for Stills, but Cuban-American relations soured and the band was not allowed to record in the United States. 'Chekere Son' (Milestone) recorded in Havana in mid-1979 by Japanese Victor engineers, remained mesmerized by disco-pop; tracks like 'La Comparsa' and the title track are underpinned with a relentless disco-groove which are contrasted by a couple of ingratiating ballads.

On 6 May 1980 alto saxophonist D'Rivera defected while Irakere was on tour in Spain. 'El Coco' (Milestone) was recorded in Tokyo later in the year with German Velazco Urdeliz his replacement. By now it was clear that leader Chucho Valdes's eclecticism was not taking the band in any specific direction as the promise of their American debut failed to materialize. By 1981 trumpet star Arturo Sandoval had left, 'Irakere recently are playing more and more dance music, which is one of the principal reasons I left them,' he said.

'Le Chemin De La Colline' (EGREM/Sonodisc) includes compositions by Cuban composer Arsenio Rodriguez while 'Catalina' (Messidor) has Arturo Sandoval as guest soloist on four of the six tracks. 'Misa Negra' (Messidor), despite the grandiose, rambling 17-minute title track, at least moved closer to the promise of their CBS debut. Live, the band was able to generate considerable excitement and continued to tour throughout the '80s, but the feeling persisted that under Valdes's benign leadership the potential of the band had been allowed to drift.

Paquito D'Rivera (b. 1948), was a child virtuoso. In 1960 he entered the Havana Conservatory and by 1973 was one of the founder members of Irakere. When he defected producer Bruce Lundvall managed to get him studio work in Madrid until he could arrange to get him to New York in October 1980. Within weeks he was attracting rave reviews; described by *Village Voice* as 'The most exciting new voice on alto', the *New York Times* urged, '[D'Rivera] should be heard . . . by anybody who likes jazz that's inventive, hot and heartfelt.'

D'Rivera soon began to establish himself in New York; during 1981 he appeared with Dizzy Gillespie's Dream Band at Carnegie Hall, was a member of Alto Summit, with Phil Woods and Arthur Blythe at the Kool Jazz Festival, New York as well as appearing with McCoy Tyner at the 1981 Montreux Festival—both festival appearances were subsequently issued as 'The New York—Montreux Connection' (CBS). Shortly afterwards he appeared on McCoy Tyner's 'La Leyenda De La Horn' (CBS).

His debut as a leader, the 1981 'Blowin' (CBS), included Hilton Ruiz alternating with Jorge Dalto (p), Eddie Gomez (b) and fellow ex-pat Ignacio Berroa (d) and went some way to showing what all the fuss was about. A fluent, virtuoso musician, his playing leapt with exuberance quite unlike any other alto saxophonist in jazz, particularly on the familiar warhorse, 'On Green Dolphin Street'. A polished musician, with Irakere D'Rivera had doubled on alto and baritone sax, on 'Blowin' he added flugelhorn, flutes and soprano sax.

In January 1982 he was featured on David Amram's 'Latin-Jazz Celebration' (Elektra Musician) and his second album as a leader, 'Mariel' (CBS) from later in the year shows him moving from the acoustic surroundings of 'Blowin' ' to incorporate electronic keyboards but the momentum of his debut is sustained. In June he appeared in Carnegie Hall as part of 'The Young Lions' (Elektra Musician), a concert of new music played by 17 young musicians as diverse as Wynton Marsalis, Hamiet Bluiett and Anthony Davis. He featured on his own composition 'Mariel', his hard-bop fluency fitting in well with the varying ensembles he found himself in.

In 1983 Helen Keane took over the management of his career; 'Live At Keystone Corner' (CBS) was the first album with her production input and was with his regular group comprising the Brazilian Claudio Roditi (t, vtb), Carlos Franzetti (k), Steve Bailey (b), Ignacio Berroa (d) and Daniel Ponce (perc). The Latin-meets-bop of 'Deja Vu', a surging D'Rivera composition set the tone of his most successful album to date. Reviewing the band during their stay at Keystone Corner, Philip Elwood wrote in the *San Francisco Examiner:* 'The music was sensational. D'Rivera's sax is not only strong and clear it is also compelling . . . D'Rivera is his own man—after one tune a listener could identify him anytime, anywhere.'

In 1983 pianist Michel Camilo joined D'Rivera's group, and the 1984 'Why Not' (CBS) from June that year included his arrangement of 'Waltz For Sonny'. Guest artist Toots Thielemans on harmonica appeared on four tracks in an album that saluted the musical cultures D'Rivera had explored since moving to New York, but like the 1985 'Explosion' (CBS) left only glimpses of his soaring, red-hot alto, D'Rivera giving in to his unashamed romanticism that detracted a little too often for comfort.

By 1986 Camilo had left and 'Manhattan Burn' (CBS) included John Hicks (p) among the cast of keyboard players plus George Coleman (ts) on two tracks in an altogether more robust session. D'Rivera as clarinettist featured on three tracks of 1987's 'Celebration' (CBS) and once again his skill and invention quotient was high on this most difficult of woodwinds, while the remaining tracks generated heat in the 'Havana/New York' style he patented. However none of his albums, except 'Keystone Corner', were really focused and other than existing as an undeniable testament to his musicianship, failed to re-create the heat and passion of his live performances.

D'Rivera established himself as an in demand New York session musician, guesting on albums such as Chris Connor's 'Classic' (Contemporary), Louie Ramirez' 'Tribute To Cal Tjader' (Ace) and the Venezuelan singer Soledad Bravo's 'Volando Voy' (Messidor). Throughout the decade he continued to perform with his Havana/New York Quintet and in 1988 he joined Dizzy Gillespie's touring carnival, his United Nations Big Band, where he was featured until the end of the decade.

Trumpeter **Arturo Sandoval** (b.1949) left Irakere in 1981 to form his own group. A Professor of Music at Havana Conservatory, Sandoval was both a piano and trumpet virtuoso. On trumpet, his preferred instrument, his style owes much to the influence of Dizzy Gillespie with whom he frequently appeared during the 1980s. In 1982 they recorded 'To A Finland Station' (Pablo), but this was by no means a good representation of either trumpeter and had all the hallmarks of a hastily cobbled-together Pablo session; the Finnish rhythm section was not an inspired production choice.

Sandoval toured extensively with his group—electronic keyboards, bass and drums. His natural exuberance, on both piano and trumpet, often led to grandstanding of spectacular proportions, and almost succeeded in concealing the obvious—that he was an excellent musician. Nevertheless Sandoval's performances were always entertaining; and if he was guilty of playing 100 notes when just one might have sufficed, it was simply because he rejoiced in the sheer pleasure of playing jazz.

Several telecasts caught him at maximum exuberance: 'Caribbean Nights' from 1988, with Dizzy Gillespie in 1987 on the John Holland film 'A Night In Havana: Dizzy Gillespie In Cuba', and extracts from the 1989 Havana Jazz Festival with pianist Chucho Valdes on 'Rhythms Of The World'. He features with Valdes again on 'Straight Ahead' (Jazz House), with a British rhythm section and with his own group on 'Tumbaito' (Messidor) and 'Just Music' (Jazz House) in two typically brash, flashy, exciting, although ultimately superficial, sessions.

Pianist **Michel Camilo** (b.1954), from the Dominican Republic, enrolled in the Dominican National Conservatory at nine and by the age of 16 was a member of his country's National Symphony. In 1979 he moved to New York and studied at Julliard and Mannes College to be closer to jazz. There he met saxophonist Mario Rivera: 'When he found out there was another Dominican in New York playing jazz, he immediately invited me up. That's where I met people like George Coleman and Jorge Dalto; that's how I broke into the scene,' he said.

His first name dates were with French horn player Peter Gordon's group French Toast. In 1983, when performing with Tito Puente at the Montreal Jazz Festival he was invited to join Paquito D'Rivera's group, with whom he stayed for two years and played on two albums, 'Explosion' and 'Why Not' (both CBS); in fact 'Why Not', a Camilo composition, became popular in New York musician circles and was recorded by several artists, including Manhattan Transfer, who earnt a 1983 Grammy for their version of the tune. In 1985 he made his Carnegie Hall debut with this trio opening for Tania Maria. His own debut on record as a leader, the 1986 'Why Not', followed by the 1987 'Suntan' (both Electric Bird/King), included Anthony Jackson (b) and Dave Weckl (d) (before he was 'discovered' by Chick Corea).

Regular performances at Michael's Pub and The Blue Note began to attract media attention; *Village Voice* said Camilo was 'rhythmically brilliant, harmonically sophisticated and given to melody both impassioned and witty', while the *New York Times* called him 'an omniverous stylist with the resources of an exceptionally rich and diverse tradition at his fingertips'. In 1987 he caused a sensation at the North Sea Jazz Festival, with both *Billboard* and *Jazz Times* hailing his performance as 'the revelation of the Festival'. Two versions of his acoustic trio appeared on the 1988 'Michel Camilo' (Portrait), one side with Marc Johnson (b) and Dave Weckl (d) and the other with Lincoln Goines (b) and Joel Rosenblatt (d). Here Camilo's flair, if not quite his power, was immediately apparent. Like D'Rivera and Sandoval there was a joy to his playing made all the more conspicuous by its absence for so long in jazz. It communicated and made audiences feel good; within weeks 'Michel Camilo' was topping the *Billboard* jazz charts. The 1989 'On Fire' (Epic) continued the momentum, more power, swirling rhythms and a deployment, *con brio,* of a formidable piano technique.

The Brazilian pianist/vocalist **Tania Maria** (b.1948) built a considerable following during the 1980s; a 'performance' artist, no recording could quite do her justice. After studying piano formally as a child she came under the influence of Johnny Alf and Luiz Eca, two important figures in modern Brazilian music plus the piano styles of Nat King Cole and Oscar Peterson. She moved to Paris in 1974 and her fluid piano, often locked in unison with her quicksilver scat plus the energy and magnetism of her personality, led to five months of packed houses at the 'Via Brasil'.

The 1978 'Live' (Accord) with a French rhythm section, recorded at the Jazzhus, Montmartre, showed her reaching for the dynamism and confidence that charged so many of her performances the following decade. In 1980 she signed with Concord Records and the subsequent 'Piquant' and 1981 'Taurus' were staging posts on the way to 'Come With Me' from August 1982, one of the Concord label's best-selling albums. Her expansive style, from the jumping 'Sangria' that opened the album, through 'Sementes, Grains And Seeds' to George Gershwin's 'Embraceable You', were stamped with her unmistakable personality, bringing the flamboyant unpredictability of Bizet's *Carmen* to the jazz of the early '80s.

Her 1983 'Love Explosion' (Concord) was better than the maudlin title suggested, but with the 1984 'Wild' (Concord), the panache of her in-person performance had the effect of overshadowing her previous work.

Recorded live at the Great American Music Hall she worked through many of the key numbers in her repertoire, several of which served her in live performance until the end of the decade. Here they were fresh, exciting and communicated easily and equally to the head and the feet. The intense momentum of 'Yatra-Ta', the delightful way she turns the beat around on 'Fiz A Cama Na Varanda' and Frank Colon's riveting virtuoso percussion display on the swirling first section of 'Sangria' was a warm breeze of serious fun blowing through jazz.

Maria's style, however, operated on the knife edge of folk-form, art and commercialism. Viewed from a social (i.e. cultural) perspective, her music was often uplifting, liberating and escapist; aesthetic considerations—how she achieved these effects—seemed less important. But when in 1985 she moved to the commercially orientated Manhattan label, what was at issue was the means rather than the end. Her albums became dominated by funk and her individualism receded under a sheen of glossy production.

From The Philippines . . .

Pianist **Bobby Enriquez** (b.1944) had his career interrupted during the mid-1980s after attracting considerable attention with Richie Cole's Alto Madness from 1980-81. A native Philippino he returned home for a brief visit in 1983 and had his passport withdrawn by President Marcos as a result of his friendship with Cory Aquino. Forced into internal exile, he remained until the Marcos regime was toppled. As a result his career lost vital momentum just as he seemed poised to establish himself.

A professional musician since the age of 14 working in Manila, Okinawa, Honolulu and Hong Kong backing visiting jazzmen such as Lionel Hampton, Chico Hamilton, Mel Torme and Tito Puente, he moved to America after a spell as musical director for the Don Ho Orchestra in Honolulu. In the late '70s he met Richie Cole and joined his band in 1980.

With Cole he proved to be a more than adequate foil and although he only appeared on the 1981 'Alive—At The Village Vanguard' (Muse) and a Ben Sidran 'Jazz Life' video at the same location, it was Cole's best group of the decade and forever seemed to link Enriquez with the altoist. In fact he was with Cole for less than a year and although too much of a gentleman to admit it, there was a suggestion that he upstaged his leader just once too often.

Cole dubbed him 'The Wild Man Of Mindano', and his style fractured the mould of Oscar Peterson's straight-ahead swing-into-bop with stride and jackhammer explosions. His debut as a leader, the 1980 'Wild Man' (GNP) was applauded by *Billboard* for his 'startling style' and 'superior keyboard technique', although the expected sparks did not fly on the subsequent 'The Wildman Meets The Madman' (GNP) from 1982. A rematch with Richie Cole and Alto Madness, Shelly Manne guested on drums, dubbing Enriquez 'the Bruce Lee of the keyboard'.

However, Enriquez seemed determined to assert a more controlled style instead of doing what came naturally and albums such as 'Ricardo', 'The Incredible Jazz Piano', 'Andalucia', 'Play Bossa Nova', 'Live In Tokyo Vols. 1&2', and 'Live At Concerts By The Sea' (all GNP) have an uncharacteristic reserve. At the 1982 Monterey Jazz Festival Dizzy Gillespie was about to go on stage without a pianist when producer Gene Norman persuaded him to use Enriquez. The result brought the house down and throughout 1983 he toured as a member of Gillespie's group.

Back in the States after his skirmish with the Marcos regime, the 1987 'Wild Piano' (Portrait) at last capitulates to the inner man with support from Eddie Gomez (b) and Al Foster (d). Percussive, swinging, energetic and humorous, Enriquez now seemed to rejoice in the 'Wild Man' tag, although not so much in tonal effects—his Kung-Fu Cecil Taylor-isms—as in his wild imagination that advanced the responsible middle ground before demolishing it with the unexpected.

The Brother From South Africa

Abdullah Ibrahim (b.1934) began his odyssey in jazz as Dollar Brand in Capetown, South Africa. He learnt piano from his mother, a pianist in the AME Church and was soon aware that South Africa represented a unique confluence of three musical cultures, African, European and American. During his formative years he adapted the popular music of his day: 'Waltzes, quicksteps, fox trots, sambas . . . what we did was put the Capetown beat underneath,' he said. Most of his South African recordings, made shortly before his conversion to Islam and his adoption of the name Abdullah Ibrahim, were made available by Kaz Records in the late 1980s. They were a valuable body of work, in essence a manifesto of the areas of music he would explore in the '80s after a period of heavy involvement in free jazz.

In 1962 he moved to Europe and in 1965 was encouraged to try his luck in the United States by Duke Ellington, an important influence on his evolving style. Ibrahim always retained a great respect for Ellington's work, which together with his love for Thelonious Monk was never far from the surface in either his small or larger ensembles. However, his

Abdullah Ibrahim. Languid, unhurried melodies over a lilting 'Capetown' beat.

formative environment in South Africa, in 'District Six' at the foot of Table Mountain, had a powerful effect on his musical conception. What emerged were folk images of Africa projected through the American jazz experience. The main characteristics of his style were hypnotic ostinatos, richly voiced chords and powerful tremolos and these modest resources were shuffled and re-shuffled to telling effect, underpinned with the spirit of *kwela,* South Africa's blend of jazz, choral music and 'Highlife'.

Ibrahim's serenity of spirit, his less-is-more ethic and his essentially 'orchestral' concept provided the unifying force that flowed through his considerable discography. There was no shortage of Ibrahim albums during the 1980s, many including different versions of his repertoire performed by his then current groups. The excellent quintet he led at the beginning of the decade with Craig Harris (tb), his frequent collaborator Carlos Ward (as), Alonzo Gardner (b) and Andre Strobert (d) were featured on 'Live At Montreux' (Enja), where the front line combined in dark, affecting tone-colours of depth and originality. The leader's concern for dynamics and pacing had a catalysing effect on Harris and Ward, whose solos assume a majesty that was not so readily apparent in their work elsewhere.

During the mid-1980s Ibrahim was featured in the Chris Austin film, 'A Brother With Perfect Timing' which showed him rehearsing and performing with his group Ekaya, formed in 1983 and with whom he made his most satisfactory albums of the decade. 'The Mountain' (Kaz) included five tracks originally issued on 'Water From An Ancient Well' (Blackhawk) with Ward (as), Charles Davis (bs), Dick Griffin (tb), either Cecil McBee or David Williams (b) and Ben Riley (d). His key soloist was Ricky Ford (ts), a fixture throughout most of the '80s whose solos had the power and emotional depth to enrich Ibrahim's compositions. The 1988 'Mindiff', with a pickup group including Ford and Billy Higgins (d), was a subtle and atmospheric deviation that provided the soundtrack for the French film 'Chocolat', named after a mountain in North Cameroon that provided the location for the film.

An all-star Ekaya produced the 1989 'African River' (Enja), and included Robin Eubanks (tb), John Stubblefield (ts), Horace Young (ss), Howard Johnson (tba, t, bs) Buster Williams (b) and Brian Adams (d). Once again Ibraham's compositions evoke the space and timelessness of the African continent; his languid, unhurried melodies over a lilting 'Capetown beat' a series of lyrical, polemic mediations.

From The Antipodes To Prague

In 1987 and 1988 Australian James Morrison (b.1963) appeared at Dick Gibson's legendary jazz party in Denver. After hearing him perform, Leonard Feather wrote: 'During several visits to the United States, audiences at clubs in major cities have marvelled at his mastery of the trom-

James Morrison. 'During several visits to the United States, audiences . . . have marvelled at his mastery of the trombone, trumpet, euphonium, flugelhorn, alto saxophone and piano . . .' Here pictured on just trumpet and trombone.

bone, trumpet, euphonium, flugelhorn, alto saxophone and piano. At Dick Gibson's . . . the general reaction left little doubt that he could be the next [jazz] superstar.'[16] Certainly there was a touch of Crocodile Dundee about the way Morrison breezed into the U.S. and began getting rave reviews; a qualified pilot and enthusiast of airplane acrobatics, in 1988 he finished third in the Adelaide Formula One Celebrity race and in 1989 he featured in a film indulging in his pastime of bungee jumping; one shot showed him hanging off a rope on Sydney's Regent Hotel 75 metres up blowing his trumpet in duet with his brother playing drums safely on terra firma!

Morrison started playing when he was seven, at nine he was in a Dixieland band, at 13 in a big band and at 16 had his own group playing the jazz spots in Sydney and Melbourne. In 1979 while studying at the New South Wales Conservatorium he made his U.S. debut at the Monterey Jazz Festival. However it was not until 1987 as a member of Red Rodney's Red Alert he began attracting acclaim. 'Postcards From Down Under' (WEA), was recorded in Sydney in 1987/8 with Red Alert pianist Garry Dial and Australian musicians, including his brother on drums, filling out the rest of the group. The theme was putting 'sound to the pictures' of artist Ken Done; the feel was of well executed mood-jazz. Morrison's tone was uniformly firm and well centred on all his instruments and his execution impeccable; but the album remained dangerously soporific.

In 1987 things began happening thick and fast; at the North Sea Jazz Festival he appeared alongside Woody Shaw, Jimmy Owens, Roy Hargrove and surprise guest Wynton Marsalis as 'Trumpets No End' and the following year appeared there with Benny Carter, described by Morrison as one of the highlights of his life. He also appeared with Bill Watrous, Phil Woods, Hank Jones, Roland Hanna and Monty Alexander at various festivals and toured with Cab Calloway, which he described as 'very interesting'.[17]

In 1988 he formed a quartet with pianist Adam Makowicz; 'Swiss Encounter' (E+W), live at the 1988 Montreux Jazz Festival, had Buster Williams (b) and Al Foster (d) backing two virtuosos who had learnt their jazz thousands of miles from the States. Morrison's fluent mainstream-into-bop style was at its best on 'Blues For Judy', a *tour de force* on trombone, including an excursion into multiphonics, before switching to trumpet. Remarkably, he duets with himself on both instruments, seemingly impervious to the problems posed by two radically different embouchures. This was no circus act, Morrison played both instruments with equal conviction and fluency; his ability was such that he could have made his mark with either instrument. In a world of earnest young neo-classicists, Morrison's buccaneering approach to the tradition and his devil-may-care recklessness was like a breath of fresh air; hell, his enjoyment *connected,* even if he hadn't satisfactorily resolved his rather gauche repertoire and a context for his playing.

Adam Makowicz (b.1941) was born in Prague, Czechoslovakia and attended the Chopin Conservatory in Krakow, Poland, before falling unashamedly under the spell of Art Tatum. Hailed by Jazz *Forum* as Europe's number one pianist in the '70s, he recorded some 25 albums before moving to the U.S. where his first album there was produced by John Hammond. However, Makowicz took a while to establish in America, initially failing to live up to his European reputation, 'From My Window' (Choice), for example, was dire.

Gradually he shed himself of Tatum-isms and 'The Name Is Makowicz' (Sheffield Lab) from 1983 with Phil Woods showed his enormous technical facility held in check and more importantly personalized by his own ideas. In 1988 he signed with RCA/Novus and 'Naughty Baby' (RCA/Novus) was an album of Gershwin tunes with two basses and a drummer. However, some of Makowicz's most exuberant playing on record was with

Morrison, including a powerful solo on 'Blues For Judy' that was simultaneously traditional and modern.

Immediately after recording 'Swiss Encounter' (E+W), Morrison boldly joined a George Benson jam alongside James Moody, Clark Terry and Randy Brecker, nearly bringing the house down with a series of powerful trombone solos that had even Benson doing double takes. In 1989 he appeared at the Rio Carnival, appeared in clubs with his own group and was a member of the Dizzy Gillespie/Phil Woods All-Star band and toured with Gene Harris/Philip Morris/Marlborough Superband, appearing on the band's September 1989 'Live At Town Hall N.Y.C.' (Concord) on trombone. But Morrison seemed at home whatever instrument he was playing. 'I'm trying to master one trade and the instrument doesn't matter that much, that's just the type of musician I am,' he said.[18]

Japan

Japan provided jazz with its biggest single audience, bigger than that of the US or that of Europe. Such an audience demanded product and Japan frequently embarrassed the rest of the world into emulating their sophisticated and well researched album re-issue programmes. Both the Original Jazz Classics and the Blue Note reissues, for example, were presaged by Japanese programmes with original liners and premium vinyl pressings. Japanese record producers also shaped the way the music was recorded by seeking out their home market's preference for mainstream/modern musicians; several Blue Note albums during the 1980s were originally instigated for the Japanese marketplace under the production control of Kazunori Sugiyama and Hitoshi Namekata.

However, the number of Japanese jazz musicians to make a mark outside their homeland were few. Musicians such as drummers Motohiko Hino and Akira Tana, pianists Masabumi Kikuchi and Aki Takase and trumpeters Terumasa Hino and Shunzo Ohno were, like so many Japanese musicians, highly competent but derivative; in a competitive music scene interest centred on the extent to which they had mastered the jazz idiom rather than their ability to advance the music.

Sadao Watanabe (b.1933) was voted Japan's number one alto saxophonist throughout the 1980s by the readers of *Swing Journal*; albums such as 'Rendezvous' (Elektra), 'Maisha' (Elektra), 'Tokyo Dating' (Warner) and 'Good Time For Love' (Elektra) were strictly in the Grover Washington/Chuck Mangione groove of pop jazz, while albums like 'Bossa Nova Concert', 'Dedicated To Charlie Parker' with Terumasa Hino (t) and 'Plays Ballads' (all Denon) were frankly disappointing.

However, in 1985 he produced a 23-day jazz festival in Tokyo where he appeared with James Williams (p), Charnett Moffett (b) and Jeff Watts (d). 'Parker's Mood' (WEA) recorded live at Laforet Museum revealed his rather stiff phrasing and less than sensational technique, despite the fact he once featured in Toshiko Akiyoshi's bop quartet before she emigrated to the States. The rhythm section performed impeccably but were on a different rhythmic wavelength, with James Williams (p) demonstrating what an underrated musician he was.

Guitarist **Kazumi Watanabe** (b.1953) was a regular visitor to the States in the 1980s with his Mobo Band, which recorded a series of good quality fusion recordings, 'Mobo 1', 'Mobo 2' and 'Mobo Club' (All Gramavision). The 1985 'Mobo Splash' (Gramavision) had Mike Brecker and Dave Sanborn providing high energy solos with Kazutoki Umezu (as) and was inspired by Watanabe's American tour. Watanabe called his brand of fusion 'New traditional Japanese music'; it certainly reflected the Japanese work ethic with its busy insistence. However, 'Kilowatt' (Gramavision), from 1989, had both power and fire more sharply focused to better effect. Watanabe showed that in a genre with no shortage of aspirants his conception and execution was among the best.

Terumasa Hino (b. 1942) was a solid and well respected journeyman trumpet/flugel/cornet player who worked with Dave Liebman in 1980 and Elvin Jones in 1982 appearing on 'Earth Jones' (Palo Alto) where his playing showed the influence of Miles Davis. Hino also led fusion bands in Japan during the early 1980s and 'Double Rainbow' (CBS) once more came under the spell of Miles Davis, this time the post-Bitches Brew variety. However, at heart, Hino remained a hard-bop musician; the 1989 'Bluestruck' (Blue Note) included John Scofield (g), Bobby Watson (as), Bob Hurst (b) and Victor Lewis (d) and while remaining typical of the mainstream bop that was being specifically styled for Japanese consumption by producer Hitoshi Namekata, was nevertheless a solid outing 'in the idiom'.

Jazz From Russia

Soviet jazz during the 1980s was one of a slowly unfolding tale; at the beginning of the decade their jazz scene was swathed in mystery. The establishment frequently blew hot and cold over attitudes to Western music with its attendant clash of ideologies. Gradually Russian jazz musicians were given sanction to play in the West, first for specific festivals; and in 1984, a tour of the United Kingdom was arranged for the Ganelin

Trio. Since then musicians such as Leonid Chizik, Victor Dvoskin and Sergei Kuryokhin have appeared in Western festivals to critical acclaim.

By 1989 Leo Fagin's Leo label was able to chart events in Russia to the end of the decade with 'Document' (Leo Records), an eight-CD set of cheerless episodes that showed Russian jazz struggling to find its identity, primarily by pushing free artistic expression to the limits as repression was relaxed. The results could be bizarre. Jazz Group Arkhanglesk performed with buckets over their heads. 'This is the musician's main response to *glasnost,*' said Fagin, 'to be more theatrical, over the top even.'[19]

Vyacheslav Ganelin (b.1944) was perhaps the most internationally celebrated Russian jazz musician during the '80s. His music, often impenetrable, with episodes in sound with no beginning, middle or end, with occasional moments of disconcertingly heavy-handed humour and theatricality was a hit at European festivals; such music emanating from

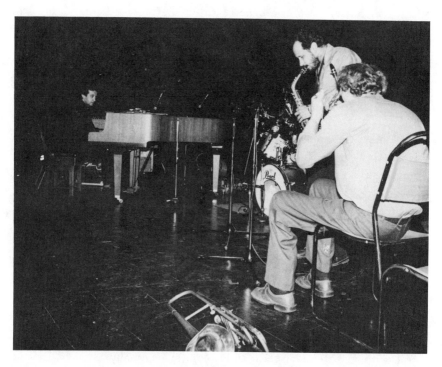

The Ganelin Trio. The most internationally celebrated Russian jazz musicians during the 1980s. (L to R Vyacheslav Ganelin, Vladimir Chekasin and Vladimir Tarasov).

Russia seemed a cause for celebration. His trio comprised conservatory-trained musicians Vladimir Chekasin (saxes) and Vladimir Tarasov (perc), the group recorded prolifically for the Leo label, including 'Con Affetto', 'Vide', 'Con Fuoco', 'New Wine . . .' and 'Ancorda Da Cappo Parts 1 &2'. In 1987 Ganelin emigrated to Israel and 'Jerusalem February Cantible' (Leo) was with a new trio.

Discography

by Tony Harlow

This discography does not claim to be complete – indeed the vast proliferation of labels and issues on a worldwide scale make such a task thankless and probably impossible. Similarly the penchant for reissue (especially in the wake of the switch to CD) makes any attempt to provide catalogue numbers redundant. We have tried to select major recordings by all artists mentioned in the text and bolster this where appropriate with the work of other relevant artists for whom no room could be found in the text. For reasons of space this discography has been confined to albums recorded during the 1980s (where possible in chronological order), even though it is appreciated albums made before and after the decade have been included in the text to provide context. It is our contention that anyone who listens to all these recordings will have a good conception of the body of work that comprised jazz in the 1980s.

CHAPTER 1: PAST MASTERS AND KEEPERS OF THE FAITH

Chet Baker
'Tune Up – Live In Paris' (Circle)
'Nightbird – Live In Paris' (Circle)
'Salsamba' (Musica)
'Leaving' (Intercord)
'Conception' (Circle)
'In Your Own Sweet Way' (Circle)
'I Remember You' (Circle)
'My Funny Valentine' (Circle)
'Peace' (Enja)
'Mr. B' (Timeless)
'The Improvisor' (CJR)
'Live In Sweden' (Dragon)
'At Capolinea' (NS)
'Blues For A Reason' (Criss Cross)
'Strollin'' (Enja)

'Chet's Choice' (Criss Cross)
'Little Girl Blue' (Philology)
'Nightbird' (Essential)
'Sings Again' (Timeless)
'When Sunny Gets Blue' (Steeplechase)
'Candy' (Sonet)
'Memories' (Paddlewheel)
'Almost Blue: Sings And Plays From the Film "Let's Get Lost" ' (RCA/Novus)
[*note*: not to be confused with 'Let's Get Lost – Chet Baker sings' (Capitol/Pacific) a compilation of material from 1953–56.]
'My Favorite Songs – The Last Great Concert' (Enja)
'Straight From The Heart: The Last Great Concert Vol. 2' (Enja)

Ruby Braff
'Mr Braff To You' (Phontastic)
'America The Beautiful' (George Wein Collection)
'A Sailboat In The Moonlight' (Concord)
'A First' [w/Scott Hamilton] (Concord)
'A Fine Match' [w/Scott Hamilton] (Concord)
'Me Myself and I' (Concord)
'Music From My Fair Lady' (Concord)

Brass Bands
Rebirth
'Here To Stay' (Arhoolie)
''Feel Like Funkin' It Up" (Rounder)

Olympia
'Here Comes Da Great' (Biograph)
Various Artists
'Down Yonder' (Rounder)
(See also Dirty Dozen)

Dave Brubeck
'Back Home' (Concord)
'Tritonis' (Concord)
'Paper Moon' (Concord)
'Concord On A Summer Night' (Concord)
'Reflections' (Concord)
'Blue Rondo' (Concord)
'Moscow Night' (Concord)

Benny Carter
'Summer Serenade' (Storyville)
'Gentleman Of Swing' (East Wind)
'Skyline Drive' (Phontastic)
'All Stars' (Sonet)
'A Gentleman And His Music' (Concord)
'Swing Reunion' (Book of the Month Club)
'In The Mood for Swing' (Lonelight)
'Meets Oscar Peterson' (Pablo)
'My Kind Of Trouble' (Pablo)
'Central City Sketches' [w/ American Jazz Orchestra] (Music Masters)
'Over The Rainbow' (Music Masters)

Doc Cheatham
'And His New York Quartet' (Parkwood)
'It's A Good Life' (Parkwood)
'The Fabulous' (Parkwood)
'Echoes Of Harlem' (Stash)
'Tribute To Billie Holliday' (Kenneth)
'Dear Doc' (Orange Blue)

Jeannie & Jimmie Cheatham
'Sweet Baby Blues' (Concord)
'Midnight Mama' (Concord)
'Homeward Bound' (Concord)
'Back To The Neighbourhood' (Concord)

Kenny Davern
'El Radio Scuttle' (Kenneth)
'The Blue 3' (Chas Jazz)
'Blue 5' (Opus)
'The Hot 3' (Monmouth Evergreen)
'Live Hot Jazz' (Statiuis)
'The Very Thought Of You' (Milton Keynes Music Series)
'Playing For Kicks' (JC)
'This Old Gang Of Ours' (Calligraph)
'I'll See You In My Dreams' (Music Masters)

Wild Bill Davison
'75th Anniversary Band' (Jaylin)
'At The Memphis Jazz Festival 1982' (Jazzology)
'And The Crown Swing Band' (Dog)
'Running Wild' (JSP)
'Plays Hoagy Carmichael' (Real Time)
'Together Again' [w/Art Hodes]

Dirty Dozen
'My Feet Can't Fail Me Now' (Concord)
'Mardi Gras In Montreaux' (Rounder)
'Voodoo' (CBS)
'New Orleans Album' (CBS)
(See also Brass Bands)

Panama Francis
'Getting In The Groove' (Black And Blue)
'Sings The Blues' [w/Jimmy Witherspoon] (Muse)
'Everything Swings' (Stash)
'Grooving' (Stash)

Bud Freeman
'The Compleat Bud Freeman' (Jazzology)
'The Dolphin Has A Message' (JSP)

Stan Getz
'Live At Midem '80' (Kingdom Gate)
'Billy Highstreet: Samba' (Emarcy)

'The Dolphin' (Concord)
'Pure Getz' (Concord)
'Poetry' [w/Albert Dailey] (Elektra Musician)
'Line for Lyons' [w/Chet Baker] (Sonet)
'Stockholm Concert' (Sonet)
'Voyage' (Blackhawk)
'Anniversary' (Emarcy)
'Just Friends' [w/Helen Merrill] (Emarcy)
'Apasionado' (A&M)
(See also Dianne Schuur)

Jimmy Giuffre
'Dragonfly' (Soul Note)
'Quasar' (Soul Note)
'Eiffel' (CELP)

Al Grey
'OD (Out Dere)' (Grey Forrest)
'With Jesper Thilo' (Storyville)
'Just Jazz' [w/Buddy Tate] (Uptown)

Scott Hamilton
'Tenorshoes' (Concord)
'Scott's Buddy' [w/Buddy Tate] (Concord)
'Apples And Oranges' (Concord)
'Close Up' (Concord)
'In Concert' (Concord)
'The Second Set' (Concord)
'Major League' (Concord)
'The Right Time' (Concord)
'Plays Ballads' (Concord)

Milt Hinton
'Just The Two Of Us' (Muse)
'The Judges Decision' (Exposure)
'Back To Bass-ics' (Progressive)
(See also under Branford Marsalis 'Trio Jeepy' (CBS); under Joey De Francesco 'Where Were You' (CBS); and under Ricky Ford 'Manhattan Blues' (Candid))

Art Hodes
'Just The Two Of Us' (Muse)
'Southside Memories' (Sackville)

'Blues In The Night'
(Sackville)
'w/Carrie Smith And Doc
Cheatham' (Parkwood)
'Joy To The Jazz World'
(Parkwood)
'Live From Toronto' (Music +
Arts)

*Discographer's Note:
The stride piano tradition
was maintained and ex-
panded in the '80s by sever-
al musician/musical
scholars. Selected recordings
include:*
Dick Hyman
'Gulf Coast Blues' (Stomp
Off)
'Stridemonster' (Unisson)
Dick Wellstood
'Live At Cafe des Copains'
(Unisson)
'After You've Gone' (Un-
isson)
Dave McKenna
'Spiders Blues' (Concord)
'The Key Man' (Concord)
'Dancing In The Dark'
(Concord)
'My Friend The Piano'
(Concord)
Harry Connick Jr.
'Twenty' (CBS)
'Harry Connick Jr.' (CBS)
'When Harry Met Sally'
(CBS)

Lee Konitz
'Live At Berlin Jazz Days
1980' (MPS)
'Dovetail' (Sunnyside)
'Art Of The Duo' (Enja)
'Lone Lee' (Steeplechase)
'Dedicated To Lee' (Dragon)
'Wild As Springtime'
(GFM)
'Medium Rare' (Label Bleu)
'Ideal Scene' (Soul Note)
'New York Album' (Soul
Note)
'Song Of The Stars' (Jazz
House)
'Blew' (Philology)
'In Rio' (MA Music)

Jimmy McPartland
'One Night Stand'
(Jazzology)

Jay McShann
'Blowin' In From K.C.'
(Uptown)
'Thou Swell' (Sackville)
'Airmail Special' (Sackville)
'Saturday Night Function'
(Sackville)
'Just A Lucky So And So'
(Sackville)

Ken Peplowski
'Double Exposure' (Con-
cord)
'Sunnyside' (Concord)
'Mr Gentle And Mr Cool'
(Concord)
(See also Loren Schoenberg,
Mel Tormé)

Oscar Peterson
'Live At North Sea 1980'
(Pablo)
'The Trumpet Summit
Meets. . .' (Pablo)
'Royal Wedding Suite'
(Pablo)
'Nigerian Market Place'
(Pablo)
'Ain't But A Few Of Us
Left' [w/Milt Jackson]
(Pablo)
'Freedom Song' (Pablo)
'In Japan '82' (Pablo)
'Two Of The Few' (Pablo)
'Face To Face' [w/Freddie
Hubbard] (Pablo)
'Meets Benny Carter'
(Pablo)

Shorty Rogers
'Re-Entry' (Atlas)
'Yesterday, Today and
Tomorrow' (Concord)
'Aurex Festival '83 Live'
(Aurex)
'Back Again' (Concept)
'California Concert' (Con-
temporary)

Bud Shank
'Explorations 1990: Suite
For Flute And Piano'
(Concord Concerto)
'This Bud's For You' (Muse)
'Plays' (Mole)
'That Old Feeling' (Con-
temporary)
'At Jazz Alley' (Contempor-
ary)
'Serious Swingers' (Con-
temporary)
'Tomorrow's Rainbow'
(Contemporary)
(See also Shorty Rogers)

Buddy Tate
'The Ballad Artistry'
(Sackville)
'The Great Buddy Tate'
(Concord)
'Tour De Force' (Concord)
'Long Tall Tenor' (Calli-
graph)
'Just Jazz' [w/Al Grey]
(Uptown)
(See also Scott Hamilton)

Clark Terry
'Memories Of Duke' (Pablo)
'Yes The Blues' (Pablo
Today)
'Mother! Mother!' [w/Zoot
Sims]
'Clark Terry/Red Mitchell'
(Enja)
'To Duke And Basie' (Enja)
'Portraits' (Chesky)
'Locksmith Blues' [w/Red
Holloway] (Concord)
(See also Horace Silver)

Warren Vache
'Iridescence' (Concord)
'Midtown Jazz' (Concord)
'Easy Going' (Concord)
'Warm Evenings' (Concord)
'And The Beaux Arts
Quartet' (Concord)

*Discographer's Note:
While this chapter was
intended to give a flavour of
the wide variety of jazz that*

could be seen during the 1980s, illustrating the whole historical perspective of the music in terms of some of its more interesting and/or visible practitioners, it can only give but a mere flavour. From the wide body of Past Masters and Keepers of the Faith active in the decade, a few more names seem worth mentioning, with one or two typical albums:

Benny Waters
'On The Sunny Side Of The Street' (JSP)
'Hearing Is Convincing' (Muse)
Teddy Wilson
on 'Swing Reunion' (Book Of The Month Club) [w/Red Norvo]
Red Norvo
'Live At Rick's' (Flying Fish)
'Just Friends' (Stash)
(See also Teddy Wilson)

Slim Galliard
'Anytime, Anyplace, Anywhere' (Hep)
Galliard also appeared in the film 'Absolute Beginners' [OST] (Virgin)
Slam Stewart
'New York, New York – Jazz Sounds Of The Apple' (Stash)
Al Cohn
'Nonpareil' (Concord)
'Overtones' (Concord)

CHAPTER 2: BIG BANDS – ANCIENT TO MODERN

Muhal Richard Abrams
'Mama And Daddy' (Black Saint)
'Blues Forever' (Black Saint)
'Afrisong' (India Navigation)
'Rejoicing With The Light' (Black Saint)
'View From Within' (Black Saint)
'Colours In Thirty Third' (Black Saint)
'The Hearinga Suite' (Black Saint)

Toshiko Akiyoshi/Lew Tabackin
'Farewell' (Ascent)
'Tanuki's Night Out' (Jam)
'European Memories' (Ascent)
'Ten Gallon Shuffle' (Ascent)
'Interlude' (Concord)

The American Jazz Orchestra
'Central City Sketches' [w/ Benny Carter] (Music Masters)
'Ellington Masterpieces' (East West)
Discographer's Note: Founder and Artistic Director: Gary Giddins Musical Director: John Lewis Assistant Musical Director and Orchestra Manager: Loren Schoenberg

Count Basie
'Kansas City Shout' (Pablo)
'Mostly Blues . . . And Some Others' (Pablo)
'Fancy Pants' (Pablo)
(See also under Frank Foster)

Carla Bley
'Social Studies' (Watt/ECM)
'Live' (Watt/ECM)
'I Hate To Sing' (Watt/ECM)
'Heavy Heart' (Watt/ECM)
'Night Glo' (Watt/ECM)
'Sextet' (Watt/ECM)
'Duets' (Watt/ECM)
'Fleur Carnivare' (Watt/ECM)

The Capp/Pierce Juggernaut
'The Juggernaut Strikes Again!' (Concord)
'Live At The Alley Cat' [w/ Ernestine Anderson] (Concord)

Buck Clayton
'A Swingin' Dream' (Stash)

Gil Evans
'Live At The Public Theatre Vols. 1 & 2' (Blackhawk)
'The British Orchestra' (Mole)
'Live At Sweet Basil Vols. 1 & 2' [w/The Monday Night Orchestra] (Gramavision)

'Bud And Bird' [w/The Monday Night Orchestra] (Electric Bird)
'Farewell' [w/The Monday Night Orchestra] (Electric Bird)

[As featured composer]
'Absolute Beginners' [Original Soundtrack Recording] (Virgin)

[with Laurent Cugny and the French Big Band Lumière]
'Rhythm-A-Ning' (Emarcy)

[with Steve Lacy]
'Paris Blues' (Owl)

[with Helen Merrill]
'Collaboration' (Emarcy)

[with Sting]
'. . .Nothing Like The Sun' (A&M) – big band track 'Little Wing'

[The Gil Evans Orchestra]
'Tribute To Gil' (Soul Note)

Bob Florence
'Westlake' (Discovery)
'Magic Time' (Trend)
'Trash Can City' (Trend)

[with Sue Raney (v)]
'Ridin' High' (Discovery)
'Flight Of Fancy' (Discovery)
'Quietly There' (Discovery)

Frank Foster
'2 For The Blues' [w/Frank

Wess] (Pablo)
'Frankly Speaking' (Concord)

[Directing The Count Basie Orchestra]
'Long Live The Chief' (Denon)
'The Legend, The Legacy' (Denon)
(See also Dianne Schuur)
Discographer's Note:
The Ellington band under the direction of Mercer Ellington also remained active in the '80s. Albums include:
'Music Is My Mistress' (Music Masters)
'Digital Duke' (GRP)

Benny Goodman
'King Of Swing – Aurex Jazz Festival '80' (Aurex)
'Let's Dance' (Music Masters)
'The Yale University Archives Vol. 1' (Music Masters) – one track from 1986.

Charlie Haden
'The Ballad Of The Fallen' (ECM)

[with his group Quartet West]
'Quartet West' (Verve)
'In Angel City' (Verve)
(See also under Geri Allen)

Lionel Hampton
'Made In Japan' (Timeless)
'One Of A Kind' (Glad-Hamp)
'Sentimental Journey' (Atlantic)
'Mostly Blues' (Music Masters)

Woody Herman
'Concord Jam' (Concord)
'Live In Chicago March 6th 1981' (Status)
'Woody Herman Big Band – Aurex Jazz Festival '82' (Aurex)
'Live At The Concord Jazz

Festival' (Concord)
'World Class' (Concord)
'A Great American Evening' (Concord)
'50th Anniversary Tour' (Concord)
'Woody's Gold Star' (Concord)

Illinois Jacquet
'Jacquet's Got It' (Atlantic)

Thad Jones
'TJ's Eclipse Live' (Metronome)
'Three + One' (Steeplechase)
(See also under Mel Lewis)

Mel Lewis
'Bob Brookmeyer Composer/Arranger with Mel Lewis and the Jazz Orchestra' [w/Clark Terry guest] (Gryphon)
'Plays Herbie Hancock: Live' [w/Bob Mintzer] (Pausa)
'20 Years At The Village Vanguard' (Atlantic)
'Soft Lights And Hot Music' (Music Masters)
'The Definitive Thad Jones' (Music Masters)

Small Groups:
'Mellifluous Quartet' (Gatemouth)
'The Lost Art' (Music Masters) – sextet with Dick Oatts (ts)

Rob McConnell
'Present Perfect' (Verve/MPS)
'Tribute' (Verve/MPS)
'All In Good Time' (Innovation)
'Atras Da Porta' (Innovation)
'Old Friends, New Music' (Unisson)
'Boss Brass And Woods' [w/ Phil Woods] (MCA)
'With Mel Torme' (Concord)
'Live In Digital' (Sea Breeze)

Gerry Mulligan
'Walk On Water' (DRG)
'Little Big Horn' (GRP)
'Soft Lights And Sweet Music' [w/Scott Hamilton] (Concord)
'Symphonic Dreams' (PAR)

Sun Ra
'Sunrise In Different Dimensions' (Hathut)
'Nuclear War' (Y Records)
'Meets Salan Ragab in Egypt' (Praxis)
'Ra To The Rescue' (Saturn)
'Love In Outerspace' (Leo)
'Dreams Come True' (Saturn)
'Live At Praxis '84' (Praxis)
'Live At Praxis '84 Vol. 2' (Praxis)
'A Night In East Berlin' (Leo)
'Live At Pit Inn' (DIW)
'Reflections In Blue' (Black Saint)
'Hours After' (Black Saint)
'Cosmo Omnibus Imaginable Illusion' (DIW)
'Blue Delight' (A&M)

Buddy Rich
'The Man From Planet Jazz' (Ronnie Scott Productions)
'The Buddy Rich Band Plays' (MCA)
'Mr Drums – Live On King Street, San Francisco' (Café)

George Russell
'Souls Loved By Nature' (Soul Note)
'Vertical Form VI' (Soul Note)
'Live In An American Time Spiral' (Soul Note)
'The African Game' (Blue Note)
'So What' (Blue Note)

Loren Schoenberg
[With his big band]
'That's The Way It Goes' (Aviva)
'Time Waits For No One'

(Music Masters)
'Solid Ground' (Music
Masters)

[With small groups]
'Mr Tram Associates – Get-
ting Some Fun Out Of
Life' (Audiophile)
(See also The American Jazz
Orchestra)

Discographer's Note:
The following is a list of
other big bands of interest
active during the 1980s:

Bob Mintzer (rehearsal
band of New York session
musicians that from time to
time included the Breckers,
Peter Erskine and Don
Grolnick)

'Incredible Journey' (DMP)
'Camouflage' (DMP)
'Spectrum' (DMP)
'Urban Contours' (DMP)
Matt Catingub
'High Tech Big Band' (Sea
Breeze)

Doc Severinson
'Facets' (Amherst)
'With The Tonight Show
Band Vols. 1 & 2'
(Amherst)

Bill Holman
'The Bill Holman Band'
(JVC)

Gene Harris
'Tribute To Count Basie'

(Concord)
'And The Phillip Morris
Superband' (Concord)

Maynard Ferguson
'Big Bop Nouveau' (Intima)

Mike Gibbs Orchestra
'Big Music' (Venture)

Mike Westbrook
'On Duke's Birthday' (Hat
Art)
'Live for Sale' (Hat Art)
'Rossini' (Hat Art)
'London Bridge Is Broken'
(Hat Art)

Bob Belden Ensemble
'Treasure Island'
(Sunnyside)

CHAPTER 3: THE HARD-BOP MAINSTREAM

Richie Cole
'Hollywood Madness' [w/
Manhattan Transfer]
(Muse)
'Side by Side' [w/Phil
Woods] (Muse)
'Cool "C" ' (Muse)
'Alive, at the Village
Vanguard' (Muse)
'Some Things Speak for
Themselves' (Muse)
'Alto Annie's Theme' (Palo
Alto)
'Richie Cole and. . .' (Palo
Alto)
'Bossa Nova Eyes' (Muse)
'Pure Imagination' (Con-
cord)
'Popbop' (Milestone)
'Bossa International' [w/
Hank Crawford & Emily
Remler] (Milestone)
(See also Manhattan
Transfer)

Art Farmer
'Isis' (Soul Note)
'A Work of Art' (Concord)
'Foolish Memories' (L & R)
'Manhattan' (Soul Note)
'Mirage' (Soul Note)
'Warm Valley' (Concord)

'My Foolish Heart' [w/John
Carter] (E-1004)
'In Concert' (Enja)
'You Make Me Smile' (Soul
Note)
'Azure' (Soul Note)
'Blame it on My Youth'
(Contemporary)
'PhD' (Contemporary)
'Moment to Moment' (Soul
Note)

With the Jazztet [w/Benny
Golson]
'The Jazztet' (Contempor-
ary)
'Real Time' (Contemporary)
'Back to the City' (Con-
temporary)
Live at the Sweet Basil Vols.
1 & 2 (Contemporary)

Tommy Flanagan
'Supersession' (Enja)
'You're Me' (Phontastic)
'Plays the Music of Harold
Arlen' (Inner City)
'The Magnificent' (Progres-
sive)
'Giant Steps' (Enja)
'Thelonica' (Enja)
'The Master Trio' (Bay-
bridge)

'Blues in the Closet' (Bay-
bridge)
'Nights at the Vanguard'
(Uptown)
'Jazz Poet' (Timeless)

Dizzy Gillespie
'Digital at Montreux 1980'
(Pablo)
'Alternate Blues' (Pablo)
'Musician-Composer-
Raconteur' (Pablo)
'To a Finland Station' [w/
Arturo Sandoval] (Pablo)
'New Faces' [w/Branford
Marsalis] (GRP)
'Closer to the Source'
(Atlantic)
'Enduring Magic'
(Blackhawk)
'Meets Phil Woods' (Time-
less)
'Endlessly' (MCA)

[With Max Roach]
'Max & Dizzy: Paris 1989'
[w/Max Roach] (A&M)

[With Stevie Wonder]
'Original Musicquarium'
(Motown)

[With Manhattan Transfer]
'Vocalese' (Atlantic)

[With The Dirty Dozen]
'Voodoo' (CBS)

Dexter Gordon
'Gotham City' (CBS)
'American Classic' (Elektra
Musician)
'At the Aurex Jazz Festival
'82' (Aurex)
'The Other Side of 'Round
Midnight' (Blue Note)
'Round Midnight' (CBS)
[See also 'In Performance at
the Playboy Jazz Festival'
(Elektra Musician) – two
tracks)

Johnny Griffin
'Return of the Griffin'
(Galaxy)
'NYC Underground'
(Galaxy)

[With Dameronia]
'Stop, Look & Listen'
(Uptown)

[With the Paris Reunion
Band]
'French Cooking' (Sonet)
'For Klook' (Sonet)

(See also Hal Willner's
Compilation, 'That's the
Way I Feel Now' – A
Tribute to Thelonius
Monk (A&M) – excellent
Griffin solo with Carla
Bley Band on 'Mister-
ioso')

Jim Hall
'Circles' (Concord)
'Live at the Village West'
(Concord)
'Telephone' [w/Ron Carter]
(Concord)
'Jim Hall's Three' (Concord)
'These Rooms' [w/Tom
Harrell] (Denon)
'All Across the City' (Con-
cord)
(See also George Shearing,
Michel Petrucciani)

Tom Harrell
'Play of Light' (Blackhawk)
'Moon Alley' (Criss Cross)

'Open Air' (Steeplechase)
'Stories' (Contemporary)
'Sail Away' (Contemporary)
(See also Jim Hall, Gerry
Mulligan, Phil Woods)

Andrew Hill
'Faces of Hope' (Soul Note)
'Strange Serenade' (Soul
Note)
'Verona Rag' (Soul Note)
'Shades' [w/Clifford Jordan]
(Soul Note)
'Eternal Spirit' [w/Greg
Osby] (Blue Note)

Ahmad Jamal
'Live at Bubbas' (Kingdom
Gate)
'In Concert' (Kingdom
Gate)
'Goodbye Mr Evans' (Black
Lion)
'Digital Works' (Atlantic)
'Live at Montreal Jazz Festi-
val 1985' (Atlantic)
'Rossiter Road' (Atlantic)
'Crystal' (Atlantic)
'Pittsburg' (Atlantic)

Hank Jones
'At the Village Vanguard'
(East Wind)
'Chapter II' (East Wind)
'Ambrosia' (Denon)
'Darji meets Hank Jones'
(Timeless)
'I'm All Smiles' (Verve)
'Lazy Afternoon' (Concord)
'Our Delights' [w/Tommy
Flanagan] (Milestone)
'I'm All Smiles' [w/Tommy
Flanagan] (Verve/MPS)

[With The Great Jazz Trio]
'Standard Collection' (De-
non)
'The Club New Yorker'
(Denon)
'Monks Moods' (Denon)

Clifford Jordan
'Hyde Park After Dark'
(Bee Hive)
'Repetition' (Soul Note)
'Dr Chicago' (Bee Hive)
'Two Tenor Winner' (Criss
Cross)

'Royal Ballads' (Criss Cross)
(See also Art Farmer)

Modern Jazz Quartet
'Reunion At Budokan'
(Pablo)
'Together Again: Live At
The Montreux Jazz Festi-
val 1982' (Pablo)
'Echoes' (Pablo)
'Three Windows' (Atlantic)
'For Ellington' (Atlantic)
Selected **Milt Jackson** al-
bums:
'Memories of Thelonius
Sphere Monk' [w/Monty
Alexander] (Pablo)
'Ain't Bit A Few Of Us Left'
[w/Oscar Peterson]
(Pablo)
'Bags Bag' (Pablo)
'Be Bop' (East West)
Selected **John Lewis** al-
bums:
'The Bridge Game'
(Phillips)
'The Garden Of Delight:
Delauney's Dilemma'
(Emarcy)
(See also American Jazz
Orchestra)

James Moody
'Something Special' (RCA
Novus)
'Moving Forward' (RCA
Novus)
'Sweet & Lovely' [w/Dizzy
Gillespie] (RCA Novus)

Frank Morgan
'Easy Living' (Contempor-
ary)
'Lament' (Contemporary)
'Double Image' (Con-
temporary)
'Bebop Lives' (Contempor-
ary)
'Major Changes' (Con-
temporary)
'Yardbird Suite' (Con-
temporary)
'Reflections' (Contempor-
ary)
'Mood Indigo' [w/Wynton
Marsalis] (Antilles)

Joe Pass
'Loves Gershwin' (Pablo)
'Live at Long Beach City College' (Pablo)
'Live at Dantes' (Pablo)
'University of Akron Concert' (Pablo)
'One for My Baby' (Pablo)
'The Living Legends' [w/ Robert Conti] (Discovery)
(See also Ella Fitzgerald, Oscar Peterson)

Art Pepper
'Blues for the Fisherman' [w/Milcho Leviev] (Mole)
'True Blue' [w/Milcho Leviev] (Mole)
'Winter Moon' (Galaxy)
'One September Afternoon' (Galaxy)
'Roadgame' (Galaxy)
'Art Lives' (Galaxy)
'Art Pepper Quartet' (Galaxy)
'Goin' Home' [w/George Cables] (Galaxy)
'Tête-a-Tête' [w/George Cables] (Galaxy)
Discographer's Note:
80's work also included on 'The Complete Galaxy Art Pepper' (Galaxy)

Emily Remler
'Firefly' (Concord)
'Take Two' (Concord)
'Transitions' (Concord)
'Catwalk' (Concord)
'Together' [w/Larry Coryell] (Concord)
'East to Wes' [w/Hank Jones] (Concord)
(See also Richie Cole)

Max Roach
'Chatternoochee Red' (CBS)
'Swish' (New Artists)
'In The Light' (Soul Note)
'Double Quartet Live at Vielharmonie' (Soul Note)
'Scott Free' (Soul Note)
'Survivors' (Soul Note)
'Easy Winners' (Soul Note)

'Bright Moments' (Soul Note)
'Max & Diz: Paris 1989' [w/ Dizzy Gillespie] (A&M)

With M'Boom [Percussion Ensemble]
'Collage' (Soul Note)

Maxine Roach
'Uptown String Quartet' (Polygram)

Red Rodney
'Live at the Village Vanguard' (Muse)
'Hi Jinx at the Vanguard' (Muse)
'Night & Day' (Muse)
'The Spirit Within' (Elektra Musician)
'Spirit' (Elektra Musician)
'No Turn on Red' (Denon)
'Red Snapper' (Steeplechase)
'One for Bird' (Steeplechase)
'Red Giant' (Steeplechase)
Discographer's Note:
Dial & Oatts recorded on their own 'Dial & Oatts' (DMP)

Charlie Rouse
'With Upper Manhattan Jazz Society' (Enja)
'Social Call' (Uptown)
'Playing in the Yard' [w/ Stan Tracey] (Steam)
'Ephistrophy' (Landmark)

With Sphere [Rouse/Kenny Barron/Buster Williams/ Ben Riley]
'Four in One' (Elektra Musician)
'Flight Path' (Elektra Musician)
'On Tour' (Red Record)
'Live at Umbria Jazz' (Red Record)
'Four for All' (Verve)
'Bird Songs' (Verve)

Horace Silver
'Guides to Growing Up' (Silveto)
'Spiritualizing the Senses' (Silveto)
'There's no need to Struggle' (Silveto)
'Music to Ease Your Disease' [w/Clark Terry] (Silveto)

Sonny Stitt
'Groovin' High' [w/Art Pepper] (Atlas)
'Sonny's Back' (Muse)
'In Style' (Muse)
'Sonny, Sweets & Jaws' (Kingdom Gate)
'Last Recordings' (Kingdom Gate)
'Last Stitt Sessions' Vol. 1 & 2 (Muse)

Phil Woods
'Phil Woods Quartet' Vol. 1 (Clean Cut)
'More Live' (Adelphi)
'Kefs Fool' (Ambi)
'Macerata Concert' (Philology)
'European Tour Live' (Red Records)
'With Lew Tabackin' (Omnisound)
'Three For All' (Enja)
'Birds Of A Feather' (Antilles)
'Live from New York' (Palo Alto)
'At the Vanguard' (Antilles)
'Piper at the Gates of Dawn' (Sea Breeze)
'Ole Dude & Fundance Kid' [w/Budd Johnson] (Uptown)
'Integrity' (Red Record)
'Heaven' (Blackhawk)
'Gratitude' (Denon)
'Bop Stew' (Concord)
'Bouquet' (Concord)
'Evaluation' [w/The Little Big Band] (Concord)
'Flash' (Concord)

Discographer's Note:
Many Bop and Hard Bop musicians continued to be active during the '80s or returned to active playing without creating quite the profile of those mentioned

in the text. A partial list of such names with selected typical recordings might include:

Kenny Burrell
'Groovin' High' (Muse)
'Togethering' [w/Grover Washington]
'Generation' (Blue Note)
'Pieces of Blue and The Blues' (Blue Note)
Charlie Byrd
'What a Wonderful World' (Concord) [w/Scott Hamilton]
Donald Byrd

'Harlem Blues' (Landmark)
'Gettin' Down To Business' (Landmark)
Herb Ellis
'Hot Tracks' (Concord)
'Doggin' Around' (Concord)
Tal Farlow
'Cooking On All Burners' (Concord)
'Chromatic Palette' [w/ Tommy Flanagan] (Concord)
Barney Kessel
'Solo' (Concord)
'Spontaneous Combustion' (Concord)
[with Great Guitars [w/

Herb Ellis/Barney Kessell]]
'At The Winery' (Concord)
'At Charlie's, George Town' (Concord)
Harold Land
'Xocia's Dance' (Muse)
[with Timeless All Stars]
'Timeless All Stars' (Timeless)
'Essence' (Delos)
Jackie McLean
'It's About Time [w/McCoy Tyner] (Blue Note)
'One Night With Blue Note Preserved Vol. 2' (Blue Note)

CHAPTER 4: WHITHER FREEDOM?

Air
'Air Mail' (Black Saint)
'80 Below '82' (Black Saint)
'New Air' (Black Saint)
'Air Show #1' (Black Saint)

Art Ensemble Of Chicago
'Full Force' (ECM)
'Urban Bushman' (ECM)
'Among The People' (Praxis)
'Live In Japan' (DIW)
'The Third Decade' (ECM)
'Naked' (DIW)
'The Alternative Express' (DIW)

Billy Bang
'Live At Green Space' (Anima)
'Rainbow Gladiator' (Soul Note)
'Invitation' (Soul Note)
'Outline #12' (Celluloid)
'Distinction Without A Difference' (Hathut)
'Bangception' (Hathut)
'Intensive Care' [w/Jazz Doctors] (Cadillac)
'The Fire From Within' (Soul Note)
'Live At Carlos 1' (Soul Note)

with The String Trio Of New York

'Common Goal' (Black Saint)
'Rebirth Of A Feeling' (Black Saint)
'Natural Balance' (Black Saint)

John Blake
'Maiden Dance' (Gramavision)
'Twinkling Of An Eye' (Gramavision)
'Adventures Of The Heart' (Gramavision)

[with Rhythm And Blu]
'Rhythm And Blu' (Gramavision)

(See also 'The Young Lions' (Elektra Musician))

Hamiett Bluiett
'Dangerously Suite' (Soul Note)
'Ebu' (Soul Note)
'Nali Kola' (Soul Note)
(See also World Saxophone Quartet, David Murray – Clarinet Summit 'The Young Lions' (Elektra Musician))

Arthur Blythe
'In The Tradition' (CBS)
'Illusions' (CBS)
'Blythe Spirit' (CBS)

'Light Blue' (CBS)
'Put Sunshine In It' (CBS)
'Da Da' (CBS)
'Basic Blythe' (CBS)
'Luminous' [w/Chico Freeman] (Jazz House)
(See also Leaders, Mose Allison, James Newton, Special Edition, 'The New York-Montreux Connection' (CBS))

Lester Bowie
'The Great Pretender' (ECM)
'All The Magic' (ECM)
'I Only Have Eyes For You' (ECM)
'Avant Pop' (ECM)
'Twilight Dreams' (Venture)
'Serious Fun' (DIW)
'My Way' (DIW)

Bobby Bradford
'Lost In LA' (Soul Note)
'One Night Stand' (Soul Note)
'Comin' On' [w/John Carter] (Hat Art)
(See also John Carter)

Anthony Braxton
'6 Compositions' (Antilles)
'Composition #96' (Leo)

'Open Aspects '82' (Hat
Art)
'6 Duets' (Cecema)
'4 Compositions (Quartet)'
(Black Saint)
'Composition 113' (Sound
Aspects)
'7 Standards 1985 Vols. 1 &
2' (Magenta)
'6 Compositions (Quartet)
1984' (Black Saint)
'With The Rova Saxophone
Quartet' (Sound Aspects)
'SKN-(B12) R10' (Sound
Aspects)
'5 Compositions (Quartet)
1986' (Black Saint)
'Quartet (London) '85' (Leo)
'Coventry Concert' (West
Wind)
'Braxton And Stockhausen'
(Hat Art)
'Moment Precieux' (Victo)
'6 Monk Compositions'
(Black Saint)
'19 Solo Compositions'
(New Albion)
'Compositions 19, 101, 107
and 139' (Hat Art)
'The Aggregate' (Sound
Aspects)
'Ensemble (Victoriaville)
1988' (Victo)
'7 Compositions (Trio)
1989' (Hat Art)

John Carter
'Night Fire' (Black Saint)
'Dauwhe' (Black Saint)
'Castles Of Ghana'
(Gramavision)
'Dance Of The Love Ghosts'
(Gramavision)
'Fields' (Gramavision)
'Shadows On A Wall'
(Gramavision)
'Comin' On' [w/Bobby
Bradford] (Hat Art)

Don Cherry
'El Corazon' (ECM)
'Home Boy, Sister Out'
(Barclay)
'Art Deco' (A&M)
[with Codona **(Collin**
Walcott and Nana

Vasconcelos)]
'Codona' (ECM)
'Codona 2' (ECM)
'Codona 3' (ECM)
[with Tim Moran and Tony
Vacca]
'City Spirits' (Philo)

Ornette Coleman
'Opening The Caravan Of
Dreams' (Caravan Of
Dreams)
'Prime Time/Time Design'
(Caravan Of Dreams)
'In All Languages' (Caravan
Of Dreams)
'Virgin Beauty' (CBS Por-
trait)
(See also Pat Metheny)

Marilyn Crispell
'Live In Berlin' (Black Saint)
'Rhythms Hung In Un-
drawn Sky' (Leo)
'A Concert In Berlin, Sum-
mer '83' (FMP)
'And Your Ivory Voice
Sings' (Leo)
'Quartet Improvisations'
(Leo)
'Gaia' (Leo)
'Labyrinths' (Victo)
(See also Anthony Braxton)

Anthony Davis
'Under The Double Moon'
[w/Jay Hoggard] (Pausa)
'Lady In The Mirror' (India
Navigation)
'Episteme' (Gramavision)
'Variations In Dream Time'
(India Navigation)
'I've Known Rivers'
(Gramavision)
'Hemispheres'
(Gramavision)
'Undine' (Gramavision)
'The Ghost Factory'
(Gramavision)
(See also David Murray,
Ray Anderson)

Chico Freeman
'Peaceful Heart, Gentle
Spirit' (Contemporary)
'Destiny's Dance' [w/

Wynton Marsalis] (Con-
temporary)
'The Outside Within' (India
Navigation)
'Tradition In Transition'
[w/Wallace Roney]
(Elektra Musician)
'The Search' (India Naviga-
tion)
'Tangents' (Elektra Musi-
cian)
'The Pied Piper'
(Blackhawk)
'Tales Of Ellington'
(Blackhawk)
'You'll Know When You
Get There' [w/Von Free-
man] (Black Saint)
'Luminous' [w/Arthur
Blythe] (Jazz House)
[with Brainstorm]
'The Mystical Dreamer' (In
+ Out)
(See also 'The Young Lions'
(Elektra Musician))

Julius Hemphill
'Georgia Blue' (Minor
Music)
'Big Band' (Elektra Musi-
cian)
(See also World Saxophone
Quartet)

Jay Hoggard
'Under The Double Moon'
(Pausa)
'Song For the Old World'
(India Navigation)
'Days Like These' (GRP)
'Jay Hoggard' (Contempor-
ary)
'Mystic Winds, Tropic
Breezes' (India Naviga-
tion)
'Riverside Dance' (India
Navigation)
'Overview' (Muse)
(See also 'The Young Lions'
(Elektra Musician))

Ronald Shannon Jackson
'Eye On You' (About Time)
'Nasty' (Moers Music)
'Street Priest' (Moers
Music)

'Mandance' (Antilles)
'Barbeque Dog' (Antilles)
'Decode Yourself' (Island)
'When Colours Play' (Caravan Of Dreams)
'Live At Caravan Of Dreams' [w/Twins Seven Seven] (Caravan Of Dreams)
'Texas' (Caravan Of Dreams)
'Taboo' (Virgin Venture)

[with Last Exit]
'Last Exit' (Enemy)
'Noise Of Trouble' (Enemy)
'Cassette Recordings '87' (Enemy)
'Iron Path' (Virgin Venture)

[with Power Tools]
'Strange Meeting' (Antilles)

Steve Lacy
'Snake Out Music' (Musics)
'Herbe de l'Oubli' (Hatmusics)
'Lets Call This' (Hat Art)
'The Flame' (Soul Note)
'Regeneration' [w/Roswell Rudd] (Soul Note)
'Prospectus' (Hat Art)
'Blinks' (Hat Art)
'Change Of Season' [w/ Misha Mengleburg, George Lewis] (Soul Note)
'Futurities' (Hat Art)
'The Condor' (Soul Note)
'Deadline' (Sound Aspects)
'Chirps' (FMP)
'Only Monk' (Soul Note)
'Hocus Pocus' (Disques du Crespuscule)
'Morning Joy' (Hat Art)
'Sempre Amore' (Soul Note)
'The Kiss' (Lunatic)
'Outings' (Ismez)
'The Gleam' (Silkheart)
'Duet' (World Artists)
'One Fell Swoop' (Silkheart)
'Your Night Is My Tomorrow' (Owl)
'Live In Budapest' (ITM)
'Momentum' (Novus)
'The Amiens Concert' (label bleu)
'Image' [w/Steve Arguelles]

(Ah Um Music)
'The Door' (Novus)
'Anthem' (Novus)

Oliver Lake
'Prophet' (Black Saint)
'Expandable Language' (Soul Note)
'Gallery' (Gramavision)
'Impala' (Gramavision)
'Otherside' (Gramavision)
'Transition' (DIW)

[with Jump Up]
'Dancevision' (Blue Heron)
'And Jump Up' (Gramavision)
'Plug It' (Gramavision)
(See also World Saxophone Quartet)
Discographer's Note:
Lake's interest in mixing Reggae and freer forms is mirrored and probably surpassed in the work of Leo Smith. His key albums include:
'Go In Numbers' (Black Saint)
'Procession Of The Great Ancestry' (Chief)
'Rastafari' (Sackville)
'Human Rights' (gramm/ kabell)

The Leaders
'Mudfoot' (Blackhawk)
'Out Here Like This' (Black Saint)
'Unforseen Blessings' (Black Saint)
'Heaven Dance' [trio only] (Sunnyside)

David Murray
'Solo Vols. 1 & 2' (Cecma)
'Ming' (Black Saint)
'Home' (Black Saint)
'Murrays Steps' (Black Saint)
'Morning Song' (Black Saint)
'Live At Sweet Basil Vols. 1 & 2' [w/Big Band] (Black Saint)
'Children' (Black Saint)
'New Life' (Black Saint)

'In Our Style' [w/ DeJohnette] (DIW)
'The Hill' (Black Saint)
'The Healers' (Black Saint)
'Lovers' (DIW)
'Deep River' (DIW)
'Ballads' (DIW)
'The Peoples Choice' (Cecma)
'Ming's Samba' (CBS Portrait)
'Lucky Four' (Tutu)

[with Music Revelation Ensemble]
'No Wave' (Moers)
'Music Revelation Ensemble' (DIW)

[with Clarinet Summit]
'Clarinet Summit' (India Navigation)
'Southern Belles' (Black Saint)

With A Tribute To John Coltrane
'Blues For Coltrane' [w/ Pharoah Sanders, McCoy Tyner] (Impulse)

(See also World Saxophone Quartet, Jack DeJohnette, James Blood Ulmer)

James Newton
'Mystery School' (India Navigation)
'Axum' [solo] (ECM)
'Portraits' [duos and trios] (India Navigation)
'James Newton' (Gramavision)
'Luella' (Gramavision)
'Echo Canyon' (Celestial Harmonies)
'The African Flower' (Blue Note)
'Water Mystery' (Gramavision)
'Romance And Revolution' (Blue Note)
(See also Anthony Davis, 'The Young Lions' (Elektra Musician))

Old And New Dreams
'Old And New Dreams' (ECM)

'Playing' (ECM)

Dewey Redman
'In Willisau' [w/Ed
Blackwell] (Black Saint)
'The Struggle Continues'
(ECM)
(See Charlie Haden, Don
Cherry, Old And New
Dreams, Pat Metheny)

Pharoah Sanders
'Journey To The One'
(Theresa)
'Rejoice' (Theresa)
'Live' (Theresa)
'Heart Is A Melody' (Ther-
esa)
'Africa' (Timeless)
'Oh Lord, Let Me Do No
Wrong' (Doctor Jazz)
'A Prayer Before Dawn'
(Theresa)
'Moonchild' (Timeless)

[with Idris Muhammad]
'Kabasha' (Theresa)

[with A Tribute To John
Coltrane]
'Blues For Coltrane' [w/
David Murray, McCoy
Tyner] (Impulse)

[with McCoy Tyner/Elvin
Jones]
'Re-United' (Blackhawk)

Archie Shepp
'Looking At Bird' (Steeple-
chase)
'Trouble In Mind' (Steeple-
chase)
'I Know About Life'
(Sackville)
'Mama Rose' (Steeplechase)
'My Man' (Impro)
'Loverman' (Timeless)
'The Good Life' (Varrick)
'Down Home New York'
(Soul Note)
'African Moods' (Circle)
'Little Red Moon' (Soul
Note)
'Soul Song' (Enja)
'California Meeting' (Soul
Note)
[with Chet Baker (!)]
'In Memory Of' (Timeless)

Bob Stewart
'In A Sentimental Mood'
(Stash)
'First Line' (JMT)
'Goin' Home' (JMT)
(See also Arthur Blythe,
Lester Bowie's Brass
Fantasy, David Murray's
Big Band, Gil Evans,
Charlie Haden's Libe-
ration Music Orchestra,
Henry Butler, Carla Bley)

Cecil Taylor
'It Is In The Brewing Lumi-
nous' (Hat Art)
'Fly! Fly! Fly! Fly! Fly!'
(Pausa)
'Garden' (Hat Art)
'The 8th' (Hat Art) [note:
edited version appeared in
1983 as 'Calling It The
8th' (Hat Musics)]
'Winged Serpent (Sliding
Quadrants)' (Soul Note)
'Praxis' (Praxis)
'What's New' (Black Lion)
'For Olim' (Soul Note)
'Live In Bologna' (Leo)
'Live In Vienna' (Leo)
'Tzotzil Mummers Tzotzil'
(Leo)
'In Berlin '88' (FMP box
set)
'In East Berlin' (FMP)
'Chinampas' (Leo)
'In Floresence' (A&M)

Henry Threadgill
'When Was That' (About
Time)
'Just Face The Facts And
Pass The Bucket' (About
Time)
'Subject To Change' (About
Time)
'You Know The Number'
(RCA/Novus)
'Slip Easily Into Another
World' (RCA/Novus)
'Rag, Bush And All' (RCA/
Novus)
(See also Air)

James Blood Ulmer
'Are You Glad To Be In
America?' (Rough Trade)

'Freelancing' (CBS)
'Black Rock' (CBS)
'Odyssey' (CBS)
'Live At The Caravan Of
Dreams' (Caravan Of
Dreams)
'Got Something For You'
(Caravan Of Dreams)
'America, Do You Remem-
ber The Love' (Blue
Note)
'Revealing' (In + Out)

[with Grant Calvin Weston]
'Dance Romance' (In + Out)

[with Music Revelation
Ensemble]
'No Wave' (Moers)
'Music Revelation Ensem-
ble' (DIW)

[with Phalanx (including
George Adams)]
'Original Phalanx' (DIW)
'In Touch' (DIW)

Discographer's Note:
Ulmer's influence touched
several bands who adopted
aspects of his style for their
own purposes; a short list
merely to illustrate his in-
fluence might include:
Defunkt
'Avoid The Funk – An An-
thology' (Hannibal)
Kelvyn Bell's Kelvynator
'Funk It Up' (Blue Heron)
Living Color
'Vivid' (CBS)
Machine Gun
'Open Fire' (Mu)

World Saxophone Quartet
'World Saxophone Quartet'
(Black Saint)
'Revue' (Black Saint)
'Live In Zurich' (Black
Saint)
'Plays Duke Ellington' (No-
nesuch)
'Live At The Brooklyn
Academy Of Music' (Black
Saint)
'Dances And Ballads' (Elek-
tra/Nonesuch)
'Rhythm And Blues' (Elek-
tra/Nonesuch)

Discographer's Note:
See also a short list of
typical European 'free'

players and their work
under the discography,
Chapter 10: 'European

Dreams and the Global
Democracy'

CHAPTER 5: MILES AND THE FUSION JUNTA

George Benson
'4 For An Afternoon' (ITI)
'In Your Eyes' (Warners)
'20/20' (Warners)
'While The City Sleeps'
(Warners)
'Collaboration' (Warners)
'Twice The Love' (Warners)
(See also Dexter Gordon)

Bob Berg
'Steppin': Live In Europe'
(Red)
'Short Stories' (Denon)
'Cycles' (Denon/Sound Pla-
net)
'In The Shadows' (Denon)
(See also Randy Brecker,
Miles Davis, Mike Stern)

Chick Corea
'Live At Midem' (Kingdom)
'Again And Again: The
Joburg Sessions' (Elektra
Musician)
'Three Quartets' (Warners)
'Trio Music' (ECM)
'Trio Music: Live In Europe'
(ECM)
'Childrens Songs' (ECM)
'Septet' (ECM)
'Voyage' (ECM)
'Live On Two Pianos' (DG)
'Akoustic Band' (GRP)
[with the Elektric Band]
'Elektric Band' (GRP)
'Light Years' (GRP)
'Eye Of The Beholder'
(GRP)
'Inside Out' (GRP)
(See also Bennie Wallace,
Griffith Park Collection)

Miles Davis
'Man With The Horn'
(CBS)
'We Want Miles' (CBS)
'Star People' (CBS)
'Decoy' (CBS)
'You're Under Arrest' (CBS)

'Aura' (CBS)
'Tutu' (Warners)
'Siesta' (Warners)
'Amandla' (Warners)
(See also Kenny Garrett;
Davis also appeared on
the rock albums of Scritti
Politti and Joni Mitchell
during the 1980s.)

Bill Evans
'Living In The Crest Of A
Wave' (Elektra Musician)
'Alternative Man' (Blue
Note)
[with Tony Reedus (Jazz
City)]
[with Randy Brecker, Tom
Scott, Robben Ford
'Echoes Of Ellington'
(Verve)]
(See also Elements)

Kenny G
'Kenny G' (Arista)
'G Force' (Arista)
'Gravity' (Arista)
'Duotones' (Arista)
'Silhouette' (Arista)

Steve Gadd
'Gadd About' (Projazz)
'Gadd Gang' (CBS)
'Here And Now' (CBS)
(See also Chick Corea,
Dianne Schuur, Steps)

Elements
'The Elements' (Antilles)
'Forward Motion' (Antilles)
'Blown Away' (Passport
Jazz)
'Illumination' (Novus)
'Liberal Art' (Novus)

[with Mark Egan]
'Mosaic' (Hippocket)

[with Danny Gottlieb]
'Aquamarine' (Atlantic)
'Whirlwind' (Atlantic)

Stanley Jordan
'Touch Sensitive' (Tangent)
'Magic Touch' (Blue Note)
'Standards Vol. 1' (Blue
Note)
'Flying Home' (EMI
Manhattan)
'Cornucopia' (Blue Note)

Jean Luc Ponty
'Individual Choice'
(Atlantic)
'Open Mind' (Atlantic)
'Fables' (Atlantic)
'The Gift Of Time' (Col-
umbia)

Pat Metheny
'80/81' (ECM)
'As Falls Wichita, So Wi-
chita Falls' (ECM)
'Offramp' (ECM)
'Travels' (ECM)
'Rejoicing' (ECM)
'First Circle' (ECM)
'The Falcon And The
Snowman' (EMI)
'Song X' [w/Ornette Col-
eman] (Geffen)
'Still Life (Talking)'
(Geffen)
'Letter From Home'
(Geffen)
'Question And Answer'
(Geffen)
(See also Mike Brecker, Jack
DeJohnette)

David Sanborn
'Voyeur' (Warners)
'Taking Off' (Warners)
'Hideaway' (Warners)
'As We Speak' (Warners)
'Backstreet' (Warners)
'Straight To The Heart'
(Warners)
'A Change Of Heart'
(Warners)
'Close Up' (Warners)
(See also Gil Evans)

John Scofield
'Bar Talk' (Arista)
'Shinola' (Enja)
'Out Like A Light' (Enja)
'Electric Outlet'
(Gramavision)
'Still Warm' (Gramavision)
'Blue Matter' (Gramavision)
'Pick Hits Live'
(Gramavision)
'Loud Jazz' (Gramavision)
'Flat Out' (Gramavision)
'Time On My Hands' (Blue
Note)
(See also Benny Wallace,
Ray Anderson, George
Adams/Don Pullen, Marc
Johnson, Mike Gibbs, Ter-
umasa Hino)

Wayne Shorter
'Atlantis' (CBS)
'Phantom Navigator' (CBS)
'Joy Ryder' (CBS)

[with David Liebman/Ri-
chie Beirach/Eddie
Gomez/Jack DeJohnette]
'Tribute To John Coltrane –
Live Under The Sky'
(Paddlewheel)
(See Buster Williams, Mi-
chel Petrucciani, Jim Hall)

Spyrogyra
'Access To All Areas'
(MCA)
'Alternating Currents'
(MCA)
'Breakout' (MCA)
'Carnival' (MCA)
'Catching The Sun' (MCA)
'City Kids' (MCA)
'Freetime' (MCA)
'Incognito' (MCA)
'Stories Without Words'
(MCA)

Steps/Steps Ahead
'Step By Step' (Better Days)
'Smokin' In The Pit' (Better
Days)
'Paradox' (Better Days)
'Steps Ahead' (Elektra Musi-
cian)
'Modern Times' (Elektra

Musician)
'Magnetic' (Elektra Musi-
cian)
'NYC' (Capitol/Intuition)

Mike Stern
'Upside Downside'
(Atlantic)
'Time In Place' (Atlantic)
'Jigsaw' (Atlantic)
[with Harvie Swartz]
'Urban Earth'
(Gramavision)
'Smart Moves'
(Gramavision)
(See also Miles Davis, Mike
Brecker, Bob Berg)

Grover Washington
'Togethering' [w/Kenny
Burrell] (Blue Note)
'Strawberry Moon' (CBS)
'Time Out Of Mind' (CBS)
(See also 'Live At The Play-
boy Jazz Festival' (Elektra
Musician) – two tracks)

Weather Report
'Night Passage' (CBS)
'Weather Report' (CBS)
'Procession' (CBS)
'Domino Theory' (CBS)
'Sportin' Life' (CBS)
'This Is This' [w/Carlos
Santana] (CBS)
(See also Joe Zawinul, Way-
ne Shorter)

Yellowjackets
'Yellowjackets' (Warners)
'Mirage a Trios' (Warners)
'Samurai Samba' (Warners)
'Shades' (MCA)
'Four Corners' (MCA)
'Politics' (MCA)
'The Spin' (MCA)

Joe Zawinul
'Dialects' (CBS)
'The Immigrants' (CBS)
'Black Water' (CBS)

Discographer's Note:
The '80s saw a large number
of artists at work whose
music in the all-encom-
passing fusion field would

perhaps better be described
as 'instrumental pop' than
jazz. However, it seems
worth identifying a few
major areas:

The GRP Sound (airplay
friendly, pop-soul-jazz
mix)
Dave Grusin: 'Migration'
(GRP)
GRP Live In Session:
(GRP)
Eddie Daniels: 'Blackwood'
(GRP)
Kevin Eubanks: 'Shadow
Prophets' (GRP)
Lee Ritenour: 'Festival'
(GRP)
Special EFX: 'Mystique'
(GRP)
Rippingtons: 'Tourist In
Paradise' (GRP)
Omar Hakim: 'Rhythm
Deep' (GRP)

The Technical Wizards
(Musician's Musicians)
Scott Henderson: 'Spears'
(Passport)
Alan Holdsworth: 'Secrets'
(Intima)
Frank Gambale: 'Thunder
From Down Under' (JVC)
Stanley Clarke: 'If This Bass
Could Only Talk' (CBS)
John Patitucci: 'On The
Corner' (GRP)
Leni Stern: 'Secrets' (Enja)
Victor Bailey: 'Bottoms Up'
(Atlantic)
Larry Carlton: 'On Solid
Ground' (MCA)
John McLaughlin: 'Live At
Royal Festival Hall'
(JMT)
Terri Lyne Carrington 'Real
Life Story' (Verve Fore-
cast)
Jaco Pastorius: 'Invitation'
(Warners)
Lyle Mays: 'Lyle Mays'
(Geffen)
Jonas Hellborg: 'Adfa'
(DEM)

Pop Jazz
Najee: 'Najee's Theme'
(EMI)
Pieces Of A Dream: 'Makes
You Wanna' (EMI)
Nelson Rangell: 'To Begin

Again' (Gaia)
Mike Stevens: 'Light Up
The Night' (RCA/Novus)
Earl Klugh: 'Solo Guitar'
(Warners)
Jamaica Boys: [Marcus

Miller/Lenny White]
(Warners)
Kirk Whalum: 'The Pro-
mise' (CBS)

CHAPTER 6: POST BOP AND BEYOND

ın Abercrombie
. (ECM)
'Five Years Later' [w/Ralph
Towner] (ECM)
'Upon A Time' (New
Albion)
'Solar' (Palo Alto)
'Night' [w/Jack DeJohnette]
(ECM)
'Current Events' [w/Mike
Brecker] (ECM)
'Witchcraft' (Justin Time)
'Getting There' (ECM)
'Abercrombie/Johnson/
Erskine: Live In Boston'
(ECM)
'Animato' (ECM)
(See also Peter Erskine, Mi-
chel Petrucciani)

George Adams
'Hand To Hand' (Soul
Note)
'Gentleman's Agreement'
[w/Dannie Richmond]
(Soul Note)
'More Sightings' (Enja)
'Nightingale' (Blue Note)
'America' (Blue Note)

[with Phalanx]
'Original Phalanx' (DIW)
'In Touch' (DIW)
(See also George Adams/
Don Pullen Quartet, Gil
Evans)

**George Adams/Don Pullen
Quartet**
'Earth Beams' (Timeless)
'Live At The Village
Vanguard Vols. 1 & 2'
(Soul Note)
'Life Line' (Timeless)
'City Gates' (Timeless)
'Decisions' (Timeless)
'Live At Montmartre' [w/

John Scofield] (Timeless)
'Breakthrough' (Blue Note)
'Song Everlasting' (Blue
Note)
*Discographer's Note:
Dannie Richmond (d), al-
though primarily associated
with the Adams/Pullen
quartet, was leader on the
following discs:*
'Plays Charles Mingus'
(Timeless)
'Dionysius' (Red)
(See also Don Pullen)

Ray Anderson
'Harrisburg Half Life'
(Moers)
'Right Down Your Alley'
(Soul Note)
'Old Bottles New Wine'
(Enja)
'You Be' (Minor Music)
'It Just So Happens' (Enja)
'Wooferloo (As Bass-Drum-
Bone)' (Soul Note)
'Blues Bred In The Bone'
[w/Anthony Davis, John
Schofield] (Enja)
'What! Because?' [w/John
Hicks] (Gramavision)

[with Slikaphonics]
'Slikaphonics' (Teldec)
'Wow Bag' (Enja)
'Modern Life' (Enja)
'Huma-Tonic Energy' (Blue
Heron)
'Check Your Head At The
Door' (Teldec)
'Slikaphonics Live'

[with Foolproof]
'No Friction' (Gramavision)
(See also Bennie Wallace,
Booby Previte, Henry
Threadgill, John Scofield)

Joanne Brackeen
'Ancient Dynasty' (Tappen
Zee)
'Special Identity' (Antilles)
'Havin' Fun' (Concord)
'Fi Fi Goes To Heaven'
(Concord)
'Live At Maybeck Recital
Hall' (Concord)

Mike Brecker
'Michael Brecker' (Impulse)
'Don't Try This At Home'
(Impulse)

[with Claus Ogerman]
'Cityscape' (WEA)

[with Gary Burton]
'Times Like These' (GRP)

(see also Chick Corea, Pat
Metheny, John Aber-
crombie)

Randy Brecker
'Amanda' [w/Eliane Elias]
(Passport Jazz)
'In The Idiom' [w/Joe
Henderson] (Denon)
'Live At Sweet Basil' [w/
Bob Berg] (Sonnet)
'Toe To Toe' (MCA)

Jack DeJohnette
'Tin Can Alley' (ECM)
'Inflation Blues' (ECM)
'The Piano Album'
(Landmark)
'Irresistible Forces' (MCA)
'Audio Visualscapes' (MCA)
'Parallel Realities' [w/
Herbie Hancock, Pat
Metheny] (MCA)

[with John Surman]
'The Amazing Adventures
Of Simon Simon' (ECM)

Peter Erskine
'Peter Erkskine' (Con-
temporary)
'Transition' (Denon)
'Motion Poet' (Denon)
'Big Theatre' (AHUM)
(See also Weather Report,
Steps Ahead, Bass
Desires, Gary Burton)

Joe Henderson
'Mirror Mirror' (Pausa)
'State Of The Tenor Vols. 1
& 2' (Blue Note)
'An Evening With' (Red)
(See also Randy Brecker,
Griffith Park Band,
Freddie Hubbard)

John Hicks
'Some Other Time' (Ther-
esa)
'John Hicks' (Theresa)
'Sketches Of Tokyo' [w/
David Murray] (DIW)
'Inc.1' (DIW)
'In Concert' (Theresa)
'I'll Give You Something To
Remember Me By. . .'
(Limetree)
'Two Of A Kind' (Theresa)
'John Hicks '88' (DIW)
'East Side' (DIW)
'Naima's Love Song' [w/
Bobby Watson] (DIW)

Dave Holland
'Life Cycle' (ECM)
'Jumpin' In' (ECM)
'Seeds Of Time' (ECM)
'The Razors Edge' (ECM)
'Triplicate' (ECM)

Freddie Hubbard
'Live At North Sea 1980'
(Pablo)
'Classics' (Fantasy)
'Outpost' (Enja)
'Rollin' ' (MPS)
'Ride Like The Wind' (Elek-
tra Musician)
'Keystone Bop' (Fantasy)
'Sweet Return' (Atlantic)
'Back To Birdland' (Real
Time)
'Life Flight' (Blue Note)
'Stardust' (Denon)

'Times Are Changing' (Blue
Note)
[with Woody Shaw]
'Double Take' (Blue Note)
'Eternal Triangle' (Blue
Note)
[with Satchmo Legacy
Band]
'Salute To Pops Vol. 1' (Soul
Note)
(See also Griffith Park
Collection, Oscar
Peterson, Art Blakey)

Keith Jarrett
'Invocations/The Moth And
The Flame' (ECM)
'Sacred Hymns' (ECM)
'Concerts' (ECM)
'Standards Vols. 1 & 2'
(ECM)
'Changes' (ECM)
'Standards Live' (ECM)
'The Book Of Ways' (ECM)
'Dark Intervals' (ECM)
'Changeless' (ECM)
'Still Lives' (ECM)
'Well Tempered Clavier'
(ECM)
'Paris Concert' (ECM)

Marc Johnson
'Bass Desires' (ECM)
'Second Sight' (ECM)
[with Bill Evans (p)]
'. . .His Last Concert In
Germany' (West Wind)
'Consecration – The Last
Bill Evans Trio' (Alfa
Jazz)
'Consecration II – The Last
Bill Evans Trio' (Alfa
Jazz)
[with Gary Burton]
'Times Like These' (GRP)
(See also John Abercrombie,
Peter Erskine)

Steve Kuhn
'Last Years Waltz' (ECM)
'Mostly Ballads' (New
World)
'Porgy' (Jazz City)
'Oceans In The Sky' (Owl)

David Liebman
'If Only They Knew' (Time-
less)
'Memories, Dreams And
Reflections' (PMR)
'Lieb Close-Up' (CVR)
'Sweet Fury' (BBN)
'Picture Show' (PMR)
'Loneliness Of The Long
Distance Runner' (CMP)
'Guided Dreams' (Dragon)
'Homage To John Coltrane'
(Owl)
'Better Leave It Alone'
(Heads Up Records)
'Trio + One' (Owl)
'Time Line' (Owl)
[with Quest, also including
the Liebman/Beirch
duets]
'Quest' (Palo Alto)
'Double Edge' (Storyville)
'The Duo Live' (Advance
Music)
'Quest II' (Storyville)
'Midpoint – Quest III'
(Storyville)
'New York Nites' (Pan)
'Natural Selection'
(Pathfinder)
'Chant' (CMP)
[with Wayne Shorter/
Richie Beirach/Eddie
Gomez/Jack DeJohnette
'Tribute To John Coltra-
ne' (Paddlewheel)]

Charles Lloyd
'Montreux '82' (Elektra
Musician)
'A Night In Copenhagen'
(Blue Note)
'Fish Out Of Water' (ECM)
*Discographer's Note:
The whole of Lloyd's recital
at the Blue Note Concert at
Town Hall, New York in
1985 was issued as* 'One
Night With Blue Note
Preserved Vol. 4' (Blue
Note)

Don Pullen
'Solo Piano' (Sackville)
'The Evidence Of Things Un-
seen' (Black Saint)

'Plays Monk' (Paddlewheel)
'The Sixth Sense' (Black Saint)
'New Beginnings' (Blue Note)
'New York Duets' (Music + Arts)
(See also George Adams/ Don Pullen Quartet)

Sonny Rollins
'Love At First Sight' (Milestone)
'No Problem' (Milestone)
'Reel Life' (Milestone)
'Sunny Days, Starry Nights' (Milestone)
'Solo Album' (Milestone)
'G-Man' (Milestone)
'Dancing In The Dark' (Milestone)
'Falling In The Dark' (Milestone)
'Falling In Love With Jazz' (Milestone)

Woody Shaw
'United' (CBS)
'Lotus Flower' (Enja)
'Time Is Right' (Red)
'Night Music' (Elektra Musician)
'Master Of The Art' (Elektra Musician)
'Setting Standards' (Muse)
'Solid' (Muse)
'In My Own Sweet Way' (In + Out)
'Imagination' (Muse)

[with Mal Waldron]
'The Git Go – Live At The Village Vanguard' (Soul Note)
(See also Dexter Gordon, Freddie Hubbard, Paris Reunion Band)

McCoy Tyner
'4×4' (Milestone)
'13th House' (Milestone)
'Reunited' (Blackhawk)
'La Leyenda De La Hora' (CBS)
'Looking Out' (CBS)
'Dimensions' (Elektra Musician)

'Just Feelin' (Palo Alto)
'It's About Time' [w/Jackie McLean] (Blue Note)
'Double Trios' (Denon)
'Bon Voyage' (Timeless)
'Live At The Musician's Exchange' (Who's Who In Jazz)
'Revelations' (Blue Note)
'Uptown/Downtown' (Milestone)

[with Pharoah Sanders/ David Murray – A Tribute To John Coltrane]
'Blues For Coltrane' (Impulse)

[with Elvin Jones]
'Love And Peace' (Trio)

[with Elvin Jones and Pharoah Sanders
'Re-United' (Blackhawk)
(See also 'One Night With Blue Note Preserved Vol. 2' (Blue Note), John Blakes Manhattan Transfer)

Bennie Wallace
'Free Will' (Enja)
'Bennie Wallace Plays Monk' (Enja)
'Mystic Bridge' [w/Chick Corea] (Enja)
'Big Jim's Tango' (Enja)
'Sweeping Through The City' (Enja)
'Twilight Time' (Blue Note)
'Art Of The Saxophone' (Denon)
'Brilliant Corners' [w/ Yosuke Yamashita] (Denon)
'Bordertown' (Blue Note)
(See also 'One Night With Blue Note Preserved Vol. 2' (Blue Note))

Jack Walrath
'Revenge Of The Fat People' (Stash)
'In Europe' (Steeplechase)
'A Plea For Sanity' (Stash)
'At The Umbria Jazz Festival Vols. 1 & 2' (Red)
'Wholly Trinity' (Muse)
'Killer Bunnies' (Spotlight)

'Master Of Suspense' (Blue Note)
'Neohippus' (Blue Note)

Discographer's Note:
Once again space has precluded dealing with some artists who, while not at the forefront of jazz during the 1980s, contributed some worthy albums that deserve a mention; a partial list might include:

Kenny Barron
'Spiral' (Eastwind)
'Green Chimneys' (Criss Cross)
'1+1+1' (Blackhawk)
'Autumn In New York' (Uptown)
'Scratch' (Enja)
'What If' [w/Wallace Roney] (Enja)
(See also Stan Getz)

Ran Blake
'Suffield Gothic' (Soul Note)
'You Stepped Out Of A Cloud' (Owl)

Paul Bley
'Tears' (Owl)
'Fragments' (ECM)
'Live Again' (Steeplechase)
'Notes' [w/Paul Motian] (Soul Note)
'Soul Note' (Steeplechase)
'The Nearness Of You' (Steeplechase)

Jaki Byard
'To Them To Us' (Soul Note)
'Live At Royal Festival Hall' (Leo)
'Foolin' Myself' (Soul Note)

George Coleman
'Manhattan Panorama' (Theresa)
'At Yoshi's' (Theresa)

Herbie Hancock
'Quartet' [w/Wynton Marsalis, Ron Carter, Tony Williams] (CBS)
'Round Midnight' [OST w/ Dexter Gordon] (CBS)
Hancock worked extensively in fusion during the '80s; among his more interesting work in this idiom was:
'Village Life' [*African fusion*

with Foday Suso] (CBS)
'Rockit' [*one of the first albums to explore hip-hop/electro/rap*] (CBS)
Ernie Krivda
'Tough Tenor' (Cadence Jazz Records)
'Well You Needn't' (Cadence Jazz Records)
Bill Saxton
'Beneath The Surface' (Nilva)
George Shearing
'Grand Piano' (Concord)
'In Dixieland' [group including Ken Peplowski] (Con-

cord)
(see Mel Torme)
Mal Waldron
'One Entrance, Many Exits' (Palo Alto)
'Breaking New Ground' (Baybridge)
'Songs Of Love And Regret' (Freelance)
'Space' (Vent Du Sol)
'Left Alone' (Paddlewheel)
'The Seagulls Of Kristiansund' (Soul Note)
'Sempre' [w/Steve Lacy] (Soul Note)

(See also Blanchard/Harrison)
Cedar Walton
'The Maestro' (Muse)
'Cedars Blues' (Red)
'Eastern Rebellion' (Timeless)
'Bluesville Time' (Criss Cross)
Larry Willis
'Just In Time' (Steeplechase)
Buster Williams
'Something More' [w/Wayne Shorter] (In + Out)

CHAPTER 7: NEO FACES

Art Blakey
'Live At Montreux And North Sea' (Timeless)
'Live At Bubba's' (Kingdom)
'In Sweden' (Amigo)
'Album Of The Year' (Timeless)
'Straight Ahead' (Concord)
'Killer Joe' (Storyville)
'Keystone 3' (Concord)
'And All Star Messengers' (RCA)
'Oh, By The Way' (Timeless)
'Art Blakey And The All Messengers - Aurex '83' (Aurex)
'The New York Scene' (Concord)
'Live At Ronnie Scott's' (Essential)
'Live At Sweet Basil' (Paddlewheel)
'Blue Night' (Timeless)
'Live At Kimball's' (Concord)
'New Years Eve At Sweet Basil' (Paddlewheel)
'Feelin' Good' (Delos)
'Hard Champion' (Pro Jazz)
'Not Yet' (Soul Note)
'Feel The Wind' [w/Freddie Hubbard] (Timeless)
'Standards' (Paddlewheel)

Terence Blanchard/Donald Harrison
'New York Second Line' (Concord/George Wein

Collection)
'Discernment' (Concord/George Wein Collection)
'Nascence' (CBS)
'Crystal Stair' (CBS)
'Black Pearl' (CBS)
[with Mal Waldron/Richard Davis/Ed Blackwell]
'Fire Waltz' (Paddlewheel)
'Live At The Sweet Basil' (Paddlewheel)

Donald Brown
'Early Bird' (Sunnyside)
'The Sweetest Sounds' (Jazz City)

Joey de Francesco
'All Of Me' (CBS)
'Where Were You?' (CBS)

Robin Eubanks
'Different Perspectives' (JMT)
'Dedication' [w/Steve Turre] (JMT)

Ricky Ford
'Flying Colours' (Muse)
'Tenor For The Times' (Muse)
'Interpretations' (Muse)
'Futures Gold' (Muse)
'Shorter Ideas' (Muse)
'Saxotic Stomp' (Muse)
'Looking Ahead' (Muse)
'Manhattan Blues' (Candid)

Kenny Garrett
'Introducing Kenny Garrett' (Criss Cross)
'Garrett 5' (Paddlewheel)
'Prisoner Of Love' [w/Miles Davis] (Atlantic)
(See also OTB, Tom Harrell)

Benny Green
'Prelude' (Criss Cross)
'In This Direction' (Criss Cross)
'Lineage' (Blue Note)

Harper Brothers
'The Harper Brothers' (Verve)
'Remembrance: Live At The Village Vanguard' (Verve)

Roy Hargrove
'Diamond In The Rough' (RCA/Novus)

Christopher Hollyday
'Reverence' (Resevoir)
'Christopher Hollyday' (RCA/Novus)
'On Course' (RCA/Novus)

Geoff Keezer
'Waiting In The Wings' (Sunnyside)

Brian Lynch
'Peer Pressure' (Criss Cross)

Branford Marsalis
'Fathers And Sons' [w/ Wynton and Ellis Marsalis, Chico and Von Freeman] (CBS)
'Scenes In The City' (CBS)
'Royal Garden Blues' (CBS)
'Romances For Saxophone' (CBS Masterworks)
'Renaissance' (CBS)
'Random Abstract' (CBS)
'Trio Jeepy' (CBS)
'Crazy People Music' (CBS)
[With Sting]
'The Dream Of Blue Turtles' (A&M)
'Bring On The Night' (A&M)
'. . .Nothing Like The Sun' (A&M)
(See also Miles Davis, JoAnne Brackeen, The Dirty Dozen Brass Band, Billy Hart, Carole King and Nancy Wilson)

Wynton Marsalis
'First Recordings' [w/Art Blakey as 'Live At Bubba's] (Kingdom)
'Wynton Marsalis' (CBS)
'Fathers And Sons' [see under Branford] (CBS)
'Think Of One' (CBS)
'Hothouse Flowers' (CBS)
'Black Codes (From The Underground)' (CBS)
'Concertos For Trumpet' (CBS Masterworks)
'Purcell, Handel, Torelli, Fasch, Molter' (CBS Masterworks)
'J Mood' (CBS)
'Standard Time Vol. 1' (CBS)
'Tomas/Jolivet' (CBS Masterworks)
'Cárnival' (CBS Masterworks)
'Live At Blues Alley' (CBS)
'The Majesty Of The Blues' (CBS)
'Crescent City Christmas Card' (CBS)
'Standard Time Vol 3: The Resolution of Romance' (Colombia)
(See also Herbie Hancock,

Chico Freeman, Frank Morgan, Marcus Roberts, 'The Young Lions' (Elektra Musician))

Mulgrew Miller
'Work' (Landmark)
'Keys To The City' (Landmark)
'Wingspan' (Landmark)
'The Countdown' (Landmark)

Ralph Moore
'Round Trip' (Resevoir)
'623C Street' (Criss Cross)
'Rejuvenate' (Criss Cross)
'Images' (Landmark)

Out Of The Blue
'OTB' (Blue Note)
'Inside Track' (Blue Note)
'Live At Mt. Fuji' (Blue Note)
'Spiral Staircase' (Blue Note)

Ralph Peterson Jr.
'V' (Blue Note)
'Triangular' (Blue Note)
'Volition' (Blue Note)

Marcus Roberts
'The Truth Is Spoken Here' (RCA/Novus)
'Deep In The Shed' (RCA/Novus)

Wallace Roney
'Verses' (Muse)
'Intuition' (Muse)
'The Standard Bearer' (Muse)
[with Chico Freeman]
'Tradition In Transition' (Elektra Musician)
[with Kenny Barron]
'What If?' (Enja)
(See also Tony Williams)

Superblue
'Superblue' (Blue Note)
'Superblue 2' (Blue Note)
Discographer's Note: Superblue is a 'supergroup' featuring current Blue Note artists playing classic tunes from the catalogue, arranged by Don Sickler.

Twenty Ninth Street Saxophone Quartet
'Pointillistic Groove' (Osmosis)
'Watch Your Step' (New Note)
'The Real Deal' (New Note)
'Live' (Red)

Bobby Watson
'Jewel' (Amigo)
'Gumbo' (Amigo)
'Beatitudes' (New Note)
'Perpetual Groove' (Red)
'Round Trip' (Red)
'Appointment In Milano' (Red)
'Love Remains' (Red)
'Year Of The Rabbit' (New Note)
'No Question About It' (Blue Note)
'The Inventor' (Blue Note)
(See also Superblue, 29th Street Saxophone Quartet, John Hicks)

James Williams
'Images Of Things To Come' (Concord)
'The Ariosa Touch' (Concord)
'Alter Ego' (Sunnyside)
'Progress Report' (Sunnyside)
'Magical Trio Vol. 1' [w/Art Blakey] (Emarcy)
'Magical Trio Vol. 2' [w/ Elvin Jones] (Emarcy)

Tony Williams
'Foreign Intrigue' (Blue Note)
'Civilization' (Blue Note)
'Angel Street' (Blue Note)
'Native Heart' (Blue Note)
[with Herbie Hancock]
'Quartet' (CBS)

Discographer's Note: Other worthy contributions to the 'neo-classic' hard-bop movement and modest post-bop explorations from other young musicians might include:

Alvin Queen
'Jammin' Uptown' [w/Terence Blanchard, Manny

Boyd, Robin Eubanks, John Hicks, Ray Drummon] (Nilva)
Manhattan Jazz Quintet
'Autumn Leaves' (Paddlewheel)
'Live At The Pit Inn' (Paddle-

wheel)
'My Funny Valentine' (Paddlewheel)
'Plays Blue Note' (Paddlewheel)
Renee Rosnes
'Face to Face (Something

Else)
'Renee Rosnes' (Blue Note)
Jon Faddis
'Into The Faddisphere' (Epic)
Steve Turre
'Viewpoint' (Stash)

CHAPTER 8: VILLAGE VOICES AND DOWNTOWN SOUNDS

Geri Allen
'Printmakers' (Minor Music)
'Home Grown' (Minor Music)
'Open On All Sides To The Middle' (Minor Music)
'Twylight' (Minor Music – reissued on Verve)

[with Charlie Haden, Paul Motian]
'Etudes' (Soul Note)
'In The Year Of The Dragon' (JMT)
'Segments' (DIW)
(See also Oliver Lake, Steve Coleman, Jay Hoggard, James Newton)

Tim Berne
'7x' (Empire)
'Spectres' (Empire)
'Songs And Rituals In Real Time' (Empire)
'Theoretically' (Empire)
'Ancestors' (Soul Note)
'Mutant Variations' (Soul Note)
'Little Trumpet Of Petra' (JMT)
'Fulton Street Maul' (CBS)
'Sanctified Dreams' (CBS)
'Miniature' (JMT)
'Fractured Fairy Tales' (JMT)

Steve Coleman
'Motherland Pulse' (JMT)
'On The Edge Of Tomorrow' (JMT)
'World Expansion' (JMT)
'Sine Die' (Pangea)
'Cypher Syntax' [w/Geg Osby] (JMT)
(See also Dave Holland, Marvin 'Smitty' Smith,

Michelle Rosewoman, Mel Lewis And The Jazz Orchestra)

Bill Frisell
'In Line' (ECM)
'Rambler' (ECM)
'Smash And Scatteration' [w/Vernon Reid] (Minor Music)
'Lookout For Hope' (ECM)
'Before We Were Born' (Elektra Musician)
'Is That You' (Elektra Musician)

[with Power Tools (Ronals Shannon Jackson/Melvyn Gibbs)]
'Strange Meeting' (Antilles)
(See also John Zorn, Paul Motian, Bass Desires)

Wayne Horvitz
'No Place Fast' (Theatre For Your Mother)
'Dinner At Eight' (Dossier)
'The President' (Dossier)
'This New Generation'
[note: This is a compilation of the above two Dossier albums] (Elektra Musician)

[with The Sonny Clark Memorial Quartet]
'Voodoo' (Black Saint)

[with Butch Morris, Bobby Previte]
'Nine Below Zero' (Sound Aspects)
'Todos Santos' (Sound Aspects)

[with The President]
'Bring Yr Camera' (Elektra)

[with Robin Holcomb]

'Larks They Crazy' (Sound Aspects)
(See also John Zorn)

Paul Motian
'It Should Have Happened A Long Time Ago' (ECM)
'Psalm' (ECM)
'The Story Of Maryam' (Soul Note)
'Jack Of Clubs' (Soul Note)
'The Paul Motian Quintet' (Soul Note)
'One Time Out' (Soul Note)
'Monk In Motian' (JMT)
'On Broadway Vols. 1 & 2' (JMT)
(See also Geri Allen, Charlie Haden Liberation Music Orchestra)

Greg Osby
'& Sound Theatre' (JMT)
'Mindgames' (JMT)
'Season Of Renewal' (JMT)
(See also Jack DeJohnette, Andrew Hill, Steve Coleman, Michelle Rosewoman, Cecil Brooks III)

Bobby Previte
'Dull Bang, Gushing Sound, Human Shriek' (Dossier)
'Bump The Renaissance' (Sound Aspects)
'Pushing The Envelope' (Gramavision)
'Claude's Late Morning' (Gramavision)

[with The Sonny Clark Memorial Quartet]
'Voodoo' (Black Saint)
(See also John Zorn, The President, Wayne Horvitz)

Herb Robertson
'Transparency' (JMT)
'X-Cerpts: Live At Willisau'
(JMT)
'Shades Of Bud Powell'
(JMT)
(See also Tim Berne)

Michelle Rosewoman
'The Source' [w/Baikida
Carroll] (Soul Note)
'Quintessence' (Enja)
'Contrast High' (Enja)

Marvin 'Smitty' Smith
'Keeper Of The Drums'
(Concord)
'The Road Less Travelled'
(Concord)
(See also Sonny Rollins,
Steve Coleman, Donald
Byrd, etc.)

Gary Thomas
'7th Quadrant' (Enja)
'Code Violations' (Enja)
'By Any Means Necessary'
(JMT)
(See also Michelle Rose-
woman, Greg Osby)

John Zorn
'School' (Parachute)
'Pool' (Parachute)
'Archery' (Parachute)
'Locus Solus' (Rift)
'The Classic Guide To
Strategy Vols. 1 & 2'
(Lumina)
'Ganryu Island' (Yukon)
'The Big Gundown' (Elektra

Nonesuch)
'Cobra' (Hat Art)
'News For Lulu' (Hat Art)
'Spillane' (Elektra No-
nesuch)
'Spy v. Spy' (Elektra)
'Naked City' (Elektra No-
nesuch)

[with The Sonny Clark
Memorial Quartet]
'Voodoo' (Black Saint)

[with Sado Michihivo]
'Rodam' (Hat Art)

[with Blind Idiot God]
'Sawtooth' (Enemy)

[with Derek Bailey/George
Lewis]
'Yankees' (OAO/Celluloid)

[with David Moss]
'Dense Band' (Moers Music)
'Full House' (Moers Music)

[with Jim Staley]
'Mumbo Jumbo' (Rift)

Discographer's Note:
A few lesser-known names
seem worth a mention in
this constantly adventurous
area:
Elliot Sharpe
'In The Year Of Yahoos'
(SST)
'Looppool' (Ear Rational)
Butch Morris
'Current Trends In Racism
In Modern America'
(Sound Aspects)
'Same Order, Long Under-

stood' (Black Saint)
Marty Erlich
'Pliant Plaint' (Enja)
'Traveller's Tales' (Enja)
Curlew
'Live In Berlin' (Rune)
Arto Lindsay
[with Ambitious Lovers]
'Envy' (Editions EG)
Bill Laswell
'Basslines' (Elektra Musi-
cian)
'Hear No Evil' (Virgin)
[with Material]
'Memory Serves' (Elektra
Musician)
'Seven Souls' (Venture)
(See Peter Brotzman)
Nicky Skopelitis
'Next To Nothing'
(Venture)
Sonny Sharrock
'Seize The Rainbow'
(Enemy)
'Live In New York'
(Enemy)
Golden Palaminos (Anton
Fiev)
'Golden Palaminos' (OAO
Records)
'Visions Of Excess' (Cellu-
loid)

Typical projects that could
be heard at the Knitting
Factory were anthologized
on:
'Live At The Knitting
Factory Vols. 1, 2 & 3'
(A&M)

CHAPTER 9: VOICE

Mose Allison
'Middle Class White Boy'
(Elektra Musician)
'Lessons In Living' (Elektra
Musician)
'Ever Since The World
Ended' (Blue Note)
'My Backyard' (Blue Note)

Betty Carter
'The Audience And. . .' (Bet
Car/Verve)

'Whatever Happened To
Love' (Bet Car)
'Look What I Got' (Verve)

[with Carmen McRae]
'Carmen McRae – Betty
Carter: Duets' (Great
American Music Hall)

Patti Cathcart
[with Tuck And Patti]
'Tears Of Joy' (Windham
Hill Jazz)

'Love Warriors' (Windham
Hill Jazz)

Jay Clayton
'All Out' (Amina)

[with The String Trio Of
New York]
'String Trio Of New York
With Jay Clayton' (West
Wind)
'As Tears Go By' (ITM)

[with Vocal Summit]
'Sorrow Is Not Forever,
Love Is' (Moers)

Chris Connor
'Love Being Here With You'
(Stash)
'Classic' (Contemporary)
'New Again' (Contemporary)

Blossom Dearie
'Simply Vol. VI' (Daffodil)
'Positively Vol. VII'
(Daffodil)
'Et Tu Bruce' (Daffodil)
'Chez Wahlberg Part 1'
(Daffodil)
'Songs Of Chelsea'
(Daffodil)

Ursula Dudziak
'Future Talk' (Inner City)
[with Vocal Summit]
'Sorrow Is Not Forever,
Love Is' (Moers)
[with The Gil Evans
Orchestra]
'Tribute To Gil' (Soul Note)

Ella Fitzgerald
'The Best Is Yet To Come'
(Pablo)
'With The Tommy Flan-
agan Trio' (Pablo)
'All that Jazz' (Pablo)
[with André Previn]
'Nice Work If You Can Get
It' (Pablo Today)
[with Joe Pass]
'Easy Living' (Pablo)
'Take Love Easy Again'
(Pablo)
'Speak Love' (Pablo)
[with Oscar Peterson]
'Ella And Oscar' (Pablo)

Dave Frishberg
'Songbook' (Omnisound)
'Songbook Vol. 2'
(Omnisound)
'Live At Vine Street'
(Fantasy)
'Can't Take You Nowhere'
(Fantasy)

'Let's Eat Home' (Concord)

Jon Hendricks
'Love' (Muse)
'Freddie Freeloader' (Denon)
[with Manhattan Transfer]
'Vocalese' (Atlantic)

Michelle Hendricks
'Carryin' On' (Muse)
'Keepin' Me Satisfied'
(Muse)

Sheila Jordan
'Old Time Feeling' (Muse)
'The Crossing' (Blackhawk)
'The Very Thought Of You'
(MA Records)
[with Steve Kuhn]
'Last Years Waltz' (ECM)
[with George Gruntz]
'Theatre' (ECM)
'Happening Now!' (Hatart)
(See also Aki Takase)

Jay Leonhart
'Salamander Pie' (DMP)
'There's Goona Be Trouble'
(Sunnyside)
'The Double Cross'
(Sunnyside)

Carmen Lundy
'Good Morning Kiss'
(Blackhawk)

Manhattan Transfer
'Mecca For Moderns'
(Atlantic)
'Bodies And Souls'
(Atlantic)
'Bop Doo-Wop' (Atlantic)
'Vocalese' [w/The Count
Basie Orchestra, McCoy
Tyner, Jon Hendricks,
Dizzy Gillespie, Richie
Cole] (Atlantic)
'Live '87' (Atlantic)
'Brazil '88' (Atlantic)
(See also 'In Performance
At The Playboy Jazz
Festival' (Elektra Musi-
cian), Richie Cole)

Susannah McCorkle
'Thanks For The Memory'

(Pausa)
'How Do You Keep The
Music Playing?' (Pausa)
'Dream' (Pausa)
'No More Blues' (Concord)

Bobby McFerrin
'Bobby McFerrin' (Elektra
Musician)
'The Voice' (Elektra Musi-
cian)
'Spontaneous Inventions'
(Blue Note)
'Simple Pleasures' (EMI)
(See also Pharoah Sanders,
Weather Report, Zawinul
Syndicate, Manhattan
Transfer, Vocal Summit)

Carmen McRae
'Two For The Road' [w/
George Shearing] (Con-
cord)
'Live At Bubba's' (King-
dom)
'Heatwave' [w/Cal Tjader]
(Concord)
'You're Looking At Me'
(Concord)
'Any Old Time' (Denon)
'Velvet Soul' (Denon)
'Fine And Mellow' (Con-
cord)
'Sings Monk' (RCA/Novus)
(See Betty Carter)

Mark Murphy
'Bop For Kerouac' (Muse)
'The Artistry Of' (Muse)
'Brazil Song' (Muse)
'Living Room' (Muse)
'The Complete Nat King
Cole Songbook' (Muse)
'Beauty And The Beast'
(Muse)
'Night Mood' (Milestone)
'September Ballads'
(Milestone)
'Kerouac, Then And Now'
(Muse)

Anita O'Day
'Mello' Day' (GNP)
'A Song For You' (Emily)
'SS' Wonderful' (Emily)
'In A Mellow Tone' (DRG)

Dianne Reeves
'For Every Heart' (Palo Alto)
'Welcome To My Love' (Palo Alto)
'Dianne Reeves' (Blue Note)
'The Nearness Of You' (Toshiba/EMI)
'Never Too Far' (EMI)

Judy Roberts
'Trio' (Pausa)
'You Are There' (Pausa)
'Judy Roberts Band' (Inner City)
'The Outer World' (Inner City)
'Nights In Brazil' (Inner City)
'My Heart Belongs To Daddy' (DK)

Dianne Schuur
'Schuur Thing' (GRP)
'Deedles' (GRP)
'Timeless' (GRP)
'And The Count Basie Orchestra' (GRP)
'Talkin' About You' (GRP)

Ben Sidran
'Old Songs For The New Depression' (Antilles)
'Bop City' (Antilles)
'On The Cool Side' (Magenta)
'On The Live Side' [w/Phil Woods] (Magenta)
'Too Hot To Touch' (Windham Hill Jazz)

Nina Simone
'Nina's Back' (VPI Jungle)
'Let It Be Me' (Verve)

Carol Sloane
'As Time Goes By' (East Wind)
'Love You Madly' (Contemporary)

Sweet Honey In The Rock
'We All . . . Every One Of Us' (Flying Fish)
'The Other Side' (Flying Fish)
'Feel Something Drawing Me On' (Flying Fish)
'Eyes On The Prize' (Flying Fish)
'Live At Carnegie Hall' (Carnegie Hall)

Take 6
'Take 6' (Warners/Reprise)

Mel Torme
'Live At Marty's' (Finesse)

[with George Shearing]
'An Evening With' (Concord)
'Top Drawer' (Concord)
'An Evening At Charlie's' (Concord)
'An Elegant Evening' (Concord)
'A Vintage Year' (Concord)

[with Rob McConnell And The Boss Brass]
'With Rob McConnell' (Concord)

[with Marty Paich]
'Reunion' (Concord)
'In Concert Tokyo' (Concord)
(See also Barry Manilow's '2am Paradise Café' (Arista))

Joe Turner
Discographer's Note:
Big Joe's Pablo Recordings are anthologized on:
'The Best Of Big Joe Turner' (Pablo)

[with Roomful Of Blues]
'Blues Train' (Muse)

Sarah Vaughan
'The Duke Ellington Songbook Vols. 1 & 2' (Pablo)
'Send In The Clowns' [w/ Count Basie Orchestra] (Pablo)
'Crazy And Mixed Up' (Pablo)
'I Love Brazil' (Pablo)
'Copacabana' (Pablo)
'Songs Of The Beatles' (Atlantic)
'Brazilian Romance' (CBS)
'South Pacific' [Dame Kiri Te Kanawa/José Carreras] (CBS)
'Gershwin Live' (CBS)
'The Planet Is Alive: Let It Live' (Gene Lees)
(See also Barry Manilow on '2am Paradise Café' (Arista))

Eddie Cleanhead Vinson
'Fun In London' (JSP)
'I Want A Little Girl' (Pablo)
'Meat's Too High' (JSP)

[with Roomful Of Blues]
'& Roomful Of Blues' (Muse)

Joe Williams
'Nothing But The Blues' (Delos)
'I Just Want To Sing' (Delos)
'Every Night' (Verve)
'In Good Company' (Verve)

Cassandra Wilson
'Points of View' (JMT)
'Days Aweigh' (JMT)
'Blue Skies' (JMT)
'Jump World' (JMT)

[with Air]
'Air Show' (Black Saint)

[with Jim DeAngelis and Tony Sigma]
'Straight From The Top' (Statiras)
(See also Steve Coleman)

Jimmy Witherspoon
'Spoon In Australia' (Jazzis)
'Sings The Blues With Panama Francis And The Savoy Sultans' (Muse)
'Live' [w/Robben Ford] (MCA)

THE BLUES
Discographer's Note:
The 1980s saw a large resurgence in Blues with multiple reissues and a wide variety of labels recording

new music. While
suggesting this is probably a
book in itself [indeed The
Blackwell Guide to Blues
Records *(ed. Paul Oliver,*
Blackwell, 1989) partially
fulfills this function), it is
impossible not to at least
acknowledge the main
developments. The
following discography
should give a very general
idea of what went on during
the 1980s as well as
supplementing the text:

Albert Collins
'Frozen Alive' (Sonnet)
'Live In Japan' (Sonnet)
'Cold Snap' (Sonnet)
(See also Robert Cray, John
Zorn)

Robert Cray
'Who's Been Talkin' ? '
(Tomato)
'False Accusations' (Highto-
ne)
'Bad Influence' (Hightone)
'Strong Persuader' (Mercury)
'Don't Be Afraid Of The
Dark' (Mercury)
[with Albert Collins/Johnny
Copeland]
'Showdown' (Alligator)

Dr. John
'Plays Mac Rebbenack'

(Fiend)
'In A Sentimental Mood'
(Warners)
(See also Bennie Wallace)

Jeff Healey
'See The Light' (Arista)
'Roadhouse' (Arista)

John Lee Hooker
'The Healer' (Chameleon)

Albert King
'San Francisco '83' (Fantasy)

B.B. King
'Now Appearing At Ole
Miss' (MCA)
'Six Silver Strings' (MCA)
'Blues and Jazz' (MCA)
'Completely Well' (MCA)
'The King Of The Blues 1989'
(MCA)

Roomful Of Blues
'Live At Lupo's Heartbreak
Hotel' (Alligator)
'Glazed' (Alligator)

Otis Rush
'Tops' (Blind Pig)

Stevie Ray Vaughan
'Texas Flood' (Epic)
'Soul To Soul' (Epic)
'Live Alive' (Epic)
'Couldn't Stand The Weath-
er' (Epic)

'In Step' (Epic)

Other Selected Titles

Johnny Adams
'Room With A View Of The
Blues' (Alligator)

Fabulous Thunderbirds
'Tuff Enuff' (CBS)

Kinsey Report
'Edge Of The City' (Alliga-
tor)
'Midnight Drive' (Alligator)

Lil 'Ed And The Blues Im-
perials
'Rough Housin'' (Alligator)

Kenny Neal
'Devil Child' (Alligator)

The New Bluebloods
[w/Various Young Chicago
Artists] (Alligator)

Joe Louis Walker
'Cold Is The Night' (Highto-
ne)
'The Gift' (Hightone)

Philip Walker
'Tough As I Want To Be'
(Rounder)
'The Bottom Of The Top'
(Hightone)

CHAPTER 10: EUROPEAN DREAMS AND THE GLOBAL DEMOCRACY

European Dreams

Stephane Grappelli
'Tribute To Blue Silver' (BS)
'At The Winery' (Concord)
'Vintage 1981' (Concord)
'Live At Carnegie Hall'
(Doctor Jazz)
'Looking At You' (JMS)
'Together At Last' (Flying
Fish)
'Live In San Francisco'
(Blackhawk)
'Plays Jerome Kern' (GRP)

'Just One Of Those Things'
(Angel)
'We've Got The World On
A String' (Angel)
'Anything Goes'[with Yo
Yo Ma] (CBS)

Philip Catherine
'Trio' [w/Escode/
Lockwood] (Gramavision)

Bireli Lagrene

'Routes To Django'
(Antilles)
'At 15' (Antilles)
'Bireli Swing '81'
(Jazzpoint)
'Live' [w/Vic Juris] (Inak)
'With Special Guests' [w/
Larry Coryell/Miroslav
Vitous] (Inak)
'Stuttgart Aria' [w/Jaco
Pastorius] (Jazzpoint)
'Inferno' (Blue Note)

'Foreign Affairs' (Blue Note)

Waso
'Gypsy Swing' (Munich)
'Live In Laren' (Polygram)

Michel Petrucciani
'Flash' (Bingo)
'Michel Petrucciani' (Owl)
'Estate' (Riviera)
'Toot Suite' [w/Lee Konitz] (Owl)
'Oracle's Destiny' (Owl)
'100 Hearts' (Concord)
'Live At Village Vanguard' (Concord)
'Note 'N Notes' (Owl)
'Cold Blues' (Owl)
'Pianism' (Blue Note)
'Power Of Three' [w/Jim Hall/Wayne Shorter] (Blue Note)
'Plays Petrucciani' (Blue Note)
'Music' [w/Tania Maria] (Blue Note)
(See also Charles Lloyd)

Barbera Dennelein
'Live At The Munich Domicile'
'Bebab'
'Tribute To Charlie Parker'
Discographer's Note:
The above are self-produced albums – labels unclear
'Straight Ahead' [w/Ray Anderson] (Enja)

Willem Breuker
'Willem Breuker Collective' (About Time)
'Music Of Ellington, Weill' (Bvhaast)
'Klap Op De Vuvrpijl' (Bvhaast)
'Bobs Gallery' (Bvhaast)
'Metropolis' (Bvhaast)

Pierre Dorge
'& The New Jungle Orchestra' (Steeplechase)
'Brikama' (Steeplechase)
'Even The Moon Is Dancing' (Steeplechase)
'Johnny Lives'

(Steeplechase)

Vienna Art Orchestra
'Concerto Piccolo' (Hat Art)
'Suite For The Green Eighties' (Hat Art)
'From No Time To Ragtime' (Hat Art)
'The Minimalism Of Erik Satie' (Hat Art)
'Tango From Obango' (Hat Art)
'Perpetuum Mobile' (Hat Art)
'Blue For Brahms' (Amadeo)
'Nightride Of A Lonely Saxophone Player Part 1/ Part 2' (Moers Music)
'Two Little Animals' (Moers Music)
'Innocent Of Clichés' (Amadeo)

George Gruntz
'Live At The Quartier Latin, Berlin' (Verve/MPS)
'Theatre' (ECM)
'Happening Now!' (Hatart)
'First Prize' (Enja)

Kenny Wheeler
'Double You, Double Me' (ECM)
'Giglo' (ITM)
'Flutter By Butterfly' (Soul Note)

Discographer's Note:
The following albums/ artists hope to provide a flavour of the European free music scene during the '80s:
Evan Parker
'The Snake Decides' (Incus)
'Collected Solos' (Limited Box Set)
'Six Of One' (Incus)
'From Saxophone And Trombone' (Incus)
Peter Brotzmann
'Low Life' (Celluloid) [w/ Laswell]
'Pica Pica' (FMP)
'14 Love Poems' (FMP)
'Go-No-Go' (FMP)
Derek Bailey

'Cyro' [w/Cyro Baptista] (Incus)
'Han' [w/Han Bennick] (Incus)
'Notes' (Incus)
Paul Rutherford
'1989 And All That' (Slam)
'Bracknell '83' (Ogun)
Albert Mangelsdorff
'Solo' (MPS)
'Live In Montreux' (MPS)
Company
'Epiphany' (Incus)
'Trios' (Incus)
John Stevens
'Freebop' (Impetus)
Lol Coxhill
'Melody Four' (Nato)
'Miller's Tale' (Matchless)
Tony Coe
'Tournée du Chat' (Nato)
'Le Chat se Retourne' (Nato)
Alexander Von Schlippenbach
'Jelly Roll' (FMP)
'Anticlockwise' (FMP)
Tony Oxley
'Tomorrow is Here' (Dossier)
London Composers Orchestra
'Stringer' (FMP)
'Zurich Concerts' (Intakt)
An important contribution to European Free was made by South African expatriots who comprised Brotherhood Of Breath. *They continued recording into the '80s and a selected discography includes:*
Chris McGregor
'Blue Notes For Johnny' (Ogun)
'Country Cooking' (Venture)
Johnny Dyani
'Mbizo' (Steeplechase)
'Afrika' (Steeplechase)
Louis Moholo
'Viva la Black' (Ogun)
Dudu Puckwana
'Live At Bracknell And Willisau' (Jika)
Harry Miller
'Down South' (Varajazz)

THE ECM SOUND
Jan Garbarek
'Eventyr' (ECM)
'Paths, Prints' (ECM)
'Wayfarer' (ECM)
'It's OK To Listen To The
  Gray Voice' (ECM)
'All Those Born With
  Wings' (ECM)
'The Legend Of The Seven
  Dreams' (ECM)
'Rosenfole' (ECM)
(See also Keith Jarrett,
  Eberhard Weber)

Terje Rypdal
'To Be Continued' (ECM)
'Eos' (ECM)
'Chaser' (ECM)
'Blue' (ECM)
'The Singles Collection'
  (ECM)

Eberhard Weber
'Little Movements' (ECM)
'Later That Evening' (ECM)
'The Following Morning'
  (ECM)
'Chorus' (ECM)
'Orchestra' (ECM)

Discographer's Note:
A sample of artists who
regularly appeared on ECM
and typified its approach:
Egberto Gismonti
'Duas Vozes' (ECM)
'Danca dos Escravos' (ECM)
Stephen Micus
'Ocean' (ECM)
'Music Of Stones' (ECM)
Azimuth
'Azimuth '85' (ECM)
Shankar
'Epidemics' (ECM)

'Songs For Everyone'
  (ECM)
Oregon
'Crossing' (ECM)
Zakir Hussain
'Making Music' (ECM)
Ralph Towner
'Slide Show' (ECM)
'Solstice' (ECM)
  (ECM)
Masquelero
'Bande a Parte' (ECM)
John Surman
'The Amazing Adventures
  Of Simon Simon' (ECM)
'Witholding Patterns'
  (ECM)
'Private City' (ECM)
Art Lande
[w/Jan Garbarek] 'Red
  Lanta'
Rainer Brauninghaus
'Freigewent' (ECM)

Jazz in Britain

Loose Tubes
'Loose Tubes' (Loose Tubes)
'Delightful Precipice' (Loose
  Tubes)
'Open Letter' (Editions EG)

Human Chain [Bates/
  Arguelles]
'Human Chain' (Loose
  Tubes)
'Cashin' In' (Editions EG)

Django Bates
'Music From "The Third
  Policeman" ' (Ah Um)
(See also with First House
  'Erendira' (ECM)

Steve Berry
'Trio' (Loose Tubes)

Ashley Slater
'Microgroove' (Antilles)

Ian Ballamy
'Balloon Man' (Editions EG)

Dave DeFries
'The Secret City' (MMC)

Courtney Pine
'Journey To The Urge

'Within' (Island)
'Destiny's Song And The
  Image Of Pursuance'
  (Island)
'Angel Heart' [OST]
  (Antilles New Directions)
'A Vision's Tale' (Antilles)
(See Jazz Warriors)

Tommy Smith
'Giant Strides' (GFM)
'Taking Off' (Head)
'Step By Step' (Blue Note)
'Peeping Tom' (Blue Note)

[with Forward Motion]
'The Berklee Tapes' (Hep)
'Progressions' (Hep)

[with Gary Burton]
'Whizz Kids' (ECM)

Andy Sheppard
'Andy Sheppard' (Antilles)
'Introductions In The Dark'
  (Antilles)
'Soft On The Inside'
  (Antilles)

Steve Williamson
'A Waltz For Grace' (Verve)

Jazz Warriors

'Out Of Many People, One
  People' (Antilles)

Discographer's Note:
Whilst media attention
focused on the 'young blood'
tenor players, a burgeoning
scene joined players of two
generations. This is a
random (and small)
selection to give a flavour:
Stan Tracey
'Poet's Suite' (Steam)
'Genesis' (Steam)
'Plays Ellington' (Mole)
'We Still Love You Madly'
  (Mole)
Clark Tracey
'Suddenly Last Tuesday'
  (Cadillac)
'Stiperstones' (Steam)
Danny Thompson
'Whatever' (Hannibal)
Peter King
'Brother Bernard' (Miles
  Music)
'Crusade' (Blanco Y Negro)
'New Beginning' (Spotlight)
Guy Barker
'Holly J' (Miles Music)
Alan Skidmore
'Tribute To Trane' (Miles

Music)
Itchy Fingers
'Quark' (Venture)
'Teranga' (Venture)
Pinski Zoo
'Rare Breeds' (Dug Out)

THE LATIN TINGE

Irakere
'El Coco' (Milestone)
'Le Chemin de la Colline'
(Egrem/Sonodisc)
'Misa Negra' (Messidor)
'Catalina' (Messidor)

Paquito D'Rivera
'Blowin'' (CBS)
'Mariel' (CBS)
'Live At Keystone Corner'
(CBS)
'Why Not!' (CBS)
'Manhattan Burn' (CBS)
'Celebration' (CBS)
'Tico Tico' (Chesky)
[with David Amram]
'Latin-Jazz Celebration'
(Elektra Musician)
[with Louis Ramirez]
'A Tribute To Cal Tjader'
(BGP)
(See also Chris Connor,
Soledad Bravo and 'The
Young Lions' (Elektra
Musician), 'The New
York-Montreux
Connection' (CBS))

Arturo Sandoval
'No Problem' (Jazz House)
'Straight Ahead' [w/Chucho
Valdes] (Jazz House)
'Tumbaito' (Messidor)
'Just Music' (Jazz House)
(See also Dizzy Gillespie)

Michel Camilo
'Why Not?' (King)
'Suntan' (Projazz)
'Michel Camilo' (CBS/Por-
trait)
'On Fire' (Epic)
[with French Toast]
'French Toast' (Elektric
Bird)

'East Rail East' (Cafe Jazz)
'Live In Warsaw' (Poljazz)
Keith Tippett
'No Gossip' (FMP)
'Couple In Spirit' (Editions

Global Democracy
(See also Paquito D'Rivera)

Tania Maria
'Piquant' (Concord Picant)
'Tarus' (Concord Picant)
'Come With Me' (Concord
Picant)
'Love Explosion' (Concord
Picant)
'The Real Tania Maria:
Wild' (Concord Picant)
'Made In New York' (EMI/
Manhattan)
'Lady From Brazil' (EMI/
Manhattan)
'Forbidden Colours'
(Capitol)

Bobby Enriquez
'The Wild Man' (GNP)
'The Wild Man Meets The
Mad Man' [w/Richie
Cole] (GNP)
'Ricardo' (GNP)
'Prodigious Piano' (GNP)
'Espana' (GNP)
'Live In Tokyo Vols. 1 & 2'
(GNP)
'Live At Concerts By The
Sea Vols. 1 & 2' (GNP)
'Andalucia' (GNP)
'Plays Bossa Nova' (GNP)
'Wild Piano' (CBS/Portrait)
*Discographer's Note:
Since Jelly Roll Morton, jazz
has attempted to
incorporate Latin elements
into its fabric. In the '80s
several Latin musicians
attempted to reverse the
process. Examples included:*
Gonzalo Rubalcaba
'Live In Havana Vol. 1 & 2'
(Messidor)
'Mi Gran Pasion' (Messidor)
Hilton Ruiz
'Crosscurrents' (Stash)
'Something Grand' (RCA/
Novus)

EG)
'Mujician III' (FMP)
Roadside Picnic
'For Madmen Only!'
(Novus)

'El Camino' (RCA/Novus)
'Strut' (RCA/Novus)
Pete Escovedo
'Yesterday's Memories,
Tomorrow's Dreams'
(Concord Crossover)
'Mister E' (Concord
Crossover)
Jerry Gonzalez
'Rumba Para Monk'
(Sunnyside)
'Yo Yo Ma Cure' (American
Clave)
Kip Hanrahan
'Desire Develops An Edge'
(American Clave)
'Days And Nights Of Blue
Luck Inverted' (Pangea)
Claudio Roditi
'Claudio' (Uptown)
'Gemini Man' (Contempor-
ary)
**Flora Purim/Airto Mor-
eira**
'The Magicians' (Concord
Crossover)
'Samba Para Flora' (Montu-
no)
Toninho Horta
'Diamond Land' (Verve
Forecast)

VARIOUS
Abdullah Ibrahim
'At Montreux' (Enja)
'South African Sunshine'
(Plane)
'Marsidiso' [solo] (Plane)
'Dukes Memories' (Enja)
'African Dawn' (Enja)
'Zimbabwe' (Enja)
'Live At Sweet Basil'
(Ekapa)
'Ekaya' (Ekapa)
'South Africa' (Enja)
'Water From An Ancient
Well' (Blackhawk)
'The Mountain' (Kaz)

'Mindif' (Enja)
'African River' (Enja)

James Morrison
'Postcards From Down
Under' (WEA)
'Swiss Encounter' [w/Adam
Makowicz] (East West)
'Snappy Doo' (WEA)
(See also with The Phillip
Morris Superband 'Live At
Townhall NYC' (Concord)

Adam Makowicz
'From My Window'
(Choice)
'The Name Is Makowicz'
[w/Phil Woods] (Sheffield
Lab)
'Moonray' (RCA/Novus)
'Naughty Baby' (RCA/
Novus)
(See also with James
Morrison)

JAPAN

Sadao Watanabe
'Rendezvous' (Elektra)
'Maisha' (Elektra)
'Tokyo Dating' (WEA)
'Good Time For Love'
(Elektra)
'Dedicated To Charlie
Parker' (Denon)
'Parker's Mood' [w/James
Williams] (WEA)

'Jazz & Bossa' (Denon)
'Meets Brazilian Friends'
(Denon)
'Iberian Waltz' [w/Charlie
Mariano] (Denon)
'Elis' (Elektra)
'Bossa Nova Concert'
(Denon)
'Selected' (Elektra)

Kazumi Watanabe
'Mobo I' (Gramavision)
'Mobo II' (Gramavision)
'Mobo Club' (Gramavision)
'Mobo Splash'
(Gramavision)
'The Spice Of Life'
(Gramavision)
'Spice Of Life Too'
(Gramavision)
'Kilowatt' (Gramavision)

Terumasa Hino
'Double Rainbow' (CBS)
'On The Road' (Toshiba
EMI)
'Bluestruck' [w/John
Scofield] (Blue Note)

Aki Takase
'ABC' [w/Sheila Jordan]
(Eastwind)

RUSSIA

Ganelin
'Ancora da Capo parts 1 &

2' (Leo)
'Vide' (Leo)
'Strictly For Our Friends'
(Leo)
'Baltic Triangle' (Leo)
'Non Troppo' (Enja)
'New Wine' (Leo)
'Can ttetto' (Leo)
'Inverso' (Leo)
'3-1-3' (Leo)
'Con Fuoco' (Leo)
'Tango In Nickeldorf' (Leo)
'Jerusalem February
Cantabile' (Leo)

Sergei Kuryokhin
'The Ways Of Freedom'
(Leo)
'Sentenced To Silence' (Leo)
'Popular Zoological
Elements' (Leo)
'Pop Mechanics #17' (Leo)
'Mad Nightingales In The
Russian Forest' (Leo)
'Introduction To Pop
Mechanics' (Leo)

Discographer's Note:
A retrospective of the 1980s
was prepared by Leo
Records comprising an 8-
CD set that attempted to
represent the whole scene:
'New Music From Russia'
(Leo)

Recommended Further Reading

Reference and Biography

Bass Line: The Stories and Photographs of Milt Hinton by Milt Hinton & David G. Berger (Temple University Press, Philadelphia)

Benny Goodman and the Swing Era by James Lincoln Collier (Oxford University Press)

Celebrating Bird: The Triumph of Charlie Parker by Gary Giddins (Hodder & Stoughton)

Chasin' the Train by J. C. Thomas (Elmtree Books)

Close Enough for Jazz by Mike Zwerin (Quartet)

Crosstown Traffic by Charles Shaar Murray (Faber & Faber)

Duke Ellington by James Lincoln Collier (Michael Joseph)

Early Jazz by Gunther Schuller (Oxford University Press)

The Encyclopedia of Jazz in the Seventies by Leonard Feather and Ira Gitler (Quartet)

The Encyclopedia of Jazz in the Sixties by Leonard Feather (Quartet)

The Freedom Principle by John Litweiler (Blandford)

The Great Jazz Pianists by Len Lyons (Da Capo)

The Imperfect Art by Ted Gioia (Oxford University Press)

In the Moment by Francis Davis (Oxford University Press)

Jazz: A History by Frank Tirro (Dent)

Jazz: The Essential Companion by Ian Carr, Digby Fairweather, Brian Priestley (Grafton)

Jazz Heritage by Martin Williams (Oxford University Press)

Jazz in Its Time by Martin Williams (Oxford University Press)

Jazz Styles: History And Analysis by Mark C. Gridley (Prentice Hall)

The Jazz Tradition by Martin Williams (Oxford University Press)

Jazz West Coast by Robert Gordon (Quartet)

Lester Young by Lewis Porter (Macmillan)

Louis Armstrong by James Lincoln Collier (Michael Joseph)

The Making Of Jazz by James Lincoln Collier (Granada)

Meet Me at Jim and Andy's by Gene Lees (Oxford University Press)

Miles: The Autobiography by Miles Davis with Quincy Troupe (Macmillan)

Milestones 1: The Music and Times of Miles Davis to 1960 by Jack Chambers (Toronto University Press)

Milestones 2: The Music and Times of Miles Davis since 1960 by Jack Chambers (Toronto University Press)

Music For Pleasure by Simon Frith (Polity Press)

The New Encyclopedia of Jazz by Leonard Feather (Quartet)

The New Grove Dictionary of Jazz edited by Barry Kernfield (Macmillan)

Night Creature by Whitney Balliett (Oxford University Press)

Oscar Peterson by Gene Lees (Macmillan)

The Penguin Encyclopedia of Popular Music edited by Donald Clarke (Viking)

Rhythm-A-Ning by Gary Giddins (Oxford University Press)

Riding on a Blue Note by Gary Giddins (Oxford University Press)

Self-Portrait of a Jazz Artist: Musical Thoughts and Realities by David Liebman (Advance Music)

The Swing Era by Gunther Schuller (Oxford University Press)

Swing To Bop Ira Gitler (Oxford University Press)

Toward Jazz by Andre Hodeir (Da Capo)

Urban Blues by Charles Keil (University of Chicago Press)

The View from Within by Orrin Keepnews (Oxford University Press)

Who's Who Of Jazz: Storyville to Swing Street by John Chilton (Bloomsbury Book Shop)

Photographic Books

The Golden Age of Jazz by William Gortlieb (Quartet)

Jazz by William Claxton (Twelve Trees Press)

Jazz: A Photo History Joachim Berendt (Deutsch)

Jazz Files by Chuck Stewart (Quartet)

Jazz Giants by K. Abe (Columbus)

L'Oeil du Jazz by Herman Leonard (Filipacchi)

References

INTRODUCTION

1 Liner notes Music Masters CIJD 20126Z/27X by Gary Giddins
2 Interview with author, 2 June 1990
3 *A Walk With A White Bushman* by Laurens Van De Post (Penguin, 1988)

CHAPTER 1: PAST MASTERS AND KEEPERS OF THE FAITH

1 *The View From Within* by Orrin Keepnews (Oxford University Press, 1988)
2 *The Making of Jazz* by James Lincoln Collier (Granada, 1978)
3 *Singers And The Song* by Gene Lees (Oxford University Press, 1987)
4 *Downbeat* – volume 56 No. 11
5 *Jazz Journal International* – volume 41 No. 10
6 *Bass Line* by Milt Hinton and David G. Berger (Temple University Press, Philadelphia, 1988)
7 *Jazz Journal International* – volume 41 No. 10
8 *Village Voice* – 4 July 1989
9 *Alec Wilder And His Friends* by Whitney Balliett (Houghton Mifflin, 1974)
10 *Jazz Journal International* – volume 33 No. 9
11 *New York Times* – 26 June 1989
12 *Close Enough For Jazz* by Mike Zwerin (Quartet, 1983)
13 *The Times* – 16 May 1988
14 Liner Notes – Enja 6020 1
15 *Drums In My Ears* by Benny Green (Davis-Poynter, 1973)

16 *Four Lives In The Be-Bop Business* by A. B. Spellman (Limelight, 1985)
17 Liner notes – Soul Note SN 1108
18 As 22
19 *Downbeat* – volume 48 No. 9
20 *Observer*- 5 November 1989
21 *Milestones 1: The Music and Times of Miles Davis to 1960* by Jack Chambers (University of Toronto Press, 1983)
22 *Oscar Peterson* by Richard Palmer (Spellmount, 1984)
23 *Oscar Peterson* by Gene Lees (Macmillan, 1989)
24 *'Night Creature'* by Whitney Balliett (Oxford University Press, 1981)
25 As 23
26 As 23
27 *The Second Lsfe Of Art: Selected Essays of Eugenso Montale* edited and translated by Jonathan Galassi (Ecco Press, 1983)
28 *Essays On Jazz* by Burnett James (Jazz Book Club, 1962)

CHAPTER 2: BIG BANDS ANCIENT TO MODERN

1 *Downbeat* – volume 49 No. 3
2 *The Big Bands* by George T. Simon (Shirmer, 1981)
3 *Downbeat* – volume 49 No. 11
4 *Riding On A Blue Note by* Gary Giddins (Oxford University Press, 1981)
5 *Good Morning Blues* – *The Autobiography of Count Basie, as told to Albert Murray* (Heinemann 1986)
6 *The Swing Era* by Gunther Schuller (Oxford, 1989)
7 *Daily Telegraph* – 27 April 1984
8 *Wall Street Journal* – 10 October 1989
9 *The New Grove Dictionary of Jazz* – edited by Barry Kernfield (Macmillan, 1988)
10 'Benny Goodman Live at Carnegie Hall' (Decca). The *Downbeat* Magazine of June 1978 commissioned two reviews of the concert by Dan Morgenstern and Arnold Jay Smith, and two of the albums by John McDonough and Don Nelson; Morgenstern for example, 'There can be no doubt that Benny Goodman's 40th Anniversary Concert at Carnegie Hall was a puzzling and disappointing event. The pacing was poor ... the sequencing of the programme made no sense, the performers frequently appeared to be as bewildered as the audience, and the show was far too long'.

11 Liner notes CBS 466620.2
12 *Ridgewood News* – 3 October 1985
13 Gene Lees – *Jazz letter* – Volume 16 No. 1
14 *Bass Lines* by Milt Hinton (Temple University Press, 1988)
15 Gene Lees – *Jazz letter* – Volume 15 No. 7
16 Frank Sinatra to Sidney Zion, 1986 quoted liner notes CBS 46620.2
17 Many thanks to Loren Schoenberg for his assistance in preparing the section on Benny Goodman
18 *Daily Mail* – 15 November 1983
19 *Meet me at Jim and Andy's* by Gene Lees (Oxford University Press, 1988)
20 *A Jazz Retrospect* by Max Harrison (David and Charles, 1977)
21 *Rhythm-A-Ning* by Gary Giddins (Oxford University Press, 1985)
22 *The Freedom Principle* by John Litweiler, page 297 (Blandford Press, 1985)
23 See 'Woody Herman: A Fan's Fan' in *Rhythm-A-Ning* by Gary Giddins, p. 111 (Oxford University Press, 1985)
24 *The New Grove Dictionary of Jazz, The Penguin Encyclopedia of Popular Music* and *Downbeat* – volume 55 No. 2, give Herman's death as 29 October 1987. However, Gene Lees, a personal friend, reports it as 26 November 1987, in *Meet me at Jim and Andy's* (Oxford University Press, 1988)
25 *Meet me at Jim and Andy's* by Gene Lees (Oxford University Press, 1988)
26 *The Swing Era* by Gunther Schuller (Oxford, 1989)
27 As 28
28 *Jazz Times* – April 1990
29 *Downbeat* – volume 49 No. 3
30 *Oscar Peterson* by Gene Lees (Macmillan, 1989)
31 The quotes by Loren Schoenberg come from an interview with author, 28 June 1989
32 *New York Post* – 26 September 1988
33 Quoted liner notes – Music Masters CIUD 201262/27X
34 *Washington Post* – 22 September 1988
35 As 39
36 *Jazz Masters of the '50s* by Joe Goldberg (Macmillan, 1965)
37 As 41
38 Interview with Mulligan by Charles Fox – BBC Radio 3 broadcast 4 May 1989
39 Barry Manilow's '2am Paradise Cafe' and 'Swing Street' (both Arista)

40 *The Wall Street Journal* – 23 January 1990

41 *Jazz Times* – April 1990

42 Liner notes – Trend TR523

43 *Jazz Journal International* – volume 42 No. 7

44 The albums are well worth the trouble of searching out: 'Kogun', 'Long Yellow Road', 'Tales of a Courtesan (Oirastan)', the two album set 'Road Time', 'Sumi-e', 'Live at Newport', 'Live at Newport II', 'Insights', 'March of the Tadpoles', 'Salted Gingko Nuts' and 'Farewell', all on the RCA label, although 'March of the Tadpoles' (1977), was re-released on Ascent in 1985

45 Conversation with author, 19 November 1983

46 *Los Angeles Times* – 6 February 1990

47 *Downbeat* – volume 55 No. 10

48 Blue Notes by Mort Goode – volume 1UU6

49 The Portsmouth Symphonia was a magnificent musical mistake, a symphony orchestra comprised entirely of enthusiastic amateurs of all ages, some with little or even no musical ability, but all charged with the ambition to make music. Undaunted, they wrestled with Beethoven and Brahms, Wagner and Mozart in a manic cacophony of sound

50 Liner notes – A & M 395 260-1

51 As 50

CHAPTER 3: THE HARD-BOP MAINSTREAM

1 *The Swing Era* by Gunther Schuller (Oxford University Press, 1989)

2 *The Recording Angel* by Evan Eisenberg (Picador, 1988)

3 *The Making of Jazz* by James Lincoln Collier (Granada, 1978)

4 *Jazz Lives* by Michael Ullman (Perigee, 1982)

5 *Night Creature* by Whitney Balliett (Oxford University Press, 1981)

6 *Long Tall Dexter,* by Stan Britt (Quartet, 1989)

7 The *Independent* – 28 November 1986

8 *The View From Within* by Orrin Keepnews (Oxford University Press, 1988)

9 Interview with author, 1 July 1981

10 *Jazz Masters of the '40s* by Ira Gitler (Macmillan, 1966)

11 As 9

12 Liner notes to 'The Complete Atlantic/EMI Shorty Rogers' (Mosaic 125)

13 Liner notes – Contemporary C-14021
14 Liner notes – Contemporary C-14026
15 As 14
16 As 14
17 *The New Grove Dictionary of Jazz* edited by Barry Kernfield (Macmillan, 1988)
18 *Downbeat* – volume 49 No. 1
19 Liner notes – Muse MR5237
20 *The Rolling Stone Record Guide* edited by John Swenson (Random House, 1985)
21 *Observer* – 30 May 1988
22 *Riding On A Blue Note* by Gary Giddins (Oxford University Press, 1981) – 'The Adventures of Red Arrow' p. 228
23 Liner notes – Blackhawk BKH50901
24 *The Times* – 2 August 1987
25 *Miles Davis* by Ian Carr (Quartet, 1982)
26 Liner notes – Portrait RJ 44394
27 *Drums In My Ears* by Benny Green (Davis-Poynter, 1973)
28 *Music In A New Found Land* by Wilfred Mellers (Faber & Faber, 1987)
29 Conversation with author, 22 April 1983
30 *The Jazz Scene* by Francis Newton (Penguin, 1961)

CHAPTER 4: WHITHER FREEDOM?

1 *The Making of Jazz* by James Lincoln Collier (Granada, 1978)
2 *All* by Philip Larkin (Faber & Faber, 1970)
3 *Musings* by Gunther Schuller (Oxford University Press, 1986)
4 *Rhythm-A-Ning* by Gary Giddins (Oxford University Press, 1985)
5 *Jelly Roll, Jabo and Fats* by Whitney Balliett (Oxford University Press, 1983)
6 *Downbeat* – volume 50 No. 7
7 *Riding On A Blue Note* by Gary Giddins (Oxford University Press, 1985)
8 *The Times,* 9 September 1988
9 *The Freedom Principle* by John Litweiler (Blandford Press, 1985)
10 Quoted in *Crosstown Traffic* by Charles Shaar Murray (Faber & Faber, 1989)
11 As 9
12 *Night Creature* by Whitney Balliett (Oxford University Press, 1981)

13 *Downbeat* – volume 51 No. 10
14 *Coda* – issue 231
15 *Wire* – issue 62
16 *Night Creature* by Whitney Balliett (Oxford University Press, 1981)
17 *The Second Life of Art: Selected Essays of Eugenio Montale* edited and translated by Jonathan Galassi (Ecco Press, 1983)
18 *Jazz Styles and Analysis* by Mark C. Gridley (Prentice Hall, 1989)
19 *In The Moment* by Francis Davis (Oxford University Press, 1986)
20 Liner notes – India Navigation IN 1029
21 Liner notes – CBS 83350
22 Iiner notes – Elektra Musician K52412

CHAPTER 5: MILES AND THE FUSION JUNTA

1 *Clive: Inside the Record Business* by Clive Davis (William Morrow, 1975)
2 *Miles: The Autobiography* by Miles Davis with Quincy Troupe (Macmillan, 1990)
3 *Downbeat Yearbook* 1973
4 *Louisville Times* – 9 December 1967
5 As 1
6 As 2
7 As 2
8 *Crosstown Traffic* by Charles Shaar Murray (Faber & Faber, 1989)
9 As 2
10 *Milestones II* by Jack Chambers (University of Toronto Press, 1985)
11 As 2
12 As 10
13 *Contact Magazine* 1981 page 24 quoted in *Milestones II* by Jack Chambers (University of Toronto Press, 1985)
14 As 2
15 As 10
16 As 2
17 As 10
18 *In The Moment* by Francis Davis (Oxford University Press, 1986)
19 As 2
20 As 2
21 *The Times* – 13 July 1989
22 As 2
23 See Discography

24 As 10
25 As 10
26 Liner notes CBS 25395
27 As 2
28 Liner notes – Elektra Musician 60298-1-I
29 *Jazz Journal International* – volume 37 No. 12
30 As 29
31 Interview in Q Magazine with David Sinclair
32 As 31
33 *Wire* – issue 43
34 *Cashbox:* Interview with Lee Jeske
35 Liner notes – Elektra Musician E1 – 160025
36 Interview with Mick Brown
37 *The Times* – 4 November 1988

CHAPTER 6: POST-BOP AND BEYOND

1 *Self-portrait of a Jazz Artist* by Dave Liebman (*Advance Music,* 1988)
2 *Great Jazz Pianists* – Lyons (Da Capo, 1983)
3 Liner notes – Milestone M-9167
4 As 3
5 John Fordham – *Wire* – issue 68
6 *Penguin Encyclopedia of Popular Music* (Viking, 1989)
7 Liner notes – Elektra Musician – MUSK 52 402
8 The quotations by Michael Cuscana are taken from his moving obituary in *Wire* – issue 65
9 See Discography
10 Liner notes – PA 8061
11 *Self-portrait of a Jazz Artist* by Dave Liebman (*Advance Music,* p. 53)
12 Liner notes – Pan Music PMC1101
13 As 11
14 As 11
15 *Garden City N.Y.* (Doubleday, 1941, pp. 290-95)
16 Interview with author 27.6.89
17 Interview with author 30.6.89
18 Interview with author 30.6.89
19 Interview with author 30.6.89
20 Liner notes – Antilles AN 1001

21 *Rhythm-A-Ning* by Gary Giddins (Oxford University Press, 1985) 22 Liner notes – Concord CJ-280

23 See Discography

24 Liner notes MCA – 5980

25 *Village Voice* – November 1988

26 Liner notes – Theresa TRCD 128

27 Liner notes – ECM 1398

28 *Rhythm-A-Ning* by Gary Giddins (Oxford University Press, 1985)

29 See liner notes – 'Duke Ellington At His Very Best' RCA 27133: 'So much goes on in a Harlem Air Shaft', said Ellington, 'You hear fights, you hear the radio: an airshaft is a great big loudspeaker . . . an airshaft has got every contrast . . . you hear people praying, fighting, snoring. Jitterbugs (dancers), are jumping up and down, always over you, never below you . . . I tried to put that in "Harlem Airshaft" '

30 See Discography

31 Interview with author, 2 June 1989

32 Liner notes – Stash ST221

33 Liner notes – Red VPA 182

34 As 31

35 As 33

36 *Downbeat* – volume 53 No. 3

37 *In The Moment* by Francis Davis (Oxford University Press, 1986)

38 Gary Giddins – from a review of the Sonny Rollins Spring 1988 Concert at Town Hall, New York that appeared in *Village Voice*

39 *Live at the Village Vanguard* by Max Gordon (St. Martin's Press, New York, 1980), See chapter 12

40 *Downbeat* – volume 55 No. 7

41 Conversation with author, 20 August 1989

42 Extracts of the Japanese concert are on the Robert Mugge film 'Saxophone Colossus'

43 Richard Cook – *Sunday Times*, 13 May 1990

44 *In The Moment* by Francis Davis (Oxford University Press, 1986)

45 Notes contained in the three album box set 'Concerts' ECM 1227 – 29

46 *Night Creature* by Whitney Balliett (Oxford University Press, 1981)

47 See Discography

48 *The Times* – 11 October 1989

CHAPTER 7: NEO FACES

1 *Self-portrait of a Jazz Artist* by Dave Liebman (*Advance Music*, 1988)
2 *Downbeat* – volume 54 No. 11
3 Interview on BBC Television, 'Catching a Snake'.
4 Extracted from Blakey's announcement at the beginning of the track 'Confirmation' on 'A Night At Birdland Vol. 2' Blue Note BLP 1522
5 *Jazz Masters of the '50s* by Joe Goldberg (Macmillan, 1966)
6 Liner notes – Contemporary C-14042
7 Liner notes – Paddlewheel K28P 6357
8 *Jazz Times* – March 1989
9 Liner notes – CDCBS 25952
10 *Downbeat* – volume 56 No. 11
11 *Los Angeles Times* – 26th March 1989
12 Liner notes – Landmark LCD 1520-2
13 Liner notes – Blue Note BL 90262
14 Liner notes – Vogue 651. 600611
15 *Downbeat* – volume 57 No. 1
16 *Art, The Enemy of The People* by Roger Taylor (Harvester Press)
17 *The Times* – 19 May 1989
18 *Sunday Times* – 11 February 1990
19 *Downbeat* – volume 56 No. 11

CHAPTER 8: VILLAGE VOICES AND DOWNTOWN SOUNDS

1 *New York Times* – 4 December 1988
2 *Jazz Forum* 121
3 Liner notes – Nonesuch 979 172
4 Interview with author – 29 June 1989
5 Interview with author – 27 June 1989
6 Kevin Whitehead – *Downbeat* – volume 57 No. 4
7 Liner notes – Enja LP5085
8 Quoted by Claudia Rowe 1989
9 Liner notes – JMT 834407
10 Liner notes – 834 420-2
11 *New York Times* 1989
12 Interview with author – 27 June 1989
13 Interview with author – 29 June 1989

14 *Jazz Styles and Analysis,* by Mark C. Gridley (Prentice Hall 1988, page 255)

15 *Musician Magazine* – 1983

16 Tiner notes – Nonesuch 979 172-1

CHAPTER 9: VOICE

1 *In The Moment* by Francis Davis (Oxford University Press, 1986)

2 *Mystery Train* by Greil Marcus (Omnibus Press, 1977)

3 *The Great American Popular Singers* by Henry Pleasants (Victor Gollancz Ltd, 1974)

4 *Downbeat* – volume 56 No. 7

5 As '1'

6 *American Popular Song – The Great Innovators 1900 – 1950* by Alec Wilder (Oxford University Press, 1972)

7 i 'The Cole Porter Songbook' charted at 15 in 1956
 ii 'The Rogers and Hart Songbook' charted at 11 in 1957
 iii 'The Gershwin Songbook' charted in 1964

8 *The Observer Magazine* – 25 February 1990

9 *Musings* by Gunther Schuller (Oxford University Press, 1986)

10 *Downbeat* – volume 49 No. 5

11 *Downbeat* – volume 37 No. 22

12 See *High Life, Hard Times* by Anita O'Day and George Eells (Corgi, 1983)

13 *The Daily News* – 16 June 1989

14 *Downbeat* – volume 37 No. 11

15 Interview with author 27 June 1989

16 As 19

17 The *Observer Magazine* – 28 February 1990

18 *Jazz – A Photo History* by Joachim Berendt (Andre Deutsch, 1979)

19 *The Times* – 22 September 1988

20 *Downbeat* – volume 48 No. 10

21 Grover Sales, liner notes – Concord CJ – 341

22 *Jazz Journal International* – volume 42 No. 7

23 *Jazz Journal International* – volume 35 No. 8

24 *Encyclopedia of Jazz in the Seventies* by Leonard Feather and Ira Gitler (Quartet, 1978)

25 *Downbeat* – volume 55 No. 2

26 *The Times* – 16 January 1989

27 Conversation with author 25 June 1989

28 *Downbeat* – volume 56 No. 2

29 *Village – Voice* – 4 July 1989

30 *Observer* – 19 January 1986

31 *New York Notes* by Whitney Balliett (Da Capo, 1977)

32 Francis Davis, liner notes – Muse 5288

33 Quoted in *Crosstown Traffic* by Charles Shaar Murray (Faber & Faber, 1989)

34 *Crosstown Traffic* by Charles Shaar Murray (Faber & Faber, 1989)

35 As 34

36 Liner notes – Fiend 143

37 *Downbeat* – volume 54 No. 3

CHAPTER 10: EUROPEAN DREAMS AND THE GLOBAL DEMOCRACY

1 Quoted in *A History of Jazz in Britain* by Jim Godbolt (Quartet, 1984)

2 *Music For Pleasure* by Simon Frith (Polity Press, 1988)

3 *The Freedom Principle* by John Litweiler (Blandford Press, 1985)

4 As 2

5 Liner notes – Elektra Musician 96.0220-1

6 *Coda* – issue 230

7 *In The Moment* by Francis Davis (Oxford University Press, 1986)

8 As 7

9 *Downbeat* – volume 47 No. 7

10 *Close Enough For Jazz* by Mike Zwerin (Quartet, 1983)

11 *The Times,* November 1988

12 The *Guardian,* 15 May 1985

13 *The Times,* 15 May 1985

14 *The Times,* 11 January 1988

15 *Close Enough For Jazz by* Mike Zwerin (Quartet, 1983)

16 Quoted in *Jazz Forum* 121

17 As 16

18 As 16

19 Interview – *Sunday Times* 1990

Index

Other DA CAPO titles of interest